UP IN HARM'S WAY

Flying with the Fleet Air Arm

UP IN HARM'S WAY

Flying with the Fleet Air Arm

Commander R.M. 'Mike' Crosley, DSC & Bar, R.N.

Airlife
England

Copyright © 1995 by R.M. Crosley

First published in the UK in 1995
by Airlife Publishing Ltd

British Library Cataloguing in Publication Data
A catalogue record for this book
is available from the British Library

ISBN 1 85310 555 4

Typeset by Servis Filmsetting Ltd, Manchester
Printed in England by Biddles Ltd, Guildford and King's Lynn

Airlife Publishing Ltd
101 Longden Road, Shrewsbury SY3 9EB, England

CONTENTS

FOREWORD

Distrust and ignorance of science is perhaps one of the most potent causes of Britain's comparative decline in engineering skills in the past century. The lack of science-based management in industry has led to many marvellous British inventions being taken overseas because they were judged by politicians or by non-science-educated managers in industry to have no commercial or military viability at the time to merit the financial outlay required to put them into production. This book mentions just a few of these instances, some of which were made at the author's expense. The book also attempts to describe how, by the brilliant instructional work of a few science lecturers at the Empire Test Pilots' School, ordinary squadron pilots could, for the first time in aviation history, become useful scientists in their own right and be able to speak on equal terms to the 'boffins' in a language that they could all understand. For the first time, we pilots knew what made an aircraft fly safely and could describe its faults or its virtues in a language that aircraft designers could appreciate and act upon immediately.

Therefore, ETPS-trained aviators are an essential part of the military aircraft Procurement Executive Department. Their understanding of the handling and performance problems likely to occur with new aircraft and their practiced liaison with the manufacturers plus their operational experience, make them a natural choice, not only to take initial action to write the Staff Requirement for new aircraft to replace the old, but to take initial command of the squadrons on their first formation to help iron out the inevitable changes which new aircraft demand in training their aircrew and in their operation ashore and afloat.

Aircraft design and the production of people to fly them is an aspect of advanced technology in which this country still excels. This book describes some of the various processes and changes that aircraft have had to pass through in the last fifty years from their first appearance as Operational Requirements on a military desk in Whitehall to their first military operations from an airfield or flight deck. The technical content of this book should need no special knowledge of the subject or more than a passing scientific interest on the part of the reader, for him to know how both living and man-made things can fly.

CHAPTER 1

THE PACIFIC WAR ENDS

It was the morning of 15 March, 1946 and HMS *Indefatigable* was about to enter Portsmouth Harbour. She had just completed a voyage of about 15,000 miles, making her way home after the Pacific war had ended. The Captain had just told us that the remains of the ship's Airgroup was to fly ashore to Lee-on-Solent where our families would be waiting to meet us. There, our remaining 24 Seafires would be pushed into the hangars and we would be sent on six weeks leave. When the Captain announced this programme over the ship's Tannoy he apologised for not being able to tell us what would happen to us after that.

So, at about 0800 we climbed into our Seafires L IIIs ranged on the flight deck, strapped in, pressed the starters, warmed up and took off. When we had shaken hands finally with our ground crews on the flight deck we had done so with much regret for we should not be seeing them again. We owed our lives to them for their work in maintaining our aircraft during 1945 in the hardest of conditions in the Pacific war with the American carriers off Japan and often in complete ignorance of what we were doing in the air or our success or failure. They had never let us down.

Ten minutes later we landed without ceremony at Lee, taxied into the area outside the 'blitzed hangars' and climbed out of the cockpits to be greeted by our families. Next day when we returned to the ship to collect the remainder of our gear we found that the Customs men were still operating. But having heard previously that they had returned to their pre-war peacetime efficiency, we had taken the precaution of stowing our attractive items in our Seafires' ammunition lockers, so they found nothing in our baggage.

To add to the success of this manoeuvre the Customs had not been told of our landing at Lee-on-Solent as the Captain there had not had sufficient time to tell them. He was much more concerned with the impending arrival at his air station of the Fifth Sea Lord – Admiral Sir Denis Boyd – who had travelled down from the Admiralty specially to welcome us. This gesture was typical of this fine man. As Captain of HMS *Illustrious* in 1941 he had organised the brilliantly successful night raid by twenty Swordfish on the Italian fleet at Taranto and had been an immense support to Naval aviation ever since. His welcome was all the more appreciated for we were but a small bunch of aviators remaining from the Navy's Pacific Airgroups and were not expecting such interest.

The voyage from Sydney had taken about six weeks. During this time we had been trying to catch up with home news. Petrol rationing and food rationing were now even stricter than they had been in wartime. Job prospects appeared to be hopeless for those unable to return to their former employers. There would be about 84,000 officers and men of the Fleet Air Arm like ourselves out of the two million returning ex-servicemen and women at this time, ten times the number serving in the Navy in 1939. We would all be clasping our 'Certificates of Post-war Credit', our free 'civvy' jackets and trousers, our latest 'flimseys' (a handwritten summary by the Captain describing our character and efficiency during the time we had been under his command) and anything else we could find to support our claim to a civilian job.

For the few of us who had elected to stay on in the Navy for a further four years, the sudden, merciful end to the war had, so far, made it impossible for the Navy to make an adequate replacement peace plan and we would be very lucky indeed to get a useful flying job.

At the time of Hiroshima on 12 August 1945, four out of the six large Fleet Carriers in the Royal Navy – *Indefatigable*, *Implacable*, *Victorious* and the flagship, *Formidable* – had just completed 36 strike days against Japan alongside the 16 American carriers. We had been hitting the Japanese mainland, sinking the remainder of their ships, wrecking their airfields and attempting to discover and destroy their remaining 4,000-strong airforce – all potential Kamikazes which were later found hidden away in the countryside – and ready to create havoc on the beaches if the planned invasion of Japan had gone ahead in September.

Implacable – the author's ship at that time – had already left the fleet a few days before the A-bombs brought fighting to a halt. She was on her way back to Sydney to collect and train replacement aircrew for the invasion – not because of fuel shortages which has since been reported as the reason. (This fuel shortage affected only a few battleships which were, of course, low priority).

The plan for *Implacable*'s two 24-aircraft Seafire squadrons had been for us to spend a fortnight at Schofields airstation near Sydney before the invasion where we would re-equip with the Griffon-engined Mark XV Seafire, absorb newly joined pilots and join up with the fleet again. The author's Squadron (880) had had five pilots killed. 801 Squadron – commanded by Stuart Jewers – had lost eight in the last two months of operations over Japan. It would not only be necessary to absorb replacements for these but a further 17 were to join – 11 Australians and six New Zealanders. The author was to take over both squadrons to form a Wing of 48 Seafire XVs and L IIIs for continued operations off Japan, allowing Stuart Jewers to train up further Seafire replacements ashore on the new Mark XV which would certainly be required for the two invasions of Japan planned for the next months ahead. We lost our Wing Leader – Cdr Colin Campbell-Horsefall. He was to return to the UK to be in charge of the School of Naval Air Warfare in Cornwall with the job of training Senior Pilots and potential COs of new Seafire squadrons which would doubtless be needed to replace us in the Pacific as the war progressed in the many months which, at that time, still lay ahead.

There were 110 firstline squadrons in the Fleet Air Arm at this time in September 1945 and about 70 of these were embarked in 25 of the Royal Navy's 41 carriers, either earmarked for, or actually in the Pacific or Indian Oceans. These 70 embarked squadrons – about 1,000 aircrew and 20,000 men – were not only poised to invade Japan's east coast in September/October but were also required to defend landings in Malaya and many other places after that. They were by far the largest and most powerful Royal Naval surface force in our entire history.

Speaking of *Implacable*'s contribution, David Royle, Lt-Cdr RNVR, serving in *Implacable* at that time writes:

> The ship's achievements in the Pacific amounted to 150,000 tons of shipping and 113 Jap aircraft destroyed. On our return to Sydney in August 1945, we flew off all aircraft and became a hospital ship. We must have been the first ship flying the White Ensign since Nelson's days to have had women aboard – 18 QARNs. Our task was to gather those poor wretches from the POW camps. We collected them from Balik-Papan, Borneo and Hong Kong. We took them to Hawaii and Vancouver, B.C. They were in a terrible condition . . .

At about this time we heard that the terms of 'Lease-lend' – whereby the American Navy had loaned our Navy nearly two thousand fighter and strike aircraft – dictated that these magnificent machines should be hurled over the side of our carrier's decks into the Pacific, or otherwise destroyed. This left the British Pacific Fleet (BPF) with about 50 Fireflys and perhaps 100 Seafires of various Marks. It showed, in stark reality, where we should have been had we not been rescued by the American Navy in 1942–4 with their huge gifts of Wildcat, Hellcat, Corsair and Avenger aircraft.

With no aircraft left to fly, the only course then open to all but a few of our carriers in the BPF was for them to make their separate ways back to UK, first out, first home. The Fleet Air Arm, having contributed the most of any Royal Navy forces in the Pacific, inevitably suffered most from the ensuing chaos of this unexpected peace, which, on our return to the UK afterwards, so reduced our contentment and our pride in our victory. The traditions of our 'Silent Service' further muted the publicity of our achievements even after wartime secrecy was no longer an excuse for doing so. We became known as 'The Forgotten Fleet.' The returning POWs had even less notice taken of them.

During the autumn of 1945 spent at Schofields – with *Implacable* engaged in rescuing and delivering POWs until Christmas – we amused ourselves learning the peculiarities of the Griffon-engined Seafire XV and converting the Australians in our squadron – having come straight from Spit 9s in the RAF – to the thrills of decklanding it on *Ruler*. We also enjoyed the delights of Bondi beach and made many visits in our Seafires to Brisbane, Tasmania and Melbourne, being welcomed wherever we went by the marvellous generosity of the Australians.

In early February 1946, ashore at Schofields, I heard that *Implacable* would not be returning to UK for another four months. Because of family reasons I applied to be allowed to return to the UK in *Indefatigable* which was leaving for the UK in a few days time. I was allowed to change places for the journey with Jack Routley, the new CO of 894 Seafires. Jack Routley took over my lot in *Implacable* which by this time had shrunk from 60 to about 36 pilots and 24 aircraft and I took over his.

Few photos exist today of Hurricanes, Swordfish, Fulmars, Seafires, Avengers, Fireflys, Corsairs or Hellcats taking off or landing on our wartime carriers. The public's ignorance of the importance and effectiveness of Naval air warfare exists even to this day, for media coverage still shows gunfire to have been the main Royal Navy's hitting power. The crowning insult to its airmen was when our carrier Admiral chose a battleship – presumably as a symbol of Naval might – from which to attend the signature of the Japanese surrender in Tokyo Bay.

To enable the reader to appreciate the difficulties that the Royal Navy has had since this date in equipping its fleet with a cost-effective air defence, it might be worthwhile to hark back briefly to the days when the Fleet Air Arm began and to mention some of the aircraft which it has used since then. Dating from 1936 and the ratification of the Inskip Report – which gave the RAF and FAA their job specifications – there was until 1942 very little attempt to provide a fighter defence. AA gunnery was considered sufficient. The Admiralty had not managed to recruit sufficient Naval pilots and observers in the five years before 1939 for it to become a proper striking force. Many admirals seemed satisfied with but 50 naval officers being trained per year, saying that this small number would be sufficient as: 'the loss of pilots would be comparatively small until some major engagement' – ie, another Jutland – 'which might not take place for a long time after the outbreak of war.'

The urgent need for carrier-borne fighters only slowly became apparent when, from 1940–42, Naval gunnery continued to show itself to be ineffectual and little more than a passing nuisance to determined and well executed air attacks. Perhaps the best example of Admiralty discouragement for the recruitment of naval aircrew was when one aspirant was told by his Captain that 'the air is poppycock' and that flying would ruin his career. The fact that the Captain's name was Phillips, who commanded the ill-fated *Repulse* and *Prince of Wales* ten years later, makes this example particularly significant.

The Fairey Fulmar had made its first flight in January 1940. It was a 'cut-down' version of the vulnerable Fairey Battle – shortly to be relegated to RAF training – and was, of course, no match for the Me 109 even when flown by the bravest and most skilful pilots in the world. The Fairey Barracuda torpedo-bomber next made its appearance in December 1940 – another dangerous failure which never sufficiently rewarded the valour of those who had to fly it.

During the war our information on the aircraft supply position was not much better than that of the man in the street. Our frustration at the lack of fighter defence would have been greatly relieved had we learnt the news, in 1941, that a relatively junior Fleet Air Arm pilot, recently the CO of a Skua Squadron – Lt-Cdr Dick Smeeton – had taken the law into his own hands in the heated atmosphere of the British Joint Services Mission in Washington and, as a junior member, had placed an order on behalf of the British government for 1,000 United States Navy fighters and 500 Avenger strike aircraft.

Similar desperate action had been taken at this time by Captain Matthew Slattery of the Directorate of Air Materiel in the Admiralty. In January 1940 he had made out an order for 50 Sea-Spitfires or Sea Hurricanes – whichever came first. The delivery of the Sea-Spitfires was delayed until the summer of 1942 because the Royal Air Force rightly stated that they would otherwise have to cancel 75 of their Spitfire Vcs needed for the Battle of Britain. There were, however, a few second-hand Hurricanes and some Grumman Wildcat Is left over from a French/US Navy order. These deliveries, plus the first of the Seafire Ibs were in time to provide fighter protection for the North African offensive in late 1942, the reinforcement of Malta from Gibraltar in a series of convoys, a chance of invading Italy and southern France and perhaps most important of all, the protection, by a few carrier-borne Hurricane IIs and Wildcats, of our North Atlantic convoys. This latter task they did by shooting down enemy maritime reconnaissance aircraft and by assisting the Swordfish in anti-submarine search and destroy missions. Their action, together with Coastal Command aircraft, accounted for the sinking of 43 U-boats in the month of May 1943 alone and forced Admiral Doenitz to withdraw his U-boats from the North Atlantic almost entirely from that date.

We in the Fleet Air Arm were not of course the only ones in ignorance of the aircraft supply situation during the war. It seems that the Board of Admiralty and Air Ministers were equally ignorant. As to the shortage of effective fighters, it appears, from a newspaper cutting pasted into 880 Squadron's 'Line Book', (now available at the Fleet Air Arm Museum at Royal Naval Air Station Yeovilton) that the First Lord of the Admiralty – at that time Mr A.V. Alexandria and a politician, of course, – had tried to throw the blame for this shortage on the Air Ministry. He said in 1941:

> The Air Ministry should persuade the Admiralty – *who are ignorant of air matters* – that the real fighting war took place in the air and not on the sea. The Navy had to thank God that the US Navy were better equipped and fitted out than the Japanese, otherwise things would be very different.

Lord Cherwell (Treasury)'s reply was illuminating:

> In the Fleet Air Arm, the Navy has special difficulties. Machines have to fly from a small, floating aerodrome with very restricted hangars and with special lifts to take the machines to the flying deck. That restricts the type of machine and the type of carrier that can be used. It must be seaworthy, defensible and made without too many man-hours, (*sic*). The type of machine to be flown must be hybrid – up to a point. They have to be ordered almost off the drawing-board in wartime. Lacking clear direction, the designers think that meeting Navy needs is more of an art than a science.

Then followed one of the more technical (?) exchanges:

Lord Beaverbrook (Air Minister): 'No, that is not the case.'

Lord Cherwell: 'In the Fleet Air Arm planes landing on the decks of carriers have to have a short run and slow landing.'

Lord B: 'What about the Hurricane?'

Lord C: 'It has a very broad arrester gear.'

Lord B: 'Why can't they all have them?'

Lord C: 'It is not possible ever to have completely up-to-date machines. This is very galling to the pilots and others using them. The government desires to give the best aeroplanes possible to the Fleet Air Arm and as many as possible'.

It was small wonder that the Fleet Air Arm's aircraft supply position was in such a mess if this rubbish was the standard of debate amongst our air-supply leaders!

The above reports appeared at the time when the Navy's memories of the battlefleet's first 'brush with the enemy' in the North Sea – as Churchill described it – was still fresh in senior officers' minds. Then there was the sinking of the *Prince of Wales* and *Repulse* in 1941. In neither of these cases were fighters available and gunnery defence was ineffective.

Following the Inskip Report detailing the job specification between the Navy and RAF's air defence tasks in 1936, the RAF had immediately ordered large numbers of Hurricane and Spitfire fighters (which had been flown for the first time – the Hurricane on 6 November 1935 by George Bulman and the Spitfire by Mutt Summers on 5 March 1936), and had begun developing some very effective *radar direction capability*. This latter facility was in operation by the start of the Battle of Britain and, according to the 'Biggin Hill' report, increased the effectiveness per flying hour of defence fighters by a factor of ten! The Royal Navy – unlike the US Navy – had made no effort to equip itself with fighters or the radar necessary for their control.

On his arrival back from the Pacific in 1946, our carrier Admiral – Admiral Vian – had been appointed to the top aviation post in the Admiralty – Fifth Sea Lord. He was asked by the press to give his opinion of the importance of the part played by the Fleet Air Arm which he commanded while it was in the Pacific. He was reported as saying that it had not been a war between battle-ships – implying that this made it somewhat unusual – but a war which employed destroyers. The use of naval air power on such a scale in the Pacific theatre had been 'abnormal' in naval warfare and should not be taken as a sign for the future.

If the Fifth Sea Lord said such things, what hope was there for the future Fleet Air Arm? However, 15 years later in 1962, after retirement, he had written a partial withdrawal of this remark. He said, in his book – *Action this Day*:

The fast aircraft carriers – the CVAs – have become the capital ships of the new Navy; the strike aircraft they carry deliver the blows which the battleships' guns have previously given; the fighters provide the principal defence against similar blows by the enemy.

On our return to the UK in early 1946, several of us ex-COs of Pacific squadrons who had volunteered to stay in the Navy on four-year short-service commissions were appointed to the School of Naval Air Warfare at St Merryn in Cornwall. This was probably in order to keep us occupied in flying until the Admiralty could think of something more useful for us to do. In August a Carrier Air Group (CAG) was formed at Eglinton in Northern Ireland and several of us were appointed as COs to the three squadrons of the group – flying Seafire LIIIs, Firefly Is and a few remaining Avengers. Production had ceased on the Seafire XVs and XVIIs but a few Seafire Mark 47s were still being produced, probably intended for the Canadian or Australian Navies who had recently bought two of our Light Fleet Carriers for their own use.

The Firefly Squadron in the CAG at Eglinton was commanded by Cedric Coxon. We had several discussions together and soon came to the conclusion that the Royal Navy's Air Branch seemed to have lost its way with Admiral Vian at the controls. It seemed to have no firm plans to emerge from its post-war limbo, perhaps by creating new challenges for our aircraft designers by asking them to produce a jet-powered, decklanding fighter of some sort, equal in performance to the Royal Air Force Vampire or Meteor jet-powered fighters which had been in service for the past three years.

Implacable was now the only operational Fleet Carrier in the Navy with but three Light Fleet carriers in addition. (All the others had been laid up, sold, returned to America or cancelled during building.) One of our CAG's tasks was to embark in her to accompany the Royal Family on their visit to South Africa in January 1947. The Royal Family used *Vanguard* – the last of the battleships – as their transport.

Halfway to South Africa, the Royal Family came across to *Implacable* by launch to pay us a visit and say thankyou for the flypast we had done for them. The King sat in the Captain's chair on the bridge and talked to us about flying. He was very interested in the Seafire and was obviously intrigued how we managed to see out of it when we were coming in to deck land and how it managed to cope with the rugged life aboard a carrier instead of the grass air-fields for which it had been designed in 1936. We replied respectfully that we thought that decklanding this lovely aircraft was by far the most difficult and dangerous job there was in the Fleet Air Arm in war or peace for a fighter pilot to have to do and no amount of training could possibly make it safe. We needed a fighter specially designed for the job and not any more hastily mod-ified, landbased fighters left over from the Royal Air Force – however excel-lent they were once they got airborne.

Our hopes for a new Naval jet fighter were not to be realised for two more years, however, as a naval pilot who had carried out deck landing trials of an elementary sort in a hooked Vampire had complained that power response from its Goblin engine was too poor to allow safe decklandings. This had dis-couraged their Royal Navy use. However, the only problem that we could see at this time when decklanding a Vampire was the added danger to the jet pilot of being seated at the front of his nosewheel aircraft with no protection whatever if he missed the arrester wires and went full tilt into the barrier.

The Navy had to wait until April 1949 before 702 Squadron received the Navy's first jets – two Meteor T7s and six Sea Vampires – for piston-to-jet conversion training at Culdrose Naval Air Station. This Squadron then embarked in *Implacable* for trials during 1949 and again in *Theseus* during 1950, achieving the world's first night landings for a jet aircraft. None of the difficulties which had been reported in the December 1945 trials (the first jet-powered aircraft to do so apart from the United States Navy's Ryan 'Fireball') were reported by 702 Squadron's pilots. This change of opinion had largely been brought about by reliance on recommendations from qualified Naval test pilots who knew much more about the problem, having attended a year's course at a new school set up by the RAF since 1943 and which was called the Empire Test Pilots' School (ETPS).

Returning from a skiing holiday in Grindelwald in December 1946 the author happened to hear of this new school for test pilots, and that up to six Naval pilots had been allowed to join each course. A Naval Test Squadron, known as 'C' Squadron, had also been formed at the Aircraft and Armament Experimental Establishment (A&AEE) at Boscombe Down airfield near Amesbury in Wiltshire. Owned by the Ministry of Supply and administered by the RAF, A&AEE's job was – alongside two RAF test squadrons, one Naval test squadron and a Civil Air Test Section (CATS):

> to evaluate the safety and performance of new aircraft types for their projected tasks in the Services and obtain clearance for their use on behalf of the Ministry of Supply, in accordance with the wishes of the Ministry of Defence and Ministry of (civil) Aircraft Production, for the list of jobs they were likely to be called upon to do.

Having immediately applied to join ETPS, the author attended an interview at Rex House in Lower Regent Street in London in February 1947, having flown back from Gibraltar to do so while returning from the South African trip in *Implacable*.

Most of us candidates who had arrived for the interview had been reading *Flight* and *Aeroplane* in case we were asked any topical questions on British and American efforts to break the 'sound barrier' – as journalists now referred to supersonic flight. The huge increase in power at high altitude which jet power had provided had, with the temporary additional thrust from a rocket, recently propelled an American research aircraft to a speed of Mach 1.1. It had been dropped from the bomb bay of a B-29 at 30,000 feet on 8 January 1947 – the Bell X-100 – and it had accelerated to its top speed in a climb! Since then our own efforts at supersonic flight had been more dangerous and much less successful because of insufficient power making it necessary to accelerate in a dive. This greatly reduced their height for recovery or for baling out whenever things went wrong – which they often did once the aircraft had entered the dense air at lower altitudes and the control forces became excessive.

'Compressibility' effects (disruptions in airflow when travelling at speeds near the speed of sound) had then increased, making it impossible for the pilots – relying on conventional control power – to pull out of the dive. Having no ejector seats they were unable to bale out after loss of control at such high speed, and crashed. This occurred to the DH108 – a delta-shaped high speed research aircraft – on 27 September 1946 when de Havilland's chief test pilot Geoffrey de Havilland was killed. Two other test pilots – Stuart Muller-Roland of 6 ETPS and 'Jumbo' Genders of 4 ETPS were later to meet a similar fate in this research aircraft.

Test flying now looked even more dangerous than before the jet age but it obviously held promise of great things. The British still had the world lead in jet engine design and it seemed that we had everything to play for. Group Captain 'Teddy' Donaldson had just done 616 mph in the Derwent-engined Meteor (September 1946). The Vampire, long in service with the RAF, had recently been flown to nearly 60,000 feet by John Cunningham (Chief Test Pilot of de Havillands who had taken over after the loss of Geoffrey de Havilland).

Those of us who were summoned for interview at Rex House for possible acceptance on Number 6 ETPS Course on 20 February 1947 faced six people round the desk opposite. Two were civilian scientists from the RAF Education Branch, two were tutors from the ETPS who had done previous courses and the chairman was the School's Commandant – Group Captain 'Syd' Ubee.

We gave our reasons for wanting to join; 'as a wish to see safer and more advanced designs for military aircraft' with no risk of repeats of the Skua, Fulmar, Barracuda or, more recently, the Blackburn Firebrand. Perhaps we would be taught some of the theory of flight and learn the boffins' language so that we could talk to them in a language that they could understand and they would not so easily reject our criticisms. We would be taught what special faults to look for, why they happened and what the scientific problems were for putting them right. Our test flying reports would no longer be a matter of opinion but a report of the facts. The same report would contain recommendations for improvement giving reasons based on these facts alone. They would not be impressions such as 'she upped and bit me' or, 'she's a bit tricky on the approach'. There would be a good partnership between design office and test pilot. The first flight of a prototype could then perhaps be much safer and never of the 'back to the drawing board' variety – a phrase which had become a music hall joke. If, during the course, we might be allowed to fly many different types of aircraft, afterwards, we might then use our own operational experience in addition to our test experience to help advise our Admirals or Air Marshals on future operational requirements. Perhaps we could convince them that aircraft design for the Fleet Air Arm was not an art – as they believed – but practical science.

A week later the author learnt he had passed the interview and was required to join Number 6 Course at ETPS at RAF Cranfield, beginning 30 March 1947. From a personal point of view, those of us chosen for this course could, perhaps, depend upon an interesting and rewarding flying career from that time forward and, having had the equivalent of about ten year's salary spent on our training, there might be a better chance of our masters at the Admiralty granting us all permanent commissions if we asked for one – if only to get their money back. In any case, the ETPS course seemed to be nothing less than an excellent training for skills necessary for us to take part in 'no-non-sense practical research into military aviation.'

Starting in 1943 in a collection of Nissen huts at A&AEE, ETPS had moved in 1947 to proper brickbuilt accommodation at Royal Air Force Cranfield near R101 airship country in Bedfordshire. The number of students for 6 course numbered thirty and included civilians and servicemen from South Africa, Australia and Canada. Our flying tutors were all ex-ETPS, the chief being Cdr 'Tiffy' Torrens-Spence, and our Commandant Group Captain 'Syd' Ubee. Our marvellous Chief Technical Instructor was Mr G. MacLaren Humphries BSc, AIP, FRAeS – 'Humph' for short.

Test-flying accidents were much in the news at that time and if we had known that 50 out of the first 200 graduates at ETPS would have been killed in flying accidents in the next five years we might have thought twice about joining. But we were not thinking on those lines at all, particularly after reading an article in the *Times* at that time which stated:

> The RAF Station at Cranfield which already houses the Aeronautical College has now become the home of the Empire Test Pilots' School. Its purpose is to provide the most highly qualified test pilots in the world, men who are not only superb flyers but capable of analysing scientifically the performance and construction of the aircraft they handle . . . (and so on!)

This improved our morale immensely after the post-war depression and gave us a clear aim for the next year or two in the Services and we thought our-selves very lucky indeed.

Having visited 'Shortstown' near Cardington and seen the R101 under construction by Short's workers at the National Airship Works, it was inter-esting to visit the huge hangar there nearly thirty years later and to meet some of those involved with its construction at the time and who waved goodbye when it left the Cardington mast on 4 October 1930, bound for Karachi via France. We were firmly of the opinion that, far from it not being airworthy, the cause of its crash into the hillside near Beauvais was nothing other than the build-up of snow and ice on its forward envelope making it nose heavy. Then, by keeping full power on, the skipper had merely driven it earthwards by the negative lift from the depressed nose. Had the skipper stopped all engines, the envelope might easily have floated skywards again – albeit at the inconve-nience of having to return to UK to refuel to have another go in better weather the next day. Any evidence of a snow/ice build-up would have immediately vanished in the white heat of burning hydrogen seconds after hitting the ground. Nevertheless, it must have been a wise move for Britain to have suspended airship production from that time, for apart from the Graf Zeppelin that had carried about 20,000 passengers across the Atlantic from Frankfurt from 1928–1937, two American airships were lost in 1933 and the *Hindenburg* finally ended her life by exploding in a ball of fire at Lakehurst, the spark having come from a huge static discharge as she approached within a few feet of the mooring mast. Imperial Airways eventually held the key to long-distance air travel by their unlocking the doors to the British Empire with Short's Empire Flying Boats – until WW 2 put an end to it. Now, in 1948, might there not be a resurgence of interest in flying boats?

CHAPTER 2

ETPS

Number 6 Course at the Empire Test Pilots' School had 14 different types of aircraft available for practice test flying. These were: Gloster Meteor I and III, Auster, DH Mosquito T3, Airspeed Oxford T 1, Harvard T 2B, Avro Lincoln B 2, Fairey Firefly FR 1, DH Dominie C 1, Hawker Tempest II, Avro Anson C 9, DH Vampire F 1, Seafire 46 (almost identical to the Mark 47 but without folding wings), a Slingsby-Sedburg 'dual' glider and two ex-German Olympia sailplanes. None of these aircraft were experimental in any way – apart from additional instrumentation – but were chosen for their availability, small operating costs and safe flying qualities. However, these qualities could be altered to produce relatively unsafe characteristics but still stay within the embryo test pilot's ability to control and report upon. To help him quantify such faults – e.g. fore-and-aft instability, poor spin recovery, insufficient stall warning, excessive changes of trim when power is applied or when lowering flaps or undercarriage or when dropping bombs etc. – he would be allowed to use additional instrumentation permanently fitted in the cockpit. These 'desyns' would measure aileron angles, elevator and rudder angles, trim tab angles, 'G' readings and fuel consumption rates. He would also be given a hand-held, spring-loaded device to measure stickforces, perhaps the most widely used of the lot. The idea of this device was to hook one end round the stick and measure the pullforce in pounds on a scale on its shaft. Voice and instrument recorders in the cockpit were yet to be invented so that all results had to be written down on a knee pad at the time.

Aircraft maintenance and repair was in the hands of the RAF while at Cranfield, but when the School moved to RAE Farnborough later in the course, maintenance was taken over by civilians.

Morning lectures in the nine-month course totalled about 250 hours. Flying time on 6 Course was only 50 hours, considerably less than in some later courses. Visiting lecturers came from a selection of aircraft and engine designers, Royal Aeronautical Society members, civilian test pilots, aeronautical engineers and safety equipment manufacturers – all organised by 'Humph' – Mr G. McLaren-Humphries, BSc, AIP, FRAeS – the School's Chief Technical Instructor. He and his team soon brought us up to what we, alone, considered to be an adequate standard of maths, physics, mechanics, aerodynamics, thermo-dynamics and structures.

'Stability and control' formed the basis of the first 20 lectures. These taught us the science of flight and how man has attempted to go one better than bird flight while still retaining sufficient safety margins. The next twenty dealt with directional control, stalling and spinning hazards and the various safety devices used to prevent resultant accidents. Finally we had lectures by aircraft designers giving us the latest information on supersonics, jet engine design, weapon performance, radar usage, cockpit design, wing shapes and sizes, power controls and flying at extreme altitudes – low or high. The author has added a further chapter on the miraculous way the Royal Navy – assisted by ex-ETPS students – transformed the machinery and landing aids on its carriers' flight decks to allow jets to deckland safely in all weathers and how, by their invention of the steam-powered catapult, made it possible to operate top performance fighter/attack jet aircraft anywhere in the world more easily and more cost-effectively than the same aircraft could hope to operate from an airfield.

During the greater part of each morning at ETPS, the blackboard in the lecture room was usually covered entirely with mathematical formulae, symbols and diagrams, such that even the two Naval Engineer officers on the course (Lt/Cdr Peter Richmond and Lt/Cdr Gordan Hawkes) had difficulty in following it all. When things became so complicated that our slide-rules began to overheat and graph paper was running short again, thought became impossible and one or the other of us would open his desklid and begin playing a tin whistle as a sign that we had had enough hieroglyphics – or 'flute music' as they became to be called – and that it was time for us to be let out into the sunshine. This was necessary because some of the less sensitive boffin lecturers could easily interpret our polite silence during the last hour of their two-hour lectures as understanding. There was the continual danger that when our lecturer entered the realms of a subject such as: 'The random vibrations associated with non-linear damping of control surfaces' (or 'flutter'), he might imagine that we could work out in our heads – as easily as he – the seven sets of differential equations necessary to discover the correct 'mean square displacement for the necessary absorber spring'.

For every hour we spent in the air there must have been five hours spent in writing reports on the ground. It was hard work at ETPS and by the end of the year when we had at last completed our 'project' reports, we were more than ready for Christmas and relaxation with our families.

One thing had become clear, however. British inventions could seldom be 'sold' to British company bosses unless the inventor could describe them to him in simple, non-technical language or – which was and still is unlikely – that the boss, on his own, had sufficient technical knowledge to appreciate the need for them and their possible commercial value. The huge separation between 'Arts' and 'Science' education which schools' curricula had imposed upon most of us at the age of thirteen seemed to be preventing science-based graduates in Britain from becoming senior management in industry. The British inventor therefore sometimes had to cross the Atlantic to sell his ideas where school education up to the age of 18 was on a much broader, if less detailed, curriculum.

As if to emphasise this divide between scientists' dreams and their practicality, a notable example occurred at RAE Farnborough at this time. This was the scientists' attempt to do away with undercarriages in aircraft altogether – and thus save at least one-tenth of its structure weight – and land it on its belly onto a 'rubber deck'. No one seemed to have worked out what to do about it after that.

During the month's gap taken to move ETPS from Cranfield to Farnborough in the summer of 1947, our two Naval 'flying plumbers' – Peter Richmond and Gordan Hawkes – were sent to Thorney Island to kill time on an air/sea rescue course. The author did a few hours on Sea Otters at Lee-on-Solent to gain experience on flying boats. This amphibian was descended from the Supermarine Walrus. Landing five tons of flying boat on the Solent was glorious fun and extremely safe and easy. The landing area was always swept clear of debris by attendant launches so that the only hazards were pilot-induced. One such hazard – ask any flying boat pilot – was landing too fast and bouncing off the forward part of the planing hull onto the rear step in a series of swoops in imitation of a porpoise. Another hazard might be when landing with drift. The 'leeward' float might then 'dig in' and be damaged if the waves were above three-foot high, and an expensive capsize might follow. Seabirds would always kindly show us the true wind direction for they never landed or took off out of wind even if this were into imminent danger.

A typical air/sea rescue instruction period on the Sea Otter might entail the following menu. We would arrive at the spot for rescue early, splash down in the oggin and then drop anchor, remove the cockpit floor boards and take out our beer, sandwiches and fishing lines. After we had 'rescued' the rest of the party, which had meanwhile arrived by launch from the shore (we did this by taxying the port float over their inflatable/aircrew dinghy and then asking them to climb along the wing and enter the fuselage by the back door on the port side), we invited them to share our beer before they departed to sunbathe on an adjoining beach. When flying back to land at Lee afterwards we had to make a special effort to remember to lower the undercarriage!

We resumed our ETPS studies at Farnborough in September 1947. The 'Royal Aircraft Establishment' had been the centre for aeronautical research as the 'Royal Aircraft Factory' since the days of Cody before WW 1 when the Royal Flying Corps had first received its Royal Warrant on 13 April 1912, with flying badges and its motto: *Per Ardua ad Astra*. Farnborough's scientists had quickly reduced the gap in Britain's aeronautical engineering and industrial progress which had, up to that time, made Britain an 'also ran' compared with the United States of America, Germany and France.

We no longer had the luxury of Cranfield's accommodation and we 'unaccompanied' officers had our 'bed-and-breakfast' in Warburg Barracks in Aldershot which the Army GOC kindly made available for us. We shared several huge dormitories above the cavalry stables in identical grey Victorian 'Alcatraz-type' barracks, surrounded by acres of parade ground.

There was much social activity on the course and frequent, mixed parties were laid on at the RAF canteen so that everyone got to know each other. Peter

Richmond had spent his 'war terminal grant' of £120 on a beautiful Rolls-Royce Silver Ghost. It had a Hooper body known as a Landaulette. The driving compartment was roofed over but had no side screens thus leaving the 'chauffeur' exposed to the elements. The passengers had a hood which could be lowered in fine weather with wind-up side windows and, of course the usual barrier-window segregating them from the chauffeur at the wheel. There was voice-pipe 'intercom' to the driver, Morocco leather upholstery and a polished figured walnut fascia to complete the luxury. 'Gate' gear change, elementary antique instrumentation plus four-wheel servo braking completed the cockpit layout. Pete, his wife, children and guests would drive up in style to the RAF Mess. The children would go to bed on the back seat guarded by the family retriever and the remaining six passengers would file out to join the party.

This particular version of the Silver Ghost was fitted with two silencers. One of these silencers could be by-passed by pulling a lever in the driver's compartment. The by-pass was operated whenever the car was taken abroad into the Colonies so that the Natives would always be able to hear the car's approach and get out of the way. Unfortunately a leak had developed over the years in the valve which controlled this bypass. As a result, when the engine was switched off, an explosive mixture built up in the exhaust system. For some reason, there was a time delay of about half a minute before the mixture ignited – with a resounding bang. Needless to say, Pete's arrival never went unnoticed because the timing of this bang always seemed to coincide with his opening the pub door.

Peter, full of drive, initiative and good humour, had also bought a London double-decker bus – minus its engine – to beat the housing shortage. He had spent much of his spare time while at Cranfield in fitting this out as a luxury caravan. It had a bath and sitting room upstairs and the kitchen and two bedrooms downstairs. The picture of this Silver Ghost towing the bus through the West End of London caused no heads to turn. However, whenever this cavalcade appeared in the country – travelling on routes carefully mapped out in advance to avoid low bridges – it was cheered to the echo. It was particularly appreciated when it turned up at car race meetings, where one of our number at ETPS – Flt Lt 'Dicky' Stoop – often performed in his much modified Frazer-Nash BMW. He had designed a streamlined body for it in 1948 which was indistinguishable from the E-type Jaguar shapes of ten years later. (Peter Richmond later joined the Australian Fleet Air Arm forming in South Australia and retired as Captain to four acres of pasture and mangos 20 miles from the coast exactly on the Tropic of Capricorn near Rockhampton).

As for our flying during the first four months at ETPS, there were very few 'incidents' or excitements worthy of note. According to my log book my first trip – on April the 1st – was with 'Cyclops' Brown in an Airspeed Oxford. Squadron Leader C.B. Brown had only one eye – like our Commandant – having lost the other in the Battle of Britain. Nevertheless, the RAF had allowed him to continue flying; but because he had lost binocular vision and could only judge his height above the ground from 'previous experience', he had developed a technique of assessing height when landing by performing a series of 'steps' until the wheels touched. He would then throttle back and make a perfect landing.

With 'Cyclops' in the righthand seat in the Oxford I was quickly apprised of the added responsibilities of flying a multi-seat, multi-engined aircraft for the first time. Not only was there the worry of having someone else's nerves and safety to think about but there was the added problem of controlling two or more engines instead of one and having to cope with far larger stickforces and slower responses. This meant that if one of these engines failed in the Oxford, far-reaching decisions had to be made instantly. Instead of making a simple decision – e.g. a forced landing or a bale-out as would be the case in a Seafire – in a twin- or four-engined aircraft you were expected to save the aircraft by flying it back to an airfield and landing it in one piece on the remaining engine(s).

If engine failure occurred in a twin, this was even more awkward than in a four-engined aircraft for it would mean that you had lost half your total power. If, at the time of failure you were not going at or above the 'safety speed' (sometimes referred to as the 'critical speed') the aircraft would either not have enough rudder power to keep straight on the good engine or would not have enough power to maintain flying speed – or both – because of the much higher drag and the much weaker rudder/fin power available at these slow speeds. (Please see Part 1 of the next chapter for a note on the 'V-squared law' which explains the effect of airspeed on aircraft controllability). If the dead engine was not equipped with a feathering propeller, its windmilling drag, even in coarse pitch, further reduced the effective power from the live engine and increased the amount of rudder needed to keep straight. If the aircraft was at its 'maximum permitted weight' and had only just taken off, with the added drag of having its flaps and wheels down at the moment of engine failure, the decision as to what to do next could be even more difficult!

Engine failure practice in the Mosquito T3 was also very exciting. Its 'safety speed' – or 'critical speed' – was 160 mph (143 knots). With the under-carriage and flaps going up it would climb away safely at this speed, the pilot nevertheless needed a bootful of rudder and needed to wind on rudder trim madly to relieve the footload as soon as possible. If engine failure occurred below this 'critical' speed – some fifty miles an hour above take-off speed which sometimes took a minute's flying time to achieve – instructions were to 'close throttle on the live engine and land straight ahead'. Needless to say, all practice landings on one engine in this particular aircraft were simulated by carrying out the procedure at a safe height.

It was small wonder, therefore, that before the arrival of jet power and multi-seat airliners, the Air Registration Board, recently set up by the government to help improve international safety standards, should insist on lower 'critical' safety speeds and much longer runways with adequate 'overshoot' areas. Designers replied to this challenge by immediately increasing rudder and fin areas and by placing the jet engines as near as practicable to the centre-line of the fuselage, so giving the modern twin-jet fighter/attack aircraft almost the same safe directional handling characteristics with a failed engine as normal flight in a single-engined aircraft. The Meteor had inexplicably been designed with 'wide-apart' engines and therefore had suffered from the same high critical speed disadvantages as most twin prop/piston-engined air-craft of World War 2. Apart from increasing fin/rudder power in piston-engined twins, Shorts designed their Sturgeon twin-Merlined 'fighter' with contra-props, their increased blade area allowing a reduction in their diameter, so reducing their needed distance from the fuselage.

The remainder of our flying during the first three or four months at ETPS was taken up by practising one or two of the more simple performance and handling tests. Best climbing speeds, fuel consumptions, rates of climb at varying weights and heights, establishing the 'speed for minimum power' (VIMP), stalling, ceiling climbs, phugoids (please see Part 4 of the next chapter), take-off distances at various windspeeds and at various weights and, of course, spinning the Harvard.

This was one of the many hundreds of American-built Harvards declared redundant by the RAF in 1948. It had the usual 600 hp, R-1340 Pratt & Whitney Wasp engine which, if its 2½ tons was flown flat out at its full 1950 rpm, was twice as noisy as any jet because its prop's tip speeds became super-sonic and it became famous for waking everyone up for miles around.

Flying jets for the first time was a great thrill. Apart from the smoothness and lack of cockpit noise and vibration, the major handling differences – good and bad – could be easily explained by its absence of propeller torque effects and the added difficulties of having to make landings on short runways without the advantages of instant propeller thrust/drag to control its higher landing speeds. We soon experienced the jets' increased fuel consumption rate, e.g., the Meteor 3 often used half a Seafire III's internal 85 gallon fuel-load by the time it had taken off and, at low altitudes, it used fuel at five times the equivalent piston-engined rate per mile. Finally, we had to learn to cope with the jets' added control problems due to 'compressibility' effects at high-Mach and high altitude. This was a whole new problem on its own.

These different characteristics between piston and jet aircraft meant all too clearly that until considerable economies could be made in the rates of fuel consumption by jets at low altitudes, piston-engined fighters would continue to be needed for ground attack/defence duties. A jet fighter sent up to combat enemy ground attack aircraft would itself need to patrol at height to preserve fuel supplies and would be going too fast to shoot at slow-moving fighter-bombers near ground level if it managed to spot them from above without its own or AEW 'look-down' radar guidance. (The AN/APS 20 radar was at this time being developed in USA for use in the US Navy's Skyraider aircraft). The only possible course of action which we saw for the jet fighter at this time was for it to dive well below its quarry and lose speed by pulling up vertically to make his attack – just as the German Me 109s did when attacking the slower-moving Hurricanes attempting to provide close fighter escort for our day bombers in the early months of the war.

Likewise, if enemy bombers were soon to make use of the greatly increased high-altitude efficiency and power of the jet engine, which would treble their *en-route* speed to their targets in future wars, jet fighters would also be required for high altitude interception duties at supersonic speeds. Then, to further complicate the situation, if jet bombers made their final approaches to their targets by diving to low level to escape radar detection in the last hundred miles or so, the defending fighters would need to be capable of very high speeds and good manoeuvrability at very low altitudes as well as at 50,000 feet. In 1948 this seemed to be an impossible requirement for the aircraft designers to meet in a single fighter design. (The problem was eventually, partly solved by 'variable sweep' in the early 1960s and later by the additional advantage of having 'fire-and-forget' or 'stand-off' weapons fired from the attacking aircraft when under the command and control of a 'look-down' radar-equipped AEW aircraft flying at a safe distance up to 200 miles away).

The Vampire at ETPS was a delight to fly, almost silent compared with the frightful noise in a Mosquito, Tempest or Seafire 46/47 cockpit. Devoid of airscrew torque effects and almost unaffected directionally by engine gyroscopic forces in steep turns, it presented the pilot – sitting at the front – with a marvellous view of his rocket or gun targets or of the flight deck/runway when landing. Control 'harmonisation' – the various in-built forces required to move ailerons, elevator and rudder a given amount – were nicely balanced throughout the speed range and remained in the popular ratio 1, 2 and 3 respectively in terms of 'heavyness'. Decklanding – with a suitably modified barrier or none at all – was found to be the easiest thing imaginable, for the Vampire sat down firmly on the runway at safe touchdown speeds 15–20 mph above its stall speed, thanks to its tricycle undercarriage. With slightly larger flaps to give more drag, engine control problems were not evident at these sensibly higher approach speeds, particularly as the engine designers of the Goblin placed restrictors in the fuel lines thus making it impossible for the pilot to 'stall' the engine by over-eager throttle opening. Later jet designs were given very large airbrakes. These were fully extended when landing, so increasing engine rpm to above the 60 per cent mark, so that power increase per rpm increase was much improved, requiring smaller throttle movements and much less delay in power response with little risk of engine stalling.

Flight deck experience of the jet soon taught us all to beware of the jet exhaust, too. Jet thrust, being spread over a hundredth of the area of an equivalent thrust from a propeller, had to emerge at very high velocity from its jet pipe. It could do immense damage if anyone got in its way, so that hydraulically operated steel barriers were provided behind the catapult positions on every flight deck from 1951 onwards and flight decks were carefully swept of all debris which, if hard and solid and then picked up by a jet's efflux, could act as a rifle bullet and kill someone.

Our first trip in the School's Meteor III – after the usual ten-minute study of the Pilot's Notes and a five-minute briefing on the controls by 'Titch' Havercroft – was uneventful. After start-up, using the usual 24-volt batteries, the pilot would wave away the chocks and move forward in the smooth silence of the closed cockpit with idling rpm of about 5,000 on both Derwent V engines. There was no warm-up, no testing of magnetos or propeller pitch controls and, apart from one or two temperature and pressure dials to keep an eye on there was nothing to do but steer with brake and rudder for the end of the duty runway, with the comforts of near perfect forward vision, a heated/cooled and pressurised cockpit surrounded with clear Perspex in all directions. Even the discomfort of having to wear 'bone-domes' had not reduced this pleasure for they were not yet mandatory.

Acceleration to 120 knots for take-off took about 15 seconds – four times as long as in a Seafire to this speed and requiring about four times the distance. Rotation and unstick occurred with a whirring sound coming from the wheels – until I remembered to brake them before retraction. The Meteor 3 climbed at about 5,000 feet per minute at an airspeed of 300 knots and at an angle of about 30 degrees nose-up. There was no vibration, the control column was steady, the instrument pointers moved slowly and smoothly and the whole aircraft structure seemed to be at one with itself. The sensation of speed and the rapid climb rate was only borne home to the pilot by the changes in cockpit pressure affecting the ears and the flashes of changing light when passing through the various cloud layers.

Flight on one engine at speeds above 160 kts was smooth and easy and, without the added effects of propeller-induced yaw, very little rudder was required to keep straight. However, at speeds below this and with landing gear down, directional control in the 'meat-box' was no better than in propeller-driven twins. (Later versions – e.g., the Meteor NF 11 and 14 – were fitted with a larger fin and rudder to partially cure this difficulty). The Meteor's aileron response at these low speeds was poor compared with the Seafire but the usual lack of positive speed control on the landing approach was more than made up for by the better view and the improved directional control and much safer braking due to the nosewheel undercarriage.

The Seafire 47 represented Supermarine's final answer to critics of earlier Marks of Seafire. By fitting contra-props in the 46 and 47, all the adverse aerodynamic, gyroscopic and engine torque effects had been cancelled out. All-round pilot vision had been greatly improved by the tear-drop hood, and rate-of-roll had been doubled at speeds above 300 knots by the fitting of spring tabs on ailerons of increased area. Fore-and-aft instability – and the dreaded effects of the large 'positive weight' in the elevator control circuit (see later), had been entirely eliminated and, to further assist decklanding, a tail hook had replaced the belly hook, and the undercarriage could now take rates of descent up to ten ft/sec at touchdown instead of the Seafire/Spitfire maximum of about seven ft/sec., without fear of collapsing.

The Seafire 46/47 series could carry twice the fuel load of the ordinary Marks of Seafire/Spitfire (without having to use surplus 90-gallon Kittyhawk tanks as we had had to do in the Pacific) and could be loaded with bombs and rockets under its wings as well as under its belly. The weapon load was, of course, suspended directly below its centre of gravity. However, the additional internal fuel could mostly only be added in tanks placed under and behind the pilot and therefore aft of the CG, thus limiting permissible G manoevres until the fuel was used. Even with this heavy load of 'stores' on board its power/weight ratio was 20 per cent higher than in the Seafire/Spitfire Ib. Its 2,300 hp Griffon 85 had the latest two-stage, two-speed supercharger with auto-change to the higher gear at about 15,000 feet. (An 'intercooler' had been inserted in the supercharger circuit to increase the density – and thus fuel content – in the intake mixture after the first stage compressor had done its job and before the second stage took over).

The supercharger system in 'high gear' used a great deal of power to drive it, so that we found on taking measurements at ETPS, that air-miles-per-gallon were better at lowish altitudes where the high-gear 'turbo' was not clutched-in, than at high altitudes.

We were allowed about six flights in the ETPS' Mosquito T3 and B35. A few hooked versions were about to be delivered to the Navy for deck trials – for some reason which we could not fathom – for they could not possibly be allowed to make single-engined decklandings in case of an engine failure. Many more unhooked ex-RAF night-fighter versions of this and the Meteor were later taken into use by the Navy at various inter-service development units ashore to improve naval experience in 'electronic warfare' aids. The RAF continued to use the Meteor NF 14 until 1961 when, at last, the Javelin came into service to replace it.

The ETPS version of the Meteor and all Mosquito versions were never of much interest to naval fighter pilots on the course as we realised that they would be dangerous to deckland with one engine failed. Any attempt to abort a single-engine approach or landing would certainly end in disaster due to lack of rudder power at these slow speeds. In fact the Mosquito's 'safety speed' (the minimum it would be safe to apply the necessary full power on one engine if the other had failed) was as high as 138 knots – or 45 knots faster than its decklanding approach speed. We could never understand why deck trials were carried out in the Mosquito or Meteor for it was surely a waste of time.

However, the Sea Hornet – which we flew at Boscombe Down on the completion of the course at ETPS – with its 'handed' propellers, (the 'inward-slanting' slipstream from which assisted rudder power in single-engined approaches) had a much lower safety speed – or critical speed – than the 'Mozzie' and might even have survived a wave-off on one engine if this were given at least a mile from touchdown by the batsman. However, a barrier accident could have been fatal due to the proximity of the propellers to the pilot's cockpit and this alone would have limited its usefulness until the angled deck made barriers unnecessary by 1953.

Whilst on the subject of the Hornet, the first Sea Hornet Night Fighter 21 with folding wings had already made its first trip. On 12 May 1947, Ken Hickson on No. 4 Course, was carrying out low level flight trials from A&AEE Boscombe Down in the second prototype when its starboard engine fell out and the aircraft disintegrated. He managed to bale out, somehow, and he walked away uninjured.

From our lectures on structures and our knowledge of mathematics – which was improved 100 per cent at ETPS – we came to the conclusion that the structural failure which originated in the rear engine bearers of Ken Hickson's Hornet may have come about because of engine/prop gyroscopic effects causing unexpected sideloads on the engine bearers, they having been mainly designed to withstand vertical loads. With Ken flying at high speed in the bumpy conditions usual at low level, the continuous 'bounce' of the high G loadings in a Hornet would have caused the engines to pitch on their rear bearers – something all of us had noticed when we flew the Hornet at A&AEE. This movement would then have been translated by propeller gyroscopic action into equally large sideloads to the engine mountings. If de Havilland's designers had not anticipated this, it seemed possible to us that the bearers would not have been designed to withstand such sideloads – which could have been up to 6G. The starboard engine would suffer more than the port as its engine rotated in the same direction as it propeller and the two would therefore have had a united gyro effect, unlike the normal Merlin/prop combination. Whatever the cause of this failure in the Hornet, it made us all feel slightly doubtful about de Havilland's wood/metal construction methods and the designers' correct remembrance of some simple schoolboy scientific principles.

The Meteor 3 was the only other jet besides the Vampire 1 available for us to fly at ETPS. The Navy were not interested in it even as a night-fighter because of its short endurance and its poor single-engined handling characteristics already mentioned. The Royal Navy seemed to favour single-engined prop-jets at this time. They were still suspicious of using pure jets for deck-landings and take-offs. They considered that prop-jets would give better low-level fuel economy and better decklanding speed control, even if this was at the expense of poor high altitude performance and a much lower top speed. Most of this thinking was due to the adverse report on the Vampire's deck-landing trials in 1945 and which gave rise to the Navy's perseverance with the Firebrand and the appearance of the Wyvern prop-jet in the early 1950s.

The United States Navy's test centre at Patuxent River had carried out trials of the 'composite' (½ jet/½ piston engine) Ryan 'Fireball' aboard their CVE *Wake Island* in the summer of 1945 and had established a liking for single-engined jets two years before the Royal Navy ordered its first jet fighter – the Attacker – and four years before it received its first jets into service in 702 squadron. (It is interesting to note that the Germans also flew their Me 262 twin jet in March 1942 for the first series of test flights with a supplementary piston-engine like the Ryan Fireball, as a much needed safety measure.)

The first prototype Attacker TS409 – single Nene jet engine of 4,500 lb thrust – made its first flight from Boscombe Down in the hands of Jeffrey Quill on 17 June 1946. It had no pressure cockpit or ejector seat. The second much improved prototype flew with Lt/Cdr Mike Lithgow – Supermarine's new Chief Test Pilot – on 17 June 1947. It went into service with 800 Squadron commanded by Lt/Cdr George Baldwin in July 1951 and embarked in the brand-new *Eagle* in March 1952. This was nearly seven years after the first jet decklanding.

Perhaps the most delightful of all the types that we flew at ETPS was the Olympia sailplane. Two of these were based at Lasham and we had a chance to have a few trips in each of them. The keen boat sailors amongst us could easily see the similarity between the driving action of the wind on a boat's sails and its lift force on a sailplane's wings; sufficient to lift one of us plus a large flying machine like the Olympia off the ground at a mere 40 knots airspeed.

We were towed off by the School's Auster – or 'winched off' if there was sufficient wind – and we released ourselves between 500 and 1000 feet. The Auster's slipstream was kept low by the towing pilot holding his tail down during acceleration to the 'unstick' speed of the Olympia. Then, with about 45 mph on the glider's ASI, we were told to pull back on the stick to take the glider *slightly* above the Auster's slipstream and hold it there until the Auster gathered enough speed to leave the ground and climb away. In this way, the risk of getting caught in the towing aircraft's slipstream was reduced to a minimum. Climbing with the Olympia above the Auster's slipstream, we would release the tow near the largest cumulus cloud in the district. We would then position the Olympia below this cumulus cloud and, maintaining an airspeed of about 45 mph, we would watch for the rate-of-climb/descent needle to nudge itself into the green (positive rate of climb) section of the dial – climbing at about 100 ft per minute; and all this energy was free of charge! We could have stayed airborne for hours in this beautiful bright silence that autumn day at Lasham just like any albatross over the Atlantic. But we were limited to about 30 minutes each so that there would be time for all of us to have a go in the perfect conditions prevailing.

Landing a glider for the first time is fairly nerve-wracking. Everyone is watching you, hoping that you will make a porridge either by too early use of the airbrakes or by overshooting. One can appreciate the difficulties that a father swan must have when landing on a small and tree-obstructed pond in a flat calm – with his wife sitting on the nest and laughing her head off if he makes a mistake and collides with a duck on his landing run.

We learnt much from our gliding experience. How a sailplane's wings are always built with a very high 'aspect ratio' (long and narrow) in accordance with the knowledge gained from windtunnel experiments and observation of the wing design of soaring birds. We learnt that such long, 'narrow' wings, although structurally weak (soaring seabirds make their nests on cliffs to allow sufficient height to gain flying speed in an initial glide rather than by energetic wing flapping for which their wings are not constructed) gave far more lift and much less drag per square foot of wing area at slow speeds and high angles-of-attack than a short, stubby wing might give. This fact seems to emphasise the vast improvement in thrust efficiency which the invention in 1923 of 'Bermuda-shaped' sails – tall and narrow – had given to racing yachts when 'close-hauled', and of the importance of jibs to assist airflow round the leeward side of the mast – where the mast would otherwise act as a serious lift spoiler to the more important leeward-side airflow of the mainsail when sailing 'close-hauled'. We could easily see the analogy between Handley Page slots in the Swordfish and the jibs' effect on lee-side mainsail airflow.

Perhaps a brief word on sailing might be of interest here, for there seems to be a natural affinity between sailing and flying, judging by the number of aircrew who have sailing boats of their own.

Modern racers make use of high aspect ratio sails (tall and narrow) with their foot close to the deck to provide an 'endplate' effect and so reduce vortex drag. Their angle of incidence to the wind can never exceed about 15 degrees without stalling, so that the 'sheets' are let out or drawn in through fairleads on the deck to keep the most efficient angle at all times when sailing 'on the wind' when maximum thrust is required. When sailing 'off the wind' – i.e. when the wind is coming from behind at an angle to the boat's hull of more than about 120 degrees – the wind enters the sails at an ever-increasing angle until it becomes necessary to set a spinnaker – at which time the sails are fully stalled at right-angles to the wind direction and make use of all its energy by reducing the windspeed in the 'belly' of the sail to nearly zero – as in a parachute.

When starting to sail and with the boat head-to-wind, the sails are 'close-hauled' to a 25-degree angle to the fore-and-aft line of the boat's hull and the boat is turned through 40 degrees out of wind to fill them. At an angle of attack of about 15 degrees to the wind, the sails are giving their maximum thrust without stalling from which the forward component is available for forward thrust and the sidethrust component being 90 per cent stopped by the lateral resistance of the boat's keel. The boat is now 'close-hauled' and sailing as near to the wind direction as is efficient in any sailing boat. Any 'closer' to the wind than this 40 degree angle and the sail will not fill with wind enough to have any worthwhile forward thrust component and the boat will merely drift sideways. Likewise, if the sails' angle-of-attack is increased to more than about 15–20 degrees (less than this if the sail is 'flat' cut for use in high wind speeds) the sail will stall, drag will increase and the boat will not be sailing at its best speed and lose the race. As the boat is turned further 'out of wind', say through another 45–50 degrees, the wind will be coming from 90 degrees 'on the beam'. If the sails are let out by the correct amount, the sails will then be at their most efficient, giving about half their 'lift' as *forward* thrust. With the wind 'on the beam' in this way, most lightly-built dinghies and some ocean racers will get enough sail thrust to allow them to 'get up and plane' like speedboats. Very lightly-built racing dinghies and sailboards can even reach a speed of twenty knots in a 20-knot wind when planing 'on a reach' in this way.

Sail 'trimming' is an art as well as a science. Too much incidence, and the sail will stall and lose two-thirds of its forward thrust. Anything less than the correct angle by a few degrees and the wind will not fill the sails properly. If the sails are hauled in too hard – say to an angle to the fore-and-aft line of less than about 15 degrees – the sails' forward thrust component will be too small and the boat will suffer from 'pinching', i.e., make excessive leeway and lose the race. If the skipper slackens off the sheets too much when sailing to windward and 'bears away' too much to keep them filled with wind he will probably then be sailing the boat too 'free' – say at 50 degrees to the wind direction instead of about 40 or 45 – and lose the race. The nearest that a boat can sail against the wind direction is about 40 degrees to one side or the other, so that on 'tacking', he needs to alter course by about 80 degrees at least. Sailing 'against the wind' is a slow business, and the dangers of a 'lee shore' in rough weather and with no auxiliary engine power available still cause yachtsmen the greatest trouble.

When sailing 'close hauled', the side thrust from the wind is perhaps five times the forward thrust component. All racing boats prevent excessive sideways motion – or leeway – by fitting deep and narrow keels, similar to the high aspect ratio fins on aircraft. Deep, narrow and thin keels have far less drag than the normal 'bilge keel' variety. Some yacht designers have taken yet another leaf from the aerodynamicist and have put 'end plates' – or fins – at the lower extremities of their racing keels to prevent excessive vortex drag – as many modern airliners have at the ends of the wings.

Just as birds recognise when their wings are stalling and inefficient – probably by feeling their top wing feathers rise – so a yacht skipper will watch wool tufts he has had fixed to the lee sides of his jib for signs of an airflow breakaway and he will adjust his helm or sheets accordingly. There are, of course, many 'wrinkles' to learn in this sailing business. Perhaps one of these is worth a mention. There is always a need to adjust the sails' shape or camber to allow maximum 'lift' when the windspeed changes i.e., the higher the windspeed the flatter the sail cut, and vice versa just as in aircraft. The sail must be trimmed so that it remains at the same, correct, angle of attack throughout its entire length from top to foot. Mast-bending can often accomplish the sail-flattening requirement in most racing yachts and in sailboards. Sail battens can also make the sail material conform to the true aerodynamic shape of an aerofoil at any windspeed. 'Kicking straps' can apply a downward pull to the mainsail boom to ensure no angle-of-attack variance between the top and foot of a mainsail and jib sheeting positions can be altered to make the jib conform. Hull shape is, of course, all-important to a boat's speed. This aspect is dealt with briefly later on when the subject is flying boats.

The final month's flying at ETPS was taken up with exercises such as 'ceiling climbs' in a Meteor 3 to 43,000 feet (10,937 feet *less* than the Bristol Type 138A achieved in 1937), crosswind landings in a Mosquito, rates of roll in a Meteor, out-of-trim dives in a Firefly, stick-force per G in a Tempest, Lincoln and Mosquito, and cross-wind landings in a Dominie – or DH Rapide.

Finally we flew over to Belfast in our two Lincolns to attend a party given by Short Brothers at Sydenham – the guests of Tom Brooke-Smith, Short's Chief Test Pilot who was on Number 6 Course with us. At this time 'Brookie' asked the author to come and join him in a year's time at Belfast as Deputy Chief Test Pilot. It was too difficult to refuse, particularly as it was at double my Naval pay and it would allow the chance of a home life at last.

CHAPTER 3

SOME BASIC REQUIREMENTS FOR SAFE AIRCRAFT DESIGN

This chapter interrupts the narrative in order to give the reader some idea of what we learnt from our main lectures at ETPS. The chapter is in four main parts.

Part 1   Longitudinal Stability

Fore-and-aft 'balance'
One of the more easily understood lectures on this subject to students on number 6 Course at ETPS was by 'Humph' himself. He explained to us the aerodynamic meaning of 'aircraft stability' by comparing an aircraft's fore-and-aft balance – or stability – to that of a see-saw. If the fuselage represented the plank of wood in a child's see-saw, its balance point would be the position of the aircraft's centre of gravity, or CG, and where the centre-of-lift from its wings had to be applied to preserve its proper longitudinal balance.

Bearing in mind that before the days of 'fly-by-wire' – which nowadays can give stable characteristics to aircraft having purposely built-in *in*stability – it was essential for the designer of a prototype fighter in those days to keep a very close check on its CG position during building and to have extensive checks in the wind tunnel of the centre-of-lift line during the building and attachment of the wings. So that, at ETPS, the subject of *fore-and-aft stability* stood out from the rest as being the most important.

Humph also gave us a simple means of understanding what is meant by: a *stable* aircraft, an *unstable* aircraft, and a *neutrally stable* aircraft. *Positive stability* can be represented by the behaviour of a ball bearing placed at the centre of a smooth saucer, *instability* – by the same ball bearing placed at the centre of the same saucer turned upsidedown and *neutral stability* – by the ball bearing placed on a level, flat surface. In the first case, if the ball is displaced it will return to its central position on its own. In the second case, it will run off the saucer completely, gathering speed as it does so. In the third case, the ball will do neither of these things and gently come to rest of its own accord and stay there.

The amount of lift required from the wings while an aircraft is manoeuvering varies from about three or four times the aircraft's weight for a bomber like the Lincoln, to about eight times – or 8 G – for a fighter. A fighter would also have to be safe to fly with up to minus 3 G being imposed on it without any risk of structural failure or loss of control.

The amount of wing lift to support these G forces is governed by a simple formula:

Lift is proportional to:
½ × Rho.V squared.Sine Alpha.S × C.

where: Rho=relative air density. V=the speed the aircraft is flying. Alpha=the angle-of-attack of the wing. S=the wing area. C=the 'lift coefficient' of the wing.

The most significant factor in this much simplified formula is that *lift increases as the square of the indicated airspeed*. This means that a wing travelling through the air at 70 miles and hour gives approximately twice the lift/drag as the same wing travelling at 50 mph – other things being equal.

The 'centre-of-lift' of any aerofoil tends to alter its position slightly with angle-of-attack and airspeed and this requires constant action by the pilot to correct – i.e., he raises or lowers the nose by pulling or pushing on the control column or, for more permanent changes in airspeed or attitude, he will need to alter the positions of the trimming tabs at the trailing edges of the control surfaces to 'trim out' any persistent stick forces not required. Most aircraft are equipped with wheels or levers in the cockpit to allow the pilot to alter the positions of these trimming tabs in flight. In some aircraft, the changes of trim during flight are so small that the pilot seldom has to use them. In others, it is essential to set the trim tabs before take-off if dangerously heavy stick or rudder forces are not to be encountered. Lateral – or aileron – trimming tabs were seldom necessary in aircraft such as the Spitfire/Seafire for changes of trim with speed or power were insignificant. Permanent tendencies for one wing to be 'heavier' than the other – usually caused by manufacturing differences – were usually offset by doping a short length of chord onto the upper surface of the trailing edge of the appropriate aileron. The chord's air resistance acted as a small tab and lowered that aileron slightly to raise the required wing to horizontal. It was unsafe to dope the chord on the lower surfaces of ailerons, as this would have increased their natural tendency to 'up-float' and be torn off due to overbalance, especially if they were fitted with spring tabs.

Almost the entire lift required by an aircraft is borne on its mainplanes. Tailplanes do not contribute lift at all in normal flight (unless, as in the case of the early Spitfire/Seafire, the aircraft is unstable and 'tail-heavy'). In fact, tailplanes, such as on the Buccaneer in the landing and take-off mode, contribute a considerable amount of *negative* lift. That is the reason why so many designers are fitting elevators *forward* of the CG in some new fighter aircraft designs where their positive angle-of-attack when the pilot pulls the stick back or when he trims the aircraft for landing or take-off, *contributes* to total lift just when it is most required. An example is the new Euro-fighter.

Wind-tunnel tests – and observation of soaring birds' wing shapes – tells us that long-span, narrow wings (i.e., wings with a high 'aspect ratio') contribute more lift and less drag for a given area than short-span, long-chord wings. High aspect ratio wings are therefore used in gliders. Nature makes use of narrow wings in all soaring birds such as the albatross – a bird having a ten-foot wingspan in some species – and which is so efficient in selecting and making use of minute rising air currents at any altitude that it can stay airborne for hours without having to flap its wings once. Racing sailing boats make use of high, narrow sails and deep narrow keels for exactly the same reasons i.e., keeping lift at a maximum and aero-drag at a minimum with such beautiful aerofoil shapes.

The *top* surface of any aerofoil contributes twice the lift of its lower surface. A smooth airflow over the top surface is essential. To help achieve this, choice of one or more of the following is desirable: (a)   Leading-edge 'slots' or 'droop' to artificially increase wing 'camber' (and therefore lift coefficient) for landing, take-off and manoeuvrability. (b)   'Boundary layer control' (BLC), described later. (c)   Extra-smooth finish. (Wing skinning in high performance aircraft is now machined out of the solid.) (d)   Careful choice of wing thickness/chord ratio.

All the above devices tend to preserve smooth, fast 'overwing' airflow, particularly as wing incidence increases. Once the upper surface's air breaks away from a smooth, close contact with a wing's upper surface it becomes turbulent, lift is lost, drag increases and a complete stall of the wing will result if the incidence is not immediately reduced by the pilot pushing forward on the stick and 'unloading' the wing as he does so. (Please see a note on 'laminar airflow' later in this chapter).

Sailmakers have long reduced the 'lift-spoiler' effect of a sailing-boat's mast by making use of the 'Handley Page Slot' effect of a tall, narrow jib. (A famous example of the automatic H.P Slot is in the Swordfish of WW 2 and can, of course, be seen at the Fleet Air Arm Museum at Yeovilton.) A sailing yacht's jib is therefore carefully placed and trimmed to guide the airflow round the lee side of the mast and will smooth out the turbulence on the lee side of the mainsail, increase its 'lift' and reduce its drag when the yacht is sailing closehauled, by a very large amount.

In sailboards where there is no jib, the 'mast' consists of a streamlined, revolving, aerofoil-shaped strut. Its bend – and thus the sail camber or thickness/chord ratio – can be altered at will by the 'pilot' to cater for changes in wind strength and varying incidence angles. The higher the windspeed, the less 'camber' he will apply to the sail. The 'V-squared' law tells him in no uncertain way that if the windspeed *doubles*, his sail will be capable of giving him *four times* the thrust and he will have to lean over much further to balance the windstrength or reduce the sail's incidence to a quarter of what it was if he wants to stay upright!

The mast of a sailboard can be swayed fore and aft to ensure the boat's lateral centre of effort is just where the 'pilot' wants it, and to help him steer without having to bother with a rudder. The sailboard skipper can also sway the mast to windward or leeward to offset the effects of sudden changes in windspeeds tending to capsize him either to windward or leeward.

Racing sailing-boat keel and rudder designers have taken advice from the aerodynamicist by designing deep, narrow (or high aspect ratio) keels and rudders for their racing boats. Some marine architects have, however, missed the advice of aircraft designers and have not learnt the importance of guarding against metal fatigue failures at the keel's joining points with the hull. Metal fatigue, as its name implies, is caused by repetitive strains at a single point in a continuous structure which eventually leads to its failure at that point. None of these strains on their own would be capable of breaking the structure. It is their number, occurring at exactly the same point, which lead to the metal 'crystaline' fatigue and its sudden, ultimate failure – as many an aircraft designer has found out to his firm's cost! Even a small notch made by a scratch on the surface of an otherwise perfect steel beam can concentrate a repetitive bending strain at this one point, and lead to its early failure. A recent case has occurred at a funfare where a light support fell across the path of a roller-coaster trolley, with disastrous results. The light support had been lashed to a framework at its base, but the continual sway-effect of the wind had fatigued the steel beam at the point of its lashing causing it to break suddenly without warning. The best method of fatigue failure prevention is for the builder/designer to ensure that built-in points of stress in any structure are kept to a minimum and if there have to be any – such as the mainplane/fuse-lage junction in an aircraft – that the repetitive loads are spread over a wide area of the joint by fairing in strengthening at these points to allow gradual changes in metal section to 'spread the load'.

Metal fatigue even affected the Buccaneer during the course of its life. The main wing/hull spar, machined from the solid, developed cracks in many places after 200 hours of bumpy low-level flying in USA and Germany. The immediate remedy to prevent the cracks from spreading was to drill small holes at their extremeties and, having detected these cracks by X-rays, by spreading the point of stress over a wider area. This allowed the Buccaneer to remain in service without further trouble for the whole of its thirty-two years of low-level flying.

Just as Mitchell found that the Spitfire went 15 mph faster with smooth hull rivets, yacht designers seek to reduce wetted area to a minimum and try to copy the lovely dolphin in the smooth shape of its body and fins.

Birds can, of course alter their wing sweepback to cater for small changes in their CG position. Hang-gliders move their weight fore-and-aft and side-ways. Kite flyers alter their string attachment points. But artists have yet to study aerodynamics, for, like Icarus, they still portray human shapes in the form of angels with their wings attached at their shoulders when CG considerations require the lift to be centred at the belly-button position!

As discussed above, designers try to choose a wing shape and an air-craft CG position which will lead to neutral longitudinal stability and will not require continuous corrective action by the pilot when he alters speed, particularly in the design of fighter aircraft. Not only must these 'centre-of-lift' position changes be small with changes in flight speed, but they must be 'self-righting' or 'positive'. That is to say they must induce an automatic nose-up change of trim when speed increases and a nose-down trim change when speed decreases.

An aircraft pushed into a dive from its 'trimmed' speed in level flight should automatically pull itself gently out of this dive and resume its original, 'trimmed,' flight speed and attitude. (As mentioned above, a 'trimming tab' is a small aerofoil hinged to the trailing edge of a flying control surface. Its angle can be altered to produce a 'bias' in the main control by the pilot winding a small wheel in the cockpit in the direction that he wants to apply the bias.) Likewise, if an aircraft is pulled into a climb and the airspeed is allowed to fall and then the stick is released, the aircraft should gently lower its nose and regain its original speed without any needed action by the pilot.

A simple check of an aircraft's 'long stab' can be made by the pilot releasing the controls in a glide, winding back a few degrees on the elevator trim tab and seeing what happens. A stable aircraft will nose-up to the stall. At the stall – which should occur gently without wing drop – the nose will fall, the aircraft will gather speed in a shallow dive, pull out of the dive on its own, climb to the stall – and repeat this manoeuvre, gradually losing height in the process. This is called a *stable fugoid*, possibly because it is repetitive and occurs, like the music, at alternate levels without any divergence in its undulations.

If the aircraft is wrongly loaded with its CG too far aft, the nose will probably drop sharply to the vertical at the stall point in the fugoid and, if the aircraft pulls itself out of the ensuing dive at all, it will do so far too steeply, end up in a vertical climb and probably enter a spin off the inevitable stall. The fugoid will 'diverge'. If, on the other hand, the aircraft is loaded with its CG too far forward, it may behave like a paper dart and never recover from the dive. Those of us who have made paper aeroplanes can study their fugoid behaviour by altering their CG or by altering tailplane incidence. Carrying out fugoids is a very hit-and-miss method of testing an aircraft's longitudinal behaviour because the results cannot be quantified accurately and they take no account of the effects of power application. Variations in engine power of propeller-driven aircraft alter the direction and strength of the slipstream over the wing roots and tail surfaces and this makes large differences in stall behaviour.

If an aircraft behaves well in its fugoid and actually returns to its original level flight attitude and speed on its own, power on or power off, it is given ten-out-of-ten marks for its behaviour at that CG position and is classed as being 'positively stable stick-free'. It would be allowed into service – other things being equal – loaded within the margin of CGs at which it behaved thus. However, if the designer had made a mistake or the aircraft has been wrongly loaded – i.e., with its CG too far aft – the aircraft might then require the pilot to take immediate action to prevent an incipient dive or stall. It would be longitudinally unstable and no test pilot would clear it for use at that CG position.

CG Margins

To test an aircraft's stability i.e., the amount its CG can be moved from a 'neutral' to a dangerously unstable position which would make it unsafe to fly – i.e., its 'CG margin' – it is necessary to plot a graph of those elevator trimmer tab positions (measured in degrees from neutral) at various speeds, which would allow the aircraft to fly 'hands off' in level flight. These measurements would then be repeated at various CG positions. The lines on the graphs would then show by how much and in what direction the elevator tabs had to be moved to achieve level flight with changes in airspeed and changes in CG positions. The CG limits for stable flight could then be decided upon. In the case of an airliner, the CG margin results would be of the utmost importance as they would be used to lay down strict rules for the safe loading of passengers, fuel and baggage.

During the war the cockpit test instrumentation used by A&AEE test pilots had been insufficient to produce accurate elevator and tab-angle data and pilots made up their own minds whether an aircraft was 'stable' or not. This was usually done by carrying out fugoids or by checking for tendencies for the aircraft to 'tighten in turns'. There was seldom enough quantitative data from such tests to convince an aircraft designer that urgent modification to his design was essential, so that little or nothing was done in some cases of longitudinal instability to put the matter right. This dangerous situation occurred with the Spitfire in 1941 and the early Seafires in 1942.

Complaints from the squadrons and, indeed from Supermarine's Chief Test Pilot, Geoffrey Quill, eventually improved things slightly with the Spitfire/Seafire by the introduction of the unpopular 'positive weight' or 'bob-weight' in the elevator control circuit. (Please see (f) and (g) in Part 1 of this chapter). However, by 1944, the introduction of a larger tailplane, a heavier engine – which brought the CG forward – and a larger fin and rudder incorporated into most Seafires after the Mark IIIs, the 'bob-weight' could be scrapped and the Spitfire/Seafire instability cured for all time.

By 1946 and by the time ETPS had been functioning for two or three years, standards of cockpit test instrumentation and test flying procedures had improved such that no aircraft received an official 'release' into service which could allow it to fly at dangerous CG positions. This was because test results were taken from facts obtained from instruments and were no longer partly dependent on a pilot's opinion.

The 'CG margin' for the Spitfire/Seafire was about seven inches – such was the sensitivity of this fighter to weight shifts. Even the insertion of extra oxygen bottles and a signal-firing gun close behind the pilot could put the CG of this magnificent fighter dangerously far aft. As the only possible place to put any 'extras' was in the aft fuselage compartment, CGs of most tailwheel aircraft tended to move aft as time went on. By the time that the Mark VC Spitfire appeared, stability had to be restored by the fitting of a six pound 'bob-weight' in place of the three-pound one. (Please see (f) and (g) in Part 1 of this chapter.)

In the case of a day-fighter aircraft – where the pilot in a dog fight would not want to be continually changing trim positions – the designer tried to inbuild almost neutral 'stick-free' stability – that is to say, fore-and-aft trim would change very little during speed and power changes in combat and would require no re-trimming on the part of the pilot between speeds of 100 and 300 mph to relieve any 'out-of-trim' stick forces. However, in the case of a night fighter where a pilot – not using his auto-pilot – needed some informative 'feel' from his stick as well as from his flight instruments to tell him what the aircraft was doing, positive stick-free stability was an absolute requirement.

Stick-force-per-G

Structural limits require sufficiently high inbuilt 'stick-force-per-G' in manoeuvring flight to prevent the pilot breaking the aircraft. In a fighter where 'G-max' might be as high as 8 G, the stick-force-per-G requirement might be four pounds of pull-force on the stick per G. The Spitfire I was designed to have about two pounds per G. When the arrestor hook was added to the Seafire Is – IIIs, the 'bob-weight, in the elevator control circuit was increased to nine pounds of lead, three times the value of the original weight in the Spitfire I. (The effects of having to fit this wartime expedient to the Seafire are discussed later in this chapter).

The positive weight idea was also fitted to the Beaufighter, the Firefly and the Spitfire from the outset, but in these three aircraft the incorporation of their light, well-positioned weights had no serious effects. In the case of the American Corsair, the Hawker Tempest and the Hurricane, the stick force was about four and a half pounds per G and in the case of the Mosquito, Barracuda and Hornet the pull force per G at normal CG positions was about six pounds. However, the Meteor – when flown at its forward CG limit – required the pilot to pull ten lb per G at indicated airspeeds above about 300 mph!

Designers of bombers also had a very difficult task to ensure that stability problems were not encountered. With very much larger control surfaces to operate, the bombers required a much closer aerodynamic balance in their controls than a fighter. Too much stability would require large trim changes and high stick forces to correct. Too little fore-and-aft stability would restrict bomb loads, fuel stowage and crew movement to very tight limits and might lower stick-force-per-G so that the pilot could accidentally overstress the aircraft – designed, as it was, for less G forces than a fighter. All 'moveable' weights – fuel, aircrew, bombs, rockets, etc. – carried in the aircraft, had to be positioned at or near its CG, otherwise, when using or jettisoning fuel or dropping bombs the change of CG position would cause a serious nose-up or nose-down pitch and could lead to disaster. (It might be of interest to recall that when Lindberg made his Atlantic crossing the necessary extra fuel load had to be placed at the aircraft's CG – i.e., right in front of him, completely obscuring his forward vision).

The ideal fighter was designed to have a smooth increase in the pull-force per G as airspeed and the amount of G increased. Starting off at about three lb/G, by the time the pilot had steepened the turn to, say, six G, the total pull on the stick might be as high as 25 lb. Sadly, in the case of the early Seafires it was found that the stick-force per G got lighter as more G was pulled in some flight conditions and there were many structural failures as a result – believed at the time to have been due to enemy action rather than the fault of the aircraft or pilot. In the case of the Mosquito, an experimental 'anti-balance' tab was fixed to the elevator in August 1945. This was intended to restrict the G that a pilot could pull. It was necessary because it had been found that in a high speed pullout manoeuvre, under increasing G, if the pilot pulled the stick further back, the force required per G *decreased* sharply. On the last test run of this device at about 380 kts, the stick was wrenched free from the pilot's grasp by elevator flutter and the aircraft broke up in seconds, discharging Fl/Lt Brooks and his test observer – Mr Becker – through the cockpit roof from which only 'Clive' Brooks survived.

The exact CG position of aircraft we tested was obtained by us students weighing the machine on the Farnborough weighbridge and then overheating our sliderules in attempting to work out its position. The most critical flight conditions demanding accurate loading were during landing and take-off, during high 'G' turns and pullouts and in rolling pullouts.

'V-squared law' effects

The V-squared law is still decidedly in charge. It means that as an aircraft gathers speed on its take-off run the lift on its wings, the effectiveness of its rudder to keep straight and the power of its ailerons and elevator to control its flight path, will actually *double* as it accelerates from, say, 50 to 70 mph and will have quadrupled by the time it is travelling at 100 mph.

This fact impressed upon us how easily an aircraft could be broken up in the air if some built-in restricters were not provided by the designers to prevent over-stressing. Control angles would need to be progressively limited by high stick forces or by some other means to make it impossible for the pilot to over-load the wings and break the aircraft.

Drag also increases as the square of the indicated airspeed. No wonder, we thought, that our car's (rationed) petrol consumption almost doubled if we tried to travel at 70 mph instead of a mere 50 mph on our journeys down the A6 to Hyde Park Corner from Cranfield. It could not all have been due to using higher revs and larger throttle openings.

But thank goodness for the V-squared law. Without it, swans would need to accelerate to 400 mph before getting enough lift for taking off and all flying as we knew it would be impossible. Birds' wings and tail-feathers are, of course, of the necessary area to allow take-offs and landing at airspeeds of about 20 mph airspeed and to allow up to 2 G manoeuvring flight. Take-offs in still air present an enormous problem to some soaring birds and to some amphibious birds such as swans. However, observance of swans taking off in a 'glassy' flat calm has shown that by flapping their wings *forward* and downward, they give themselves more wing-tip V-squared and, by using foot thrust on the water, they are then able to 'get over the hump' and lift themselves clear of the water after a reasonably short distance.

A small boat hammering her way close-hauled against a strong wind is wet and uncomfortable especially in the short, steep seas of the Channel and North Sea. But when chasing away before the wind she is a different vessel altogether, sailing upright and dry and lessening the force of the wind and sea by giving way to them; whereas close-hauled she increases the power of the wind and sea, to the discomfort of those on board. 'Running before the wind' gives most racing sailing boats (over-canvassed as they usually are) a reduction in wind force of perhaps twenty knots – say from fifty to thirty knots – thus reducing the windforce in their sails and rigging to nearly a third of what it was before.

Another of nature's example of wind force is the fate of so many poorly-designed roof shapes in some fashionable modern architecture. The mushroom-shaped roofs of some holiday homes look pleasing enough but if a wind of fifty miles an hour happens along, they are the first to take-off. The Indians in America with their wigwams, the Chinese in the Pacific and the architects of our cathedrals were much wiser in their roof designs, for they incorporated lift-spoilers in the sharp, sometimes hollow edges of their roofs, ensuring that they would not take-off and disappear into the forest – even if a tornado hit them. Unlike the Tacoma bridge. This structure not only supplied itself with 'lift' from a passing hurricane but its suspension allowed this lift to vary in a cyclic manner, leading to oscillations similar to control 'flutter' in aircraft, such that the whole bridge disintegrated.

A Seafire 47's wing is about 240 square feet in area. (This is about half that of a Buccaneer or Phantom F4H which have to lift eight times the weight of a Seafire 47.) Each square foot of the Seafire 47's wings lifts about 40 pounds off the deck at 75 mph at take-off. In a tight turn at seven G, each square foot has to lift seven times this amount – or 280 pounds, for which it needs a minimum airspeed of at least 200 mph. At 400 mph, each square foot of a Seafire's wing could in theory lift nearly half a ton. Each square foot of jet thrust from a J-79's exhaust in afterburner gives about seven tons of thrust. Such is the immense power required to accelerate a fighter aircraft to very high speeds.

Basic control design

Built-in safety devices to limit control movements are necessary to prevent excessive G as speed increases. Luckily, the V-squared law usually acts as this limit, because of course, the control forces themselves increase as the square of the airspeed flowing past them and make it difficult for the pilot – not equipped with power-operated controls – to overload the wings and break the aircraft. The situation is therefore self-regulating and present-day 'fly-by-wire' systems – where electronics have control of stability and give 'artificial feel' to the pilot's control column and often take entire charge in all circumstances except final landings and initial take-offs – should not be necessary except in emergencies or where civil or military aircraft performance may depend upon them. In that case, the 'fly-by-wire' systems should always be capable of easy disconnection at the demand of the pilot in such a manner that he can safely assume immediate conventional control under all flying conditions if he wants to.

But in all conventional aircraft controls, the designer makes sure that the pilot's movements of the controls are progressively limited as aircraft speed increases so that overstressing of the aircraft structure cannot occur. It is only when the control forces do not increase as the square of the speed that trouble occurs. The shape of the control surface and its position in the airstream is therefore all-important so that this V-squared relationship is always preserved, and control 'harmonisation' – i.e., the relative heaviness of rudder, elevator and aileron forces – remains as the designer intended.

As aircraft engine powers and aircraft speeds increased in the 'forties and, as their size and that of their control surfaces increased in proportion, it was necessary – before the days of power-operated controls – for the *aerodynamic balance* to be closer and closer, so that the pilot would have sufficient strength to move the controls at all.

By the end of the war, aircraft which weighed about 40 tons were flying at indicated airspeeds of 300 mph, but they were still fitted with manually-controlled ailerons, elevators and rudders. Like the swan, the area of their wings and controls was mostly governed by landing and take-off requirements. Elevators were sometimes the size of barn doors. To ensure any movement at all on such large control surfaces – especially at high indicated airspeeds – the designers not only had to set-back the hingelines towards the control's centre-of-lift position as far as possible but they had to add 'servo' tabs at the trailing edges of these controls. These were geared to the main control movement such that they moved in the reverse direction to the main control to assist it. The more the control movement, the more the tabs stuck out in the airstream and the more they aided its movement in the direction that the pilot wanted.

By 1947 and by the time that the jet power further increased airspeeds and had perhaps quadrupled aerodynamic load on the controls, designers began fitting what were known as 'spring tabs' in place of the geared 'servo' tab variety. These tabs only came into action to assist pilot's stick or rudder forces to move the ailerons, elevator or rudder, when the pilot had to use *considerable* force at any time i.e., at high indicated airspeeds. The more force he used, the larger the tab movement and thus the greater the help he received from it.

Apart from a tendency to allow aileron 'upfloat' (which reduced effectiveness) and to encourage 'flutter' (which was sometimes fatal) the spring tab was a brilliant stopgap between the geared tab and the *hydraulically-powered control-with-feedback* which came into general use in the 1950s. However, it was the Miles M.52 experimental jet project which was first fitted with power-operated flying controls in 1945. It also had an after-burner added to its Whittle W2/700 engine and had wings of only 7½ per cent thickness/chord (t/c) ratio. It was, however, cancelled early in 1946 by the Ministry, much to the disappointment of Aero Flight at Farnborough, for it was confidently expected to have achieved transonic flight more reliably than the DH 108 which made the attempt a few years later.

But in 1946, Short's Chief designer was so worried about excessively high or dangerously low stickforce-per-G results in large aircraft – and whether John Lancaster-Parker would be strong enough to move the controls of Shorts' latest huge 60-ton Shetland flying boat – that he connected the pilot's stick straight to the 'servo' tabs themselves, leaving the main controls free to flap about on their own during the taxying out periods. (David Keith-Lucas – Short's Chief Designer after 1948 – also used this tab system in the Sperrin, an intended four-jet 'V'-bomber, which Brookie first flew in 1951). Tom Brook-Smith had already flown the Shetland flying boat at Felixstowe before joining ETPS. He told us that the rudder tended to 'jybe' when taxying down wind on the water but otherwise the controls were exceedingly pleasant once the flying boat was in the air.

When designing close-balance controls, wind tunnel results – even in full-scale trials – were sometimes unrealistic. This was because of the inability of most windtunnels to reproduce the turbulent airflow – such as in propeller slipstreams – which the full-scale elevators and rudders sometimes experienced. This sometimes led to *overbalance* of the controls in prototype testing, with catastrophic results.

An example of this difficulty had occurred two years before the start of ETPS 6 Course and was still in everyone's thoughts. The prototype Handley Page Hermes airliner was taking off on its first trip from Radlett airfield. The manually-controlled elevator overbalanced in the fully nose-up position at the end of the take-off run and the pilot was unable to find enough strength to push the control column forward to prevent the aircraft rearing up into a stall – from which all aboard were killed. Fast taxying tests would possibly have exposed this overbalance design fault but in this case the runway at Radlett was too short for the test pilot to have checked the behaviour of the elevators. This accident probably gave new impetus to the proposal to extend Boscombe Down's main runway to more than 3000 yards.

During 6 ETPS Course, there was yet another example of a pilot losing elevator control in flight which we read about in the press. This fatal crash occurred when an Avro Tudor 2 (a 'stretched' Tudor 1) was bringing back a full load of footballers to Cardiff. At about 2,000 feet on the approach to the airfield, on lowering the flaps and undercarriage for landing, the pilot reported in a panic that he was unable to apply sufficient nose-down elevator to prevent the airliner rearing up and stalling. The catastrophic nose-up change of trim was probably caused by too many passengers queueing up to use the toilet in the rear of the aircraft before landing, so moving the aircraft's CG dangerously far aft. Seatbelt discipline and careful loading of passengers – especially in long-fuselage aircraft – was the order of the day from that time onwards.

We have seen above how designers had been able to reduce stickforces by the addition of geared tabs, spring tabs and, of course, by setting back the hingeline about one-third back on the main control itself. (This position also corresponds to the approximate centre-of-lift position of most conventionally shaped aerofoils – as any hang-glider knows.) Then, by extending the elevators' leading edges outboard so that they were no longer shielded by the tailplane itself, the designers were able to use this 'unshielded horn balance' to alter the elevator's trail angle to assist 'positive stick-free stability'. This device was used in addition to the 'bob-weights' in the Spitfire. The lead weights fused into its leading edges also acted as a mass balance for the control itself and reduced the chance of 'flutter'.

Also, to further prevent unwanted movement of the entire control circuit extending all the way back to the pilot's cockpit – particularly in 'bumpy' weather when the 'positive weights' or 'bob-weights' tended to take charge – the entire control linkage and the ailerons, rudders and elevators were mass-balanced at various places along their control runs. This meant that whatever 'G' the pilot might require to impose on the aircraft or whatever horizontal G forces might be imposed during catapult take-offs, the control remained in exact balance about its hinge line. If this were done correctly there would also be less likelyhood of control 'flutter' occurring – a frightening phenomenon where undamped control oscillation induced large aerodynamic and aero-elastic forces in the main structure sufficient to break the aircraft itself. This state of affairs often arose when flying at high speeds at high mach numbers, in turbulent conditions and when flying near the stall. Very few of these conditions could be reproduced this side of the Atlantic in the small wind tunnels at our research establishments so that the British test pilot was often caught out.

Aircraft designers also continually reminded us of Hook's Law which we had learnt at school – which dealt with stress and strain loadings – repetitions of which in bumpy air could lead to 'fatigue' failures at wing junctures, engine mounting attachments and control hinges – as mentioned above.

Wartime expedients to cure instability – the 'bob-weight'

Due mainly to the exigences of war, very few of the wartime aircraft in the Fleet Air Arm met these strict longitudinal stability requirements. To secure almost neutral longitudinal stability – and thus light elevator forces for the fighter pilot – in the Spitfire, Mitchell had designed an aerodynamically neutrally stable aircraft. However, as we have seen in previous paragraphs, when additional equipment was added aft of the CG – wireless sets, flare tubes, tail strengthening, etc., and which could not be compensated forward for fear of overloading the engine bearers, aerodynamic means had to be used to restore the balance. 'Bob-weights' were added to the elevator control circuit in such a manner as to give it a small 'downfloat' angle when G was applied, so preventing the tail-heavy effects of the aft CG. This small 'positive weight' was intended to give the Spitfire the highly desirable characteristic of a positively 'stick-free' stable fighter aircraft in all the – then – foreseeable combat conditions.

Mitchell had given the Spitfire a very light 2–2½ pounds of pull force per G, about half the usual for fighters of that period. When the Navy – desperate for some effective fighter defence in 1940 – needed to hang a 100 pound hook some 12 feet aft of the Spitfire's CG, true stability could only be restored by Mitchell's team adding an even heavier balancing weight to the front of the aircraft. The engine bearers were already loaded past their original design limits by the additional weight of a constant-speed propeller and a heavier and more powerful supercharger and could not take more than about 40 pounds of lead attached to the front bearers without risking structural failure of the rear bearers. Furthermore, more weight to the front of the Spitfire would have risked its nosing-over when the pilot applied brakes. Other devices had to be used. The elevator had its area increased forward of its hingeline outboard of the tailplane – an 'unshielded horn balance' and an aerodynamicist's nightmare. This increased the elevator's tendency to 'float' downwards – already held thus by Mitchell's original Spitfire three-pound weight. This three-pound weight was now increased to about nine pounds for the Seafire. All photographs taken of early Seafires in flight show the elevator's droop of about four degrees by the action of this nine pound 'positive' weight and the 'unshielded horn balance' – an exceptional state of affairs in any aircraft. It helped to make the Seafire the world's most difficult aircraft to deck land and caused more casualties than the enemy by a large margin.

Dangers of longitudinal instability
All makeshift cures tend to have bad side effects. It was the job of us test pilots to find out what these side effects might be. In the case of the early Seafires, the 'unshielded horn balance', when combined with the positive weight – or 'bob-weight' – in the elevator control circuit, had four potentially very dangerous side effects, not all of which had been properly discovered and put right during wartime.

One of these side effects became apparent when decklanding the Seafire Is, IIs and IIIs. Provided propeller slipstream was maintained over the tail surface, the device known as the 'unshielded horn balance' on the elevator did a good job. However, on 'cutting' the engine at the batsman's behest when decklanding, the slipstream over the tail vanished and the elevator was no longer held at its usual 'in-flight' position, i.e., drooped at an angle of about five degrees. When the pilot 'cut', the slipstream vanished and the elevator raised itself, its 'upfloat' assisted by the ground effect. Lift on the tail surfaces was consequently reduced and the tail lowered itself giving the impression that the pilot had pulled the stick back and had initiated the familiar 'float, float, float – prang' series into the barrier. The pilot always got the blame for such occurrences.

The second side effect had fatal results. As we have noted above, in an effort to restore longitudinal stability after the fitting of the arrestor hook in the early Seafires, Mitchell had added an additional six pounds of lead to the three pound weight in the early Spitfires' elevator control circuit. This nine pounds of lead was fixed to a nine inch steel shaft with its other end welded in a horizontal position to the foot of the pilot's control column. When the pilot applied G, the lead weight in the Seafire would force the stick *forward* with a stick force of about three pounds for every G the pilot applied. In other words, the harder the pilot pulled back, the more the stick moved of its own accord forward.

Apart from the annoyance of the stick moving itself backwards and forwards when flying in bumpy air, the 'positive weight' usually did a good job in preventing the aircraft self-tightening in turns. The Seafire's large 'bob-weight' therefore applied a nose-down stick force of about 20 pounds during a 7 G steep-turn or pull-out and so gave the pilot the impression of stability. However, had we known what was going on and had we cared to look down at the stick during the somewhat stressful time of a pullout from a dive or during a steep turn over Japan in 1945, we would have seen the stick actually *move forward* several inches as we applied the pull force!

However, this marginally acceptable state of affairs turned sour when other manoeuvres were attempted – and which, before the days of ETPS – obviously had not been anticipated by Supermarines or Boscombe Down test pilots when the Seafire was undergoing acceptance tests in 1942.

First: The much heavier 'positive' weights in the control circuit sometimes came unwelded or bent their shafts beyond the horizontal. Our maintenance crews discovered two such cases during after-flight inspections during the Pacific operations in *Implacable*. At the time this occurred, the pilot would have been pulling out of a strafing or bombing dive and would seldom have been able to reverse his pullforce quickly enough to avoid a disastrous pitchup and the instantaneous breakup of the aircraft.

Second: Pilot's Notes recommended that we inverted our Seafires to allow us to 'fall out', rather than risk getting hung up on the hood closing lever if we climbed out, when baling out in emergency. When the Seafire pilot attempted to bale out by inverting the Seafire in a 'failed-engine level glide' situation (where the lack of slipstream over the elevator trimming tab would largely nullify the action taken by the pilot to trim fully 'nose forward'), the 'positive' weight would then have the *reverse* effect and pull the aircraft into the completion of a loop. This would effectively pin the pilot half in and half out of the cockpit until the aircraft hit the sea in a vertical dive. Even when 'negative-G' fuel supply was available, engine-failed bale outs were often necessary in the case of the Seafires operating in the tropics when carrying long-range tanks, as fuel supply lines overheated during combat at low altitude and boiled the petrol in the delivery pipes near the overheated supercharger casing, thus permanently stopping the engine. Thus, on changing tanks on the way back to the carrier after about two hours in the air, the engine sometimes failed to pick up on the fresh tank selected and engine failure necessitated a 'power-off' bale out over the sea. The tragedy was, no one ever got back to tell us of the dangers of an inverted bale out so we persisted with this method until the end of the war when – too late – we learnt of its dangers from our ETPS lectures.

Third: The most disastrous effect of this 'bob-weight' device was during the steep dives we made during our bombing and strafing operations in Norway and the Pacific. No one had realised at Supermarines that the 'positive' weight would cease to have its 'positive' stability effects in steep dives. The loss of stability which then occurred was due to the near-zero gravity acting upon it in dives as steep as 65–75 degrees, for it was merely hanging down like a pendulum at the time and had no effect on the stick's position whatever. Thus, on any backward pressure being applied to the stick, G forces could sometimes be in excess of structure limits *before the weight itself started to push the stick forward to prevent them.* The wings came off four Seafires in such circumstances on operations in the Pacific and the pilots were killed.

Fourth: In order to prevent the stick from falling forward in the cockpit when not flying, the Supermarine design office had prevented this misplacement by applying a 'negative spring' in the elevator circuit equivalent to a pull of about four pounds. This worked well during all positive 'G' manoeuvres, but when the bob weight's effect was reduced in negative 'G' manoeuvres, the spring took charge, adding its effect to the pull of the now 'negative' bob weight, leading to overstressing during pullouts from steep dives and effectively pinning the pilot in the cockpit in spite of his applying full nose-down trim when attempting to bale out inverted. We discovered afterwards at ETPS that Fireflys and Beaufighters also had 'positive weights' of a small size in their elevator control circuits. As the war progressed and as the Firefly was required to be loaded with more and more electronic equipment for use by the observer, the aft movement of its CG was inevitable. However, in the case of the Firefly, its 'positive weight', placed at the foot of the control column, was cocked up at a 45 degree angle to the horizontal so that it retained a positive force throughout a steep diving attack and retained its beneficial effects. It was not fitted with a 'negative' spring and the control column was allowed to flop forward in the cockpit when the aircraft was not flying.

Although RAF squadrons in Britain were apparently fully aware of the purposes of the 'bob-weights' and the rigid rules governing CG positions in their Spitfires, Seafire squadrons in the Pacific war were given no information about dangers of instability in the Seafire or its possible causes. Not knowing the purpose of the bob-weight at the time, I and several other pilots often reported 'overstressing' during high G manoeuvres and, on inspection in several cases, our mechanics found that the wingfold bolts were 'notched' to a depth of 1/16th of an inch and were just about to shear. Two – at least – of the bob-weights had come unwelded from the control column and were lying in the bottom of the fuselage under the cockpit. It was thought at the time that when a Seafire crashed in such circumstances that it was due to pilot error. Luckily, the introduction of the much heavier Griffon engine in the Seafire XV – with a larger tail, fin and rudder which its extra weight forward allowed to be added aft – cured the stability problem. The extra weight of the engine balanced the tail-heaviness and turned the Seafire into a longitudinally stable aircraft – 'stick free' – for the first time in its history. There were, however, some more equally serious structural and handling problems in the Mark XVs and XVIIs but these were completely cured by the arrival – too late for the war – of the beautiful contra-prop Seafire 47.

Part 2   Directional Stability

Effect of engine failure

This was probably the next-most important item in the ETPS syllabus, particularly where multi-engined aircraft were concerned. The most exciting twin on the Course was the Mosquito. Produced by de Havillands in November 1940 as a private venture, it was still the RAF's favourite twin night and day fighter/recce/intruder aircraft in 1948 and its only fault – compared with some of its American contemporaries – was its lack of directional control when flying on one engine at low speeds. Of course it had none of the delightful feel of a single-engined fighter like the Seafire in its element, neither the light stick forces, the high rate-of-roll or tight turning circle in a dogfight nor the good view from the cockpit.

As already described, if an engine fails in twins, the aircraft loses half its total power – all from one side. If this occurs at slow speeds in the take-off configuration – i.e., below about 160 mph in the case of the Mosquito B 35 and T 3 at ETPS, the full power of the live engine is immediately required to maintain flying speed. If low altitude prevents a dive to gain speed, at this slow speed the rudder is often not sufficiently effective to prevent an uncontrollable swing towards the dead engine, particularly if the 'critical' engine fails – where the live engine propeller torque decreases available fin/rudder power even more.

A test pilot's task was to find out the minimum 'safety speed' at which full directional control and a positive rate of climb could still be safely maintained following engine failure at take-off. As windspeeds and air temperatures affected the results (the higher the air temperatures, the higher the altitude of the airfield and the lower the speed of the natural wind down the runway, the longer the take-off run would have to be), these tests were always finally repeated in the tropics to make sure that the correct answer for the 'safety speed' had been found in all circumstances. This speed was not often reached in our Mozzie until at least 50 seconds after 'wheels roll'. If engine failure occurred after the 'safety speed' was reached (i.e., after it had achieved a speed at which it could be controlled directionally and its drag had become less so that it would gain speed and thus altitude on the live engine), there were no problems, provided, of course, that the flaps and undercarriage had been retracted quickly and the dead engine's propeller had been feathered at once.

If, however, power was lost on one engine in the 50 seconds *before* the aircraft had accelerated to its known safety speed, the pilot had to decide what to do very quickly. If he was lucky enough to have taken off from Boscombe

Down's 3,000 yard runway into a fresh wind, there would be room to land straight ahead with undercarriage down. On a shorter airfield, such as Radlett, a wheels-up overshoot might be attempted in a light aircraft but in a Mosquito or any high-performance twin, the pilot might have to crash-land off the airfield with the undercarriage retracted. Much would depend on the quick-thinking and skill of the pilot. In 1948, Shorts' concern over lack of directional control in twin-engined fighters made them fit contra-props to their new Sturgeon, thus allowing shorter prop blades and the twin 1,600 hp Merlins to be positioned nearer to the aircraft's centreline.

Sometimes, if the pilot banked the aircraft towards the live engine the side thrust of the prop's slipstream against the fin and rudder would help the pilot to retain considerably more power on the live engine without losing directional control. So that, if the aircraft was lightly loaded, it would still have enough power to accelerate to its safety speed and climb away slowly and recover full control from speeds a few mph below the critical speed. Pilots' skill and knowledge had much to do with the outcome of such occurrences.

One of the most difficult twin-engined aircraft to operate safely in the early days of World War 2 had been the Avro Manchester. It had twin Vulture engines of about 2,000 hp each. As these engines were in their early stages of development at the time the heavy bomber force was being assembled for its night onslaught on Germany, engine failures in the Vulture were common. In 1941 an Australian crew were collecting a Manchester from A&AEE to take it back to their squadron. The Manchester required at least 1,000 yards of take-off run into a 20 knot wind, even when lightly loaded to 40,000 lbs AUW (i.e., the weight of a lightly-loaded Buccaneer). The port engine cut as it flew over the hangars and with the pilot in a left-hand climbing turn, with insufficient speed or height to retain control, a crash was inevitable. The aircraft was fully inverted before crashing into the countryside north of Amesbury. It seemed to us at ETPS that a single-engined aircraft was far safer to fly than an overloaded twin, anyday, for you would be able to land straight ahead in such emergencies and, in the case of a Seafire with or without overload tanks, only 100 yards of runway into a twenty-knot wind would be needed to unstick.

The Manchester was withdrawn from service in January 1942 and the two 24-cylinder Vultures were safely substituted by four Merlins. The bomber's name was changed to the Lancaster and it became by far the best of the three wartime bombers, beating the Short Stirling in load, height and ease of landing and the Halifax in accident reliability. It seems likely that some of the 'unexplained' accidents in the Halifax may have been due to insufficient fin and rudder area leading to fin stalling and loss of directional control on 'engine out' approaches to land. Likewise the Stirling's accident record may have been because, being the first of the heavy bombers, it had had its wing clipped by six feet so that it would fit into the RAF's standard-size hangars. It was this increase in its wing loading which ruined its climb performance above about 12,000ft and which made it necessary to fly it on bombing missions at such a dangerously low altitude within accurate AA range.

Engine failure effects in the Oxford and Lincoln compared

In the case of the Oxford, the limiting factor – as to whether to crash-land straight ahead or to try to continue – was the airspeed that you happened to be doing at the time of engine failure. If this was below 125 mph, directional control would be lost immediately – even with full opposite rudder applied – and, if the undercarriage and flaps were down at the time of the failure, the aircraft would not gain height on the live engine at this slow speed. Unless power on the live engine was immediately reduced, directional control would be lost and the aircraft would spiral into the ground within seconds.

The Lincoln II was almost identical to the Lancaster bomber with about six feet of extra wingspan. It could easily maintain height on two engines at any weight, and on one only at very light weights. Landing it was far easier than in a Mosquito – or a Stirling, for that matter – its stall being gentle and with tail-buffet warning, without any risk of a wing drop occurring. Control loads were, of course, far heavier and, for a fighter pilot used to good visibility from the cockpit, the view all round was very poor but that was our only criticism. If one engine was 'practice-failed' on take-off, the Lincoln would climb away on the other three at any speed above 125 mph, flaps and wheels going up, at weights up to 50,000 lbs. Rudder trimmers were powerful enough to relieve the entire footload at this speed. If engine failure occurred below 125 mph on take-off, the remaining three engines' throttles were closed immediately and full brake applied directly the aircraft could be touched down again on the runway. This procedure could only be tested on a very long runway such as at Boscombe Down.

Although the Lincoln's 'engine-failed' handling qualities showed an improvement in safety standards compared with wartime bombers and the Airspeed Oxford, there were signs that the Civil Air Registration Board would soon insist on further safety improvements in all new passenger aircraft in the next few years. Luckily, the change to jet power allowed engines to be placed closer to the centreline – a major factor in reducing safety speeds – and airline operators were insisting on having runways and overshoot areas of twice the length of wartime airfields before they would agree to operate jet aircraft in Europe. It was the possibility of having to provide exceedingly costly runways all over the world that re-stimulated Shorts' and the Brabazon Committee's interest in the large flying boat, for a flying boat's beautifully level 'runways' stretched for miles and miles worldwide and were comparatively free of charge and could often be used without permission from the adjoining countries in time of war.

Directional control in some other aircraft

Perhaps the safest twin-piston-engined fighter of this period was the DH Hornet – quickly adopted by the Navy in small numbers. It had 'handed' propellers and a very effective dorsal-finned rudder. This improved the tail fin's ability to withstand large angles of yaw without stalling, and its exceptional power/weight ratio of 1:4 allowing quick acceleration off the catapult to its comparatively low safety speed. It would certainly have become very popular if the Korean war had continued and we had had sufficiently large carriers at that time to accommodate them. Its advantage over other twins in the 'one-engine-failed' condition was due to the makers having 'handed' the propellers. By this is meant – when the props are viewed from the tail – that the port propeller in the Hornet revolved clockwise and the starboard propeller revolved anti-clockwise. The advantage lies in the fact that both propeller slipstreams increase the fin/rudder effectiveness. (Please see below). However, even DHs could get it wrong; for a start they sent a Hornet to Boscombe with the props going round the wrong way!

The rudders and fins of all aircraft usually project into the *upper* portions of their propellers' slipstreams. This slipstream has a vicious twist in the direction that the propeller is turning. (Seafire XV and XVII pilots know how frightening this can be for the direction of 'swing' on a deck take-off took them towards the island!) Thus by 'handing' the propellers in the Hornet so that both the upper half of each propeller's slipstream was 'twisted' *towards* the fin/rudder, the live engine's propeller's slipstream was made to assist rudder and fin effectiveness in correcting yaw after an engine failure. In the case of the Mosquito and all other twins of that period, only one of the propellers assisted in correcting yaw. The other *added* to it and the pilot had to remember to add a few mph to his safety speed when the 'critical' engine failed.

When an engine fails in a multi-engined propeller-driven aircraft, the resultant yaw caused by asymmetric propeller thrust is not the only problem, for the dead-engined wing loses lift from its propeller slipstream and drops away, so adding to the pilot's difficulties. If the failed engine is far outboard, the loss of lift is powerful enough to cause a rapid roll towards the dead engine. By applying corrective aileron, the pilot adds further to the drag on that wing (and reduces it on the other) and, if the aircraft happens to be very near the stall, the very act of a sudden application of down-aileron to lift the wing may induce a premature stall on the dead-engined wing, adding to his troubles. Added to all this is the drag of the dead-engine's nacelle and its cooling arrangements and the huge drag of a windmilling propeller if this is not immediately feathered.

The arrival of the jet engine changed all this. Not only could the thrust be placed much nearer the fuselage (as no propeller clearance was needed) but the engine's nacelle drag was far less – two factors which did much to reduce the need for large angles of corrective rudder to keep straight. Furthermore, because a jet engine's power/weight ratio was almost double that of an equivalent-powered piston engine, the twin jet's available single-engine power was far greater than that of its piston-engined equivalent, particularly at high altitude. Although it could be argued that jet engines were relatively inefficient at slow speeds during take-off, and, when landing, tended to give rise to far longer landing runs due to their lack of propeller drag when throttled back, the overall picture was that jets had a lower – and therefore more satisfactory – safety speed and were far safer to operate near the ground than multi-engined piston-powered aircraft.

With the arrival of reverse jet thrust and very large airbrakes and lift spoilers in the late fifties, landing and take-off safety – a flight regime responsible for half of all aircraft accidents – improved beyond all recognition and the increased safety of air travel encouraged the building of much larger seating capacities, greatly reducing the cost per passenger/mile of jet travel within a few years. Handling with one jet engine failed was improved to such an extent that the huge Boeing 747's safety speed on take-off, even under the worst conditions of zero wind, maximum weight, tropical temperatures and on high-altitude airfields, is now achieved *before* the aircraft leaves the ground. Reverse thrust, lift spoilers, airbrakes and non-skid brakes on numerous tyres ensure that it will then stop within the runway length.

Part 3   Lateral Stability

Dihedral effect

All aircraft are designed to have a small amount of inbuilt lateral stability. This is normally provided by 'dihedral' – that is to say the slight upward-slanting of the wings from root to tip as seen in most low wing monoplanes. If, in level flight, one wing hits an airbump and becomes banked one way or the other, the lower wing will recover of its own accord to a laterally level position without any action being needed on the part of the pilot. The aircraft will naturally yaw towards the lower wing. Due to the wing's dihedral, more lift will then automatically be generated on the lower wing – for it is then at a slightly higher angle of attack than the other wing – and the aircraft will right itself.

If the aircraft has been designed with too much dihedral – or insufficient fin area or a poorly balanced rudder – there is a risk of a 'Dutch roll' developing. Try launching a paper aeroplane having too much dihedral and it will not only carry out a dutch roll (an oscillation in rolling and yawing planes simultaneously) but, if it lacks an adequate fin and rudder, it will enter a spiral dive and crash. This clearly demonstrates the care that is needed on the part of aircraft designers to get the balance right. Highwing monoplanes need no inbuilt dihedral. They may even carry *an*hedral, as in the Tornado.

Low wing monoplanes normally require considerable inbuilt dihedral. If, as in the case of many jet aircraft, a slight 'Dutch roll' occurs in normal flight (feature of the early versions of the Boeing-707) – particularly at high altitudes where aerodynamic 'damping' forces are much lighter – the designer may have to connect the rudder and ailerons to an autostabilisation system using part of an autopilot to achieve the necessary very small corrective control movements. (e.g., the Buccaneer).

If an aircraft is purposely yawed sideways for any reason – such as by the application of rudder – it will tend to get more lift on the side which is opposite to the direction of turn. Thus, if right rudder is applied, the nose will swing to the right and the airflow over the aircraft will no longer be straight fore-and-aft but at an angle of a few degrees, coming from the left. Provided that the aircraft has dihedral, the lift on the left wing will now be greater than that on the right as it will be at a slightly higher 'angle of attack' to the airflow than the right wing. The aircraft's left wing should then start to rise slightly, but return to level flight directly the rudder bias is removed. However, because control friction tends to prevent small, automatic adjustments to control surfaces uninitiated by the pilot, inbuilt stability of this nature is never relied on and hands-off flying can only safely be carried out after plugging in the autopilot.

Birds teach us how to fly

An aircraft in a turn gets more lift from the faster, outer wing than the slower-moving inner wing. It therefore tends to increase its bank angle automatically and enter a spiral unless this is checked somehow – either by rudder or by 'opposite aileron' to 'hold off bank'. Birds can do without rudders and separate ailerons for any of these purposes for they are adept at correcting yaw and applying the correct bank for an accurate turn by altering wing incidences, areas and appropriate 'airbrake' drag as necessary to induce an accurate turn. When gliding, they can be seen to 'hold off bank' in a turn by applying tailplane twist. The Phantom F4 was one of the first fighter aircraft to use 'twist' in its 'all-flying' tailplane to correct small lateral misplacements in this way.

Birds never stall accidentally or get out of control, for they sense the rising feathers on the top surfaces of their wings whenever the normal, smooth, indeed laminar airflow begins to break away at very high incidences – such as when coming in to land – and they take immediate action to prevent this poor airflow from spreading, probably by locally reducing wing angle-of-attack for a few micro-seconds.

We human pilots have to make do with ailerons to apply bank in order to initiate a turn and we have to use rudder to prevent skid in the turn. We then have to 'hold-off bank' to prevent the turn from self-steepening. This 'adverse yaw' as it is called, is usually eliminated by the aircraft designer using differential aileron gearing whereby the upgoing aileron travels through twice the angle of the downgoing one. In the case of the modern jet, small lateral control adjustments can be applied by 'tailerons' – like the birds twist their tails to 'hold off bank' in a turn. Only at very low speeds do modern jets make use of inboard ailerons. At high speed and in transonic or supersonic flight, differential use of lift spoilers and airbrakes are employed in a similarly efficient manner to that of the birds, but for entirely different reasons.

Predatory birds can, of course, cater for the large changes in their CGs – perhaps caused by carrying food in their beaks or by clasping it in their feet. They do this by sweeping their wings forward or backward slightly in flight. When coming into land they are able to increase the lift coefficient of their wings by puffing out the feathers (i.e., increasing the thickness/chord ratio of their wings and so increasing their lift coefficients). They can, in addition, lower the trailing edge feathers to form landing flaps and droop the leading edges of their wings to act as leading edge flaps – as fitted to most high-performance aircraft today.

Swans are particularly clever in using the forward and downward movement of their wings to add to the V-squared factor when landing and taking off. Some of the 'weight-lifters' – such as eagles – make use of small, midspan leading edge Handley Page slots to assist smooth airflow at high angles of attack when coming into land. To reduce 'wingtip vortex drag', rather than use pointed wing tips as in swallows and soaring birds (and the Spitfire), the 'weightlifters' have evolved separated wing-tip feathers, each aerodynamically balanced along its hollow main spar – the quill – and each obtaining lift from the upward part of the vortex from the feather in front. Perhaps the most beautiful example of this is in the Bald Eagle – the American Symbol – which is one of many such powerful birds that use the 'flipper' action of their wingtip feathers to help low-speed forward thrust with both upward and downward wing movements.

Birds in Vee migration formation also use this 'wave-vortex' effect to obtain free lift from the bird in front. When diving after prey on the ground – and to avoid excessive speed build-up – predatory birds reduce their wing area and further increase their drag in the dive by lowering their undercarriages which are often fitted with airbrakes in the form of feathers. The Golden Eagle has particularly large and long 'airbrake' feathers on its undercarriage. They compensate for the nose-down drag from their undercarriages by selecting full nose-up elevator. All such action can be seen on TV wildlife programmes.

The Pterodactyl

Professor Hill, a skilled designer of the 1930s–1950s, designed a small aircraft having elevons hinged about their centres of lift, projecting from each sweptback wingtip. The elevons' shafts were a continuation of the aircraft's main wing spar, so he called the entire structure an 'isoclynic' wing, as all tendency for it to twist with the usual aileron application was eliminated. It could therefore be built much lighter than the usual 'box-spar' construction of most wing designs. Furthermore the wingtip elevons could actually *contribute* to lift in normal flight conditions – unlike the average tailplane and elevators.

The elevons also acted as elevators – being placed aft of the CG – so that the aircraft was tailless, being called the Westland-Hill Pterodactyl. The full-moving wingtip elevons were the only controls – apart from a small rudder – which were needed to control the aircraft. The design not only saved weight but was designed to eliminate wingtip stalls and make it impossible for a pilot to enter a spin. If a pilot in a conventional aircraft were to pull the stick back too hard at too slow an airspeed, one wing or the other might stall and the aircraft would 'flick' over on to its back and crash. If the Pterodacyl's stick was pulled back too hard in such circumstances the elevons actually *decreased* their angle of attack so that, even if the wing itself stalled, the elevons themselves would not be stalled and full lateral control to prevent a sudden wing drop could be retained by the pilot. However, in practice it was sometimes found necessary for the pilot to have to push the stick *forward* to lower the nose to recover from a stall. This unexpected requirement *increased* elevon incidence and stalled them too – a requirement which Professor Hill may not have fully foreseen.

This danger could only have been eliminated by permanently rigging the elevons with about 20 degrees of 'upfloat' – or negative incidence – and this necessity cancelled out their additional winglift possibilities and reduced one of the major advantages that wingtip elevons might have had over tailplanes which do not normally contribute to lift. No doubt the disadvantages of tailplanes are now being avoided by the use of canard controls placed well forward of the aircraft's CG and well clear of any mainplane 'wake' effects, too; e.g., the Euro-fighter.

The 'aero-isoclinic wing' fitted with wingtip elevons was considered to be such a 'weight-saver' in 1951 that Shorts carried out some tests in a specially designed glider – the SB 1. Towing it off the runway with a Sturgeon on a long tow at 70 knots, the high-wing glider got caught in the Sturgeon's slipstream on its second trip and crashed at 100 knots, injuring 'Brookie' at the controls of the SB 1. The over-sensitive longitudinal control was the probable cause and Shorts' proposal to incorporate these in a new jet-bomber project of theirs was scrapped.

The only other 'flying wing' at this time was the AW 52. This, too, had suffered from poor elevon control on its first trip from Boscombe Down in November 1947 and eventually crashed with the pilot – Joe Lancaster – being the first pilot to have to use the Martin-Baker ejector seat in anger. The remaining AW 52 eventually found its way to Aero-flight at Farnborough, the usual accommodation for problem aircraft for which there was no obvious service requirement.

To return to the subject of lateral control in more conventional aircraft designs: most designers avoided the dreaded wingtip stall by making sure that the wing *root* stalled first as speed was reduced – as this had less roll 'leverage' and the ailerons remained unstalled and fully effective for a little while longer. They did this by providing an inbuilt 'washout' to the outer wing's angle of attack. This reduced the overall lift efficiency of the wing but cured the wingtip stall. In the early years of monoplane design, the Blackburn Skua/Roc aircraft – the Navy's 'torpedo-fighter' of 1936–9 – had such a vicious slipstream-induced starboard wing drop at the power-on stall that the designer had to attach a permanent lift spoiler to the port wingroot leading edge to cause that to stall at the same time as the starboard when making a landing.

Aileron reversal

Airspeeds more than doubled in fighter aircraft in the war and rates of roll became slower so that aileron-geared, servo or spring tabs had to be invented to increase aileron power and reduce the stickforces. In the case of the Seafire XVs supplied to us in Australia in 1945, we found that at speeds approaching our permitted maximum – 450 mph (395 knots) – when a rapid roll to the right was attempted, the aircraft refused to do so. The harder we tried to force the stick over to the right the more the aircraft tried to roll to the *left*! Following a tragic accident to one of our Australian pilots when his Seafire XV broke up over the airfield and in full view of his fiancée, we grounded all our Seafire XVs and reported it to the Admiralty. Within three weeks we were descended upon by a working party who stripped the top wingroot surface from our Seafire's wings and rivetted-in a replacement skin of double the thickness. We had no more trouble. Had we gone to war without this modification, as we would have done if the A-bomb had not rescued us, many more Seafire losses would have occurred.

At the time of 1945 that we had struck this phenomenon of 'aileron reversal', we could only guess what the cause of the wing failure could have been i.e., the aileron was acting as a tab to the wing which was twisting. In other words, when the pilot applied aileron to bank to the right, the action of the ailerons was to twist the mainplanes. The left aileron twisted its mainplane up at its trailing edge giving it less lift, and the right aileron twisted its mainplane down, thus increasing its lift. The Seafire XV would either refuse to roll at all or slowly roll in either direction, heedless of the pilot's attempts to control it. Then, with the aircraft pointing earthwards – half-inverted by now and the pilot using all his strength on the aileron control – structural failure due to wing twist would cause instant disintegration and the pilot would be unable to save his life by baling out.

Part 4   Stalling

Wing 'angle-of-attack,' or 'incidence'
The fourth most-practised piece of 'handling' that we were required to perform at ETPS was stalling. Wing incidence – usually referred to as 'angle of attack' – is the angle the wing's chord makes to the approaching airstream. If lift is to remain the same, the wing's angle of attack must remain the same and the indicated airspeed must not alter. If the airspeed is allowed to decrease, to preserve the same lift and to prevent the aircraft from losing height from level flight, the pilot must then increase the wing's angle of attack by gently pulling back on the stick, allowing the whole aircraft to adopt a more nose-up attitude. If the airspeed is allowed to increase, to preserve the same lift and so prevent the aircraft from climbing, the pilot must *decrease* the wing's angle of attack by gently pushing the stick forward and lowering the nose a few degrees.

The Hurricane and Seafire wings could manage about 20 degrees of 'angle of attack' (or 'alpha') before showing signs of stalling. The nose-up attitude at the stall corresponded roughly to the aircraft's 'three-point-landing' attitude required for a perfect three-point landing. As this would only correspond to 15 out of the 20 degrees, the remaining three to five degrees were 'added on' by setting the wing at a three to five degree positive incidence to the aircraft's normal flight line. Even then, with the wing's chord-line at an angle of, say, five degrees 'angle-of-attack' to the airflow in normal, one-G flight, the aircraft plus wing would have to be rotated a further two or three degrees nose-down before the wing would give up all its lift: for the 'no-lift' incidence of most wings is about *minus* three degrees. This is why pilots in a steep bombing or strafing dive often found themselves having to depress the nose to well beyond the apparent vertical, with the engine 'cutting' through zero G causing fuel starvation, and they themselves 'hanging on their straps' in the cockpit as they pushed the stick further and further forward to keep the gun-sight on the target. Yet, during such uncomfortable manoeuvres the aircraft's *path through the air* would often not be anywhere near vertical.

Thin wings of normal shape stall at angles-of-attack less than 20 degrees and their 'lift coefficients' (the theoretical maximum lift available from each square foot of wing per knot of windspeed) are much less than thick wings. Leading-edge slots, drooped noses and trailing edge flaps of all kinds tend to increase lift coefficients by artficially increasing wing thickness – just as birds do when they land and take-off. Such 'camber' increases make the upper wing surface more curved and so increase the distance travelled – and therefore the speed – of the wind flowing over it. This further reduces its pressure (see Bernoulli's theorem) and so increases its suction – or lift – on the upper wing's surface.

Stalling Characteristics

Power-off stalls in most aircraft occur with lift on both wings failing at the same time and with no 'wing drop' occurring. With 'power-on' from a pro-peller-driven aircraft, a straight stall is the exception rather than the rule due to the 'twist' in the propeller's slipstream affecting the wing lift unequally. This 'twist' effect can usually be overcome in a monoplane by fitting leading edge slats or contra-props. If the stall is 'straight' and otherwise innocuous and the pilot then takes no immediate action, the nose will fall gently into a shallow dive from which gentle recovery action can be taken whenever the pilot con-siders that sufficient flying speed has been attained to cope with the extra 'G' of the pullout.

In order to prevent 'tipstalling' which causes 'wing drop' and a spin ten-dency, and to retain a measure of aileron control near the stall, most mono-plane aircraft – particularly of the 'flying wing' and hang-glider variety – are designed to have considerable 'washout' – or reduced angle-of-attack – towards their wing extremities. As we have seen above, the main advantage of this modification is that it ensures that the wing roots stall first and the resul-tant breakaway of the airflow inboard causes minimum lateral instability. Wing root premature stall will also cause pre-stall tail buffet (as the tail passes through the stalled wing root's turbulent wake) which is a useful way of warning the pilot of an approaching stall. Furthermore, in the case of a hang glider with sweptback wings, the fact that the wing centre section stalls first in a straight stall causes a nice gentle nose-down change of trim and automatically avoids a wing drop leading to a spin, making stall recovery easier.

In some aircraft a 'wing-drop' stall can be accompanied by 'aileron snatch' or overbalance and this can make matters worse. Unless immediate wingdrop recovery action is taken, (never by attempting to use aileron but by centralising the stick, applying 'opposite rudder' and then easing the stick further forward to unstall the wings), the aircraft's stalled wing (i.e., the wing on the inside of any possible spin rotation) can administer such drag to that side of the aircraft that it can not only pull the aircraft round into the first turn of a spin but retain it in the spin, in some types of aircraft, against any recovery action on the part of the pilot. Unless the stick is eased forward immediately to 'unload' the wings and unless opposite rudder is immediately applied, most aircraft will continue to spin. However, elementary trainers are usually capable of spin recovery on their own, providing that the aircraft controls are released and they are trimmed for normal level flight.

Rudder/fin stalling can also be a problem. The Harvard's fin and rudder tended to stall when the aircraft was purposely sideslipped, giving the pilot the impression that rudder 'overbalance' was occurring. Many aircraft designers built-in dorsal fins to delay fin stalling. To improve fin/rudder control at high Mach and to prevent Dutch rolling and erratic yaw effects, they introduced area-rule 'bullets' at the front and rear of the tailplane junctures.

There are many causes of 'wingdrop' at the stall. 'Dissimilar lift' characteristics between one wing and another (due to poorly fitted cowlings and turbulent wakes behind engine nacelles on the wings' upper surfaces) are two of the many reasons. The 'twist' in propeller slipstream (locally increasing airflow incidence to the wing which lies behind the up-going prop blades) is another common reason for 'power-on', 'wingdrop' stalls. The cure for the latter is to fit contra-props or in multi-engined prop-driven aircraft – 'handed' props. The Short Sturgeon 1, built for the Navy and intended as a day/night fighter/bomber, was fitted with twin contra-props and had a very easy stall and recovery, power on or off.

In the case of the early Merlin-engined Seafires, the port wing root was subjected to the propeller slipstream meeting it at a much higher incidence than it met the starboard wing root. This, together with a poorly-fitted cine-gun-camera hatch on the port wing's top surface a few inches from an equally poorly fitted engine cowling which fed high-pressure air on to the wing root's top surface, all this promoted an early and complete 'power-on' stall of the port wing. This often led to a port undercarriage collapse at the 'cut' when decklanding. Worse still, it could lead to a 'flick' stall into the sea at about the batsman's position on the flight deck. (This occurred for the last time on the very last decklanding made by a Seafire before the Squadron disbanded in Portsmouth at the end of the war and the pilot – Lt D. Hatton – was killed.)

Although 'power-on' stalls occurred at slightly lower airspeeds than 'gliding stalls' – due to slipstream lift benefits – they were always much sharper and occurred with much less warning to the pilot. 'Glide' – or 'power-off' stalls – are always much smoother in prop-driven aircraft and usually give the pilot good warning signs.

The first indication of a stall in the Seafire – and most other aircraft – with 'engine-off', would be a gentle buffet felt on the tail surfaces. This buffet was caused by the turbulent wake from the semi-stalled wing roots striking the tailplane and it was felt by the pilot as a vibration on the stick. This gave him a very effective warning that his aircraft was only a few mph above its stalling speed.

When 'power-on' stalls were tested in the Merlin-engined Seafire – with its prop turning clockwise when viewed from the tail – the aircraft would drop its port wing sharply at about 65 knots. (In the case of the Griffon-engined Seafire XVs and XVIIs in which the prop turned round the other way, these aircraft dropped their *starboard* wing very sharply). As we have seen in the paragraph above, slipstream 'twist' effects were mostly responsible for this early, engine-on, port wing stall. The stall could be made even more vicious if, at a speed about two knots above the stall, considerable power was then suddenly applied as might be required in a decklanding approach in turbulent air astern of the carrier. The sudden increase in engine torque reaction in having to 'twist' the prop round faster with more power and in a clockwise direction, would tend to roll the aircraft in an anti-clockwise direction to port and overload the port wing and, at the same time, locally increase wing incidence in the rear of the upgoing propeller blades. If the pilot then attempted to use aileron to lift the port wing – which would be the natural reaction – instead of instant right rudder, the aircraft would 'flick' stall and dive into the sea in a second. When power application was sudden – as in a last-minute wave-off from a decklanding approach – or when, as was often the case, the engine's accelerator pump failed to supply an instant increase in fuel supply direct to the cylinders and the engine momentarily cut out entirely so that the pilot mistimed his application of starboard rudder, the aircraft would once again immediately flick over to port and into the sea. At least three Pacific Seafire pilots lost their lives in this way when decklanding. Needless to say, all these torque effects were eliminated when Supermarine produced their beautiful contra-prop Seafire 46 and 47.

Although aircraft designers could use models to reproduce spinning characteristics of prototypes before full-scale versions were built and flown (in a vertical-flow wind tunnel at Farnborough into which was inserted a free-fall model), they were not always able to reproduce stalling behaviour. When approaching the stall, as we have seen above, the ideal aircraft should have an inherent tendency towards a reduction of its angle of attack, thus making it easy for the pilot to return to normal flight conditions. The very least that a pilot should expect at this stage is that his controls should remain effective.

As such 'suck-it-and-see' trials cannot be carried out in the wind tunnel – particularly in 'power-on' conditions of model flight – the initial stalling trials of a prototype are approached with considerable caution and much crossing of fingers. The test pilot might be looking for the following characteristics:

Any deterioration in control effectiveness as speeds reduce to within five mph of the stall should be progressive rather than abrupt, yet distinctive enough to allow the pilot to recognise their limiting condition before an uncontrollable stall occurs. The ideal warning consists of gentle tail buffeting, wings remaining level and a tendency for the nose to drop – thus tending to unstall the aircraft automatically. If the pilot continues to apply gentle back stick regardless of the warning signs, an ideal aircraft would not drop a wing but would carry out a small fore-and-aft pitching motion – or a small amplitude *fugoid* motion – losing height but maintaining a degree of aileron, rudder and elevator control throughout.

In the stall tests that we carried out on the Harvard, the aircraft was purposely loaded at its aft CG limit i.e., about 12 inches behind the aircraft's designed centre of lift. This tail-heavy loading increased its tendency to stall without the pilot having to pull-back on the stick at all and for it to enter a spin on its own. It therefore showed us what to expect in other aircraft but with the certainty that in the case of the ETPS Harvard, our lives would not be at risk as this aircraft always came out of a spin on demand, provided of course we took the correct recovery action. Even if we did not take immediate recovery action by centralising the stick and easing it forward with full opposite rudder, and the Harvard then entered a full spin instead of the 'incipient' variety, it would always come out on the correct demand from the pilot – an ideal training aircraft in this respect.

Aerodynamic and hydrodynamic drag
There are two types of aero-drag affecting objects flying through the air. The first – and the simplest to understand – is called 'form drag' and is mostly a function of the object's frontal area facing into the airflow. Streamlining, smooth finish and 'fineness ratio' all tend to reduce form drag as any cyclist, tobogganer, downhill skier/racer – where seconds count – will know.

The second most common form of aero-drag is called 'induced drag'. This is mostly a function of the drag caused by wing lift. As 'G' increases in a turn, the lift required – and thus the induced drag – increases in like proportion until it reaches a maximum. A Seafire 47 could maintain about 5 G in a level turn at full throttle without losing speed at its best operating height. Jets, such as the Sabre had insufficient power to overcome their increased induced drag above G values of about 4 G and a dive had to be initiated to maintain airspeed. A Phantom in after-burner could usually maintain 7 G in a turn at medium altitudes in subsonic flight without having to dive to maintain speed. In spite of variable sweepback and huge increases in variable direction engine thrust available from the modern jet, induced drag is still the main limiting drag force to a fighter plane's manoeuvring performance, especially at high subsonic Mach values where there is a very steep increase in drag. Perhaps the easiest way to understand why this huge drag increase occurs at about 0.85 Mach in most aircraft designs is to compare the drag behaviour of a 30-foot yacht. The maximum, practical top speed, V, for a conventional sailing yacht always works out roughly as:

$$V \text{ (knots)} \approx 1.3 \times \text{square root of its waterline length in feet}$$

If pushed above this speed, its bow wave increases to immense proportions because the water builds up in front of the boat's bow and uses up much more of the boat's energy in pushing it out of the way. Likewise, an aircraft approaching the speed of sound is travelling too fast to 'warn' the air of its arrival and to give it time to begin to get out of the way. The air builds up a 'bow wave' of air pressure in front of the aircraft's fuselage and wings, sharply increasing the drag at this point in the Mach scale and heating up its leading surfaces. This is known as the compressibility drag rise. A sharply pointed 'bow' and thin, sweptback wings greatly reduce this drag rise, so allowing the aircraft to enter supersonic flight – where the rate of drag increase falls off – with minimum delay or reduction in control effectiveness.

Needless to say, the sailors who operated their canoes in the Pacific thousands of years ago soon found out that a long, narrow hull went faster and easier through the water than a heavy, conventional 'displacement' hull design i.e., a light canoe with its waterline length about ten times its maximum beam. (The Polynesian canoeists were also the first to achieve lateral stability in such hull shapes under sail by building outriggers.) Flying boat and speed-boat designers – followed by sailing boat designers such as Uffa Fox who designed the Flying Fifteen – soon adopted a hull shape of sufficient lightness and water-plane area so that when it had reached its maximum/efficient speed *through* the water (i.e., 1.3 × square root of the waterline length) and if it were kept upright, it would then have sufficient 'waterplane' area to get up and plane like a speedboat with very much reduced drag. Lateral stability was provided either by the crew or by a streamlined fin keel with its weight very low down e.g., the Flying Fifteen.

Skin friction was reduced by flush planking and smoothed varnish finishes. By 1948, weight was reduced by using stressed skin aircraft construction methods and materials. Moulded plywood was used for the ¼-inch thick hull and deck using 'Aerolite' gap-filling, waterproof glue as the main fastener as in the de Havilland Mosquito.

By 1955, cheaper and lighter glass-fibre replaced wooden hulls and yachting became even more popular than before. Sixty-foot ocean-going racers can now keep up an average sailing speed over 24 hours of 15 knots or more in a following sea when the hull 'gets up and planes' for short distances, with their sterns high on the crests of 50-foot following seas. Robin Knox-Johnson's catamaran plus his crew circumnavigated the world in 74 days and 20 hours at an average speed through the water of 14.75 knots.

Once the hull 'gets up and planes', the hull has no need to divide the water at its bow or pass *through* it like a liner, a merchant ship or a Twelve-metre Class yacht. It can now easily attain very much higher speeds *over* the water, reducing the skin friction as it does so by raising its hull out of the water, allowing air through a suction hole in its bottom to 'lubricate' the hull/water contact. This is referred to as a 'ventilated step' in flying boat design which also uses a flared V-section in its hull shape to take advantage of the reduced displacement as winglift raises it out of the water as speed increases.

It is interesting to see how ski jumping champions prolong their 'airborne' time by using the lift from their body and by moving the toes of their skis out to form wings in the 70 mph airflow. Watching the Olympics on TV it is easy to see that the longest jumps are consistently made by light-bodied contestants who slope their bodies smoothly between their broadened skis, holding an incidence to the airflow of no more than 20 degrees to achieve maximum lift. They wait as long as the rules allow – like swans do on a calm-air-water take off – for any chance of a wind gust to increase their V-squared lift and so prolong their 'glide' distance. Likewise, downhill racers use their skis to *reduce* lift whenever possible in jumps, for time in the air in downhill racing is time wasted. When the first five bob-sleighs' finishing times are within a tenth of a second of each other, the reduction in 'form' drag to a minimum during their 1½ minute descents at 70 mph is also essential. Likewise cyclists, racing cars, speedboats and all other objects required to move at anything over about 30 mph through the air try to copy the birds and present a smooth entry and exit with minimum skin friction in their dress and in the designs of their vehicles.

The Stable Stall

In the case of many new jet designs having high tailplanes, the rudders and elevators – urgently needed at their maximum effectiveness at the time of stall recovery – were found to be ineffective in prototype stall tests. Having entered the stall, the test pilot applied full nose-down elevator to recover from the stall and this had no effect whatsoever. Even if the pilot attempted to enter a spin – from which he thought he might have a better change of recovery – he could not do so. Four such cases occurred in airliner prototypes with high tailplanes in the next few years and it took these tragedies to force action by the Ministry of Supply to build much larger and more effective wind tunnels at RAE Bedford and elsewhere, whenever money could be found.

The reason for the 'stable stall' phenomena was mostly because the tailplanes had been placed at too shallow an angle above the turbulent wake from the stalled mainplane and, because of jet power, the tailplane itself no longer had the benefit of increased airflow from propeller slipstreams if and when the pilot opened up to full power when attempting to recover from a stall. Later designs increased this angle by reducing the distance between tailplane and mainplane and so allowing the tailplane to remain above the wake from the mainplane at all times. In twin jet airliners, their jet engines were often placed on struts either side of the rear fuselage, forward of the tailplane, so that, if a 'stable stall' occurred, full jet power would tend to 'straighten out' the airflow past the tail surfaces and full control would be maintained. The power-operated, all-moving, 'slab' tail was another major improvement in 'back-end' controllability and this may have solved the 'stable stall' problem – but not before three high-tailplane airliners had crashed and one delta fighter, killing their crews. The American 'fighter' – the Cutlass also suffered from the stable stall phenomenon and was very unpopular with the Naval crews who flew them. (The BAC 111, the DH Trident, the Handley Page Victor and the Gloster Javelin were the main British offenders).

Some other aerodynamic effects

Our aerodynamics lectures explained a host of reasons for past accidents in the types of aircraft that we had flown during the war. The 'positive weight' saga in the early Seafires was a case in point. The G-stalling of the Barracuda – with its high tailplane in the wake of its airbrakes on the pullout from a bombing dive – was another of these dangerous faults which had not been diagnosed during wartime trials in UK.

'Humph's' explanations taught us how dangerous it was for a pilot to approach to deck-land with skid applied. Decklanding has always been the most demanding exercise for any pilot and the manner in which decktrials had to be entrusted to non-test-pilots during the war and before ETPS got going, and who had little or no knowledge of the aerodynamics involved, was a major cause of unnecessary accidents during the war. One such naval pilot actually recommended the use of a 'crabbed', or skid, approach in the Seafire – to allow the pilot to see the deck on a straight-in approach! Such 'in-spin' misuse of the controls a few mph above the power-on stall could have caused innumerable accidents if this method had not been ruled out by more experienced pilots.

When discussing aerodynamcis, 'Humph' almost placed us in the position of a morsel of innocent air as it approached the wing of an aircraft and how it had to decide whether it wanted to pass over or under the wing. Then, whether it could remain in company with its friends surrounding it in a 'laminar-flow' manner or whether it would have to break adrift from them and be swept away in a whirl of changing pressures and directions, doing no good whatsoever.

Humph explained that the faster and farther that air flowed over the top of an aircraft's wing, the more its 'boundary layer' tended to slow down and thicken, the less it retained any 'laminar flow' characteristics and the more turbulent it became. By the time it reached about halfway towards the wing's trailing edge, it was producing about half the lift per square foot than when it started. The thicker the wing and the flatter its undersurface, the greater the distance the upper-surface air had to travel to catch up with the lower-surface air, so the faster it had to go. This meant more 'V-squared' and, of course, more lift, but *only* if it could be encouraged to stay in a smooth airflow *in close contact* with the wing's upper surface all the way to its trailing edge. As the upper-surface airflow was 'sucking' upwards, it could more easily lose contact with the wing's upper surface than higher-pressure air 'pushing' upwards on its lower surface, particularly if the upper surface had any unevennness or irregularities. (The Spitfire/Seafire's flush riveting was a major improvement over other contemporary fighter aircraft in this respect).

A quick look at the shape of the backs of most saloon cars will immediately tell us that the airflow behind the average rear window of a production saloon or hatchback car is so turbulent that any aerofoil intended to straighten it out or 'spoil' the airflow to reduce over-all drag or increase rearwheel roadweight adhesion (as do the download 'tailplanes' on racing cars) is, for all practical purposes a complete waste of time.

Our wind tunnel lectures told us that thinner wings gave less lift but much less drag. The Hurricane wing had a thickness/chord (t/c) ratio or about 14 per cent (Hawkers needed this thickness to produce the necessary strength). Mitchell's Spitfire wing could be manufactured by Supermarines with an average 12 per cent t/c ratio. By halfspan, this was reduced to ten per cent t/c ratio, a 'thinness' made possible by using the structural strength of the wing's skin – a system of 'stressed skin' construction which he had used for the first time when building the floats of the Supermarine S series of Schneider Trophy winners of 1934. The Spiteful/Attacker wing was thinner still – ten per cent.

Roughly speaking, the thicker the wing the higher its 'lift coefficient'. The thinner the wing, the lower its low-speed lift capability but the less its drag at high speeds. Furthermore, as we shall see, a thin wing, especially one having its maximum thickness at about mid-chord instead of one third chord, could be flown much faster without encountering the 'sonic' drag rise – i.e., compressibility effects when approaching the speed of sound. By the end of the war, wings were being designed with sweepback. This not only decreased the thickness/chord ratio in the direction of the airflow to as little as three per cent but delayed the early onset of the 'compressibility' drag rise and allowed better control during the transonic speed range.

G-stalls

The stalling behaviour of the aircraft discussed above referred only to the 'one-G' stall in straight and level flight. Stalling speeds obviously increase as the aircraft's weight is increased. In a turn, with the pilot applying, say, 2 G in a Seafire 47, each square foot of wing has to produce about 80 lb/sq ft instead of the usual 40 lb. To enable the wing to do this – and in accordance with the V-squared law – the pilot must increase his speed from 75 mph to at least 110 mph before it is safe to make this turn. Woe betide him if he does not.

By 1946 new aircraft for the Fleet Air Arm were about to be flown for the first time having wingloadings of 65 lb/sq ft (e.g., early prototypes of the Westland Wyvern). This loading was more than double that of the Spitfire. This meant that their final, 'over-the-rounddown' approach speeds would have to increase to about 110 kts if no 'lift augmentation' could be added in the landing configuration and assuming the same wing efficiency and lift coefficients which had applied to the Seafire or the American Corsair of WW II. Of more importance, especially in the jet age, all carrier take-offs would have to use the catapult – for there would be insufficient deck run or rocket assistance to attain the necessary high speeds which high wingloadings required – and these catapults would require to be longer and deliver up to 20 times the total energy of wartime catapults.

Vortices

Whilst flying in the high-temperature, humid air in the Pacific, we had noticed condensation trails from the 'clipped' wingtips of our Seafires. We were used to this in high-G, high-humidity conditions of flight near the cloud base but we had not seen it during a normal take-off or decklanding. ETPS aerodynamics lectures fully explained these 'tip trails' as being caused by reduction in air pressure – and thus its temperature – at the centre of the wingtip vortices – by the centrifugal action of the revolving air. It thus became visible as locally condensed air extending for a short time from each wingtip. The larger the 'G' forces on the wing, the more vicious would be the power of the vortex. In the case of a 747 landing at Heathrow, the wingtip vortices stretch for several miles astern of its approach path and woe betide any aircraft caught up in them.

The cause of the vortex – or air rotation – at the wingtips is simply that the top surface, low-pressure air at the wingtip meets the lower surface high-pressure air. Nature abhors a near-vacuum so that in trying to get into each others' space, a rotation or mini-whirlwind is set up. This trails behind the wingtips, propeller tips, or helicopter rotor tips, as the case might be. The vortex from a port wing rotates clockwise when looked at from astern – and *vice versa* for the starboard. This is because there is in-flow onto the top surfaces and outflow from the bottom surfaces in all cases. The whole object of 'wing fences' is to stop this 'inflow/outflow' from occuring and to avoid the drag that it causes. Most birds reduce wingtip vortex generation when gliding by drooping the outboard halves of their wings, so retaining any spanwise lower-surface outflow and making it more difficult for it to rotate onto the upper surface at the wingtips. They offset the negative dihedral or anhedral, effects of this by *increasing* the dihedral of the *inner* half of their wingspan, giving rise to the well known 'gull wing' description.

Vortex drag is not only a source of drag in modern wing designs but causes similar drag in boats' sails and, hydrodynamically, on their fin keels and rudders.

To return to the subject of aircraft wing design – vortex drag had to be eliminated as far as possible. One method was by pointing the wingtips – which can be seen in the Spitfire/Seafire and in many of the beautiful, soaring, migratory and insect-eating birds. Another method was by straightening the inflow and outflow tendencies at the wingtips by erecting small 'barriers' at the wingtips. In the case where wingtip tanks were fitted to the DH Venom aircraft, these acted as vortex barriers so efficiently that, in spite of the increased drag and weight of the fuel tanks, the Venom did more mpg with them in place than without them! Vortex 'generators' – usually about the area of a ten-pence piece – were welded on edge at an incidence to the airflow on the wings' top surfaces in areas where the boundary layer showed early signs of breakaway. (These were used in the Sea Hawk and in the Attacker. The Navy's Jetstream prop-jet transport also uses them on its wing root to preserve a smooth airflow either side of the engine necelles.) The 'mini-rotating-turbulence' so created, speeds up the airflow velocity near the wing surfaces from that moving faster a few inches above it and so retains a measure of laminar flow for a greater portion of the wing area further aft, reducing drag and increasing lift.

Some aspects of high altitude aviation

Anyone knows the effect of high altitudes and how pressure is reduced and air – and thus oxygen – becomes 'rarified' the higher we go. By the time that an aircraft has climbed up to about 15,000 feet above sea level anywhere in the tropical or temperate world, the temperature has gone down to near freezing and the air-you-feel has about halved its density. Not only is the oxygen pressure reduced and the 'thinner' air gives less lift, but the lower temperatures reduce the speed of sound. Cockpit airspeed indicators depend upon 'air-you-feel' for their readings. An airspeed indicator is nothing more than a barometer, its capsule being connected to a suitably designed and positioned open-ended tube held out into the airstream called a pitot-head. It does not therefore register the *true* airspeed of the aircraft except at sea level and at standard temperature and pressure, but only the pressure difference between the air from the open-ended tube and a 'static' air pressure source obtained from another tube suitably placed to give static, outside air pressure. By the time an aircraft has climbed to about 37,000 feet, the ASI reads a mere fraction of the actual speed that the aircraft is going, while the temperature has probably gone down to the stratosphere norm of about minus 47 degrees Centigrade.

Piston-engine powers are maintained by supercharging their air intake pressures as far as possible up to the pressure they are supercharged to at sea level. This is usually done by varying the speed of an engine-driven turbine in the air intake and by the pilot altering his throttle settings as required to maintain boost pressures with increase in altitude. The piston engine does not know the difference, except perhaps from its having to drive its 'turbo' faster the higher it goes, so giving up some of its propelling power. Jet engine intake pressures depend for their maintenance with increase in altitude, on the use of multi-stage compressor turbines plus the ram effect of the air entering their air intakes. There is, of course an equal or greater fall-off in airframe drag with altitude so that miles-per-gallon-per-ton and cruising speeds for jets are greatly increased compared with piston-engined aircraft.

In 1947, human oxygen supply was assured between 10,000 and 50,000 feet by pressurising the cockpit and by the aircrew breathing 100 per cent oxygen through their masks. Pressure waistcoats were sometimes used. These were filled with oxygen under pressure which was fed through a special oxygen mask to the pilot when he was required to fly at 40,000 feet and above in unpressurised aircraft.

The 'rarified' air at high altitudes does not therefore limit jet power as much as that from piston engines so that jet aircraft can be flown at very high true airspeeds while avoiding the huge air forces which increase the drag and the structural hazards if these speeds were attempted at low altitudes. However, as an aircraft depends upon the value registered on the indicated airspeed dial for its lift, unless it can greatly increase its true airspeed – and so retain the same indicated airspeed as it had at lower levels – its manoeuvrability becomes less with increase in altitude and by the time 25,000 feet is reached it often takes twice the turning radius to complete a 360 degree turn that it takes at sea level. At the stage of development reached by 1947, even the use of flaps did not help much, for their increased drag required more engine power, which at these extreme altitudes was not forthcoming at that time.

As an example of the large differences that reduction in air pressure/density make in aircraft speeds and behaviour at high altitudes I can quote the Phantom. When, in 1963, I was flying a United States Navy Phantom at 45,000 feet. Although the machmeter registered Mach 2, and the true airspeed indicator read about 1350 mph, the airspeed indicator – the air-you-feel – only registered about 450. At ground level, the noise at an indicated airspeed of 450 mph would be incredible at this airspeed and it would be a very bumpy ride. But turning the aircraft through 180 degrees would only take about 2 miles of countryside to accomplish at about 7 G – using an airpressure 'G' suit to maintain the blood supply to the head and eyes. The same turn at 45,000 feet at the same indicated airspeed would take about six miles of airspace to accomplish, but would be in comparative silence and without air turbulence – sharp-edged, stratospheric 'gusts' permitting.

Because of the much lower air temperatures and pressures at high altitude, the speed of sound and athmospheric drag are much reduced the higher we go, so that supersonic testing above about 45,000 feet is relatively safe, particularly if available jet power allows such investigations to be carried out in level flight or a climb.

With their use of rocket power in addition to jet turbine power, the Americans were able to take full advantage of high altitude in their speed-quest trials and, using a form of capsule rescue rather than an ejector seat, with its own supply of oxygen and automatic release which was being evolved by our own Martin-Baker, they quickly achieved world speed records in their research aircraft operating from Edwards Airforce Base in California. The other advantages of high altitude testing at speeds well in excess of Mach 1, were that structural limits could not so easily be exceeded if the aircraft became uncontrollable and sufficient height would usually remain in which to bale out or recover from a dive if this became difficult.

Some new ideas – Farnborough, 1947
At ETPS in 1948 we hoped that someone would soon come up with some sensible ideas, for the boffins were talking about prone pilots and landing jets without undercarriages on an air-inflated mattress instead of on a steel flight-deck with arrester wires. This last idea, nicknamed the 'magic carpet', was

being assembled at Farnborough at the time our course was due to move down to Farnborough from Cranfield in September 1947. It struck us all as being entirely unworkable for it entailed lifting the aircraft off the 'mattress' after each landing and then supporting it without an undercarriage until it was loaded again into a special cradle for a catapult take-off. Its first trial-landing at Farnborough ended in anticlimax as the pilot came in far too slowly, misjudging the ground effect and stalled the aircraft onto the ramp. The idea was abandoned a little time afterwards.

Another very interesting investigation by the aerodynamicists at Farnborough was into the exact behaviour of airflow over a wing. They knew, as we all knew, that the longer the airflow could be encouraged to move fast and stay close to the upper wing's contour, the more lift and the less drag would be encountered. Bearing in mind that about two-thirds of the lift from any normally shaped aerofoil comes from its top surface in unstalled flight, scientists at Farnborough were very keen indeed to prevent early 'breakaways' of top-surface airflow, particularly when using 'laminar flow' aerofoil shapes – those which they hoped would give less drag at high speeds and which were about to be used for 'flying wing' prototypes (e.g., the Armstrong-Whitworth AW 52 Flying Wing, September 1948 first flight). Thinner wings could then be built with smaller spans and longer chord measurements. By studying airflow patterns fullscale, air behaviour at transonic and supersonic speeds could perhaps be encouraged to be more predictable and fullscale supersonic manned flight could be made safely and not just in American supersonic wind tunnels using models. Smooth 'laminar flow' wings might also remain unstalled at much slower speeds and have much more predictable stall characteristics.

The aircraft wing initially chosen for this experiment was a Hurricane wing. Its upper surface had been smoothed to an accuracy of 1/100th of an inch – much smoother than a Spitfire wing. Two such wings were then flown through artificial smoke clouds in still air and the exact airflow pattern photographed. Squashed insects on the wings' leading edges were unpopular as they wrecked the results, so the wing was coated with cartridge paper until the aircraft had climbed to an insect-free height and the sheet was then removed by the pilot pulling a wire to cut its leading edges so that it fell away. We could hardly believe all this, for what possible hope would there be of such a wing surviving in practice. However, it was all done for a good purpose. Aero Flight at RAE Farnborough had no adequate, fullscale wind tunnel of its own to study such matters and recourse had to be made to such alternatives if scientific knowledge was to keep pace with events.

Supersonic flight – first attempts

In 1945/6/7 there were strong feelings going round the Ministry of Supply that manned supersonic flight investigations were too dangerous for humans to undertake so that free-flying models would have to be used instead. This was in spite of the American success in achieving supersonic flight in the Bell X series of aircraft – which were fully manned – and, two years later the appearance of the American F-86 Sabre jet fighter.

The first English test pilot to 'go supersonic' was R.P. 'Bea' Beamont. He did so in the Sabre F-86A in May 1948, but this was kept secret by the Ministry of Supply so that we did not hear about it until three months later by which time the brave John Derry – perhaps accidentally and out-of-control – had exceeded the speed of sound in the second prototype of the DH 108 – 6 Sept 1948).

Unfortunately for Britain, our early transonic research attempts – made in the DH 108 – had to be made in dives in order to get up enough speed. Neither did our pilots have the essential assistance of 'all-flying' tailplanes and power-operated, 'irreversible' ailerons and rudders which the Americans had been quick to adopt. Derry told us that although the DH 108 could be test-flown up to a Mach reading of M.98 in a dive from 45,000 feet, its normal safe limit should be set at about 0.7 Mach!

Boundary Layer Control (BLC)

'Humph' explained to us that from time immemorial, aerodynamicists had known that a smooth surface encouraged the air to remain in perfect contact with the upper surface of the wing, with its various airlayers sliding smoothly over each other in a manner described by the aerodynamicists at Farnborough as 'laminar flow'.

Signor Bernoulli had expounded a theorem which said categorically that *if air was made to move faster than its surrounding air, it would always be at a lower pressure*. The faster this difference in speed, the more 'suck' there would be on a wing's top surface and the greater its lift would be. Likewise, Bernoulli's theorem worked equally well for air travelling under a wing. The air under a wing, meeting it at an angle, would be compressed and slowed down. It would push the wing up. The air over the wing, having to travel farther and thus faster to keep up, would be at a lower pressure and 'suck' the wing up. Lift is generated in this way.

It was this low pressure air on a wing's top surface – responsible for no less than two-thirds of the total lift of the wing – that was always trying to break free of the surface and become turbulent, particularly when the wing was of the so-called 'high lift' shape – its top surface steeply curved – or its surface not entirely smooth, or when the airflow's angle-of-attack as it met the wing was higher than about 20 degrees.

All manner of devices were being tried out to encourage the top-surface airflow to remain in smooth 'laminar flow' as long as possible. The latest device in 1955 was in addition to vortex generators to assist airflow near the stall or at slow speeds and high angles-of-attack – and without increasing the total drag – was called 'boundary layer control' (BLC). This American idea consisted of high pressure air blown from spanwise slits along the wing's top surface at about quarter chord distance from the wing's leading edge. This re-accelerated the airflow in contact with the wing and – in accordance with

Bernoulli – sucked it back onto the wing's top surface before it could break away any further. It thus reduced the thickness of the boundary layer being 'dragged along' by the aircraft, increased the wing's top surface airflow velocity and effective lift, and so enabled an aircraft fitted with BLC to fly at a much reduced approach and landing speed at greater wing angles-of-attack.

Other slots, also on the top surface – this time sucking slow, turbulent air from the wing's trailing edges just ahead of the control surfaces – also reduced turbulence and boundary layer thickness and greatly increased aileron/elevon control effectiveness, especially in transonic and stalling regions. At least, this is what the scientists were hoping it would do. As large quantities of compressed air would seem to be available from jet powered aircraft, this idea made sense.

It was clear that something like this would have to be done to improve wing lift coefficients if large naval jets were ever to be economically used from the small British carriers, otherwise the RAF might quite rightly say that they should be allowed to do the job from a mass of new airfields which they would be obliged to build round the world, and we Navy flyers would all be out of a job.

The immense advantages of BLC compared with normal wing design not only lie in its ability to increase lift sufficiently to reduce the landing speed of a Buccaneer by 15–20 knots and reduce its required 'end-speed' off a catapult launch by the same amount, but BLC also stops wing icing which can upset the airflow on take-off over the entire wing.

In spite of every device intended by the designer to keep the air in laminar flow, the smallest irregularities at a wing's leading edges or in the first third of its upper surface will so upset the airflow over the entire wing that take-offs have to be aborted and crashes still happen. If snow or ice settles on the wing during a taxi out to take-off, by the time the airliner is halfway down the runway, enough irregularity in the wing shape has occurred to lead to a stall as the aircraft is rotated to maximum lift-angle-of-attack and it will then refuse to leave the runway. When an aborted take-off occurs in these conditions on a short runway in nil wind conditions, a crash is always a probability as, with a slippery runway to cope with as well as excessive speed and in spite of reverse thrust and airbrake extension, a heavily loaded airliner is in great difficulty if it is to avoid a fatal overshoot.

Bernoulli and the cricket ball

In addition to 'leg-breaks' and 'off-breaks' being initiated by a bowler imparting spin to the ball as it leaves his hand, we have also seen how some bowlers manage to swerve the ball *before* it hits the ground. Likewise we have noticed how a footballer, a tennis player, a table-tennis player and a golfer can do likewise. This swerve is Signor Bernoulli at work. All the player is doing is to cause the air round one side of the ball to travel faster than it is round the other. According to Bernoulli *The faster the air compared with its surroundings, the lower its pressure.*

We can obtain this necessary pressure difference by spoiling the airflow more on one side than the other of the cricket ball or football, so that the 'spoiled' side has less suction effect than on the other side. Air on the 'suction' side can be also be encouraged to go faster and cling longer in smoother flow by *smoothing* its contours and giving it a polish on the trousers whenever possible. Perhaps the most effective way to encourage air to flow faster on the 'suction' side is for the bowler to rotate the ball as it leaves his hands so that its surface rotates with the airflow on the chosen 'suction' side and against it on the other. Most fast bowlers do not use ball rotation to swerve the ball but do so by polishing one side of the ball and projecting it from their hands such that the polished side is not obstructed by the lift-spoiler effect of the seam, but the roughened side, is. Thus, when it leaves their hands the seam lies fore-and-aft, but with a slight tilt towards one side or the other to use the seam itself as a further means of spoiling the 'lift' on the 'slow' airflow side. The skill of the seam bowler lies in his ability to ensure the presentation of one side or the other throughout the ball's flightpath to the batsman.

The other very effective way of swerving a ball is by setting it turning as it leaves the hand, club, foot, raquet or bat. The air will then flow faster round that side of the ball whose surface is moving in the same direction as the airflow, due to its reduced skin friction. Likewise, the opposite side will be moving against the airstream and will slow down the air on that side, causing a pressure increase. Likewise, 'topping' a ball can cause it to dip – as in a table-tennis service – or in a badly hit golf ball. Football championships are won by clever swerving of free kicks. They can also be lost by the kicker's inability to keep the ball below the goal cross-bar, which he can sometimes do by imparting a forward rotation to it as it leaves his foot from a free kick near the goal.

Only a few ounces difference of 'suck' is required on a five-ounce cricket ball to make it move sideways in its one second flight to the batsman and a relatively slow rotation is all that is required to make a football or a golf ball swerve out of line, particularly when it is travelling very fast. Bernoulli and the V-squared law can take over completely.

The boomerang comes back because its rotation gives more lift on the outside of its turn than on the inside. It performs a smooth roll to the left to a vertical bank if thrown from the right hand and, depending on the skill of the thrower to impart the correct elevation and rotation/throw speed – and, of course, taking into account the wind direction – the boomerang should come back by completing a full circle before striking the ground if it misses its target.

CHAPTER 4

BOSCOMBE DOWN

Thirty students of 6 ETPS received new postings by Christmas Day 1947. Ten of us had the luck to be told to report to Boscombe Down. 'C' Squadron was fully booked up at that time so that the author, Nick Goodhart, Ian MacLachlan and later, Peter Richmond, temporarily joined the 'Intensive Flying Development Unit' (IFDF) on the South side of the airfield until last August 1948 when some room became available for us at 'C' Squadron. Our Naval CO was Lance Kiggell – another Taranto veteran, who had recently relieved Cdr J.A. Ievers RN. (Later Rear-Admiral J.A. Ievers CB, OBE). Kiggell had had none other than Lt/Cdr Dick Janvrin as his Observer over Taranto harbour that famous night. (Janvrin later became Vice-Admiral Sir Richard Janvrin, KCB, DSC. He was one of the few pre-war Fleet Air Arm officers who survived the high casualty rate in the early months of the war over Norway and in the Mediterranean and who became such valuable Fleet Air Arm members of the Naval Staff in the late 1960s who were able to persuade the Admiralty Board to introduce 'through-deck cruisers' – now known as the 'Invincible' Class of aircraft carriers – after much vigorous lobbying.)

Our Senior Pilot at 'C' Squadron at Boscombe Down was 'Spike' King-Joyce and I knew him well. He had been the author's Hurricane Flight leader in 1942 in the old *Eagle* before she was sunk in Operation PEDESTAL, and again, in 800 Squadron in *Biter* for the Oran landings with Hurricane IICs and IIBs.

The purpose of IFDF was for ourselves from 6 ETPS – plus Lt (E) Peter Wilson plus three RAF pilots – to report on any further engineering or performance defects not discovered in the initial clearance testing of early production or prototype aircraft. This saved operational squadrons from having to do this disruptive task. Our CO was Sqn/Ldr Jim Starky – a New Zealander from 2 ETPS.

The purpose of the four test squadrons at Boscombe Down was to clear prototype military and civil aircraft for service use after they had been tested initially by the manufacturers' test teams at their own airfields, and to discuss with them and with our own boffins at Boscombe any alterations necessary to their design if they fell short of the customer's operational and safety requirements. For this we were able to use the scientific knowledge gained at ETPS together with our knowledge of operational flying gained during the war and afterwards, guided and assisted as necessary by our own 'private' civilian scientists attached to each test squadron.

Our job at Boscombe was entirely different from that of the four ETPS test pilots posted to 'Aero' Flight at RAE Farnborough. Farnborough's test flying programme, carried out by six or seven RAF/RN ETPS graduates, was in the charge of research scientists. These scientists were intent on pushing forward the frontiers of aviation performance in all its aspects, often using 'failed' prototypes as their workhorses. Their chief 'customers' were aircraft designers and scientists working in the four or five aircraft factories in Britain. Our main customers at Boscombe Down were the three Services, the Navy's chief being the Director of Naval Air Warfare (DNAW) at the Admiralty whose job it was to 'dream up' new operational requirements to place before the aircraft industry. They, in turn, would then offer a 'project' to meet this requirement and would then approach the Board of Admiralty through the 'Procurement Executive' (PE) in the Ministry of Supply – as it was called then – for the money to build them. A contract would then go out to a firm chosen by the Ministry of Supply to build it – starting with a few prototypes and, hopefully, ending up several years later with a production order once Boscombe had given its initial OK.

Interservice competition for money was severe, of course, so that the Commanding Officer of 'C' Squadron together with his own technical adviser needed to have the best possible engineering advice to correct the inevitable faults in the prototype design. He did this through regular meetings with the manufacturers involved and by carrying out a comprehensive test programme giving clear results which would help the Admiralty with PE's advice to make up its mind whether it was worth the money or whether some other manufacturer's offerings should be tried out instead.

During the time we spent at IFDF, we had the opportunity to fly many types of aircraft. Among these were: Firebrand Mark IV, Bristol Brigand, DH Hornet, Percival Prentice, Meteor NF II, Sea Fury FB II, Wyverns of various Marks, the Fairey Trainer, the new Seafang and several marks of Firefly and Seafire. Only four of these are commented upon in this chapter. First, the Percival Prentice, chosen by the RAF to be their new *ab initio* trainer. It had the habit of turning on its back in steep turns and then entering a flat spin and failing to recover! A larger rudder, 'anti-spin' strakes and up-turned wingtips had been added to it, but pilots were still demanding spin-recovery parachutes to be attached to its tail before they would carry out further trials. However, we heard later that after a major alteration to its elevator, it was allowed its clearance and many were built. When we flew it however, it had been guilty of continually dropping a wing sharply at the stall – with or without skid applied and while in a glide as well as with power on. It had none of the well-mannered behaviour of a Tiger Moth or even a Miles Magister.

The next aircraft of any note was the Bristol Brigand. It had first flown in October 1944. This was Coastal Command's replacement for the Blenheim or Beaufort and it had taken four years to appear in its present form and was not yet in production. Bristols had fitted large dive brakes to allow it to slow down after a dive to sea level so that it could drop its torpedoes at their 200-knot maximum permitted speed for water entry or allow it to be used as a daytime dive bomber. But after the RAF's wartime experience with the Fairey Battle, steep-angle dive bombing as a means of accurate bomb delivery had never found favour with the RAF because they had always lacked sufficient low-level fighter cover over the enemy battlefields. We therefore suspected that the Brigand would be consigned to Coastal Command where its huge divebrakes might come in useful for the dropping of torpedoes. We were aghast to hear this for we had hoped that the Navy had at last ceased to imagine that the air-dropped torpedo was still a practical proposition in modern warfare.

The Brigand's airbrakes were extended pneumatically by inflating huge bags hidden in the wings' trailing edges. When the pilot wanted to lower the dive brakes – perhaps on entering a dive over the sea at night before dropping his two torpedoes at some, hopefully, unsuspecting enemy ship – he was required to pull a lever in the cockpit. This opened a valve to admit air from an open-ended tube facing into the slipstream which inflated these bags which then pushed the airbrakes down. There was no mechanical interconnection between the two dive brakes – one on the trailing edge of each wing outboard of the engine nacelles – and we were waiting for the next time that one bag inflated before the other – or failed to inflate at all – so repeating a tragedy which this dangerous system had already caused a year previously.

I took my turn to fly the Blackburn Firebrand Mark 4. After four years in the semi-prototype stage this aircraft had still not gone into production. Its poor lateral control had not been improved by the fitting of spring tabs on the ailerons. These had 'up-floated' at slow speeds and had therefore reduced lateral control on the landing approach when it was most needed, a disadvantage which offset any advantage they might have had at high speeds. However, the one we flew at IFDF was fitted with experimental power-operated ailerons with 'spring feel' which we found too heavy at slow speeds and too light at high speeds and which destroyed the necessary harmony of the control forces. What we had asked for was a progressive increase in stick forces with increased indicated airspeed – perhaps by some sort of aero-dynamic/hydraulic feedback. This was later installed 'in series' with the spring feel and because its input was proportional to air density – and thus proportional to indicated airspeed – it was labelled 'Q' feel.

Fitted with dive brakes, the Firebrand was to have been the Navy's torpedo/bomber replacement for the Barracuda. It was yet another attempt at a 'multi-role' aircraft, a concept which was bound to fail but which was still considered by many as a necessary means of saving money on the air defence bill. The Services were told they could either have a multi-role aircraft or nothing! In this case, the Navy was told it could not have the Sea Fury and the Firebrand, but one or the other. Directly the Firebrand had dropped its bombs or torpedoes at the enemy battleship it would then become a fighter – like the Blackburn Roc or Skua was supposed to have done – and be able to fight its way back to the carrier for another go – a concept which most of us thought ridiculous.

The reason for the Firebrand's latest resurrection was probably because the new Westland Wyvern – another multi-role Fighter/Strike aircraft which met the Navy's insistence on propeller-driven aircraft rather than pure jets – would be late getting into production and the American Avenger – which had taken over the Navy's maritime strike role in the latter stages of the war – was no longer available in Britain.

We were all petrified at the thought of having to fly the Firebrand operationally and to have to dive this heavy and under-powered, single-seat contraption down to sea level at night and, at a mere 200 mph, approach a Russian aircraft carrier or cruiser to within 2000 yards, drop the torpedo and then retire – somehow – find our way back to the carrier in radio and radar 'silence' and make a night decklanding.

America was at that time carrying out the final tests on a 'look-down', Airborne Early Warning (AEW) radar to allow low level fighter direction of its carrier-borne fighters and had recently installed radar-controlled gunnery with 'proximity' fused shells. These defences made the prospect of a torpedo attack on a Russian Sverdlov cruiser – with the Russian Navy never far behind the Americans in technical improvements – look suicidal.

Although the Wyvern was yet another multi-role aircraft – originally designated as a Strike/Fighter – it at least had a pressure cabin and the new Martin-Baker ejector seat. As we had all been squirted up the Farnborough M-B test rig and survived without broken backs, we were entirely sold on the idea, for if we got lost or shot down, we would at least survive baling out if the water was not too cold up north and be able to climb into our auto-inflated dinghies and wait for one of the new rescue helicopters to home in on our new 'Mayday' dinghy radios.

One of our tasks at IFDF had been to carry out 'gun heating' trials in the Meteor IV. Because of the effects of sunheating on the wings, the tests had to be carried out at night. This entailed a climb to the troposphere – up to about 45,000 feet where the outside air temperature was about minus 47 degrees C – and hanging around there taking thermometer readings until fuel shortage made it necessary to descend and land again at Boscombe, still in darkness.

One night, the vibration during the high-speed descent (it was essential to maintain engine power – and therefore full airbrakes – to prevent loss of cockpit heating and icing up of the interior) dislodged the black metal cover and the 'Woods' filter from one of two experimental UV-A source lamps, six inches from the pilot's eyes just below the gunsight. Realising the radiation danger at such close range, the pilot (the author) turned them off, only to realise that the same rheostat turned off all the UV. The remaining cockpit 'floodlighting' was no longer effective because of approaching blindness caused by the UV radiation, so that, in order to see anything inside the cockpit – including the flying instruments – it was necessary to turn the UV on again at maximum intensity.

Landing as soon as possible – the iced-up canopy further impairing runway lighting visibility – I climbed down out of the cockpit and groped my way to the crewroom. Semi-blinded unknowingly by UV radiation, the crewroom appeared to me to be in semi-darkness. I remember asking for the lights to be turned up fully while peeling off much warm clothing and the 'pressure waistcoat'. (We wore these waistcoats for two reasons: One, it would supply us with enough oxygen to breath to stay conscious long enough if we were to bale out at high altitudes – provided we 'free-falled' to 15,000 feet before pulling the ripcord. Two, it provided oxygen under mild pressure, so increasing our intake and delaying the effects of anoxia at high altitude when flying without the benefit of a pressure cabin.)

Next day the flying doctor – unaware of the possible future effects of UV radiation on the eyes – pronounced the damage as trivial and did not grant a 'Hurt Certificate' which I was advised to ask for by my CO. This would have allowed me to claim for compensation when, in 1970, the cataract, which it was agreed in 1983 ensued from this exposure, first took its toll on my eyesight.

The purpose of the UV high-intensity installation in this Meteor was to try out a new scheme of cockpit lighting intended for the nightfighter Meteor NF II. This scheme used the invisible radiation from UV-emitting mercury lamps 'shining' through black Woods filters and exciting the radium-painted instruments to glow in the otherwise totally dark cockpit. This preserved the perfect night vision of the aircrew. The twenty or thirty cockpit instrument dials in the 'experimental Meat-box' that the author flew that night at IFDF had been extra-heavily coated with radium-based paint – like the dials of our new service stop-watches. The UV source lamps had been moved closer to the flying instrument panel into the pilot's direct line of vision as he watched his flying instruments. Their power had been increased by three times the normal wattage. All UV systems were quietly discontinued a couple of years after this episode but the 'normal', relatively harmless installation can still be seen by looking into the cockpits of the Meteors, Sea Hawks, Wyverns etc., in the museums at Duxford and at the Fleet Air Arm Museum at Yeovilton.

At the time of this UV incident I wondered whether it was worth worrying about? The Russians were blockading Berlin, the American fighter – the F-86 A Sabre – had just flown supersonic, the MiG 15 was about to do so (it used the German 'swept-wing' design dating from 1946 and an engine derived from the Rolls-Royce Nene made available to the Russians by our government in 1947), and to show just how small my problems were compared with others, I and many others were about to attend the funeral of 'Spike' King-Joyce who had just been killed in an Attacker.

At the beginning of August 1948 Lance Kiggell told us in IFDF to come and join him in 'C' Squadron. Gordan Hawkes and Lt C.E. Price (waiting to join number 8 ETPS Course) were already there, as was Lt Ian MacLachlan. The change came about partly because of poor 'Spike' King-Joyce's death. He had been killed while investigating high-speed flight in the second prototype Attacker. He may have got into transonic difficulties and then he may have attempted to bale out – using the newly fitted 'lightweight' ejector seat in the Attacker's new pressure cockpit. This obviously had not worked for he had not got clear of the aircraft before it hit the ground. From the wreckage it was learnt that the forward belly tank attachment had been released but the tank had not dropped away cleanly from its aft attachment which had then jammed, causing the tank to break away uncontrollably during the dive. We went to his funeral – held at the nearby church at Upavon – and we were sad at his loss for long afterwards.

Early the following year, Gordan Hawkes was due to carry out the deck-landing trials of the third Attacker prototype. Flying down to meet *Illustrious* off the Cornish coast he called in for some fuel from RNAS Culdrose. When lining up for take-off he noticed Pat Chilton doing some Dummy Deck Landing practice with his boys so he thought he would join for some last-minute practice. On reaching the ship he could get no 'undercarriage locked down' green light to show for his starboard leg. He wrote:

> Thinking, perhaps wrongly, that it would be safer, and rightly, that it would be less trouble, I decided to land ashore alongside the runway at Culdrose rather than continue out to the carrier. I asked over the radio for Phil Illingworth – the Air Engineer Officer at Culdrose – to arrange for about 100 or so men to stand by to turn the aircraft face up if I did a cartwheel when I landed with one mainwheel locked up. Luckily it didn't and slid along or its belly for about half a mile, slowly turning round through 180 degrees as it did so. The firm's 'rep' was soon on the scene with a screwdriver. He released the stuck catch, used about thirty men to lift the starboard wing as he pumped the undercarriage leg down and allowed the aircraft to be towed away on its wheels. Meanwhile I was invited – despite my protestations – to ride back to the sick bay in the ambulance where I was given a medicinal dose of brandy.

They say that 'all Jack and dull work make a boy' – or something like that. Our leisure activities at Boscombe included an invitation from the Commandant to join his weekend shoot – on the airfield. He had cleverly planted acres of kale round the southern perimeter of this 2,000-acre airfield. The birds from adjoining farms thought themselves equally clever and would wait for the weekend lull in flying before nipping over the fences for a good, weekend feed. With MacLachlan's black Labrador, we would set off on a Saturday – about eight of us including beaters – and by lunchtime we would all have a brace of pheasant dangling from our waists, with the retriever flat on his back and too tired even to notice the inquisitive hare on the other side of the perimeter track.

Lance Kiggell sent me up to do some 'out-of-trim' dives in a Sea Fury XI – the type which we were to use in Korea in a couple of years time. In one of these dives, the Fury turned on its back at 2,000 feet in a 60-degree dive with 25 degrees yaw. Being a superb product of Sydney Camm and his team at Hawkers, the aircraft had stayed in one piece. This was in spite of its under-cart's starboard leg having sheared its up-lock and lowered itself at the bottom of a dive at 540 mph. It was flying again by next day with a new fairing fitted!

One day, I looked out of the crewroom window across the main runway and saw IFDF's Meteor being towed back to its hangar by the station tractor/crane. Apparently Dicky Stoop had been doing 'measured take-offs' at maximum all-up-weight (AUW) in still air, and the very high tyre speed had whirled off bits of rubber into the wing and these had ruptured the Derwents' fuel systems. We had recently been his guest at his pit-stop at a car-racing circuit near Bournemouth – where some of us got to within a few feet of Stirling Moss, Fangio and Mike Hawthorne on occasion – and Dicky was therefore interested in tyres, braking and tread design. He said it was essential to check tyre behaviour at speed up to 160 knots on take-off runs, as jets would soon require to attain such speeds on long runway, still air, take-offs if they were to compete with catapult take-offs in carriers without having to use rocket assistance.

Halfway through October 1948 we carried out the deck trials of the Sea Vampire in *Illustrious*. We each did about 20 decklandings and free take-offs without any trouble. We wondered what could have made it so difficult three years previously. This decklanding session for us at 'C' Squadron was a good move by Kiggell for it established the right of 'C' Squadron at Boscombe Down – with its ETPS-trained pilots – to be the main deck-clearance authority for new types of aircraft in the Navy from that time onwards.

In September and October we flew the Seafang and Seafire 47. The Seafang was the navalised version of the RAF's intended Spitfire replacement which they called the Spiteful. These trips in the Seafang were mostly concerned with gunnery, rocketry and bombing. It had a similar fuselage layout and shape to the Seafire 47 but was fitted with what the boffins referred to as a 'laminar-flow' wing with a thickness/chord (T/C) ratio of about ten per cent, the thinnest wing of any British aircraft in service at that time. An almost identical wing was later used in the Attacker.

At about this time, a few of us were becoming intrigued with the flying boat business and I thought that it might have a good future in the Navy as well as the civil air transport market. We had all been very impressed with the Saunders-Roe Saro A-1 flying boat jet fighter demonstrated by Westland's Chief Test Pilot – Geoffrey Tyson – at the 1948 SBAC Show. With the cloud base at about 800 feet he had appeared at one end of the runway at 100 feet travelling at about 600 mph. At the other end of the runway he momentarily disappeared into the clag again only to reappear but this time upside down, travelling along the whole runway with his hood almost scraping the ground. Someone had seen him put his arm over his head at this time and when questioned later, he told us that he was trying to pick up his pencil which had fallen into the hood from the cockpit floor!

Just before Christmas 1948, I received an official letter from Admiral Slattery – the Managing director of Shorts – offering a three-year contract as Deputy Chief Test Pilot under 'Brookie'. I immediately accepted and resigned the last year of my four-year Short Service Commission in the Royal Navy. The Admiral had enclosed a three-year contract for me to sign. He also included the offer of a house in Holywood, Co. Down, removal expenses and nearly double the pay of a Lieutenant in the RN.

CHAPTER 5

SHORT BROTHERS

Shorts' contract for a three-year period as Deputy Chief to 'Brookie' said:

> Mr Crosley shall perform the duties which from time to time may be assigned to him by the Chief Test Pilot, shall devote the whole of his time, attention and abilities to the business of the Company and shall obey the orders from time to time of the Chief Test Pilot of the Company.

Although this wording was a trifle peremptory and gave no impression of a happy and relaxed atmosphere, Brookie was one of the most friendly and thoughtful bosses for which anyone could work and with the air-minded Admiral Matthew Slattery in charge and his personal assistant being none other than Captain St. John Fancourt – a well known former CO of the wartime Naval Air Station at Hatston – a former Fleet Air Arm fighter pilot such as myself could only do anything wrong with the greatest difficulty.

After Brookie had shown me round the firm and introduced me to the Production Controller – George Gedge – and the Chief Designer – David Keith-Lucas – we went to our office on Sydenham airfield. It was right by the quayside where an unfinished 20,000-ton 'Unicorn' class carrier had been tied up since the end of the war and was further overshadowed by the huge Shetland flying boat prototype shortly to be disposed of. Brookie told me what my duties might be. He said that I was employed for development test flying – not salesmanship or production testing, although if things were slack, this might be an additional requirement.

The aircraft production situation at Short Bros & Harland's new Belfast factory was a trifle dull. About 25 Sunderland Mark Vs came in each year from the RAF for major inspection and repair. This government contract was on a 'cost plus . . .' basis, so however long Shorts took to do the job they would always make a profit. The other five projects they had in progress were:

First: the Sturgeon TT Mark 2. This twin-Merlined contra-prop was intended – somewhat surprisingly – to be a torpedo/bomber. However, following the cancellation of the building of large carriers at the end of the war, its task was changed to 'fast, carrier-based target-towing aircraft.' Having first flown in June 1946 from Shorts' Rochester-based factory airfield with Geoffrey Tyson as pilot, the production of two more prototypes was now proceeding at Belfast.

Second: a more powerful version of BOAC's Solent 2 flying boat – the Mark IV. The prototype ZK-AML was launched on 26 May 1949 by Princess Elizabeth. She christened it *Aotearoa* on behalf of Tasman Empire Airways of

New Zealand who had ordered four, and half Harland and Wolff's shipyard – who were our next-door neighbours and now back to work on the unfinished *Eagle* – watched the proceedings from her flight deck.

Third: was Short's contribution to the V-bomber contract – the Sperrin – still under construction and not to fly before August 1951 in two and a half years time. It was an unswept 'thin-wing' design with four Rolls-Royce Avon engines, wing-mounted in pairs one above the other.

Fourth: and perhaps the most interesting of all, was the Sealand twin-engined amphibian. Brookie had made the first flight of the Sealand a year previously on 19 January 1948. He had since test-flown it nearly 100 times but it still needed improvement in its performance before it could be granted a Certificate of Airworthiness to allow it to carry any of its full load of seven passengers.

Fifth: construction had just started on a variant of the Sturgeon to Specification M6/49. This was for a search-and-destroy anti-submarine aircraft powered by two Mamba prop-jet engines instead of the two 2,000 hp Merlin 140s in the Sturgeon.

Just before I arrived at Shorts, the second prototype Sealand had flown to Norway on a sales tour but it had crashed in poor weather and the crew of three were lost. The pilot – Fl/Lt D.G. McCall – had been on our Number 6 ETPS Course and had joined Shorts immediately afterwards in 1948. Hopes were still high when I joined, that the Sealand would steal a large part of the world-wide medium-range amphibian market from the Americans who were busy promoting their Grumman Goose and Mallard amphibians.

Grummans were already famous for their Goose – the Dakota of the amphibian world at that time. It was an almost indestructible Wasp-engined seven-seater used throughout the war. Their latest amphibian design was the Mallard G-73 which had first flown two years before the Sealand. It was powered by two 'Pratt and Watney Wisps' – as we called them – and, with a structural weight only 25 per cent above that of the Sealand it had nearly double the Sealand's power: 2 × 600 hp Wasp R-1340s instead of the Sealand's 2 × 340 hp Gipsy Queen 70s and could carry up to twelve passengers to the Sealand's seven. It could cruise at 180 mph to the Sealand's 150 and operate over distances of 1,000 miles compared with Sealand's range of 750 miles. However it cost dollars and few European airlines could afford dollars at that time.

At the end of the war BOAC were looking for a replacement for their old 'C' Class Empire flying boats, none of which had survived the war. Shorts had replied by converting about ten wartime Sunderlands into Sandringhams or Seafords. BOAC were still interested, so Shorts again re-designed the Sandringham's interior, enlarged the tail surfaces, increased its engine power and the area of the planing bottom to take more weight – and called it the Solent Mark 2. They had completed about 16 of these during 1947 before they moved their entire Rochester factory to Belfast.

Having taken delivery of these Solent 2s – now a luxury 34-seater – BOAC re-opened their old 'Empire' routes from Southampton Water, through Augusta in Sicily, stopping off in Khartoum to refuel, then an overnight stop at Victoria Falls and finishing up in Jo'burg or Capetown. The RAF also showed every intention of retaining their Coastal Command flying boat stations: Calshot, Kalafrana in Malta, Aden, Capetown, Sydney, Auckland and Singapore. They had recently used their Sunderlands to help break Russia's blockade of Berlin by landing on an adjacent lake. BOAC's market research had told them that if the British Empire remained in being, flying boats would be the most sought-after method of air transport over this third of the world's 'low-altitude' surface. A flying-boat safari through Africa – along the bits marked red on the map – might still be considered a romantic and genteel adventure. As late in the day as September 1949 – and with the 120 ton, eight-engined Brabazon about to make its first flight from Filton with Bill Pegg at the controls – Shorts were hoping that new orders for their latest Solent 4, the Sealand and the M 6/49 would keep their factory – and Brookie and me – busy for many years to come. With the Brabazon likely to need two miles of costly runway to be made available almost everywhere, before it could operate worldwide, but with flying boats able to land almost anywhere free of major construction charges or political barriers, Shorts reckoned they were on to a good thing.

The first Solent 2 had flown at the 1948 Farnborough airshow – showing off its perfect handling characteristics by behaving like a fighter and doing the display almost entirely on two out of its four Bristol Hercules 637s of 1,690 hp. By the time I joined Shorts, Tasman Empire Airways' order for four of the more powerful Mark 4 Solents was well under way. In this version, engine power of the four Hercules 733s had been increased to 2,040 hp and its 'all-up weight' had increased from 68,000 lb to 79,000 lb – carrying 50 passengers instead of the Mark 2's 34. There were no serious handling problems with the Solent 2s and 4s and, apart from possible engine cooling problems caused by longer take-off runs in the tropics in the Mark 4 version, Brookie was not expecting any delays in delivery.

Tasman Empire Airways were intending to use the Mark 4s to replace the Sandringhams they were operating on the Fiji/Wellington route. They expected that with drink bars, bunks and a VIP lounge as standard accommodation on two decks they would attract many more holiday-makers, top executives, oil magnates and Royalty to this form of air travel. It seemed that the only thing now missing from the Solent's luxurious furniture was a 5-piece orchestra complete with Bechstein and double bass – as perhaps we might have seen in the ill-fated R 101 had it survived its first journey.

Squadron-Leader Johnny Booth had replaced Fl/Lt McCall as Short's salesman/pilot. He was engaged in his first Sealand sales tour of South America at this time – so far without success. Having drawn a blank with Shorts he later joined Saunders-Roe at Cowes who were also entering the large flying boat market. They had not been discouraged by the failure in 1947 of the Howard-Hughes 'Spruce Goose'. The 'Goose' was an eight-engined wooden construction costing as much as ten Solents and whose first and only flight, reaching a height of ten feet lasting for four minutes, was made entirely in order to qualify for American government financial support – for the airlines were not interested in it and did not order it. Saunders-Roe had also been given Ministry of Supply financial support to produce their own giant Princess – launched from their Cowes slipway on 19 August 1952 – using half-a-dozen or so of the new 'prop-jet' engines as its power source. They called it the Saro Princess – and it was as potentially beautiful as its name. Apart from its huge size it had fully pressurised accommodation for 75 passengers. It could therefore travel *over* the weather – not through it like the low-altitude Solent – and with much greater speed, without expensive overnight stops and without the need to use more than half-a-dozen landing places worldwide.

As for the Sturgeon, this easily-handled twin-Merlined contra-prop fighter-bomber unfortunately had no significant merits over the Sea Mosquito apart from its easier single-engined handling and, having a power/weight ratio a third lower than the DH Hornet, we all knew it stood no chance in the RAF or Naval market for future fighter/bombers. It had already been declared redundant in its original form a year previously in 1947 although the Navy placed an order for 24 target-towing Mark 2s in 1949. This was not only to try to give Naval gunnery practice more realism but to take advantage of willing government support for this nationalised industry.

Following carrier trials in *Illustrious* in April 1949, the Sturgeon target-tug was cleared for service by September 1950. It did not embark aboard a carrier – possibly because by this time the Navy had been correctly advised by ETPS-trained test pilots about the dangers of attempting to deckland a conventional twin with one engine failed. Instead, it was employed entirely for shore-based, 'Fleet Requirements' duties. By 1952, from the remainder of the original order of 24 Sturgeons, yet another variant was devised – the TT Mk 3. The long 'camera-pod' nose of the Mk 2 was replaced by a shorter one and all equipment needed for carrier operations was removed. These were also attached to shore-based 'second line' Fleet Requirements Units where they were used until 1961 alongside a few Sea Mosquitos, Hornets, Meteors and Fireflies for gunnery assessment and target towing for the Navy and Army, based mainly in the Mediterranean area.

The third variant of the Sturgeon nearing completion at Belfast was the M 6/49 anti-submarine prototype. Brookie told me that the firm was hoping this might become a useful competitor to the new Fairey Gannet A/S Mark 1 and the Blackburn GR 17/45. The Gannet prototype had first flown at Fairey's on 11 September 1948 – about four months before I joined Shorts – but it had struck stability and structural problems. Likewise the Blackburn prototype had started its clearance trials at Boscombe a few days later – with Pete Lawrence at the controls. Pete had been an original 813 Squadron Swordfish pilot in *Eagle* in 1942 at the same time that Spike King-Joyce and myself were on board flying Hurricane 1s. He told me over the phone that the GR 17 was late in getting to Boscombe in its final form because the Navy had asked for a third seat to be added and for its 2,000 hp contra-prop Griffon to be replaced by an Armstrong-Siddeley Double Mamba driving two contra-rotating six-bladed, 13-foot propellers on a central shaft, similar to those already fitted to the Gannet. Shorts would have until May 1950 to produce the M6/49 at which time the Admiralty could choose which of the three it wanted.

After a dozen trips in the M6/49, I realised that we would have no chance of selling the M6/49 to the Navy as a carrier-based anti-submarine aircraft if only because of its unsafe single-engined handling characteristics. The two Mambas were wing-mounted and therefore a very likely cause of single-engined handling difficulties when deck landing. Our rivals at Blackburns and Faireys had fitted a Double-Mamba contra-prop on the *centreline* of their two Gannet designs, so avoiding directional handling problems entirely.

The two rivals to the M6/49 had yet another advantage. Pilots could save fuel at any time by shutting down one of the engines entirely and feathering the propeller. Ground start-ups could also be made easier by 'windmill-starting' the second engine from the slipstream of the first. The M6/49 could not compete with these advantages at all. It not only had the torque difficulties of un-handed single propellers (at least the Sturgeon had contraprops) but it had a tailwheel undercarriage as well. It would therefore have to be decklanded at speeds much nearer the stall than the nose-wheeled Gannet and GR 17. This, alone, would probably rule it out in the competition without consideration of further handling faults.

In order to gain some prop-jet flying experience before I had taken on the job of flying the Mamba-engined M6/49 I had had a couple of trips in the Balliol 2 – also fitted with a Mamba prop jet. Because of the very high idling rpm in jet engines – three times the relative idling speed of piston engines – most prop-jet propellers had to have their fine-pitch settings at about six degrees instead of the piston engine's 16–20 degrees, otherwise the propeller would give much too much thrust when idling on the deck. In the Mamba-engined Balliol, this caused some awkward drag effects in the air whenever the pilot closed the throttle. The same situation arose when the Westland Wyvern was fitted with the Python prop-jet. An even more serious situation arose if the prop-jet engine were to fail in the air. When engine or prop failure occurred in a prop-jet, the prop would usually enter fine pitch and the phenominal drag so caused reduced the aircraft's speed to such an extent that it had to be held in a near vertical dive to maintain a safe flying speed and to maintain enough airflow over the tail surfaces for the pilot to have any response from his rudder or elevator when attempting to pull out of the dive to make a forced landing. If the failure occurred at slower speeds and lower altitudes, the Wyvern entered what was known as a 'phantom dive', where the tail surfaces were so blanketed by the prop that the pilot lost all elevator control and the aircraft dived earthwards out of control.

The M6/49, having two such engine/prop combinations had a very large nose-down change-of-trim when the pilot required to reduce power. This nose-down pitch was made worse by the large reduction in jet-pipe thrust because the jet pipes had been placed with their thrustline well *below* the aircraft's CG position, so rotating it nose up when power was increased and rotating it sharply nose down when power was reduced.

Shorts' design office's attempt at a remedy – by adding about two feet of jet exhaust to each jet pipe and turning them to point aft through a right angle – showed that they seemed to have no idea what the problem was or how to cure it, for it made matters worse.

In fact, looking back at this episode, it seems quite extraordinary that anyone in the naval procurements branch or in the design office at Shorts could ever have thought that this layout could have passed through Boscombe's 'C' Squadron for service afloat. Short's designers did not blame their pilots for their failures, of course, but it must have been very humiliating for their design office to be told that the M6/49 had this serious design fault and Brookie's and my remarks on it in our reports to their chief designer must have gone down like lead balloons. In fact, it never went to 'C' Squadron and it was subsequently scrapped.

Apart from the military aircraft at Shorts which required our attention, the most interesting and urgent jobs we were given by the chief designer was advising him on what design changes he should make to give the Sealand a chance of getting a CA Release (the legal document allowing an aircraft to fly in public) so that it could be safely flown by airlines or by members of the public and command a place in world markets.

My second trip in Sealand G-AIVX – the first prototype – was quite useful. Brookie told me that G-AIVX was under-performing to such an extent that it would scarcely climb at all on one engine with more than half the equivalent ballast-load of its intended seven passengers – even in the cold air over Belfast Loch.

During the next two years I carried out about 100 flights in addition to Brookie's to try out the many alterations thought up by our design office to improve Sealand's performance – both at water take-offs and in single-engined climb performance. We carried out flights with locked flaps, new intake scoops, propellers changed, extra smooth finish, re-designed cooling ducts, engines lowered nine inches, wing leading-edge slats fitted, retractable lift-spoilers fitted, ejector exhausts fitted, new floats, de-icing on wings and hull and water rudders.

A report dated 4 April 1949 noted that G-AIVX flew that morning at a take-off weight of 8,970 lb, its CG was at 26 per cent SMC, (about neutral), the air temperature was +11 degrees C, the barometer was 995 millibars at sea level and the mainplane centre section had had a specially modified fairing fitted to reduce drag. I reported that the 'speed for minimum power' (VIMP) was 89 knots and the minimum speed at which directional control was still possible on one engine was 85 knots. The report also admitted that the only way in which I could get the Sealand to climb on one engine at maximum power – with the other feathered – was to cheat by using the rising wind gradient over

Holywood Hills like the local seagulls. The Air Registration Board (ARB) officials who handed out Civil Airworthiness Certificates (the CA Release) would not be amused if they read this in my report, of course, but it was included in order show how 'marginal' things were with the Sealand. Very little could be done to increase engine power or reduce structure weight to compensate for this serious fault so that further measures to reduce aerodynamic drag would have to be taken.

One day when trying out a new propeller and doing the usual performance check on one engine in the Sealand, a loud bang came from the port engine exhaust. Looking to the left I saw that part of its silencer/manifold had fallen off. I also noticed that the height had increased from 6,180 feet to 6,320 feet in the space of one minute and that the airspeed had also increased a couple of knots too. The increased rearward thrust from the chance opening of a couple of exhausts had so improved Sealand's single-engined performance that it allowed the issue of a restricted CA release in time for it to be demonstrated at the Farnborough SBAC Air Show in August 1949. Ejector exhausts were fitted to all Sealands from that time onwards and the passengers had to put up with the extra noise.

At this time we were also trying to find out the reason why Sealand buried its starboard float in the water during calm-water take-offs, making it impossible to keep it straight. We thought that it might be caused by 'dissimilar stall' characteristics between the port and starboard wings at the moment of maximum incidence (the 'hump') during take-off, caused by propeller slipstream 'rotation' effects. The 'swing to starboard' was abnormally strong for a flying boat and was not caused by propeller torque reaction alone – which we found could be balanced by adding 80 lb of sand in the port float. Sealand's trouble was far more serious than that – perhaps equivalent to a thousand pounds loss in lift on the starboard wing causing the starboard float to bury itself and drag the aircraft round to the right.

Brookie finally settled for an offset skeg – or mini water-rudder attached to the rear planing step – to help keep Sealand straight on take-off. This was placed just forward of the retractable tailwheel and it was accompanied by a slight redesign of the hull shape. However, 'dissimilar stall' characteristics between the port and starboard wings during water take-offs remained a feature of the Sealand throughout its history and led to at least two serious accidents in its early life.

One day the Revd Lewis, a member of a Canadian Missionary Society operating in northern New Guinea, visited the flight office and asked Brookie for a trip in the Sealand. Here was a brilliant opportunity to sell our first Sealand. Revd Lewis said he needed it to operate amongst the head hunters in the jungle hills of New Guinea to convert them to Christianity. The Sealand would be used to transport missionaries and medical aid in a civilised manner instead of having to risk the crocodiles and rapids in canoe journeys. It was dangerous aviation country as Amelia Earhart had tragically found out in 1937.

Brookie told me to take Revd Lewis up in our second 'production' Sealand – which had dual control – and show him the aircraft. As he was an experienced seaplane pilot I was to allow him to do a few take-offs and landings in Belfast Loch, finishing up with a runway landing opposite the office so that all could see.

In my report after the flight I said:

My knowledge of Rev. Lewis' terrestial flying ability is still very slight. However, as he told me that he was used to flying Beechcraft biplanes with floats – and therefore lacked experience of the roll tendencies of flying boats – I thought I would show these first.

Mr Lewis' seating position in the Beechcraft would have been much higher than in the Sealand. So that when he came to fly the Sealand, this may have accounted for Mr Lewis' mis-judgement of height during the 'hold-off' before splashdown a little later. Among the things that Rev. Lewis wanted to find out was Sealand's short take-off performance. He had shown me photographs of his proposed landing areas in the rivers and lakes of New Guinea. One of his likely landing areas was to be in a fast-flowing river, 100 feet wide, with steep overhanging banks and with a 20 degree bend in it halfway along the take-off run. He said that it was about 3,000 feet above sea level and the normal daytime temperature was about 95 degrees and usually obstructed with turtles!

I demonstrated a minimum-length take-off. This was measured by counting the channel markings in Belfast Loch as they wizzed by. I reduced the take-off length as far as possible by selecting full flap directly an airspeed of 55 knots showed on the ASI. Unstick speed was reduced to 62 knots and a take-off distance of 450 yards was achieved, a saving of about 150 yards over the normal, zero wind distance at today's temperatures.

Rev. Lewis then took over the controls for a bit to get the feel of the aircraft before doing two water landings and take-offs himself. His first landing and, as it turned out, the only one which could be described as such, was 15 degrees out of wind and made in a steep glide approach – something which he said he usually did in the Beechcraft. He left his 'flattening-out' until the last possible moment, misjudged it slightly and zoomed up to hold off ten feet too high. On the stall occurring, the splash must have been seen for miles. As we porpoised to a standstill I remember his saying: 'I wanted to see what would happen if I dropped her in a bit.'

'Oh good, I replied,' remembering just in time that the customer is always right and good salesmanship must be allowed to triumph over everything else.

The next two take-offs which Rev. Lewis tried were abandoned before the aircraft reached 40 knots waterspeed – ie, before we were at water-plane speed. He was attempting a crosswind take-off – about 15 knots at 25 degrees from the port side. The approximate paths of the aircraft on his two attempts are sketched below. (Here I had marked two unsteady curves to the right, one ending a few feet from a sewer outfall, the other ending two feet from shallow water, having missed a fairway pile by about 6 inches. I continued:)

The two attempts at take-off were somewhat haphazard due to the fact that the starboard float was in the water from the time the throttles were opened until the aircraft porpoised to a standstill. I now have even greater faith in Sealand's stressing, for, at times on these 'take-offs' the aircraft was thrown clear of the water in a stalled condition. It then landed of its own accord on its starboard float with a large amount of yaw, bouncing forward onto the main step – and so on, finally coming to a standstill 90 degrees to the original landing direction, the windscreen covered in seaweed, various Irish fishermen standing up in their boats applauding, and myself, pale and shaking, picking up my goggles from the cockpit floor, crossing myself and trying to preserve a momentous calm.

I had to be careful what I said. I had to avoid saying it was difficult, for this might make Rev. Lewis decide to buy something else. Neither could I say that it was easy, for this might imply that he was a poor pilot. I thought of the words of Churchill when he described Admiral Jellicoe's quandary during the battle of Jutland: 'Anxiously peering at the menacing curtains of the horizon or poring over the contradictions and obscurities of the chart, Jellico held on his course for another eight minutes.'

After a further eight minutes 'flying' and a satisfactory touchdown on land at Sydenham, the Revd Lewis recovered his faith in Sealand and recommended to his Society that they should buy our fourth aircraft. This was sent out in packing cases to New Guinea where Shorts' engineers assembled it and maintained it for a month's flying among the headhunters without incident. In fact our customers reported joy and wonderment and many more converts to this angelic form of transport. They described totally naked passengers – complete with daggers slicing into the seat upholstery as they sat down with their wives and children – wide-eyed with a mixture of pleasure and fright and grateful to their pilot for being taken to church in this way and all wanting to become missionaries themselves as quickly as possible.

Then came bad news. The Revd Lewis had tried to take a left-hand turn in the local river during a take-off in zero wind and had finished up on a sand-bank, high-and-dry, surrounded by turtles. There the Sealand had remained and, although a replacement was sent out, it crashed a few months later into a mountain like the Norwegian Sealand had done. Sadly, none of the crew or passengers survived this last crash.

Towards the end of 1949 we heard that British West Indian Airways had ordered four of the lower-engined version of the Sealand and, while I was away doing the tropical trials of the Mark IV Solent on the Nile in Khartoum, Brookie had taken Sealand G-AKLM on sea trials to the West Indies. Spirits rose a little more when the Indian Navy later ordered ten Sealands and Johnnie Booth's tour in G-AKLP in South America began to stir up interest within the Argentinian Navy.

The Short Solent Mark IV prototype – named *Aotearoa* and launched by Princess Elizabeth – was a beautiful development of the Sunderland/Sandringham series. It had passed its temperate performance and handling trials in 16 flights, all of which we had completed on the prototype in ZK-AML in only three weeks. It had not put a step wrong, turning up fully serviceable each morning at 0800, with the ARB, design office and Mr Gedge – our engineer – in attendance and behaving like the thoroughbred it was.

Tropical trials on the Mark 4 Solent were next on the list. These were to be held on the Nile upstream of Khartoum. Not having a Commercial Licence, I was flown out from Southampton's flying boat terminal by Captain Upton of BOAC. Flying time to Khartoum was 17 hours, the last leg over the desert took nine hours – all below 8,000 feet in perfect weather.

We splashed down in the glassy Nile at Gordon's Tree, a few miles south of the city of Khartoum – with nothing but sand all round us stretching for hundreds of miles in all directions. We taxied back the mile of our landing run and were taken in tow by BOAC's launch. Our bow rope was tied to one of their moorings in midstream, about 100 yards from their small pier/jetty crowded with interested passengers who had just come ashore from a Solent 2 arriving from Victoria Falls. Captain Upton then quickly took his leave and left us to introduce ourselves to our hosts, to BOAC's Chief Engineer and to Mr Nelson, BOAC's Manager at Gordon's Tree.

Native labour was employed throughout. One of their jobs was to keep the moorings and take-off/landing runs free from rafts of driftwood and weed descending the Blue Nile – which usually had natives asleep on them – and for guarding the boats left overnight at their moorings. Our Mark IV *Aotearoa* was purposely left unlocked at its moorings overnight in case emergency access was required to tow it to safety.

As BOAC was in the middle of an economy drive, only one mooring launch was available. We therefore had to leave our hotel in Khartoum at 0500 each morning to be sure of arriving in time to complete a test flight before the launch would disappear to collect BOAC's arrivals – who naturally had priority. We were nearly passing out with the heat during these waiting periods, particularly as BOAC did not allow us to take our shirts off as this was considered improper for Europeans. They also insisted upon our chaps talking quietly so that they would not attract the attention of the 50-or-so passengers who came ashore complete with their multi-coloured sunshades, summer dresses and floppy hats to cool off while refuelling was in progress. Five years before independence, the Sudan was a peaceful place and the beautiful city of Khartoum by the Nile was a visitor's paradise – provided he did not cross the river into Omdurman where living conditions were very different.

Records of cylinder-head temperatures on the two starboard engines' number two cylinders showed that we might expect overheating when fully-loaded take-off trials were begun. The reason for the starboard engines' overheating was, of course, because these two engines were the only ones at full power throughout the take-off run. The two port engines had to be throttled back in order to prevent the swing to starboard due to the usual prop slipstream effects. (This swing was gentle compared with the Sealand's behaviour and was never a problem with Solents or Sunderlands.)

It was essential for the pilot to 'lead' with the starboard throttles when opening up to take-off throughout the first half of the take-off run until the boat was riding smoothly on its main step and until its airspeed had risen to about 60 kts and the rudder became fully effective. Sometimes, during the two-mile take-off run necessary when loaded to 79,000 lb, the wind at the start of the run might have been from behind at five knots. By the end of the run two miles further up the Nile, the wind could be blowing from ahead at ten knots, or so. Photographs of each run – at 'hump' positions, at 'unstick' positions, aborted take-off positions, 'engine-failure' positions etc. – were required, but these were difficult to obtain with but two photographers.

Following two wasted days – due to unscheduled BOAC's arrivals at Gordon's Tree utilising the only launch available – we decided that we would not carry out a circuit after each take-off test but land immediately straight ahead after a momentary 'unstick'. This would need an extra mile of landing run to be cleared of debris, but BOAC agreed to do it for us immediately. This not only reduced the time we had to spend in BOAC's airspace but halved the amount of valuable fuel we used as well.

But this attempt to save time and money had a most unfortunate consequence. On one such take-off made at the maximum weight of 79,000 lb, the wind had altered through 180 degrees at the far end of the take-off run so that it was blowing up our stern. After a very long run and having throttled back to splash down again, being unable to use full flap owing to lack of time for it to operate, the rear step touched the Nile first and we started a slight porpoise. Then, holding the stick back as prescribed under such circumstances, the down-wind (port) float touched first from one of the slight porpoises which had started and, on turning round to taxy back for another run I noticed that the port float's rigging wires were slack. This denoted some serious distortion in its attachment to the mainplane.

In case the float had hit some driftwood and might have sprung a leak, I told the crew to get out on the starboard wing to prevent the crosswind from dipping the wounded port float into the water – which, if it did, might fill and cause a disastrous capsize. I cut the two inner engines so the crew could lie on the wing in reasonable safety – without falling off into the Nile and providing lunch for the crocodiles, that is – and, keeping the boat exactly head-to-wind, I taxied back towards the moorings about three miles downstream.

The wind changed as we neared the moorings so that to keep the damaged float clear of the water I had to turn the boat through 180 degrees to keep her head to wind. At the launch pickup position, I saw that the launch skipper, unaware of our trouble, was intent on turning *Aotearoa* down-wind bringing us across wind and so capsizing us. Unable to hear our shouts asking him not to do this, our bowman had to dive into the Nile and swim over to his launch to tell him personally of our wishes – which were to be allowed to drift down to our mooring stern first and to attach the bow line ourselves.

Our bowman's action not only saved *Aotearoa* from a capsize but earned the cheers of the multitude watching from the pierhead. The launch then disappeared to attend to a BOAC arrival and left us on board for two hours, bemoaning our fate at now having to stay an extra fortnight waiting for spares to arrive from Belfast so that we could repair the float.

For the remainder of that day our engineers with George Gedge's brother as foreman, attempted to assemble repair resources from RAF Khartoum and Sudan Airways. They were very willing to help but without telephones or our own river or road transport this was a tedious business. It was late evening before we managed to remove the port float. We then had to weigh down the starboard float to prevent the boat from capsizing and then take the float plus its struts ashore for their ends to be removed and replaced with new pins in place of the ones which had sheared and which had caused the rigging wires to go slack.

Their removal was easier said than done. Eventually, by heating the strut/plug ends and hanging a four-ton weight from the struts plus the added pull from a twenty-ton chain lifting tackle (which bent the overhead steel beam it was attached to) the plug ends came adrift and were riveted back in position with hardened steel taper pins. (A few months later, the same thing happened to *Awatere* – the second production Mark 4 – shortly after her delivery to TEAL in New Zealand. The engineers found that her float struts – like all the others – had been fastened with *soft* stainless steel pins and not hardened ones. This was why *Aotearoa*'s had sheared so easily at Khartoum.)

Fate now intervened with us at Khartoum. It had been too late to take the repaired float out to the aircraft and refit it that night. The boat had to be left on the moorings without it, guarded by a 'duty watch'.

During that night, as luck would have it, a *haboob* (a local whirlwind) sprang up and our sentry-watch crew were too late to prevent the boat blowing over against its *good* float. The sudden high wind had 'got under' and lifted the floatless wing higher still from its raised position above the Nile and this extra 'dihedral' lift had been sufficient to submerge the starboard float. Once submerged, of course, it stayed down, resting on the river bottom – the shallow water luckily preventing a complete capsize.

By dawn, having been unable to secure a launch under the starboard wing – or to find and inflate *Aotearoa*'s own dinghy supposedly stowed in her port wing – the 'good' float could not be raised without risk of further damage so that a gentle tow ashore was necessary. Summoning up the crane and its launch and arranging for twenty natives to weigh down the port wing to prevent the starboard wing and float from scraping too hard on the river bottom – and entreating BOAC not to allow their newly arriving passengers to photograph *Aotearoa* in her predicament – we eventually dragged her ashore where by now, the port float was ready for refitting.

The Nile was in flood and its margins were hard sand instead of soft mud. We were afraid that damage would occur to the float and wingtip as they dragged it along the bottom. Increasing the number of natives arranged along the port wing was fraught with the danger of their 'seesawing' the boat dangerously, falling off, hurting themselves and then, their weight no longer holding the weight off the starboard float, this would crash down and ruin that float as well. Eventually, we found a native who spoke the language and some sort of seesaw balance-control was possible, much to their immense amusement.

After replacing the port float and towing *Aotearoa* back to her moorings after all the water had been pumped out of her starboard wing and starboard outer engine, we spent the next four days riveting a new leading edge to the starboard tailplane where water splash had dented it during our last landing. The new skin sent from Belfast matched perfectly, even to the positioning of several hundred rivet holes which they had drilled for us.

On the first trip after repairs had been completed, the starboard outer engine had overheated and I had to shut it down. This had happened because a small amount of Nile water had remained in its lubrication system when the engine was dried out. It had turned into steam within the crankcase and this had blown about ten gallons of oil out of the breather into the desert, doubtless to the annoyance of passing camels underneath. Luckily, no damage was done.

The trials were completed by 28 July – having taken a month – and we were back in Belfast by 2 August with my apologetic report already in Admiral Slattery's in-tray.

Brookie and I continued for the next year to check out the half-dozen or so modifications to Sealand dreamed up by the drawing office to try to correct its poor performance. Brookie's trip to the British West Indies for sea trials in the Sealand had not succeeded. It had performed so badly in the hot, calm conditions amongst the islands and lagoons that BWIA cancelled their entire order. Next we heard that the results from Johnny Booth's sales trip to South America had been equally disappointing and that our customers were more interested in the more powerful Mallard.

Another possible rival – the Italian Piaggio 316 – had recently attracted much media attention at the Paris Air Show – probably because of its smooth lines, its 'pusher' props and its very pretty inverted gull wings. It seemed to be just what the international playboy wanted and the Italian Airforce was interested, too.

I took a Sealand alongside *Implacable* on one of her visits to Belfast and took her Captain for a brief splash round the Loch. He was much more interested in a Flying Fifteen sailing boat I was building than making any recommendations to Their Lordships that the Sealand might make an excellent Admiral's Barge.

World politics, the communist assault in Korea in June 1950, the U2 'incident' and the appearance of US forces in Britain in large numbers to defend the West against the growing power of Russia, had unsettled the civil air market in Africa and the Far East. BOAC announced its withdrawal from flying-boat operations in November 1950 and that its London-Sydney route would be taken over by Lockheed Constellations. The latter took four days to the Solent's ten for the same journey and Connie tickets cost about half as much per passenger as flying boat tickets as no expensive night stop-overs were required.

Things suddenly looked bad in the flying boat business and history now shows that Shorts produced only half-a-dozen more Sealands – making about 25 in all – and a further ten Solent conversions. The RAF, Aquila and Pacific Airways continued to use flying boats where landplane facilities were lacking, but when support for the Saunders-Roe Princess was withdrawn and the even more beautiful Comet came on the scene (first flight 24 July 1949 and it having just flown 34 passengers from London to Cairo in five hours) it must have been then – late 1951 – that Shorts decided to cancel plans for a Mark 2 Sealand with the more powerful Alvis Leonides engines – and to transfer the interests of their design-office staff to less aquatic ideas.

With the demise of the M6/49 and stagnation in the Sealand production line, there was little flying activity for us pilots at Shorts during the first four months of 1951 when a strike was also in progress. I worked during off-duty hours at building my Flying Fifteen in one of Short's stoke-holes, using very expensive wood veneers and Aerolite glues from Short's stores. They sold me this beautiful silver spruce veneer and minutely-thin mahogany plywood – used for lining 'C' Class boats – at a tenth of the price I would have had to pay for it in the shops if it had been available. The boat – Number 48 in its class – was one of Uffa Fox's lovely designs. It turned out to be far lighter than the rules allowed. Being a planing boat, to race fairly with the others on Strangford Loch, I had to load *Iff* with 50 lb of lead shot. There are now over 3,000 of this design racing round our coasts – which seems to prove that Uffa Fox must have been years ahead of the other yacht designers in 1948/9.

We also started Short's Sailing Club. We built about half-a-dozen 'Wildcats' ourselves. Such light, fast, planing dinghies built of marine ply had not been seen before in Northern Ireland. Many of the yacht club members at Cultra were somewhat doubtful of their safety. One mother, talking to her child, was heard to say when coming face-to-face with my Wildcat on the beach: 'Don't spit in it Willy, you'll sink it.'

Flying was a scarce commodity during 1951. The only high spot during this slack period was a trip in the Short Sperrin. Brookie had made its first flight from Aldergrove on 10 August 1951. It was a beautiful flying machine, with light and effective controls – using servo-tabs with a computed, variable 'Q'-feel stickforce mechanism which prevented over-control at high speeds. There were no awkward trim changes with flaps or power alterations, it had an innocuous stall and, seemingly, no compressibility handling problems at Mach numbers up to M0.78 – the fastest we flew it. However, as the Vulcan and Victor 'models' had already proved that they could probably fly much faster and higher than the straight-winged Sperrin, Shorts were not allowed to proceed further and the only one built was eventually turned over to Aero Flight at Farnborough for research use.

Late in 1949 Shorts had received a Naval Staff Requirement for a cheap, light, single-engined, two-seat, fixed undercarriage, anti-submarine aircraft, capable of decklanding in all weathers on short flight decks. By the end of 1951, this project was taking shape in the hangar at Shorts. While it was building I had submitted an idea for a 'head-up display' of the airspeed indicator and other vital instruments on the windscreen of the Sea Mew – as this A/S aircraft was to be called – so that pilots could retain a constant gaze at the flight deck during the approach to land and see their airspeed written on the batsman's stomach and would not have to continually glance down in the cockpit to see their flying instruments when low-flying over the sea. This was the first of its kind in Britain by about seven years, a mock-up of which Shorts had already installed in the first Sturgeon TT Mark 2 prototype VR 363. Shorts had then applied with me for the Patent (No. 662,987) on 13 May 1949. It was filed at the Patent Office on 12 May 1950 and the 'Complete Specification' was published 12 Dec. 1951. We could all become rich if it caught on.

Shorts could not give Sea Mew a nosewheel because it got in the way of the nose-mounted radome. They give it a 'long-stroke' tailwheel instead, extendable for decklandings, thus giving it some of the decklanding attributes of a nosewheel layout. About 60 Sea Mews were ordered but owing to the unexpected cancellation of the RAF's share and many minor problems discovered by 'C' Squadron at Boscombe – plus the intense competition for this edge of the A/S market by helicopters which were beginning to be produced in quantity in the States – only seven out of the 60 ordered were completed and, after Sandys' Axe had been wielded in 1957, these went to the scrapheap too.

By the end of 1950 it seemed obvious there was no further use for two expensively trained ex-ETPS test pilots at Shorts. There was no development work coming up in the future apart from some shared research into vertical take-off in conjunction with Rolls-Royce and boffins at RAE Farnborough – and nothing to keep both myself and Brookie busy. Even the flight testing of a glider with Professor Hill's Pterodactyl 'aero-isoclinic wing' with wingtip elevons intended for a bomber project, had recently been cut short by its crashing on its second flight, injuring Brookie in the process. Nearly all the Sturgeons had been delivered. Jock Eassie had just joined – relieving Johnny Booth who was leaving Shorts to fly the Princess Flying boat at Cowes – but after his glider-towing job had ceased, he too, had nothing much to do.

So I decided I would have to rejoin the Navy if they would have me back. This would be a return to a Short Service Commission but, with my useful experience, the Navy might still sign me on permanently if I behaved myself.

So I had a meeting with Admiral Slattery. He saw my problem and wrote to the Second Sea Lord at the Admiralty. Captain Percy Gick replied:

> Provided he is fit, we can take him back into flying in the Navy as soon as he likes to come. The maximum seniority we can give him is five years as a Lieutenant. For a man of his age (31) this may not seem very much but we are very rapidly accumulating a surplus of Lieutenant Commanders. It would obviously be unfair to bring Crosley back and put him straight in command of a Squadron or Air group but there is no reason why he should not qualify for the acting rank of Lt/Cdr which he held whilst commanding squadrons in the Pacific.

Alternatively, if he would prefer to continue as a test pilot we would be only too willing to keep him in such an appointment. I enclose the terms of the present Short Service Scheme for ex Naval Pilots . . .

I signed on, dated 7.10.51. I was granted a Permanent Commission by 10.5.54., promoted Lt/Cdr 7.10.54. and Commander 31.12.57. I could not have asked for more.

However, before I left Shorts I asked Admiral Slattery whether I could retain the Patent for my 'head-up display' idea. He said that, unfortunately, the rights would be retained by Shorts and the Patent would be renewed as necessary by them when the existing Patent lapsed after seven years.

The Patent Specification dated 12 December 1951, can be seen at Appendix 7. But in 1982, having seen a virtual copy of my invention installed in a Service fighter aircraft I wrote to Shorts to ask them why they had allowed my Patent to lapse in 1958. Their disappointing reply was:

> The normal reason for failing to renew a patent is that the Company has decided that no likely advantage will accrue from the maintenance of the protection.

Rear-Admiral Sir Matthew Slattery left Shorts in 1960 – at about the same time as 'Brookie' – to be appointed chairman of the nationalised BOAC. None of the subsequent management had seen the necessity for this invention. Today, of course, all modern military jet aircraft use the HUD principle. It is doubtful whether they could be safely flown without it.

It might be of interest here to mention some of the reasons for the water take-off problems associated with Sealand, for these were perhaps typical of all flying boats of that type at that time.

Brookie and I were certain that the cause of the starboard wing-drop on a calm water take-off in the Sealand was due to asymmetric stalling of the wing initiated by propeller slipstream effects. The *directional* slipstream rotation behind the two anti-clockwise props was easily offset by 'opposite' rudder application and Sealand's directional behaviour on take-off was the same in this respect as in any other aircraft not fitted with contra-props. However, slipstream rotation behind the two propellers occurring in the *vertical* plane could not be offset and it had the effect of locally increasing wing incidence by a few degrees in that part of the wing lying behind the *upward*-moving propeller blades. This stalled that part of the wing whenever wing incidence was at its maximum – during the 'hump' nose-up attitude just before planing speed was reached. Because the stalled part of the wing was more outboard on the starboard wing than the port, the aircraft's right wing dropped sharply during this 'hump' period and nothing could be done to right it for the loss in lift represented the weight of about six people.

One day Brookie flew the Sealand near the stall and I flew alongside it with Keith-Lucas in the Dominie for him to observe what happened to some wool tufts on the Sealand's upper wing surface. This showed that a large area of the wing centre section was stalled – even in normal flight! When speed was further reduced to near stalling incidence, the wool tufts behaved very badly indeed, some pointing forwards! When full power was applied at this time, the stalled area on the starboard wing was twice the area of that on the port wing and was farther outboard.

The normal basic conditions for a flying boat to get airborne from the water can be summarised as follows:

(a)   she had managed to accelerate to waterplaning speed – say 40 knots, and had come off the '*hump*'* and had started to plane while maintaining full directional and lateral control.
(b)   she had then accelerated to an *airspeed* of at least 55 knots, so that rudder control became effective.
(c)   she had reduced incidence and was planing bow-down on her fore-body with the rear step clear of the water in the minimum waterdrag planing attitude. This would allow easy acceleration to 'unstick' speed.

Except in the case of floatplanes, lateral control of flying boats had always presented a problem to designers. Even when planing on the main step, the slightest crosswind requires corrective use of engines plus rudder – for the hull is balanced on little more than a pin-point. Furthermore, being highwing monoplanes, they suffer from dihedral effects when taking-off the water in crosswinds much more than other aircraft.

Even when floatplanes take-off, directional and lateral problems can still occur. In the case of the Schneider Trophy Supermarine S5 and S6, I remember having seen the pilots starting their take-off runs pointing initially towards Calshot when their final take-off direction into wind was towards Ryde and at right angles to their initial take-off direction. This uncontrollable 90-degree swing-to-port was caused by engine-torque reaction burying the port float in the water until planing speed was reached.

Short's design office's trials to cure this 'dissimilar stall' characteristic of the Sealand included the fitting of full-span leading-edge slats. Had these slats been placed only in the affected areas, it may have worked well; but by placing them conventionally across the entire wing leading edge their corrective benefit was much reduced and they were discarded.

After so many unsuccessful attempts to remedy matters, Keith-Lucas was now convinced that there was a serious design fault. He now lowered the engines nine inches to improve 'over-the-wing' airflow behaviour near the stall. This produced a much larger improvement, but still not enough.

I suggested fitting a small lift spoiler outboard of the port engine nacelle. This would stall that part of the port wing equally with that on the starboard side. I said that this sort of cure had worked in the case of the Blackburn Skua and that it might have ironed out the Seafire's wing root stall problems, too.

---

*   The '*hump*' is a name given to a critical high drag, nose-up condition during a water take-off where maximum water-drag and aerodynamic drag coincide – and therefore at the time when acceleration is at its minimum.

No designer likes admitting defeat by having to 'subtract' lift in this philistine manner and it was never a popular addition. In Sealand's case, the retractable spoiler – of about the same size as a twelve-inch ruler and pneumatically operated by a small lever on the control column – was placed in the wrong position, that is to say it was placed *inboard* of the port engine nacelle in an area which was already fully stalled so that it had much less effect than if it had been placed outboard.

The fitting of 'handed' props was considered. However, their necessary direction of rotation to secure maximum rudder control in the 'engine out' case was the opposite of that required to cure the dissimilar stall, so that idea was also discarded. Contra-props might have cured Sealand's troubles – as they cured the Seafire's – but these might have been costly and added further to the weight. It was a very great pity that in spite of its rugged construction, its serene flying silence, its excellent cockpit view and, even, its reversible-pitch propellers which greatly improved its water handling, it was not able to compete with the Mallard or later editions of the Goose in its passenger-carrying role and it could not compete with the de Havilland Dove, either. The Dove was a similar-sized aircraft designed for short-haul, unpressurised passenger transport, using identical engines. Yet it had nearly double the range of the Sealand, could fly 30 mph faster with double the number of passengers and weighed 2000 lb less. Not all of this weight and performance difference could be ascribed to the necessary extra weight of the planing hull in the Sealand.

Looking back at this period in aircraft construction and at the difficult problems which stress engineers were having, it seems that, at this time in the middle fifties, they may have taken a leaf out of the boatbuilding industry's book by using 'man-made' materials instead of metal and wood. The hulls of many small, racing boats were, by 1955, being made with fibre-glass – bonded with gap-filling, waterproof resin glues – instead of wood or metal 'planking'. It was not until a few years later – in 1962 – that RAE Farnborough began experimenting with carbon-fibre structures for aircraft in place of duralumin/steel alloys. These materials were not only more economical in man-hours and demanded less skills to work with but they were found to be capable of mass-production within very close limits, were stronger for their weight, were free from corrosion or electrolytic action and, perhaps most important of all in the light of the Comet crashes, were free from fatigue failures.

Perhaps, if the beautiful Sealand had arrived on the scene ten years later, Shorts might have been able to improve its power/weight ratio and might have had a great success.

CHAPTER 6

BE A SAILOR FIRST

Directly it was decided that I should leave Shorts in October 1951 and rejoin the Navy, I called in at ETPS to learn the latest news. Bill Sear and Peter Lamb on 10 Course said that Hawkers had sold their Sea Hawk fighter to the Navy and it had already completed its Service Release trials at 'C' Squadron, including decklandings. A hundred had been ordered and they were to have pressurised cockpits and Martin-Baker ejector seats. Later versions were to have fully-powered ailerons with 'regulated' or 'Q' spring feel and were to be fitted for the carriage of rockets and bombs. The first 'production' Sea Hawk came off the lines in November 1951.

George Baldwin was to take 800 Squadron's Attacker FB Mark 1s aboard the newly launched *Eagle* by March 1952 after completing trials in 787 Squadron (the Naval Aircraft Fighter Development Unit (NAFDU) at RAF West Raynham). I was sad to hear of the death of Andrew Lindsay (6 ETPS) and Bob Orr-Ewing (8 ETPS), both killed in Attackers.

About a hundred Attackers were on order. It was not as popular as the Sea Hawk, not only because it was thought by some to be more difficult to deck land with its tailwheel configuration, but its handling at high Mach – up to about M0.78 maximum – was no better than the Seafang and even less predictable. Les Colquhoun (9 ETPS) – one of Supermarine's test pilots – had landed an Attacker at Chilbolton with its starboard outer mainplane having folded in the air. On 23 May 1950 Les had just completed a fast run over the airfield at about 450 knots (520 mph) when he heard a loud bang and on looking out saw the outer three feet six inches of wing standing up vertically. The aircraft still flew on, and realising that he still had some lateral control due to the positive dihedral effect of the folded portion of the wing compensating for the loss of lift in the starboard wing, he decided to try to control it with rudder and elevator alone – the ailerons having self-locked when the wing folded. Coarse use of rudder was just sufficient to control bank at speeds above 230 knots so he decided not to bale out. He crossed the airfield boundary at 230 knots (265 mph), touching down at 200 knots (230 mph), twice the normal approach speed of the Attacker. He said:

> By juggling with the elevator and brakes to keep the aircraft on the ground I pulled up ten yards short of the end of the 1,800 yard runway.

By landing this aircraft intact, the fault could be discovered and put right so that it could never happen again. For his good work, Les was awarded the George Medal to add to his DFM and DFC. He still interests himself in aviation as the Chairman of the Southern Region of the Spitfire Society.

I also met Dicky Martin who had spent some time at Aero Flight at Farnborough as CO after the death of Stewart Muller-Roland while flying the notorious DH 108 on 15 February 1950. Apparently Stewart Muller-Roland – a very highly regarded ETPS graduate of No. 6 Course and about to become CO of Aero Flight at the time of the accident – had taken off in the high-speed version of the DH 108 to check its longitudinal stability at high Mach. Someone thought that Stewart had lost his life because he had forgotten to check his oxygen supply – a most unlikely omission by a pilot of his experience.

Bar gossip at ETPS also revealed the news that the Navy was about to have its own 'look-down' radar defence. John Treacher was about to form the first AEW Squadron at Culdrose, using American Skyraiders fitted with American AN/APS 20 'look-down' radar. These Skyraiders became 'front line' aircraft – of 849 Squadron – by November 1952. They embarking in *Eagle* in January 1953 – but too late for the Korean war.

The ability to see enemy aircraft approaching the fleet 'on the deck' 150–200 miles away instead of the twenty miles that mast-head radar allowed, was the most significant improvement in air defence over the sea since the introduction of Fighter Command's radar chain round Britain in 1940.

My next job was a non-flying one. The post-war Navy was keen to give all its new Fleet Air Arm officers a dose of genuine 'sea time' as early as possible in their career. This was in continuation of their philosophy: 'Be a sailor first', written on the door of the canteen at St Vincent in 1940 and which we were often told to read by Chief Petty Officer Wilmott on first joining the Fleet Air Arm as 'Naval Airmen Second Class', determined to become aviators.

So my first job as a 'retread' was to report to 'Pompey' Barracks for a course in seamanship. I was issued with a free copy of the Admiralty's *Manual of Seamanship Vol. 1* and, if I wanted to pass my Watchkeeping Certificate I was told I had to learn it.

It mostly contained the elementary jargon necessary to make myself understood aboard ship. After a few weeks marching round the parade ground at Pompey I received a signal telling me to report to *Loch Scavaig* – an anti-submarine Frigate stationed at that time in Malta as part of the Mediterranean Fleet.

Brevity was the watchword when using radio in aircraft. I now had to get used to giving no less than 11 separate orders and receiving 12 separate responses every time I might want the helmsman to alter the ship's course by a few degrees. It also taught me the importance of Naval Ceremonial, especially when entering or leaving harbour and the methods the Navy used to come to a buoy, moor ship, 'come alongside', anchor and pay proper marks of respect to other ships – all so different to my usual 'messing about in boats' up the river Hamble.

So I reported to my Captain – Commander Sir David Macworth Bt – aboard *Loch Scavaig* moored off Sliema in Malta and spent an interesting, instructive and exceedingly comfortable time aboard her for the next five months cruising round the Mediterranean between Aden and Gibraltar and attempting to carry out duties as a junior watchkeeper.

I also had other duties. One was 'correspondence officer', where I fought with an Admiralty Pattern – and therefore entirely indestructible – typewriter. I was also appointed 'fo'csle cable officer', 'boats officer' and, believe it or not 'gunnery officer'. Perhaps a story about each might suffice to explain the difficulties of each job and the immense strain placed upon our 'fish-head' brethren in the Navy whenever they had us airmen under their instruction.

One of my duties as 'correspondence officer' and Captain's secretary was to pay the ship's company on the quarter deck each Friday. One Friday morning I was walking on the upper deck in the sunshine, whirling the two keys of the ship's safe round and round when one flew off its string and disappeared. The ship's pay had to be available in a few hours and I had to get about £2,000 out of the safe and put it into about 150 envelopes. Panic-stricken, I went ashore – at Venice – and got an Italian safe manufacturer to try to drill his way through the two locks. His drill could not cope with the Admiralty Pattern steel so I walked aft to tell the Captain that there would be no pay that day until I could get the safe ashore to have it cut open with a diamond saw – the nearest one being in Rome.

Luckily, when walking aft with trembling gate for this interview and with eyes cast down in shame, they fell upon the glistening key perched upon the lower-deck awning, two inches from falling off into the harbour. Reaching with the boat hook and with the whaler alongside to catch the key if it slithered down into the harbour – with twenty anxious hands upstretched to receive it – I recovered the key and unlocked the safe.

My duties as 'foc'sle cable officer' were mostly confined to taking the blame if anything went wrong on the fo'csle when entering and leaving harbour or when anchoring or mooring. I had a most understanding and patient First Lieutenant – Lt/Cdr Josef Bartosik (later CO of RNAS St Merryn near Padstow in Cornwall) – plus an equally good Leading Seaman – and provided there were no outward and visible signs of chaos which could be seen by the Admiral's staff keeping watch from the castle on Manoel Island when *Loch Scavaig* entered and left Sliema Creek in Valletta harbour in Malta – these two were only too willing to leave me alone to make my own mistakes and learn from them.

Once, when entering Sliema, with the ship going astern at about five knots, with the fo'csle crew in the whaler being towed from our bow and ready to receive the two heavy mooring cables to tie on to the buoy, and the Leading Seaman having just that moment 'slipped' the cable to them through the navel in the bow, I happened to notice that one of the anchors was missing. Luckily the Leading Seaman had noticed that its 'Senhouse Slip' had been knocked off when the cable had 'run out' through the navel, and because we had forgotten to put on the 'Blake Stopper' (designed to secure the anchor to the ship, come what may) the anchor, plus a short length of cable had disappeared through the hawse pipe into Sliema Creek.

Reporting this tragedy to the Captain, he told me that we had to get it back quickly as KR & AIs (*King's Regulations and Admiralty Instructions*) forbade us to go to sea without both of them. A diver from the dockyard soon arrived, disappeared beneath the ship for a few minutes, asked for the cable to be lowered which he then attached under water to the anchor and we raised it, making sure our motor cutter shielded the goings-on from the Admiral's spies in the castle on Manoel Island.

The third incident of note occurred next day, when I and a few others of the ship's company were attending Captain's 'request-men and defaulters' behind closed doors on the upper deck. Halfway through 'defaulters', there was a crash and the ship suddenly accelerated forward at about five knots, coming to an equally sudden halt after travelling about ten feet. We all fell over – including the defaulter – except the Captain, who had his upright desk to hang on to. The ship's navigator – Lt Michael Roope – and the senior watchkeeper, started off for the door, only to be summoned back by the Captain: 'Where d'you think you're going?' Instantly came the reply: 'Damage control stations, sir'.

We had been rammed in the stern by the next-in-line destroyer – HMS *Saintes* – as she entered harbour. She had come in astern at about 15 knots and much too fast – hoping to impress the population lining Sliema front – and, forgetting the crosswind out of Grand Harbour, had first of all drifted her bow into our starboard 'whisker' boom as she passed us, sinking our two sailing dinghies. Next, her skipper, having probably been put off his stride a little by this near-miss, forgot to 'ring down' to his engine room for less rpm when 'going ahead' (which he had to do to stop his ship neatly by his mooring buoys). The result was that *Saintes* not only stopped rather quickly but gathered way at full-speed-ahead again before the skipper had realised his mistake. With her 130,000 hp steam turbines flat out, she then came charging into our stern, cutting a neat hole four feet deep. *Saintes* then went astern once more, then ahead once more and, passing us too close on our port side this time, completed the damage to our boats by carrying away our *port* whisker boom. As this nearly sank our ship's liberty boats and the Captain's motor 'skimmer' as well, it ceased to be a laughing matter.

Next day the Captain of *Saintes* came up the quarter-deck gangway full of apologies, no doubt hoping that the inevitable Board of Enquiry would be run on gentlemanly lines.

As 'boats officer' it was my job to keep all five of our ship's boats smartly turned out. One day the Captain's wife got oil on her dress from the seat in the motor skimmer. Next evening she got more oil on her shoes as oily bilge water welled over them as the 'driver' let in the clutch. The ship's engineer officer and I tried to do something about it.

Because of the fire hazard, the Navy had removed all the petrol engines in their ships' boats which Vospers and Scott-Payne boatbuilders had originally installed in them, and had replaced them with very large and heavy diesel engines. This meant that most of the Navy's fast boats were now far too heavy to plane, especially when overloaded with returning 'liberty men'. They tended to stick on the 'hump' like an overloaded flying boat in a flat calm take off and they refused to get up 'on the step,' their bow waves slowly filling the 'driver's' forward watertight compartment with water. The coxwain's language up for'ard in the officers' motor boat returning from shore leave at midnight from Valletta could be heard in the flagship, miles away.

As our skimmer had a hull leak as well as an oil leak, she was even less likely to succeed in planing properly particularly when both the Captain and his wife were aboard. Things got so bad at Sliema one day that I had to sail the Captain ashore in our 14-foot sailing dinghy – which he quite enjoyed.

In order to cure the trouble with the Captain's 'skimmer' I used my ETPS instinct and carried out a series of test flights with the ship's plumber watching the engine. He, with his bottom upwards staring into the engine and trying to find the oil leak, and me in the bow, with throttle wide open and trying to avoid the *dheisas* – the very beautiful two-oared mini-gondolas much used for everyday transport in the harbour – we tore round Sliema Creek one beautiful sunny morning, trying to get the boat off the 'hump' and on to its step so that the Captain and his wife could travel in style once more.

It proved necessary to remove the 'safety gate' on the throttle and allow a bit more power. We came to the conclusion that it was that little bit extra which made all the difference for we then had the fastest skimmer in Sliema Creek and oil leaks became a nasty memory.

The fifth episode of note occurred one day in beautiful Venice. We were alongside the quay, hoisting the ship's motor cutter into the davits. The manoeuvre was being watched by a few Venicians. Whether it was the beauty of the scenery or some other distraction I do not know, but one of the sequence of my, hopefully, clear, crisp orders to the man on the fo'csle steam-windlass did not get through to him, and instead of 'hook on', the order arrived on the fo'csle as 'off turns'. The winch driver cast off the boat's falls from the 'warping drums' on his steam-windlass and the ends ran out, allowing one of them which had not yet been 'hooked on', to drop the cutter's bow back into the canal from its fully hoisted position. This emptied all the crew from the bow into the stern and all the stern crew over the transom into the water – to the cheers of the multitude. Luckily, Captain 'D', our Flotilla CO, did not hear about it and we told the 'multitude' ashore that a rope had parted owing to the weight of Venician wine on board.

Very little of our time at sea seems to have been taken up with submarine hunting – which was our main task. Apart from making routine Asdic searches – in which no aircraft were involved – the only other under-sea device we used apart from a few depth charges, was the 'bathy-thermograph'. We lowered this into the Mediterranean wherever we went to record the temperature of the water at various depths and sent the results to the

Admiralty. The Navy was still investigating where and how the German submarines had been able to avoid our Asdic detection during the war by hiding below – or above – the sharp changes in water density which occurred in the western Mediterranean.

Michael Roope and Joseph Bartosik – the First Lieutenant – instructed me in the use of the ship's ancient sextant and how to use several of the stars for position finding. I was shown the Navy's latest radio and radar sets – about ten cubic feet of glowing valves, revolving 'condensers' and humming transformers – which took so much power to drive them that the main generator had to be switched on before they would operate. In any case, the Flotilla was still making use of flag signals, hand semaphore and morse lanterns – as in the Battle of Jutland – for the electro-magnetic energy coming from our aerials would not only have fried a passing seagull but would have given away the position of the fleet to the enemy for miles around. Naval navigation purposely made use of basic methods to ensure safe arrivals in ships which had suffered enemy action and which could not use electronic methods of knowing where they were. Nevertheless, it is worthy of note that for half the cost of a sextant, yachtsmen can now press a button in their cockpits and see their position, speed, course, and time-to-next-mark come up on a small screen, within an accuracy of 50 feet, anywhere round the British Isles or the coast of northern France.

My efficiency as Gunnery Officer was put to the test when we had a practice shoot off Malta with the main armament – a single 4.7-in. gun. This stuck out from a small gun turret on the fo'csle. A tug towed a large wire-netting target a few miles out to sea and, standing on the bridge and reading from a book hidden from the eyes of the gun crew, I gave the complicated series of orders through an Admiralty Pattern 'sound-powered' telephone for them to loose off about a dozen rounds at it.

Two weeks later we were sent the results in the form of a large and beautiful parchment sheet, with the hits and misses marked on it. The nearest we got to the target was about 60 yards, but most were at least a quarter of a mile away. This did not surprise anyone at all as we had no 'interrupter gear' to offset inaccuracies due to the ship's pitching or rolling, and no allowance was made for cordite temperatures, ship or target movement, or wind. It seemed a pity to waste the beautiful solid brass shell cases plus a dozen shells for such poor results, especially as each shell cost half as much as the latest Italian 'Vespa' motorscooter which I was saving up for.

Every airman is sceptical about Naval long-range AA and surface gunnery accuracy, its usefulness in war and its cost-effectiveness in delivering destruction to the enemy compared with aircraft delivery methods. During the Normandy landings in 1944, from 'D' Day and for six weeks afterwards, 48 Seafire pilots of 3 Wing under the Command of Cdr 'Buster' Hallett – of which I was one – had been employed from Lee-on-Solent to act as 'bombardment spotters', directing the 14–16 in. guns of of our remaining battleships anchored offshore at the Germans at distances up to 20 miles inland. This we did from 'D' Day 6 June until 20 July. In our Seafires we were given a unique view of Naval bombardment effectiveness.

The poor results we saw when these big guns were fired at long range allows us all to dispel, with good authority, the huge myth surrounding the might of Naval gunnery. As very little science is involved in unfolding this myth it seems extraordinary that the truth has not come out before – especially after Admiral Jellicoe himself had failed to satisfy Beatty's and Churchill's complaints that the big guns at Jutland had only hit their huge, slow-moving targets once out of every 450 shells they had fired at them and few of those that had hit had pierced the German armour anyway. (As the subject of 'Air Defence – Gunnery or Fighters' can be somewhat technical – I have included a short discussion on the subject at Appendices 1 and 2.)

In May 1952, when I had nearly completed four months aboard *Loch Scavaig* and our Captain – David Macworth – had already given me my 'watchkeeping certificate', the ship was sent for a period of 'self main-tenance' in Grand Harbour, leaving us sufficient time for off-duty sporting activities – with the ship's company – rugby, rowing and, of course, sailing. Following this, the ship made a brief tour of eastern Sicily, calling in at Taormina for a week – then up to Venice again before returning to Sliema once more by 1 June.

I had read in *Flight Deck* that the new *Eagle* had just been commissioned and I wondered whether the Navy would use her alongside the Americans in Korea or whether she would be considered too valuable. I watched my letter box each day for a signal telling me when I should be getting back to flying. I was hoping to get a worthwhile job in test flying – as I would probably be more use doing that – although I had a suspicion that I might be required to 'work my passage' back into the Navy by doing some ordinary squadron work first – perhaps off Korea.

CHAPTER 7

KOREA

Directly it had been decided by the United Nations to land forces in Korea to defend it against the communists, the Admiralty had given Number 738 Naval Air Squadron at Culdrose in Cornwall the job of training up Sea Fury pilots for ground attack duties, after which they would be sent to whichever carrier happened to be 'on duty' off the west coast of Korea at the time. The author was now one of these. We assumed that all our efforts would be to try to force the communist enemy to retire from whence he had come – to the north of the Yalu river in North Korea.

Our flying rate in Sea Furies at Culdrose was about three trips per day per pilot – practise-firing rockets, low level bombing, dive bombing and strafing exercises with live ammunition at the gunnery ranges over Treligga and working very hard at airfield dummy decklandings (ADDLS). The Sea Fury fighter was a magnificent aircraft for this sort of warfare. With 200 gallons of internal fuel compared with the Seafire's 135, plus two × 500 lb or 1000 lb bombs – depending on available wind speed, plus carrier's speed plus cata-pult's 'end-speed' – the Sea Fury, loaded to 14,650 lb in this way had almost the same ground attack capability as the Avenger and able – unlike the Firefly – to revert to its designed fighter/intercepter role at a moment's notice after dropping its load of bombs or rockets.

The flying standards required in bombing, rocketry and ground strafing at Culdrose in 1952 were similar to those demanded in wartime from Seafire pilots in 1943–5, and the Sea Fury used identical weapons. The course took a month and about 30 hours of flying time, ending with a few decklandings and the usual 'tail-down' catapult launches in *Illustrious*.

Travelling out via Singapore, Bangkok and Tokyo with Lt/Cdr Peter London, who had been appointed CO in place of Lt/Cdr S. Shotton, DSC, – who had just been killed – the author learnt a little about the military situation and why Britain was involved.

Korea had been a Chinese colony until the Japanese had usurped it as a 'protectorate' in 1894 after their victory at Tsushima. In 1910 the Japanese annexed it as a colony for themselves until it was declared 'neutral' by the Allies in 1943. In 1945 Russia gained a foothold in Korea in competition with the returning Chinese by declaring war against Japan a few days before the Japanese armistice was signed. Russia thereafter annexed the northern half of Korea (of which one-third produced industrial raw material with the remain-der farming) and the United States forces in Japan crossed over and occupied the southern half (the economy of which was mostly agricultural in undeveloped farming country). The 38th parallel acted as an approximate dividing line between the communists in the north and the non-communists under the Americans in the south – the latter now setting about rounding up the remaining Japanese in the south and returning them to their country.

In 1948 Russia obstructed attempts to unify Korea and refused to accept the West's proposal to make Syngman Rhee an independent President of all Korea. Instead, the Russians organised a communist puppet government in North Korea and called it the Korean People's Republic (KPR) of *all* Korea. By 1950 the KPR was in firm control of the North and was threatening to extend its influence southwards. As the Russians and the Americans had, by this time, left Korea to its own devices, the situation was becoming very unstable with Communist China under Mao having defeated the Kuomintang and, being paid by Russia, was beginning to take advantage of the 'vacuum' in the north.

During 1949–50, Russia armed the communist North with about 180 tanks, 175 aircraft – including the MiG 15 – and trained 90,000 well-armed troops under their puppet leader Kim Il Sung. In June 1950 these troops invaded the South without declaring war. They reached Seoul two days later and Syngman Rhee fled 100 miles south to Taejon with the remnants of his untrained army, retiring to the port of Pusan in the south-eastern corner of Korea, only a hundred miles from Japan and the Americans.

The conflict had now begun in earnest. The UN Security Council – in the absence of Russian representation – voted to repel the North Korean communists and President Truman sent the ill-prepared US 24th Division to carry out this task. After a few setbacks – but having total air superiority – the South made an unopposed amphibious landing at Inchon north of Seoul, advanced northward and took up positions by the Yalu river.

The Chinese communists now took a firmer hand and advanced from the north and drove the US army back from where it had started in South Korea. An important feature of this battle under General Ridgeway – and later under General van Fleet – occurred in May 1951, when a major Chinese re-offensive was stopped in its tracks by the 1st Battalion of the Gloucestershire Regiment when they held on to a key section of the south bank of the Imjin River. Van Fleet called this 'the most outstanding example of unit bravery in modern warfare.' Its effect was to stabilise the Allied line just north of the 38th Parallel – which had been the situation for the past year when I and Pete London joined 802 Squadron aboard *Ocean* on 13 August 1952.

Further details of the military position may be of interest here – very little of which we knew at the time, of course. On taking up positions against the UN troops along the 38th Parallel the enemy had probably failed to take into account the effect that allied air superiority would have over his land and sea supply routes. This air support was supplied by the United States Air Force, United States Navy and Royal Navy. So that, when, in July 1950, the Allies had begun their air blockades from carrier aircraft operating from both sides of the Korean peninsular and from the USAF in Japan, the North Koreans were unable to sustain an offensive in the south in spite of huge advantages in man power, as they had no food or weapon reserves for such ventures and their 300-mile supply lines were under continuous, daylight air attack.

The Royal Navy with an LCV plus a cruiser, destroyers and minesweepers, assisted by the Royal Australian and Canadian Navy and an occasional American carrier, took over the blockade and interdiction of the western coast in the Yellow Sea, from the river Yalu – the Chinese border – to 60 miles south of Pyonyang, the Korean capital city. The United States carrier force – armed with Corsairs and a few Skyraiders – took over the eastern shores. The USAF soon found their F-80 Shooting Stars lacked the necessary range and had to resurrect their F-51D Mustangs until the end of 1950, when the MiG 15 made its appearance over Korea making the return of the F-80, and a few F-84 Thunderjet attack bombers and later the F-86 A Sabre, essential to preserve allied air superiority. By early 1951 the USAF had replaced the F-86 As with 86 Es having power controls and the 'all-flying' tail. They mostly flew on routine B-29 escort missions up to the river Yalu boundary, flying from air bases to the south of the 38th parallel.

The RN's initial part in the war was to prevent the enemy from reinforcing his army by sea, so that, to start with, half the usual complement of 12 Firefly aircraft aboard our carriers were used for minespotting and A/S patrols. The remainder – including some of the Seafire 47's in *Triumph* under Ian MacLachlan (No. 6 Course at ETPS) in 800 Squadron – carried out Combat Air Patrols (CAPs) over the carrier and occasionally over our in-shore naval force of minewsweepers, destroyers and cruisers, the latter being used as bombardment ships.

A succession of our Colossus class Light Fleet Carriers patrolling 150–200 miless off the western shores of Korea then took over the interdiction of enemy supply lines ashore, operating nine days on and seven days off. First there was *Theseus* – substituting 24 Sea Fury FB IIs of 807 Squadron for *Triumph*'s Seafire 47s. *Theseus* was followed in April 1951 by *Glory* with more Furies and Fireflies (804 and 812 Squadrons). Then five months later she was relieved by HMAS *Sydney*'s Furies and Fireflies (805, 818 and 817 Squadrons), then by *Glory* again from January 1951 until May 1952 (804 Squadron and 812 Squadron). This patrol was then taken over by ourselves in *Ocean* (802 and 825 Squadrons) from 17 May 1952 to the end of September 1952.

By the time *Ocean* took over on this sixth operational tour of British carriers, the interdiction tasks had become less productive and it was easy for any 'war veteran' to see that our Korean ground targets were of less military value than WW 2 targets. Moreover, as we were fighting a primitive economy and a peasant army, such targets as there were moved only at night if they moved at all and the full benefits of daylight air superiority could not be exploited.

To secure twenty-four-hour stoppages along their supply routes, all we could do was to blow up their river and rail bridges wherever they could be found in daylight, and hope that they could not be repaired in time for use the following night when we were unable to hit them. Even then it was difficult – as our army commander General Van Fleet said:

> Although we can win the battle of the bridges we can lose our objective – which is knocking out the traffic – because the enemy is building by-passes and leaving us nothing but flak traps.

Meanwhile, lacking a clear military aim and politically tied to operating south of the Yalu, all that our armies could do was to occupy fixed, defensive positions dug into hillsides from which they could deploy their vastly superior firepower and hope to convince the communists of the hopelessness of their position and encourage them to make peace at the 'Armistice Conference' set up in November 1951 at Panmunjon – seemingly, to us aboard *Ocean* – in continuous but unproductive political argument.

Therefore, when Pete and I joined *Ocean*, 75 per cent of our targets were nothing more important than the remains of the enemy's road, rail and river links. Although these were mostly static and lifeless during daylight hours, they were always potential 'flak traps' if attacked, with their main concentrations of light and medium flak at river bridges and entries to towns and villages. Only very seldom could we 'find, fix and kill' any 'targets of opportunity' during our 'armed recce's,' not only because these targets were so few, but being so well camouflaged, they required 'stereo' analysis from air-to-ground photographs to show us, at briefing, where they were. By the time we got there next day they had probably moved on somewhere else.

The UN politicians had forbidden us to do any fighting or bombing north of the Yalu river, so that the communists used this area as their safe military store-house and a home for their MiG 15 fighters – mostly flown quite well by the Chinese – which had, by 1952, increased in number to 400.

Although we were operating our carriers within range of these MiGs, lacking low level radar control (AEW) – which was at that time being installed in Skyraiders in the form of AN/APS 20 back home – the enemy air activity over our portion of the Yellow Sea was minimal and CAP (Combat Air Patrol) over the carrier was only necessary night and morning. Nevertheless, just in case, our Furies were sometimes sent to provide air support for our inshore shipping – including bombardment spotting for the cruisers *Newcastle* and *Belfast* – and we always supplied Close Air Support (CAS) for any landings of friendly troops – including guerrillas. These landings were made in an attempt to attract the enemy out into the open, to make him use up his reserves and to give us airmen some genuine military targets.

Even then, 90 per cent of the traffic that moved by day in *Ocean*'s operating area was in the form of heavily camouflaged animal or human transport. Cattle pulled ox-carts along hundreds of miles of farm tracks and hundreds of men and women from the countryside trekked south carrying 'A-frames' on their backs loaded with food and ammunition.

However, four days before Pete and I had arrived on board there had been a bit of good news to raise morale. One of 802's division leaders, Lt 'Hoagy'

Carmichael, (a division' consisted of two pairs of aircraft who normally flew together) was leading a division of 802 Squadron's Sea Furies on a morning recce of the railway-line from Pyongyang to Chinnampo. His four Sea Furies were in open 'finger' formation at 4,000 feet and flying down-sun at about six o'clock in the morning when they were 'jumped' by about six MiG 15s coming out of the rising sun. One of them, having missed with his own guns, flew into Hoagy's field of view and instead of retracting his air brakes and 'getting to hell out of it', the MiG pilot had started to turn back to have another go – a serious mistake when once a jet has slowed down to 'piston-engine' speed.

At these low speeds the Fury could easily out-turn the MiG – which had a much higher wing-loading than the Fury – and Hoagy, using the Fury's gyro gunsight at short range, soon secured enough hits with his 4 × 20mm cannon on the MiG – whose pilot had by now retracted his air brakes and was trying to climb back to safety – to see it crash into the hillside ahead of him.

So this was the position when Pete and I arrived on board *Ocean* on 13 August – each 'counting our beads' in the back of a Firefly of 825 Squadron driven by Pete Reynolds (later 15 ETPS). (We met at the 40th anniversary lecture of Boscombe's Royal Aeronautical Society given by Dennis Higton in November 1993 and he still remembers how shagged-out we both looked at the time he collected us from Seoul.) We had had a boring and uncomfortable flight out to Tokyo in a Lancastrian. I had found myself sitting alongside James Cameron, a distinguished journalist who told me he was 'covering' the Korean war for the *Express* and the *Picture Post*. He told us he was opposed to our presence in Korea and if taken prisoner, we would deserve all we got. It turned out that, having witnessed the Bikini atoll nuclear test in the summer of 1946, he was a founder-member of CND, so that this would have explained his attitude to the Services at that time.

On our arrival on board, the Captain (later Vice-Admiral Sir Charles Evans, KCB, CBE, DSO, DSC), sent a message down to Pete and the author on the flight deck to tell us to report to his sea-cabin where he welcomed us and, it being bar-opening time, he gave us both a gin and tonic. Being one of the very few fighter-pilot Captains in the Navy and having been Cdr (Air) of *Implacable* at the same time that the author was CO of 880 Seafire Squadron, we were very lucky to have had him as our boss in *Ocean*. Before our first trip, we new arrivals were given a short briefing by Nigel Bailey – Commander (Air). We were warned about the dangers of being taken prisoner-of-war by the North Koreans and told how we might be able to survive a month of inter-rogation in solitary confinement. We were told that if we did not co-operate at once, we might be taken out one morning, asked to dig a hole and then be lined up with others to be shot. If we agreed that we were criminals and would not fight against communism and become 'one of them', we might then be taken to a proper PoW camp and survive until peace was declared and the commu-nists triumphed. (This treatment of PoWs – plus routine torture – had been the common practice in the Chinese wars to their own people for the past century and history now shows that we should not have expected anything better.)

We were issued with a '38 revolver, a mass of 'rescue' aids, silk maps, mini compasses, water purifiers and bribe money. We were told whenever possible to bale out over the sea where we would stand a near-certain chance of rescue by the marvellous American air-sea-rescue organisation based at Chodo, an island complex off the west coast.

Provided the hood jettisoned cleanly, baling out – from the inverted position – in a Fury was nothing like attempting the same feat from the early Seafires. The Fury was longitudinally stable under all conditions of flight and it was possible to trim 'nose forward' before inverting, and with the hood already jettisoned, to drop out easily and clear all obstructions – even with a cumbersome dinghy and water-carrier attached to the parachute.

To get used to flying from a carrier again my first trip was a routine CAP. Next day I led a strike of four Sea Furies on a (Tactical Armed Recce CAP) TARCAP – where our job was to provide fighter cover while some Fireflies bombed a bridge target near Charyong – after which we could go and bomb it ourselves if it was still standing.

One of my 500 lb bombs failed to explode. When I returned on board I was told that this was a common occurrence with these wartime bombs. We were shown photographs of our bridge next day and both spans were down, but as we had not destroyed the upright stone-work, the Communists would easily repair it during *Ocean*'s next refuelling period. So, on the 17th we had another go at it and managed to flatten it properly. My division's second trip on 15 August had been a bridge at Chinampo and another four Sea Furies had come along as well under 'Paddy' McKeown. We completely missed it this time, possibly because the cloud base was too low to get enough aiming time in the dive.

Flak was worrying, too – the first I had seen so far. Bursts could be seen at about 4,000 feet – probably 37mm – and some tracer was also flying about at heights up to 2,000 feet – probably 20mm. Apart from our second bash at the bridge at Chinampo I was told to carry out another bridge-busting strike at Cheryong which we shared with Peniston-Bird's division. One of us carried an F-24 oblique camera so that we could bring back a few pictures of any damage we had caused.

I had told my division that I would only make a single pass at any target and never, ever, go back to it. I had also told them we would always make combined attacks – all of us diving within a few seconds of each other and all from different directions. The chance of ricochets from our own bullets or bombs hitting us at our pull-out height of 1,500 feet were so slight as to be negligible compared with the dangers of coming in one behind the other and presenting an easy target for light flak. In theory, our method might reduce by a factor of 16 the number of guns firing at a four-aircraft diving attack. (This method was written in to Naval Fighting Instructions by 1958).

The F-24 camera was fitted with a 24 in. telephoto lens and could take pictures at 1/5th sec. intervals at a 90 degree angle to the aircraft's flight path up to distances of half a mile and, depending on the light values, at shutter speeds up to 1/2000th sec. and iris settings as wide as f2. Thus, when using this camera, the pilot would have to make a 90-degree turn after his dive to get a fleeting picture of the damage – if any. He was not under any circumstances to return to the target area to do this. It was common knowledge that there wasn't a Sea Fury target in the whole of Korea worth a pilot's life.

The second strike on the 17 August was to coincide with an USAF Sabre sweep just in case our presence might attract a few MiGs into the area. Reading the map as best I could and spotting a river here and a road at the bottom of a valley there, I managed to point out the target in good time to my Division and we spread out to enter our 45-degree dive – from about 6,000 feet, in clear weather. I squinted into the gunsight – its graticule depressed to allow for a shallow dive angle. I set the release height – to warn me over the r/t when to press the button – and started the dive into-wind, calling over the r/t for the others to start theirs. We judged the 'push-over' point by making a diving turn to port directly the target appeared from behind the port wing root. Throttling back to about +2 boost, trimming forward on the elevator trimmer, adjusting the rudder angle to prevent any yaw in the dive (we had warning lights either side of the gunsight to tell us when we had excessive yaw or skid in the dive) and trusting that the enemy shooting was poor, I pressed the bomb release on the r/t signal at about 1,500 feet, climbed to about 4,000 feet in a steep left-handed turn at full throttle and, having a look round for the others – and finding them there – set course for home, keeping in 'finger fours' and on the look out for MiGs.

We resisted the temptation of strafing a few likely-looking patches on the roadways – which could have been ox-carts – for we were already late for our land-on time after two hours and ten minutes in the air and the communists would have heard the noise of the bombing and would be ready for us. Calling Paengyang-do radio – the United States Naval rescue organisation – to tell them where we were, we took a course back to *Ocean* using our ZBX radio beacons and, in spite of the ship pitching badly into the swell from the approaching Typhoon 'Karen', we landed on without mishap.

Apart from two wheels-up landings on Chodo beach, two barrier prangs, three Furies hit by light AA and Sub-Lt R.J. Clark, RNVR getting into trouble after a RATOG (Rocket Assisted Take-Off Ground) launch with two × 1,000 lb bombs on board) the carrier's sixth Patrol had been remarkably free from accidents. Two 'barriers' in 600 landings – the last 100 made with the ship pitching some ten feet at the round down – was about one third of the decklanding accident rate of the average Seafire squadron in the Pacific and about one tenth of the Seafire accident rate in the Mediterranean in early 1944.

S/Lt Clark was one of six 'force-on' RNVR officers in 802 Squadron. They had all left their jobs in UK to come out and fight. I had the good fortune to fly with them in my Division, off and on. They were Lieutenants: Buxton, Adkin, Belville and Clark, the last three continuing their service in *Glory* with 801 Squadron after we returned to UK in November.

Clark's RATOG problem had arisen a day before I joined. He may not have offset the strong nose-up change-of-trim which occurred when the RATOG rockets were fired. Such crude methods of obtaining flying speed on a carrier take-off were very unpopular in *Ocean*, but failing enough natural wind to bring the windspeed over the deck to about 35 mph and not having a catapult of sufficient power aboard *Ocean*, a loaded Fury could not accelerate to the 100 knot airspeed required in a 'free take-off' without RATOG. (Chapter 8 describes some of the problems associated with catapult take-offs and gives a few possible reasons for Clark's accident.)

Clark's Sea Fury was loaded to its maximum AUW of 14,650 lb and needed every bit of RATOG assistance to achieve full flying speed by the end of the four-hundred-foot deck run. His aircraft had zoomed into the air, lost flying speed in a very steep climb, stalled, and had landed nose-first in the sea abreast the ship. The whole lot then disappeared from view beneath the waves for 90 seconds – when Clark's head miraculously appeared and he was rescued by our helicopter, just in time. He had had trouble getting free from his dinghy attachments but had probably remained fully conscious under the water by breathing oxygen through his mask – which we all did throughout all flights – and which miraculously stayed put during his stay under water. He was off flying for two days.

I heard the sad news that Ian MacLachlan – 6 ETPS – and who was CO of 801's Seafire 47s in *Triumph* at the time, was killed on 29 August 1950 by a piece of aircraft propeller which crashed through the ship's Operations Room scuttle where he was sitting. How unlucky can you be?

Ocean's sixth patrol ended on 17 August and we retired to Kure in Japan for a week alongside, to replenish ourselves and the ship. Five hundred and eighty-four sorties had been carried out in seven days, spread amongst forty-two pilots, eight observers, six aircrewmen for the Fireflies and two hard-working air/sea/rescue helicopter pilots. My total of seven trips had therefore been par for the course for my first four days on board.

Perhaps one of the greatest improvements in safety during deck operations was the introduction of the S.51 Dragonfly helicopter into service in January 1951. 'All-weather' trials of this American designed 'chopper' had been held aboard RFA *Fort Duequesne* and the first Air-Sea Rescue Unit had embarked in *Glory*, relieving *Theseus* in April 1951. The S.51 had immediately proved its worth by rescuing four of *Glory*'s pilots from the sea and another four from behind enemy lines during her time off Korea. By the time *Ocean* arrived off Korea, the latest version of the S.51 having metal rotor blades and hydraulic servo controls was in service aboard several carriers. Later versions of the Dragonfly – the HR3 – were also used for ASR, communication and 'Fleet Requirement Duties' ashore and afloat throughout the 50s and early 60s where they set the standard for all future users of this versatile, but highly vulnerable, form of air transport.

Charles Evans addressed us in the Wardroom after we arrived in Kure at 1745 on 19 August. He was worried about a case of a certain disease occurring on board and he enjoined us to be careful when we went ashore and to take precautions. The temptations were immense, he said, and 'although fighting-men are seldom celibate' (and our 'parson' was nodding his head), 'I will have no further visits to the sickbay for this reason, apart from those who wish to collect "the necessary", just in case.'

So, I hardly knew what to expect when I got ashore with some of the boys in the Squadron. Geisha girls abounded, taxies lined up with the Japanese drivers demanding extortionate fares to take us to the various 'swimming parlours'. The only deterrent was lack of money and the sight of the inevitable American shore patrols – sometimes known as 'snowdrops' and wearing white helmets and leather flak jackets, with guns, radios and grim faces; ready to arrest anything that moved out of line and return it to its ship forthwith – so unlike the British 'Bobby'. But we had no trouble with *Ocean*'s 'runs ashore'. The only incident that I can remember was when Paddy McKeown collected a damaged eye from a Japanese taxi-driver's starting handle when he, quite rightly, refused to pay double the agreed fare back to the ship, one night.

I wrote to my father on 16 September. I said:

I have now done 58 sorties over Korea and on the next partrol we shall all get in another dozen. *Ocean* will then have completed 3,800 sorties. It really is one of the 7 wonders to watch a land-on. Twenty-five aircraft coming in to land at intervals never more than twenty-five seconds between each. The barrier seldom in position for more than a few seconds at a time – just sufficient in case the fellow on his approach overshoots a bit and misses all the wires and might then go into the deck park forward.

There is very little that an Englishman likes doing in Kure. It is really a 'Little America' and has all the usual gaudiness of an American film set in a goldrush town – flash cars and popsies. Last time in harbour we spent in Sasebo – the Commonwealth Forces HQ. The Japanese are hardworking and clean but not as pleasant as the Chinese or Siamese we have met. Even the South Koreans are really beautiful in their way. Trouble is they let themselves down in the eyes of us westerners as they use human droppings for manure and their drainage arrangements need gas masks. The men are cruel to their women but they seem to expect it and are wonderfully plucky and hardworking in spite of it all.

I cannot imagine why the ship has not been attacked by MiGs yet. We are well within range of them but there seems to be a gentleman's understanding about the way the war is being conducted which helps to add to the farce of it all. Perhaps the communists don't mind us here at all because we are doing ourselves more damage in men and materials than we are inflicting upon them. For instance, we shoot off 10,000 cannon shells per day at 17/- each at ox-carts. Our cruisers shoot off 3,000 shells a month at open countryside, when each 6" shell would buy a complete Vespa.

On 26 November I wrote again and said:

The rivers are drying up now and the nights are getting longer, too. So we are getting very hard up for targets. In the last patrol we lost no one at all, although a few aircraft got shot up and force-landed due to flak or engine failure.

I am looking forward to seeing you – it will have been about six months, won't it. We play a few games – both on board and ashore. Carole Carr is coming on board to-night to entertain us. She is going to sing and is bringing her own piano – wisely – as ours is out of tune having had beer poured into it, of course.

Some of the all-night attractions ashore – not for me, I hasten to add – include meeting Turks, Dutchmen and Americans in Geisha girl establishments where things go on behind closed doors after midnight. Hope to get a good camera for a fiver tomorrow as the price will be at its lowest as we leave tomorrow. I have only got a mere fiver left over after paying my mess bill this month. Still, the car (a 1928 Rolls-Royce) will have been paid for by now.

Our next patrol will be the last and after that we come straight back via Singapore and Suez to Malta on our way home. A 'patrol' works out at about 45 hours of flying – about thirty offensive sorties over Korea – with bombs or rockets. It is hard going, but the standard of flying is far higher than in the war albeit with far less danger. Some of the boys come back shot up. The CO, – who, incidentally was far junior to me in the war – was very lucky to get away with it as he had an explosive bullet in his main spar and another in the port aileron. Another one, still, cut a hydraulic drain valve stop and was within ½" of his main pressure fuel line to the carburettor.

The war out here is like nothing that has happened before. When ground-strafing in the war there was either flak or fighters or there was nothing. Here, the peasant himself is armed with a gun and he takes a pot shot at you at any time or place just as he would a rabbit in the garden. The law of averages says you will be hit, sooner or later, if you fly within their altitude range for more than a few minutes each sortie.

Life aboard during our rest periods is almost unreal. We have marvellous service from our Chinese (ex-Hong-Kong) stewards – hot tea each morning, water run in our cabin basins at the right temperature for washing, knife edge creases in our pants, snow-white tropical shoes and shorts, long socks invisibly darned, names sown on our clothes for laundry idents, tropical 'Number 10s' kept a blinding white, medals burnished.

Rest periods are also an opportunity for us to get to know the men who maintain our aircraft. We are not allowed the pleasure of flying our 'own' aircraft on operational trips – as this is obviously too difficult to arrange – so that complete trust in all the squadron ratings is essential, not just those who we know especially well, but all those involved in looking after our aircraft.

Off duty, we visit *Unicorn* – our air maintenance carrier – where Ted Ray and company gave us a show full of good British humour. While on board *Unicorn* we heard about the immense 'black' she put up – by entering Japan's Inland Sea by an unaccustomed route and carrying away the entire overhead electrical supply to the Island of Kyushu with her mast and plunging it into darkness for several weeks.

So ended this rather long letter to my Dad. On returning to Japan in the Inland Sea in October the flight deck was repainted – removing the hockey markings

– and we paraded on it for an inspection ceremony by our Admiral – Sir Roderick ('Wee') McGrigor. During this parade the RAF were doing circuits and splashes overhead in their four Sunderlands – their contribution to the Korean war – and the noise they made was not very popular.

On our next-to-last patrol, the accent had shifted from interdiction of enemy transport to more industrial targets. Industrial and semi-military targets in built-up areas had hitherto been forbidden by the UN politicians because we might hurt civilians more than the communist army and the inevitable media publicity that this would afford could make us even more unpopular with the socialists in Britain than we were already. Our new targets were sluice gates and dams near Haeju and Yonan.

So 802 was to go Dam Busting! The North Koreans were producing rice in sufficient quantities to supply their frontline troops without recourse to the use of the main supply route – or the 'Delegates Road' – and therefore totally banned from our attention. Rice needs fresh water, so that our task was to breach the dams with bombs to let in salt seawater to ruin the crops for the next three years. Our 'Air Weapons Officer's' scheme was to drop about 10 × 500 lb and 1000 lb, 30-second delay bombs in a 20 degree dive along the line of these sluice gates, trusting that when they blew up they would collapse the barriers and flood the rice crops alongside.

Although we had set time delays on our bomb fuses so we were not blown up by our own bombs, we had underestimated the hardness of water when a bomb hits it at a shallow angle at 500 mph. Most of the bombs we dropped on our first sorties bounced on the water and disappeared into the undergrowth. Some reappeared above wing level to the surprise of the pilots. (Thirty years later the Argentinian pilots had similar trouble. The British landings at San Carlos were allowed to take place with minimum casualties not only because the Argentinian A-4 Sky Hawks chose the wrong targets but nine of the bombs that hit our ships failed to explode because of the incorrect arming of their fuses and by the very low level of their release.)

The Korean dam job was finally completed on 17 November when we were joined by 825 Squadron Fireflys to drop about a dozen 12-hour delay bombs – which we did as near to the dams as we could – using a 45-degree dive. This last series of attacks was to discourage their attempts to repair them at low water. The Fireflies of 825 then followed up again with photo/recce details. These showed widespread damage to the dams, the water having drained in from the sea over thousands of acres of rice crops.

On 20 September it was my turn to get up at 0300 for a dawn strike. The targets were the usual ox-carts and sampans plus a really worthwhile one – some motor transport. We spotted their headlights along a hilltop road north of Tae Dong Gang. I did 21 trips on this patrol totalling about 40 hours in the air, flying, as we all did, three times on two days of the nine day period.

On *Ocean*'s ninth patrol a typical division did 20 trips, three of which would be 'Close Air Support' (CAS) over our army lines north of the 38th parallel. CAS consisted of flying to a given map reference position and waiting for the army 'Air Observation Post' (AOP) – usually an Auster – to appear and mark the target by dropping a yellow flare and then giving us a bearing and distance over the radio from it where the army AOP pilot estimated his chosen target to be and on which he hoped we would drop our bombs. These targets were usually on the 'reverse slopes' of hills opposite our lines, and where the army's gunfire – for which the Auster AOP pilots spotted – could not therefore reach. The army later told us that we had had '50 per cent coverage' of our target. Bearing in mind the long time we had been flying over the target area waiting for the army's AOP marker plane to appear and consequently waking up the communists' artillery, we were lucky to have escaped their AA fire.

On 13 October, while we were 'flak suppressing' for Pete London's division while they bombed some road bridges west of Chaeryong, Chris Jenne (now farming in Devon) who was leading my second pair, was hit by light flak and skilfully made a wheels-down landing on hard sand on the beach at Chodo. He could not restart the engine to taxy above high water mark when the tide came in later, but waded out afterwards to retrieve the valuable gyro gunsight, bomb carriers and instrument panel, flying back with them to the ship by US Navy helicopter the same evening to continue flying next day.

The tenth and last patrol included bombardment spotting for *Birmingham* on a coastal village south of Chodo Island. *Birmingham* managed to get very near the village after four ranging shots, but this was to be expected as the range was only seven miles.

On 27 October we went on a dawn lorry hunt, with 2 × 500 lb bombs and without wing tanks, (as wind speed was insufficient for anything heavier off the catapult at that time in the morning) looking for headlights in the area Hanchon – Cinnampo, west of Pyongyang, about 20 miles inland from the coast. The timing of the take-off from *Ocean* was critical as the aim was to arrive over our target just as the dawn sky was lightening. This limited amount of light would be sufficient to see the ground and see ourselves, but still sufficiently dark for us to pretend to the enemy we were not there so that he would not dim his lorry lights or reach for his guns and we could still see them to aim at them with our bombs.

When crossing the coast on the way to the target, Lt Tim Adkin, RNVR, my number 3, came up on the radio and suggested his pair – i.e., himself and Lt 'Pug' Mather – should have a go at some headlights of lorries he had seen below. I told him to 'peel off' and tell the shore radio he was doing so. (The shore radio station, 70 miles south, would not have received Adkin's message as he was, by that time, at too low an altitude and his VHF transmission would have been screened. I do not think that either of us realised this at the time.) I then told Adkin that I and Buxton (RNVR), would continue up north to our briefed target area and would make our own back to the ship.

Still in almost pitch darkness, at about 2000 feet above high ground, about 30 miles north of Chinampo, I watched the ground for lorry headlights. At last I saw some on a hill top about two miles ahead. I and Buxton immediately dived together, unloaded our bombs and turned for home as we had to be back by 0530 and we had already used nearly half our fuel. Buxton kept in visual contact with me by silhouetting me against the dawn sky. None of the head-lights were visible when we turned back, so they had at least heard us!

I could not raise Tim Adkin or Mather on the VHF radio (it transpired that he was at low level and thus screened from us) so I went over to the rescue fre-quency as I had heard someone mention the word 'trouble' in a very indistinct transmission. Climbing up to 6,000 feet where I could contact Rescue at Chodo about 60 miles south, I gave them what I thought was Adkin's last known position. Luckily another Sea Fury strike led by Lt Davis was crossing that piece of coast at the time and he heard my call and went to the position I had given Chodo, telling them and myself what he intended to do.

Tim Adkin then told us the news that it was 'Pug' Mather who had been hit by AA and had baled out and that he (Tim) was circling overhead. The posi-tion I had given must have been quite near Mather as he was joined by Lt Davis' four Furies, six Fireflies and eventually by two RESCAP Corsairs, sent up from Chodo. The US rescue helicopter set course at the same time as the Corsairs, arriving about half an hour after. The USN S.51 immediately landed and picked up Mather who was, by this time, getting more than anxious as the growing daylight had revealed some approaching enemy guerrillas. Mather's position turned out to have been about 15 miles north of Taedong Gang estuary, and roughly where I had left Tim Adkin.

I found out on landing aboard after this trip that 'Pug' Mather had had some excitement the day before as well. He had force-landed at Paengyong-do with engine trouble!

As if to complete Mather's misfortunes, he was shot down again three months later when operating from *Glory* in 801 Squadron, having been hit by a 76mm shell. He was not so lucky this time, being taken prisoner. (Please refer to John R.P. Landsdown's book – *With the Carriers in Korea* – for the full story of his capture and subsequent treatment by the communists as a PoW.) Apparently, the helicopter sent from Chodo was unable to find Mather and to make matters worse, one of the RESCAP Fury pilots died when he crashed into a snow-covered hillside in cloud, nearby. Neither could Ted Anson, Mather's number 2, do a thing to help for he had apparently lost sight of Mather after he had seen him bale out. Mather spent the next eight months as a PoW. Although he survived in reasonable health, he looked 'absolutely awful' when he was at last released with thousands of others in September 1953, some two months after the signing of the peace treaty itself. He had been told that he would be given leniency (i.e., not summarily executed) pro-vided he took advantage of: 'the opportunity he would be given to reach a state of remorse and repentance for his crimes'. As this was the sort of treat-ment which Mao's 'officials' meeted out to many of their own people in civil life in China who had disobeyed the communist rules, it should not perhaps come as a big surprise.

The ship returned to Sasebo by 4 November and after refuelling there we set sail for Hong Kong and peace. There we exercised *Glory*'s 801 and 821

Squadrons' strike capabilities in exercise TA PAN before they set off for *Glory*'s third session off Korea, taking four of 802's RNVR pilots with her. A feature of our arrival in Hong Kong was Charles Evans' using a few of our aircrafts' slipstream on the flight deck to turn the ship round in harbour rather than using the tugs, in an operation which came to be known as 'pinwheel'.

Those of us taking our aircraft ashore to refuel during our flying exercise with *Glory* had to land at Hong Kong's main airfield. In those days it was very small with a right-handed approach down a steep incline. A few feet below our approach path we could see a thousand upturned faces in the narrow streets as we descended to sea level on the very short runway. A 'run ashore' after work was a marvellous experience, using rickshaws as transport, going into the Chinese quarters and sampling their cut-price food and drink, seeing private enterprise working at its primitive best before the huge building programmes had started and before western technology had begun to take over. We were encouraged to visit the yacht club where I found my request for a loan of a Swallow sailing yacht included a spare Chinese crew – if needed – with the boat held alongside for Tim Adkin and I to step daintily aboard, the boat's sails ready hoisted and it pointing in the desired direction. The ship's tailors – F.C. Khoo and Co – had by this time finished a suit I, and many others, had ordered while in the Yellow Sea at a price one fifth of Savile Row's best. It fitted perfectly and I still wear it today, 43 years later. The ship's tailor was referred to as 'Jelly Belly'. He and his Chinese staff worked a few inches above the ship's keel in an ill-lit, watery and grey-steel environment with the shattering noise of the ship's screws turning a few feet from their hand-operated Singer sewing machines. It said much for the Chinese on board *Ocean* that they could produce such beautifully made clothes in such primitive conditions – did it not?

We then set sail for Malta, via Singapore and Suez, arriving there on 4 December. *Ocean* again used Sea Furies to manoeuvre into Grand Harbour but some were badly overheated – having to run their engines at high power while pointing downwind on the flight deck – and these had to be put ashore for repair. Numbers 802 and 825 Squadrons then walked on board *Theseus* for the journey home to UK. *Theseus* had already done seven months of patrols off Korea from September 1950 to April 1951 and during this time she had won the Boyd Trophy for carrying out 150 sorties in one day. (She had also achieved a thousand successive accident-free decklandings). *Ocean* had equalled this sortie record and she also received the trophy – for the year 1952. (The silver trophy was a model of a Swordfish and was presented to the pilot or squadron which had achieved the finest feat of naval aviation during the previous year and was in memory of Admiral Sir Dennis Boyd, KCB, CBE, DSC, one of the FAA's fighting Admirals).

Our Squadron disbanded on arrival in UK on 10 December and I see from a copy of the 'flimsey' that Charles Evans wrote for me that I had done 76 sorties from *Ocean*, 57 of which were over Korea.

The signing of the armistice in Panmunjon on 27 July 1953 had brought the fighting to an end. The FAA had flown about 23,000 sorties, the 70 RN and Commonwealth ships taking part had fired about 150,000 rounds of ammunition and had steamed about two million miles while doing it. Twenty-eight RN officers and 45 Ratings had been killed or were missing. In spite of the self-imposed limitations set upon us in the air war, targets, such as they were, were insatiable and demanded continuous flying effort on the part of FAA aircrew – unlike the more dangerous but much more rewarding requirements of WW 2 which tended to come only in separate operations with large gaps in between. The conspicuous role played by the Commonwealth Colossus class Light Fleet carrier force in co-operation with the USN, and the almost entire absence of the RAF, re-stated the case for a strong FAA. But in spite of this, *Glory* was scrapped in 1961 and *Theseus* and *Ocean* in 1962. They were but three of the 80 carriers which had, by that time, been sent to the breakers since the end of the war.

The Russians' puppet leader – Kim Il Sung – has continued to rule North Korea in strict communism for the past 40 years. North Korca is probably the only communist state which remains an enemy of democracy. There is even a suspicion that it is now about to develop its own supply of A-bombs. The war in Korea may not be over yet and we may be required again some time in the future!

CHAPTER 8

DECK LANDING AND THE CATAPULT

Before continuing with the narrative, this might be the time to include a brief description of the improvements in flight deck operations which the advent of the jet aircraft had made essential in aircraft carriers.

Some of the skills needed

When assessing skill requirements for naval aviators, that required for deck-landing must still be amongst the most exacting, sometimes demanding a boldness beyond the call of duty. The ability to carry out 'spot landings' made with 'three-point' touch-downs in tailwheeled aircraft has usually been taken as a sign of a good pilot. Decklandings are routine 'spot landings', but with frequent unpractised difficulties added – such as poor visibility, a pitching deck, a damaged or malfunctioning engine or flight control system or fuel shortage – very few of which can be foreseen or practised beforehand.

For safe deck-landings to be guaranteed for all except nosewheeled aircraft, in addition to directional and rate-of-descent accuracy, the most demanding requirement must be speed control to within very few mph of the engine-off stall. American naval aircraft in WW 2 – such as the Corsair, Hellcat and Avenger – were purposely equipped with large landing flaps set at large angles to the airflow. Not only could the wing then produce high lift at low speeds but the engine rpm could be kept high on the approach, and the propeller in fine pitch, to impart extra slipstream lift the instant it was desired. Control of the airspeed to within very narrow limits could thus be attained. In the case of the Seafire, none of these design advantages were available. This beautifully slim, drag-free aircraft could best be semi-glided in to land at an airspeed well above the stall or 'three-point-attitude' and on a straight approach to its grass airfield, with the pilot able to see over the nose for most of the way in. Decklanding the Seafire, on the other hand, required a 'nose-up', curved approach, with the turn steep enough to allow the pilot to see through his port exhaust efflux and catch sight of a frantic batsman on the edge of a tiny deck-space about 200 feet long and 90 feet wide, ending in a formidable wire barrier. To allow such a beautiful flying machine to settle on its three points within its low structural limit of seven ft/sec and to limit its desire to leap sky-wards and float over the six arrester wires, the pilot needed to control his air-speed to plus-or-minus two knots at an approach speed centred around 1.05 Vse (Vse='engine-on stall speed' for the Seafire L III which was 63 knots at normal weights). Then, on receiving the signal from the batsman to 'cut', the loss of slipstream lift over the wing would promote a gentle 'engine-off' (Vs) stall – which occurs in most propeller driven aircraft about five knots above its Vse – so making it reasonably certain that his Seafire (which in any case had additional stability problems compared with the Spitfire which are mentioned elsewhere in this book) would stay down and catch an arrester wire in the one and a half seconds of flying time still available before it hit the barrier.

Most of us would not attempt to glance inside the cockpit to see the airspeed indicator's needle quivering round the 63–65 knot mark – which was half a needle's width on the dial – but would keep our eye on the carrier's centreline and the batsman's frantic signals, using the nose angle to the horizon as a gauge of our attitude/airspeed.

From 1948 to 1954 – the difficulties of operating jet aircraft from aircraft carriers, their higher landing speeds, their slower take-off acceleration, their quadruple weight increase for less endurance and their poor speed control on the landing approach – would have led to the end of all carrier aviation if it had not been for three British inventions – the angled deck, the mirror/projector landing sight and the steam-powered catapult.

To advance a few more years to the 1959 position, the problem of speed control on the decklanding approach for jet-powered aircraft was solved by the addition of large airbrakes – which maintained high engine rpm and so allowed high BLC energy to lower stall speeds by up to 15 knots and allowed the engine to operate where smaller throttle openings gave larger power increases – plus various devices which limited the possibility of engine compressor stall if the pilot required rapid throttle opening on the approach. The best example of these aircraft improvements was the Blackburn Buccaneer. Its huge airbrakes behind the rudder were extended fully for landing, the extra drag being overcome by use of very high engine rpm not only giving high BLC pressures but also giving the jet engine the same instant power response to small throttle movements as from a constant speed prop-jet or piston/prop engine. Speed control was thus made simple in the Buccaneer, perhaps the easiest-ever aircraft to deckland in the 1960s if all the other modern aids and the advantages of its nose-wheel layout were taken into account as well.

The difficulties of decklanding the Seafire during WW 2 led to many caustic comments by the admirals-in-charge, but such was its excellence in the air – if properly directed by our own radar – that pilots' morale did not suffer much, even after the allied landings at Salerno and Anzio where lack of windspeed over the decks of the 'Woolworth' carriers involved caused more Seafire decklanding casualties than these marvellous fighters could inflict on the enemy. However, by the time *Implacable*'s 48 Seafires had arrived in the Pacific and had carried out their first operation against Truk on 14–15 June 1945, the Seafire had an equal or better decklanding record than the Firefly and, with 90 gallon drop tanks, could go as far and at a greater speed towards the enemy on its ground attack duties as the Corsair and Hellcat.

Up to 1949, the take-off from a carrier – whether by catapult or by a free run up the deck – had been simple. In the case of the Seafire, use of a catapult was not necessary in our thirty-knot carriers owing to the Seafire L IIIs very high power/weight ratio. For us the routine – after the usual cockpit checks and warm-up – was 'chocks away', taxy to within about 250 feet of the carrier's bow and open the throttle when the green flag dropped. The tail could be raised almost immediately to allow a view over the nose and, in full right rudder was not enough to prevent the usual Seafire IIIs swing to the left, power could be reduced until the rudder became fully effective. About half-a-pound pullforce was required on the stick to climb away after leaving the bow. We knew that once committed to a take-off there was no turning back and we trusted entirely in the work of our groundcrew that nothing would go wrong.

We formed up in fours, eights or sixteens and proceeded to our target. The first to take-off would climb straight ahead for two minutes. The leader – usually the first off the deck – would then turn 180 degrees left and fly down the port side of the ship at a pre-arranged form-up height and speed, collecting the remainder of his flight who could cut the corner to join up with him.

After a couple or three hours we would return, find the right carrier and circle it in fours and wait with twenty or thirty others for the fleet to turn into wind. The moment it began to do so we had to judge our circuit so that we would land 20–30 seconds behind the man ahead. In addition to the usual cockpit checks we had to remember to drop the arrester hook, tighten our harness, disconnect our dinghy, lower the undercarriage, open and lock the hood, raise our seat, select fine propeller pitch, select rich mixture, check two greens on the undercarriage and a single green for the arrester hook position indicators, check brake pressure, loosen off throttle friction, lower flaps as the speed dropped to 85 knots or so, open radiator, call 'downwind' on the radio after changing to the landing frequency, trim nose-up elevator and right rudder bias to offset torque, and, if any time remained, to count our beads. (We would normally use a simple memory code such as TUMPH. These letters would stand for Trim, Undercarriage, Mixture, Pitch, Hook, Hydraulics, etc.)

On 'finals' we reduced speed still further to fly our Seafires at 1.05 Vse on a curved approach, hoping not to meet too much turbulence over the round-down which might ruin all our efforts to straighten up over the deck centreline – this after three hours of sweating in the air and perhaps after two earlier trips starting at 0430 that morning.

The Americans used a different approach path to ourselves when deckland-ing their 'purpose-built' aircraft. They approached in level flight to within about 200 feet of the carrier's stern at a height corresponding to about 50 feet above flightdeck level. On receiving the 'cut' sign from the batsman the sudden loss of slipstream lift (much greater than in the British descending approach) plus the increased drag of American-designed aircraft, immedi-ately slowed the aircraft to a speed below its engine-off stall speed and it rapidly descended in its three-point attitude to the deck without exceeding its vertical velocity limit of about 12 ft/sec. There was never any confusion between the batsman and pilot as to who might be to blame for any accident as the American batsman's signals were advisory and not mandatory like the British.

The three-point touchdown is of great importance when landing aircraft with tailwheels. No amount of 'long-stroke oleos', fully absorbant hydraulics or high pressure tyres can prevent an aircraft from leaping into the air again if there is suffficient lift still on the wings. It can be shown that if an aircraft – whether tailwheel or nosewheel – can be landed so that *the first wheels to touch are aft of the aircraft's CG*, provided it is allowed to flop onto the remainder of its undercarriage, *it will not bounce*. (To this end, the Chance-Vought Corsair had its tailwheel strut lengthened by a foot so that the first wheel to touch would be the tailwheel even if the aircraft itself was not yet at stalling incidence. This modification made the Corsair acceptable to the US Marines and so saved it for our 'lease-lend' programme along with the thousands of Avengers and Hellcats, making it possible for our Navy to take a full part in the Pacific war.)

However, if a *tailwheel* aircraft is landed mainwheels first – which are forward of the CG – the tailwheel will go on going down and this will *increase* the 'angle of attack' of the wings and it will take-off again in the ground effect, even if it is only a few knots above the stall speed. This will result in the 'float-float-float – *prang*' sequence.

Likewise if any *nosewheel* aircraft is, somehow, landed *nosewheel first*, it being forward of the CG, the aircraft will immediately go nose-up, increase its lift and take-off again. This is somewhat difficult to do, for nosewheel struts are designed of such a length as to allow the aircraft to flop forward after mainwheels' touchdown. In doing so, incidence and therefore lift, is much reduced or removed altogether and the aircraft stays down – with the pilot immediately able to apply brakes if needed without risking a 'nose-over' and able to apply directional control through a steerable nosewheel.

All of us at 'C' Squadron at Boscombe had already landed a Vampire on a carrier at speeds between 1.1 and 1.2 Vs – between 10–20 knots *above* the Vampire's stalling speed – and without the slightest difficulty in engine control, speed control or bounce. However, the much higher approach speeds needed for jet aircraft having higher wing loadings required the pilot to maintain his view of the deck continuously as there was no time for him to lower his gaze to glance at his airspeed indicator in the cockpit, for this caused considerable disorientation. More assistance was therefore required than the mere fitting of a 'head-up' airspeed indicator display (which the author invented while at Shorts in 1949).

Jet engine handling and the difficulties which had to be overcome
Jet engine power response without a propeller was much slower than in piston engines. The latter required little or no engine speed-up, for it was normally within the constant-speed propeller rpm range. Power increases were therefore transmitted straight to the propeller which immediately coarsened off its pitch to absorb it and not only thrust the air rearwards at an instantly increased speed but gave extra lift to the wings as it flowed past them. Jet engine power response is very different. The jet exhaust extends over a much smaller area

than a prop slipstream so that it has to be thrust rearwards at a much greater velocity. Large rpm increases are necessary, particularly at low-power settings, to produce any significant power increases which can suddenly be required in a typical decklanding 'wave-off.' Likewise on reducing power, the jet applies no instant drag to slow the aircraft as does a 'constant-speed' propeller-driven aircraft. In a jet engine, only the top 25 per cent of rpm produce large power increases. There is also a very large rpm range to speed up and slow down – say, from about 4,000 'idling' rpm to 12,000 rpm.

When decklanding, throttle movements are continuous and sometimes urgent. In the early jets, trouble usually started whenever a jet pilot opened his throttle too fast. The sudden surge of fuel igniting in the combustion chambers caused a huge increase in gas pressure whose exit through the jet pipe was largely obstructed by the slow-turning turbine rotors. This high-pressure gas, keen to make its exit somehow, would either stall the turbine blades – thus ensuring a reduction of rpm rather than an increase – or try to get out forwards through the compressor, appearing as flame from the intake. This process might be repeated in a series of 'bangs' – known as 'surging'. The pilot could only recover engine power by closing the throttle completely and starting again.

Eventually, auto-restrictors were introduced in the throttle linkage which governed fuel increase demands to what the engine could handle at the time. Variable-pitch compressor stators were also introduced so that higher pressures due to overfuelling would not stall any stages in the 'multi-stage' compressor turbines.

Some further advantages of nosewheels

There are one or two further advantages that nosewheel aircraft have over those fitted with tailwheels. With more and more single-runway landing grounds being provided for commercial use, crosswind landings are becoming frequent. If a crosswind landing is made in a tailwheel aircraft and the aircraft touches down without the pilot having corrected the necessary yawed approach to the runway by the required amount of 'last-minute' rudder, the tailwheel aircraft will tend to weathercock and swing into wind and off the runway. Tailwheel locks can help, but in strong crosswinds, even the use of full rudder and brake cannot always correct a swing into wind. If a swing begins and sidewise inertia is not immediately checked by action with brakes and rudder, the tailwheel aircraft will tend to tighten in the turn and 'ground-loop' like any motor car. However, in the case of the nosewheel aircraft, its CG is forward of its main landing wheels and any tendency it may have to swing off the runway will be immediately corrected by the 'positive' sidewise inertia straightening the aircraft up again. Not only does the CG position stabilise the direction of the landing run, but nosewheel steering can often be used and full brake applied – consistent with overheating – without fear of a nose-over. Faced with all the advantages from a nosewheel layout, it seems all the more unfortunate that Joe Smith – Supermarine's Chief Designer – had to design the Navy's first jet fighter, the Attacker, with a tailwheel, against the advice of his Chief Test Pilot.

A disadvantage of jet nose-wheeled aircraft was soon discovered to be the extra landing run they required ashore. The extra expense of providing longer runways worldwide was avoided in all naval airfields by the installation of runway arrester gear which could be quickly rigged whenever a naval aircraft had brake failure, flap failure or some other defect. By lowering its hook – using its emergency release gear if necessary – it could guarantee pulling up in time without damage. Chain Arrester Gear (CHAG) was rigged at all naval airstations from the early war years, making use of redundant anchor cable attached to each end of four wires stretched across the 'duty' runway whenever required. The next improvement – to cater for much higher arresting energy requirements as landing speeds and aircraft weights increased – was to attach the wire ends to pistons sliding up long pipes filled with water. The wire pulled the piston up the pipes, squirting water through exit holes drilled in the pipes, the number of holes remaining automatically reducing as the speed of the aircraft reduced during its landing run. This gear was known as Waterspray Arrester Gear (SPRAG) and was permanently rigged at all Naval airfields. Changi airfield near Singapore was one of a few RAF airfields overseas rigged with SPRAG on its single, 8,000 ft runway, and allowed Naval jets in the Far East to make use of the adjoining Malayan jungle for low-flying exercises and for LABS bombing and rocketing practice (for a description of LABS see Chapter 9). The final answer arrived in the sixties in the form of 'Purpose-use Arrester Gear' (PUAG). This was a permanent part of all naval airfield's furniture and so allowed the Navy to use small airfields worldwide which could not accommodate high performance land-based aircraft having no arrester hooks.

Some changes in flight deck machinery

The only class of carrier to see much operational service immediately after the war had ended was the Colossus class of Light Fleet Carriers used off Korea from 1950 to 1953. These mostly employed the Firefly and the excellent Sea Fury. The latter had a structural weight limit of 14,650 lb at take-off. The only factor effecting its use at this weight was whether it could get enough flying speed at take-off, either from the ship's catapult or with the assistance, on a free take-off, of RATOG. (Rocket Assisted Take-Off Ground.) Once it was safely airborne and climbing away, there were no handling problems and if it were 'jumped' by enemy fighters *en route* to its ground attack target, if given sufficient radar/radio warning to allow it to gather speed and height after jettisoning its load of bombs and rockets, it could perform as an interceptor/fighter once more. It was a single-role aircraft, only able to carry out an additional role because of the 'external' power assistance at take-off from the carrier's catapult, the only time in the whole flight that it would need it.

Catapult launches in the 'tail-down' mode in the Sea Fury were – unlike the early Buccaneer – safe and easy. All the pilot had to do was to ensure that the stick did not move backwards at the moment of 'squirt.' He could do this by holding the flat of his hand against the back of the stick and wedging his elbow in front of his waist. The stick or hand could not then move very far backwards during the 4 G catapult acceleration as it was prevented by the elbow wedge, just as the pilot's head was restrained by the headrest and his legs by the foot rests on the rudder bars. The same precaution was necessary with the left hand. The throttle friction nut was fully 'wound up' – so that the throttle lever would not come back and close the throttle on its own. Likewise, the flat of the pilot's left hand was held behind it so that he should not grasp the throttle lever itself and inadvertently pull the throttle rearwards. The pilot also pressed his head hard back against the headrest and sometimes 'squeezed' his breath to ensure blood-flow to the retina during the horizontal 'G' forces.

Catapult and RATOG trials ashore were carried out to test the strength and positioning of the various strop fixtures and 'holdback' attachments. A small mistake in the vertical positioning of either could result in the thrust from the RATOG or catapult imparting a nose-up or nose-down pitching moment to the aircraft as it left the deck and so cause the pilot to lose control. When Lt Clark crashed following his unaccustomed RATOG (he suffered no injury and was picked up by helicopter two minutes later) the stick may have moved aft accidentally pulling the nose up as it did so or the elevator circuit in his Sea Fury was not properly mass-balanced. Perhaps the cause of his pitch up and crash into the sea might have been due to the out-of-balance forces caused by a slight change in the *vertical* position of the Sea Fury's CG when loaded with wing bombs and with less internal fuel than normal. Then perhaps Clark may have been partially 'blacked out' at the time due to the high and long-sustained *horizontal* 'G' forces in a RATOG take-off starving the blood supply to his retinas. (There was a suspicion that such G forces tended to starve the retina and the front brain of blood supply, causing semi-blindness and semi-consciousness unless the blood was 'compressed' by the pilot applying temporary lung pressure. Some time later, Surgeon Lieutenant Ellis at the School of Aviation Medicine at Farnborough tried to investigate this phenomenon while travelling along a small 'homemade' railway track assisted by some spare RATOGS, much to the delight of the rest of the doctors there. Whatever the real cause of Clark's crash, it shows the risks involved when large external forces are applied to flying machines of any sort and the high standards of design skill required to foresee and overcome them before they are used in anger.

Eleven Colossus class carriers were completed between 1945 and 1953. These ships could do no more than 24 knots and their BH 11 air/hydraulically powered catapults' 'end-speeds' were little better than the wartime Fleet carriers', giving but 66 knots shuttle speed with aircraft weighing 20,000 lb or less. Although faster through the water than the Woolworth's 18½ knots such as *Biter* or *Dasher*, the Colossus class were slower than the next class of Light Fleets (i.e., the four Centaur class which operated from early 1955–1965) which did 27 knots. These, in turn, were slower than the four Audacious or

Eagle class of armoured Fleet Carriers which could do 31 knots. This class, which included the rebuilt ex-WW II *Victorious*, was conceived as a 'follow-on' to the late wartime Implacable class. At least two of the Eagle/Audacious class were operational at one time or another from 1952 when *Eagle* was commissioned, until 1970, by which time she was operating the F-4K Phantom, Buccaneer S2s, and Gannet AEW3s for the two years before her final paying off in January 1972.

Ark Royal's entry into service had been delayed until February 1955 to allow inclusion of a five-degree angled deck, a mirror sight and two steam catapults. Twin projector sights with gyro stabilisation were added in her 1959 refit, replacing reflected light from a single source. This greatly increased the power and range of the sight in poor visibility conditions. In 1966 the 'Ark' replaced her first set of steam catapults with longer and more powerful ones capable of launching the Phantom F-4K at a weight of 50,000 lb in zero natural wind in the tropics. By 1974 the latest American carriers could launch their magnificent variable-sweep F-14 Tomcats with their more powerful engines and armed with heatseeking Sidewinders, 'fire-and-forget' Phoenix missiles with a 100 mile range plus other stores and fuel adding up to a total take-off weight of 68,000 lb, of which 28,000 lb was useful load. The *Ark* was the most powerful British carrier up to the time of her death in 1978. Her catapult was similar in performance to the minimum required from all American Navy Fleet Carriers.

Returning for a moment to the 1950s, even before the arrival of jet aircraft, the important feature for satisfactory operation of piston-engined fighters in the ground attack role had been the carrier having sufficient catapult power capable of giving heavily loaded aircraft sufficient 'end-speed' in low wind conditions. The carrier's speed through the water was of great importance. Thus the 'Woolworth' carriers were almost useless in the Mediterranean in hot, calm conditions in the war as their speed through the water was insufficient to create a high enough windspeed over the flight deck to make deck-landings and take-offs safe.

In the 1950s, the Sea Fury could be catapulted quite comfortably from the large Fleet Carriers' catapults at its maximum weight of 14,650 lb in calm wind conditions because they could give the aircraft a vital few knots extra wind speed with their 31 knots through the water. (On Buccaneer Mark 2 trials, the *Ark* did 33 knots – using some boilers normally reserved for electrical generating. However, this was at the cost of increasing Ark's fuel consumption by a factor of three at 25 knots.) But when catapulted from Light Fleet Carriers of the Colossus class capable of only 24 knots – and that with all available steam going to the ship's turbines – between ten and fifteen knots of natural wind was needed to make sure the Sea Furies had about 105 kts 'on the clock' at the end of their catapult run. This was because the catapult could only accelerate an aircraft of this weight to 66 knots by the time it had reached the end of its run. When a natural windspeed of at least 15 knots was not blowing over the water, a rocket-assisted free take-off (RATOG) was necessary. This reduced take-off time between aircraft but required them to be ranged aft from where they could take the whole 600-foot deck-length to accelerate, using the additional acceleration from four rockets which the pilot fired at a point in the take-off run just aft of the island. When RATOG was used at short notice in this way, the accident rate increased and RATOG was unpopular with the pilots.

It is extraordinary to note that a mere 15 knots of extra wind over a flight deck could allow a 50 per cent increase in a Sea Fury's offensive load. We can appreciate the workings of the V-squared law even better by watching a swan trying to get airborne in a flat calm compared with his performance with five knots of natural wind blowing over the water. A swan can get airborne with an airspeed of 20 knots. In zero wind over the pond, he will need double the take-off run – and perhaps four times the effort – in getting airborne than if he had the benefit of taking off into a five-knot wind. This is because the extra five knots would double the lift available at the time his 'water-speed' had reached the exhausting speed of 15 knots (when his foot-thrust becomes less effective) and this extra lift would have allowed him to leave the water and climb away in half the distance he would have needed if the wind had been a flat calm.

We can thank those engineer/test pilots of the 1950s for being the first to realise that the extra take-off thrust necessary to get an overloaded jet or piston-engined fighter airborne could be more efficiently supplied by ship's power than by the fighter itself. Why carry around huge additional flaps, increased wing areas, heavier structures, November-the-fifth RATOG attachments and associated strengthening when these would only be required for a few seconds of every flight when operating in the fighter-strike role? Ship's power is *steam* power and this was logically chosen to replace hydraulic reservoirs and RATOG as the source of catapult power.

To test the practicability of launching 'overloaded' fighters during the 1950s, the US Navy propelled an over-loaded wartime Corsair to its 150 knot take-off speed from a 350-foot, on-shore, catapult driven by the inertia energy obtained from a huge flywheel speeded up for five minutes by a Wright Cyclone engine! By 1957 they had substituted this with their TC-7 – a scaled-up version of the brilliant British steam-powered design first tested in HMS *Perseus* in August 1951. The TC-7, used in the USS *Forrestal* by 1961, was capable of accelerating a 42,000-lb aircraft to 150 knots in zero wind, some 20 knots faster than the equivalent British steam catapult in *Ark Royal* at that time.

By 1953, all American CVs were being designed with a catapult power sufficient for their aircraft to be 'squirted off' in harbour in *zero* wind conditions with enough fuel on board for them to reach the local naval air station ashore. In 1952 the US Navy laid keels for two more 50,000-ton attack carriers. These had four deck-edge lifts, a 8–10-degree angled deck to allow overshoots without a barrier and four steam catapults fitted with jet efflux deflectors to allow launches at the same time as landings and allowing eight aircraft to be launched per minute. From 1952–1964, the USN built six more carriers with

Aotearoa, a Short's Solent Mark IV, beached during tropical trials at Khartoum to repair the port float in July 1949.

We had full confidence in our Short's Solent IV aircraft and its auto-pilot!

Above: The prototype Short's Sealand amphibious aircraft seen landing in 1949.

Opposite top: A Short's Solent Mark II taxying on Belfast Loch in 1950.

Opposite bottom: The Short's Sturgeon Mark II.

Below: A Hellcat being armed prior to take-off some time during 1944.

One of 802 Squadron's Sea Fury XIs over Korea in August 1952.

RAF Manby in November 1953.

The air starter is plugged into a Wyvern S4.

The author in a Wyvern S4 in 1955. Note the jet exhaust above the wing root.

HMS *Eagle* entering Gibraltar.

Wyverns of 813 Squadron during rough weather aboard HMS *Eagle* in the winter of 1955.

Wyverns stacked neatly at the stern of HMS *Eagle*.

The RN historic flight – a Firefly V, a Swordfish and a Sea Fury X.

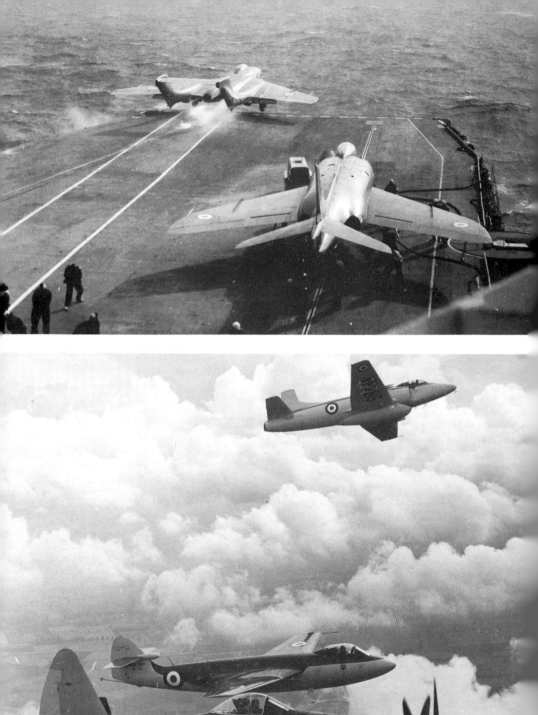

Above: A Gannet AEW takes to the air without catapult assistance.

Left: A Sea Vixen is catapulted from the deck of HMS *Eagle* during carrier trials in July 1957. A Scimitar is shown in the foreground with its deck crew in attendance.

Left: An Attacker shows clearly its 90-gallon belly fuel tank as it pulls away from a Sea Hawk and a Wyvern.

Below: This photograph was taken during DH110 carrier trials on board HMS *Ark Royal* in 1956. It shows the tail-down catapult launch arrangements.

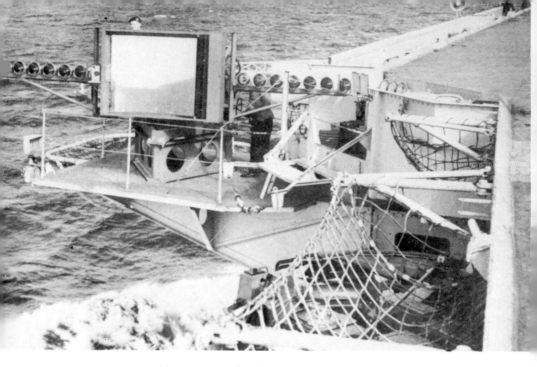

The port mirror in HMS *Albion*. It can be raised or lowered and is gyro-stabilised in pitch and roll. Datum lights are green. Source lights shining into the mirror are 160 feet aft of the mirror position.

A Scimitar with four long-range fuel tanks and flight refuelling probe launching from HMS *Ark Royal*.

A Scimitar takes the barrier before the invention of the angled deck made this unnecessary.

The author and Lt Coleman climbing out of XK527 after their arrival in the Buccaneer at Hal Far to start deck trials. 3 November 1960.

Buccaneer Mark I deck trials on 28–30 August 1961 aboard HMS
Hermes in Lyme Bay. Buccaneer XK529 is shown on the flight deck.

HMS *Hermes* at speed as a Buccaneer prepares for take-off during
deck trials in Lyme Bay in 1961.

A Buccaneer alongside the trusted and faithful Swordfish. It is difficult to remember that there was only about 20 years between the biplane leaving service with the Fleet Air Arm and the arrival of the Buccaneer.

A line-up of the aircraft flown in the USA at the US Navy Test Center at Patuxent River in 1963. Shown from left to right are Lt-Cdr Nick Bennett, Dennis Higton, the host, Commander Powell, US Navy and the author. The aircraft in the background from left to right are an A4D Skyhawk, an A3J Vigilante and an F4 Phantom II.

The author, Dennis Higton and Nick Bennett in front of an F4H
Phantom II at Patuxent River in July 1962.

The handwritten message on the photograph reads:

Happy day's Mike, I guess you were clearing the Buccaneer on ARK in Feb 1963 when I arrived with this strange V/STOL animal. XP831 NOW sits in the new FLIGHT gallery Science Museum — proudly wearing the crest of Ark Royal.

All the best

Bill Bedford

"26.1.93 (THIRTY YEARS ON!)"

Inset top:
The "Flying Bedstead" was an early research vehicle employed in testing vertical take-off by use of vectored jet thrust. Here the Bedstead is seen in 1951.

The prototype of the Harrier arrives on the deck of *Ark Royal* in 1963. The message written on the photograph is as follows: 'Happy days Mike, I guess you were clearing the Buccaneer on *Ark* in Feb 1963 when I arrived with this strange V/STOL animal. XP831 now sits in the new Science Museum Flight Gallery – proudly wearing the crest of *Ark Royal*. All the best, Phil Bedford 26.1.93 (30 years on)'.

The third production A35-1/A-5A, number 146694 which the author
flew at Patuxent River on 10 July 1962.

The W2F Hawkeye in 1963 – and still in service with the US Navy.

even better performance and in the 1960s they commissioned the 80,000-ton nuclear-propulsion *Enterprise* having a crew of 4,600 and a complement of 85 aircraft.

Decklanding and catapulting machinery

The decklanding situation by 1949 was very worrying. The Navy had still not come out in favour of the nosewheeled aircraft for some obscure reason. Their solution to retain speed control on the decklanding approach and to secure adequate acceleration for deck take-offs was to retain the propeller as the driving force rather than the pure jet. Compared with prop-driven aircraft, the jet-engined decklander had none of the benefits of instant propeller drag or thrust on demand that came from the equally instant power response from a constant-speeding piston engine. Neither did a jet pilot have any extra lift from a jet's slipstream when he wished to go faster or recover from a stall. A jet's only advantage was its absence of engine-propeller torque effects when altering power rapidly (plus, of course, less vibration, less noise and much more power). But even these advantages were reduced in importance once the contra-prop Seafire 47 came into service in 1946. The 'straight' slipstream and the high thrust or drag when required from its contra-prop allowed a safe decklanding approach to be made at a speed of 1.07 Vs instead of the usual 1.05 Vse for the Seafire III. The Mark 47 would doubtless have remained the world's outstanding fighter for many years more had it been used in the Pacific war in sufficient numbers.

Supermarine's designers had still not hoisted in the decklanding benefits of a tricycle undercarriage by 1946. Aircraft such as the Short Sturgeon and – wait for it – the Blackburn Firebrand and the tailwheel Wyvern were still in the list of likely future aircraft required to deck land in all weathers, night and day. Wing-loadings were also increasing. By 1946, the Seafire's wingloading was 35 lb/sq/ft, Shorts' new A/S Mamba/prop/jet aircraft – named Seamew – was to be 38, and the prop/jet Wyvern was designed to be a frightening 57 lb/sq/ft.

Catapulting speeds would also have to increase if any of the new naval aircraft were to compete with the RAF weightlifters. Urgent need existed for catapult powers and 'end-speeds' to be increased. The normal maximum 'end-speed' for a type BH3 catapult was about 66 knots with a maximum aircraft weight of about 20,000 lb – e.g., a Hornet's weight. However, by 1949, to achieve the 100 knots *airspeed* necessary, a wind speed of 28 knots over the sea was a necessary addition before any of the post-war jet aircraft could operate at all from a carrier.

The next generation of British catapults – which would have to allow zero wind/harbour-launch capability to keep up with the American 1949 carrier design – had yet to put in an appearance. Luckily, we had Commander (E) C.C. Mitchell to invent the *steam catapult* for ourselves and the Americans. It was his invention – *the C 11–1 steam catapult* – using four times the energy over 211 feet, that allowed large jet-powered aircraft to continue to operate at all from any carrier after 1951. We also have to thank the CO of 703 Squadron – Jack Glaser – who was the first naval aviator ever to be squirted off a trial steam catapult in *Perseus* alongside Sydenham airfield in 1951.

So far as deck-landing aids were concerned, approach airspeeds had now risen from the 68 knots for the Seafire Mark 47 to 100 knots for the Wyvern/Hornet. (By 1963 they had risen to 140 knots in the McDonnell F-4 Phantom and night landings in these aircraft were controlled by 'approach-path compensator auto-throttles' automatically disconnected by 'weight-on-wheels' at touchdown and with its deck-landing approach airspeed – usually around 130 knots – continuously transmitted to the deck control officer throughout his approach.)

As wind-speed-over-the-deck minimum had remained the same at 20 knots (i.e., the economical speed of the carrier itself) the actual approach speed to the deck had therefore increased by nearly 100 per cent. But necessity is the mother of invention and another ETPS 'plumber-aviator' – Nick Goodhart – saw the need and invented the gyro-stabilised mirror sight which he further improved to the 'Projector Sight' by 1954.

Not only could the pilot now see the necessary deck-landing signals clearly but, far more important, the sight gave an instant and progressive image of where the pilot's aircraft was on the approach path and in what direction he had to fly to get back onto it if he strayed off it by a few feet. All the pilot had to do apart from keeping a straight approach path down the centre of the deck, was to adjust his height up or down to keep a central light in the 'mirror' level with two horizontal bars either side of it. The instant information from the mirror sight cut out the inevitable second's delay for a batsman to realise the pilot's error and for a further second's delay before the pilot could alter the approach path of his aircraft to conform with the batsman's wishes.

Speed control by throttle adjustment had become much more difficult with the jet engine. Assistance was soon forthcoming, however. Pilots were now given progressive, continuous *audio* signals of any required changes in airspeed on the approach through their radio earphones – higher/faster sounds for too high an airspeed and the reverse for speeds which were too slow. A steady medium-pitch tone would come through a pilot's earphones if his speed was correct.

Then, to compensate for weight alterations so that the pilot could retain the same, safe margin of airspeed above the stall, an incidence (or 'angle-of-attack') meter was placed in his easy line of vision in the cockpit with the 'safe' approach incidence clearly marked on its dial. This was an outstanding improvement – first fitted to the Phantom in 1962 – because it *compensated for any weight condition* at which the aircraft happened to be landing and, if the pilot was in a turning dogfight, he could immediately know how hard he could pull the stick back in a steep turn without reaching stalling incidence and getting out of control.

Then, in order to help the pilot retain this correct airspeed, the *'auto-throttle'* was invented. This 'automated' the necessary throttle movements on one of the two engines – in a 1970s Sea Vixen installation initially – to maintain an exact airspeed on the approach in order to allow the pilot to concentrate on other matters. This device was especially useful when landing at night or in poor visibility and when using radar homing and landing approach facilities.

Clear-view windscreens – essential in all aircraft where hoods could not be opened in flight – were also becoming available. They used hot jet efflux to clear both rain and ice formation – the earlier versions capable of cracking windscreens occasionally, too!

Perhaps the next most significant improvement to damage avoidance, deck-landing safety and ease of rapid carrier operations was the deletion of the crash barrier and the invention of the *angled deck*. In order to check the feasibility of this arrangement, British carriers were modified by stages, from a four-degree angle to start with, ending up with a full angle of eight or ten degrees. Apart from allowing overshoots if a mislanding occurred, the deck-landing pilot had no need to 'cut' engine power over the round-down, so avoiding delay in jet power application to go round again if he missed the wires. The eight-degree angle also allowed much more space forward on the flight deck so that catapulting, parking and refuelling with engines running could proceed at the same time as deck landings. The 'inventor' of the angled deck was Captain Dennis Campbell who was the Deputy Chief Naval Representative at the Ministry of Supply in 1951. He was assisted by Mr Lewis Boddington CBE who was Head of the Naval Air Department at RAE Farnborough. It was Boddington who forced the Admiralty to take notice of this brilliant invention and it was he who was mostly responsible for putting the idea into effect before the Americans.

The steam catapult was shown to the Americans as fitted in HMS *Perseus* in February 1952. This ship had already done 900 launches alongside at Sydenham and at sea, with 703 Squadron, the 'Service Trials Unit' under Jack Glaser, supplying the pilots. By 1953 the Americans had modified the USS *Antietam* which then operated such aircraft as the Douglas Skyraider, McDonnell F-2H2 Banshee, Grumman F-9F2-5 Panther and the Douglas F-3D Sky Knight. The US Navy said, at this time:

> Without the British, the steam catapult would not have been invented in time to save carrier aviation from extinction.

After landing on an angled-deck carrier, there was no danger of being 'attacked' by other aircraft if they missed the wires for their flight line took them clear of the foredeck. All we had to do on arrestment was to close throttles, stop engines by cutting fuel supply, engage nosewheel steering, retract flaps and arrester hook, select wingfold, open the hood and, when the chocks were in place, release the harness, check armament switches were 'safe' once more, turn off oxygen supply and cabin air-conditioning, climb down the ladder onto the flight deck and turn the aircraft over to our 'Plane Captain' engineer.

By 1962, the requirement to carry out all-weather day/night carrier aviation by fighters had further added to the hazards of deck-landing. By 1970, the smallest class of US Naval attack-class carriers – the Essex Class of 46,000 tons – were being replaced with 60,000–68,000 ton giants in order to operate the F-4s, the A-6 medium attack Intruder, the more powerful version of the F-14 and, by the 1980s – the still more powerful F/A-18 McDonnell Hornet strike fighter.

A night landing in a Crusader F-8E fighter would be semi-automatic. Auto-monitoring of 'angle-of-attack', approach path and airspeed was also relayed to the deck control officer by 'meatball' lights shining from the approaching aircraft. Engagement of the auto-throttle by the pilot was mandatory. Maintainance of this accurate approach path at the correct airspeed was ensured by gearing the F-8E's airbrakes/flaps/spoilers and throttle settings to the approach path requirements. The system worked so well that, by 1964, a Phantom, approaching at 140 knots could be made to catch number 3 wire five times out of five in weather conditions which would have made similar operational flying impossible from an airfield.

Had it not been for these important improvements in deck and aircraft operating aids in the 1950–1970s, large aircraft carrier operations in the jet age would probably have come to a halt as being far too hazardous and non-cost-effective compared with the use of landplanes. Whereas the US Navy has made full use of these inventions ever since, the Royal Navy were told in 1966 that they could no longer afford large aircraft carriers.

But hope was at hand. Lance Kiggell's observer at Taranto had been Dick Janvrin. The latter was Deputy Chief of Naval Staff at this fatal time in FAA history in 1966, and it was due to this brave airman's vigorous lobbying in arguing the Navy's case for continued air power that gave us the 'through-deck cruiser,' the first of which was *Invincible*.

A few years later, necessity was again the mother of invention and Doug Taylor gave us the 'ski-jump' method of launching the brilliant Harrier VSTOL fighters from *Invincible* with a useful load and without the need of a catapult or a long flight deck.

Meanwhile, the USN continued to develop the power of their steam catapults to the point where they could operate fighters in the strike role – by squirting them off in what would be a hopelessly overloaded condition for a fighter if a runway take-off was all that was available. The huge advantages of the catapult do not apply on a free, runway take-off. First, a runway take-off can never rely on at least thirty knots of windspeed to reduce the take-off run. Even if 3,000 yards was available, the runway speeds necessary during the latter part of a take-off run would increase the centrifugal forces on a fighter's tyres sufficient to whirl them off and cause serious damage to the aircraft – as occurred twice during 'still-air' Meteor 7 overload take-off trials at Boscombe Down in 1948.

The USN now has no need of purpose-built strike aircraft in its large carriers. They use the British inventions of the steam catapult, the 10-degree angled deck, the gyro-stabilised 'mirror' landing aid and the 'hands-off' catapult launch technique with the aircraft's auto-control 'fly-by-wire systems' in complete charge during the catapult run, until safe flying speed is attained. In fact, F-18 fighter pilots now have to be seen by the catapult control officer to be grasping two handholds above the cockpit coaming before he will give a green light for them to be launched. Once airborne they are immediately controlled by 'look-down' radar from a carrier-borne AEW aircraft – such as the Hawkeye – and have no need whatever for land-based aircraft support.

CHAPTER 9

PILOT'S NOTES

The author's next job after learning to be a sailor in *Loch Scavaig* was to be 'Officer-in-Charge' of RN Handling Section – attached to No. 4 RAF Squadron based at RAF Manby in Lincolnshire – writing 'Pilot's Notes.'

This was back to test flying with a Naval detachment of twelve ratings under the technical management of Chief Aircraft Artificer Derek Tunks. During the 20 months of this appointment which began in February 1953, this small detachment carried out the maintenance work on seven different types of aircraft. No. 4 Squadron RAF, attached to the Royal Air Force Flying College and Commanded by my boss – Squadron Leader L.J. Roxburgh AFM – had three RAF pilots and 30 RAF technicians, doing the same job over the same period for the RAF's five aircraft.

The succession of seven different Naval aircraft were as follows:

> the Seahawk F2 and FB3, the latter destined for seven Squadrons due to form from July 1954;
> the new Wyvern S4 with an Armstrong-Siddeley Python prop-jet engine destined for 813 Squadron due to form at RNAS Ford in three months time.
> the Sea Venom FAW20 due to enter service with 890 Squadron in March 1954;
> the Gannet AS Mark 1 due to enter operational service with 826 Squadron in January 1955;
> the Attacker FB 2 due to enter service with 803 and 800 Squadron aboard *Eagle* in January 1954;
> the Sea Vampire T 22 and about half-a-dozen other types.

The author was also able to fly the RAF's Sabre F-86, the Hunter 1 and the Canberra B 2, the introduction of the last two having been greatly accelerated by, but too late for, the start of the Korean war.

Way back in the '20s', flying safety standards and the finer points of how to fly new aircraft were largely left to pilots' private opinions, expressed over the bar in flying clubs or breathed tactfully into the ear of its owner. When an accident occurred in which the reason was not obvious, the pilot was seldom asked why or how it could be avoided in the future, for the chances were he did not know. As time went on and more complicated and expensive operational and auxiliary machinery were added to aircraft – resulting in dozens of new levers and switches in the cockpits of military aircraft – so the demand came for a standardised method of using them and setting limits and suggesting emergency procedures if they failed. There was even a demand for 'a standardised cockpit', with every lever, switch and instrument dial to be of the same shape and size and in the same relative position in all types of military aircraft.

The outcome was that in 1939 the Central Flying School of the RAF started 'Handling Flight' at Manby with the job of writing up a set of Pilot's Notes covering 'the handling behaviour and expected performance – including emergency procedures – for every type of aircraft in service'. The 'Notes' would also include a full description of its equipment, why, how and in what conditions it was to be used and how to correct it in the air if it failed – i.e., emergency procedures.

Engineers employed by RDT3 Department of the Ministry of Supply were responsible for Part 1 of the Notes – which was mainly engineering information. We were responsible for Parts 2, 3 and 4, dealing with Handling, Limitations and Emergencies. Although ATA pilots managed with a single card each for the fifty types they flew in the war which they attached to the instrument panel for easy reference in flight, by the late fifties we were beginning to see the future need for much more information than was possible in a 50-page notebook – or even in *Pilot's Notes General* (AP 2095) or in *The Pilot's Flying Manual* (AP129) – if we were to get the best out of new aircraft costing fifty times as much to build and operate and having speeds and power three or four times those experienced in 1939 when 'Pilot's Notes' was first started.

We had a good liaison with the scientists and engineers in RDT3 and we also kept in close touch with the manufacturers and to A&AEE at Boscombe Down. We were normally alloted the second or third production aircraft in a new type and, on arrival at Manby it would be given a thorough '30-hour' inspection by CPO Tunks before being taken into the air. The pilot responsible for the Notes would then put it through the entire 'flying envelope' likely to be required of it in service, keeping a diary of events and making separate reports, giving recommendations, facts and figures. Check flights might then be made by other members of the squadron if there were any points not ironed out by discussions on the ground. Finally, firms' test pilots would be brought in to the meetings held in the Ministry before draft copies of the Notes were made and the results sent to TF2 Dept for printing and distribution. The job of the Squadron at Manby did not end there. Any small changes in an aircraft's method of use and every modification and addition to its weaponry would require amendments to the Notes. These could involve interesting visits abroad and to the manufacturers which added much to the job's enjoyment.

The author was 'handed over' the job at Manby by Lt Frank Cawood who had been doing it for the past two years since completing No. 8 ETPS course and who was now joining a Sea Venom squadron as Senior Pilot.

The first job was to collect Wyvern S4 VX754 from RNAS Stretton. This was the fifth production aircraft from about 60 on order since October 1952. As it needed to have 'zero-length' rocket launchers fitted under the wings – which took a fortnight – the waiting period was spent gaining a bit of experience in the Attacker, Meteor 7, Venom NF 1, Provost, Avenger, Athena, Vampire T22 and the Mark 13 Meteor.

The Wyvern presented a considerable challenge to engineers and pilots alike. Not only was it the first single-engined prop-jet in the Navy – but it had a shocking history of engine/propeller and airframe failures which had already caused the death of five test pilots, one rating and two civilians. In addition to these tragedies there had been a further loss of eight Wyverns, in non-fatal crashes believed to have been caused by these design failures rather than by the pilots themselves.

Typical of these fatalities was the accident, on 15 October 1947, to Pete Garner (ETPS No. 4) who was flying the first prototype for Westlands and 'posing' for a publicity photo alongside a Naval Firefly. During this flight the Firefly pilot reported over the r/t to Yeovilton that he had seen the Wyvern's prop stop, then he had seen the aircraft enter a straight dive from which it had failed to fully recover before crashing into a field near Yeovil.

The cause of Pete's crash was failure of the contra-prop's 'translation' bearing. This 16-inch diameter contra-rotating, double ball-race not only has to cope with a three-ton propeller thrust but the large centrifugal forces and opposed gyroscopic forces of the 16-foot contra-rotating propellers. It also had to ensure that each of the $200 \times \frac{1}{2}$ in diameter steel ball bearings received copious amounts of lubrication throughout their highspeed journey round the grooves of this bearing. Derek Tunks sympathised with these ball bearings and imagined that it was when they got confused as to which way to go round that things could go wrong!

Failures of the Wyvern contra-props were probably due to inadequate lubrication in the extremely heavily loaded 'centrifugal' and gyro-stressed environment – particularly in high-G manoeuvres – within the ball races designed to 'translate' 4,000 hp turning at about 12,000 rpm to the propellers turning in opposite directions each at about an eighth of this speed.

Jeffrey Quill had suffered an identical failure in the Seafire 47's contra-prop, but had managed to retain sufficient thrust – at full throttle – to make an emergency landing at Middle Wallop. But Wyvern propellers were four times the size of the Seafire's contra-props and when their 'translation' ball-races seized through lack of lubrication, the results were catastrophic. The resultant huge drag from the propeller seizure required the pilot to dive steeply to retain flying speed. Unable to pull out in time – probably due to insufficient speed to cope with the G and the Wyvern's very high wingloading in addition to the 'blanketing' of the tail surfaces by the stationary propeller – Pete Garner's Wyvern hit the ground hard, the aircraft caught fire and he did not get out. This first prototype, with the Rolls-Royce 3500 hp Eagle piston engine, had no ejector seat. It is probable that Pete's harness release catch sheared on impact with the ground and that he hit his head on the gunsight, knocking himself out.

The Naval requirement for the Wyvern originated in the minds of DNAW in 1945 following a Naval pilot's adverse report on deck-landing the Vampire in December 1945. They preferred an aircraft with a propeller for their new

Torpedo/Fighter project to replace the Firebrand. The RAF soon lost interest in the prop-jet solution and, by early 1945 they had had enough experience with pure jets to realise that, particularly with afterburners, they alone would give sufficient power for all future military attack aircraft.

The Navy had persisted in its desire for a dual-purpose – or multi-role – prop-driven 'fighter/torpedo aircraft' capable of dropping a torpedo at enemy battleships into the bargain! This impossible dream – that of being able to design an aircraft for the strike role with it able to turn itself magically into a fighter once it had dropped its load on the enemy – may have had its origin when most of the brave Swordfish crews led by Lt/Cdr Eugene Esmonde VC had been shot down by Me 109s when attempting to torpedo the *Scharnhorst*, *Gneisenau* and *Prinz Eugen* before they could get into firing range. The remainder were then shot down by the same Me 109s on their way home as most of their Spitfire fighter escort had failed to find them as they had no radar direction.

So the first Wyvern Mark 1 piston-engined prototype with the 3,500 hp Eagle engine had been completed at Yeovil and flown from Boscombe Down by Harald Penrose – Westland's Chief Test Pilot – on 12 December 1946 – seven years before its final version arrived at Manby.

The Eagle-engined prototype's first flight was on 12 December 1946 from Boscombe Down with Pete Garner at the controls – seven years before the Python-engined version eventually arrived with us at Manby. Initial carrier trials were carried out in May 1948 in *Implacable* using TS 378, one of six Eagle-engined prototypes then flying. A prop-jet engine – the 4,300 hp Rolls-Royce RB-39 Clyde – was substituted for a short time, before the Python became available. This Admiralty decision was a wise move, for, like the Manchester bomber's Vulture engine (which was virtually a couple of Merlins placed one under the other and driving the same propeller shaft), the Eagle piston engine had already shown itself to be unreliable and had some poor design features. For instance, when Harald Penrose was flying the second prototype Mark 1 one day, *both* magnetos failed in the Rolls-Royce Eagle and the engine stopped dead. He made an exceedingly skilful forced landing – having no ejector seat fitted – and inspection of the engine revealed that Rolls-Royce had designed it with a *single* shaft drive to the duplicated magnetos and this had fractured, so nullifying the duplication-for-safety reasons inherent in having two independently-driven magnetos and twin sets of spark plugs for each engine in all aircraft from the time of Wilbur Wright. This design error had therefore caused the loss of another aircraft, a single one of which cost the Navy its weight in solid silver to build.

Although we knew little of the Rolls-Royce Eagle engine's history at that time – for everything was secret and fatalities were seldom discussed – we were not surprised at the Eagle's cancellation for we knew that the piston engine was becoming obsolete where very high powers were needed. Moreover, the Eagle's rpm had to be kept high when taxying to prevent oiling up the lower cylinders in this 24-cylinder engine. A plug change would then be necessary – all 48 of them – and this usually took the entire day by the time things had cooled down sufficiently for work to start. The over-worked but very patient Rolls-Royce 'rep' had also warned us that when taxying down wind, the overheating that this caused could also damage a few of its 24 'sleeve' exhaust valves – due to *lack* of lubrication. The engine would then seize up and one or two connecting rods might appear through the crankcase and the whole aircraft could become shrouded in blue and black smoke.

After the cancellation of the Eagle-engined Mark 1 it took until late 1951 before the Python prop-jet version was sufficiently developed for it to begin its Naval clearance trials. Even then it was still suffering fatally from power and/or prop failures, a subject still of some interest to us at Manby in May 1953.

The last three Wyvern fatalities had occurred in October 1949, June 1952, and May 1953, the latter to Lt/Cdr A.C. Poplewski, a US ETPS student. The first of these was to Mike Graves while he was demonstrating the Wyvern to a crowd of Navy and Ministry of Supply officials. His prop stopped at the top of a loop and the aircraft overshot Yeovil airfield while Mike was attempting a dead-engined forced landing, killing Mike and two occupants of an adjoining house. The second was to Dave Hanson (9 ETPS and a Seafire pilot in 718 Squadron with me at Eglington in 1946) on a test flight from C Squadron. His hood broke free in a dive and it may have hit him, knocking him out. The same thing had nearly happened to Nick Goodhart at Boscombe, but he had survived his injury and made a successful landing.

Another tragedy struck us at this time. Pete Lawrence was carrying out stall tests in the RAF's prototype Javelin fighter/bomber (the Javelin was shortly to be the RAF's choice instead of the Navy's Scimitar) and it entered a 'stable stall' similar to the high-tailed' V-bombers etc., and Pete failed to get out in time, his ejector seat being found near the wreckage. P.G. Lawrence, MBE, ex-824 Swordfish Squadron in the old *Eagle* with me in 1941/2 had joined Glosters in 1952 as number two to Bill Waterton after working on the Firebrand and GR 17 – the Gannet rival –for Blackburns. It seemed to us at the time that Pete was unable to eject in time perhaps because the hood would not come free at the very low airspeed and flat descent which the aircraft was in at the time.

Later aircraft were fitted with hood-breakers welded to the tops of all ejector seats so that through-hood ejections were possible. Explosive bolts and/or powerful springs to assist hood jettison were also fitted. Further improvements by 1964 made it possible for Sqn/Ldr Svensson (16 ETPS), flying the Delta Mirage 1110 of the Royal Australian Air Force, to eject at supersonic speed. (Please see Appendix 4 for the story of this remarkable escape.)

By 1958, ejecting from a Wyvern was also becoming much easier and flying it was much safer, too. It had been fitted with a taller dorsal fin and rudder, small outer fins to improve its spin recovery, spring tabs on the ailerons to improve high speed lateral control, a Martin-Baker ejector seat, better air conditioning and cockpit pressurisation and a stiffer canopy which could be jettisoned easily without it hitting the pilot. Buffeting with airbrakes extended had been reduced and, perhaps most important of all, the propellers' translation race was now force fed with oil and no further failures had occurred since.

Other important and life-saving improvements were also made to the Wyvern's engine handling to give smoother power response and to avoid engine stalling. Being the most powerful single-seater in the world at that time and with its huge prop-jet combination, this subject was of great interest and the following few paragraphs describe some of the problems the deck-landing pilot had to cope with.

To cure the inevitable delay in power response to rapid opening of all jet engines' throttles, the engine makers had devised their ACU – acceleration control unit. Although this achieved a smooth rpm engine response to rapid throttle opening and avoided engine stalling, it introduced another fault when fitted to prop-jets like the Wyvern. It was found in the case of the Wyvern with its props weighing about half a ton, that there was a dangerously long delay before the propeller thrust itself became available – so urgently required when 'going round again' on being 'waved-off' at the last moment in a deck-landing approach in carriers not yet fitted with the angled deck. This delay was caused by the need to first speed up the heavy propeller and second, to coarsen off its pitch so that it could turn the extra rpm into thrust. To remedy this defect the propeller makers invented their 'anticipator'. This pre-coarsened the propeller pitch as the throttle was moved open – or *vice versa* – so that thrust/drag responses kept in time instantly with the pilot's required power alterations.

The Python Wyvern then had almost identical handling characteristics to any piston-engined aircraft. However, another snag then raised its head. This was the large nose-down trim change caused by the 'blanketing' effect when the huge propeller fined its pitch as power was *reduced* on the landing approach. This slowed down its slipstream over the tail surfaces, reduced elevator and tailplane effectiveness and caused a repeat of the 'phantom dive' tendency.

To cure this, an extra fine pitch stop was fitted – six degrees instead of the usual 16 degrees – so that the much higher jet idling speeds would not give excessive propeller thrust. When power cut out completely – such as in engine failure – the result was a repeat of the sort of dive that had already caused several fatal crashes. Even on the landing approach, if the pilot closed the throttle a little too much, the same 'phantom dive' could start to occur. This behaviour was very similar – but much more extreme – to that of the Mamba-engined Sturgeon M6 I had flown in 1950 at Shorts.

The simple remedy for the Wyvern was for Rotols to put in an extra 'flight fine pitch stop', preventing the propeller from fining off to more than 16 degrees whenever the aircraft was in the air. After touch-down with the weight on the wheels and, of course while taxying, the 'flight fine pitch' stop was removed automatically by a switch on the undercarriage legs so that the propeller was free to fine off to six degrees if the pilot closed the throttle fully when the aircraft had landed and engine rpm could be maintained without excessive prop thrust or compressor stalling when taxying or at start up. The pilot was prevented from unintentionally closing the throttle to the 'ground idle' position in the air by the fitting of a special 'gate' to the throttle quadrant.

In this way all the attractive deck-landing features of a piston-engined contra-prop aircraft were transferred to the Wyvern – albeit at some cost in time and human life – making it in conjunction with the improvements brought about by the mirror sight and the angled deck and the Wyvern's good view over the nose, a relatively easy tailwheeled aircraft to deck-land, day or night. The contra-props also removed the risks of torque-induced swings on take-off, yaw effects with changes of speed and power when firing weapons and allowed a smooth, straight approach to the deck when coming in to land. These advantages – coupled with a gentle nose and wing drop at the power-on stall, easily held longitudinal trim changes with increase in speed and power to the maximum indicated dive airspeed of 550 knots, small trim changes when selecting flaps, airbrakes or undercarriage and a good spin recovery – all had been obtained in their excellence by first-class test flying and designers' co-operation of which ETPS would have been proud.

At this time we had noticed the demise of the windmill as a working concern in the British countryside. If a propeller the size of a Wyvern's could absorb 4,000 hp, why couldn't a windmill of ten times the propeller area do likewise and impart this sort of power to an electrical generator? We noticed that the average windmill in Britain and Holland had large area 'sails' set at a fixed angle of incidence whatever the windspeed. It had consequently often suffered structural failures in windspeeds over 30 mph, particularly if the farmer had not turned it round 'edge-on' to the wind or had not 'reefed' the sails to avoid damage in storms. A brief study of the immense power absorbed by the Wyvern's propeller had told windmill designers how it was possible to harness nature's free energy by making variable-pitch windmill sails, the blades of which were contoured to that of a propeller rather than to the rough-and-ready shape of a boat's sails and which would automatically alter their pitch to cater efficiently for all changes in windspeed and loads. We now have 'wind farms' and we can watch with interest who will win the battle for their survival: those who wish to preserve nature's countryside or those who wish to reduce air pollution from man-made sources of energy needed to produce electricity.

Although the Wyvern S4 had taken six years since its first flight before receiving even a partial service clearance from 'C' Squadron in October 1952, (the first Wyvern allotted to 813 Squadron at Ford arrived 18 May 1953), it had exceptionally been one of the few aircraft in history that had overcome the enormous disadvantage of having had to combine a prototype airframe and prototype engine in the same initial package. But by the time the Navy placed its first order for delivery of the Python Wyvern S4 in 1951 (the prefix F for fighter had been dropped from its type number by then), John Cunningham had already flown its replacement – the first prototype de Havilland Sea Vixen 110 – to supersonic speed.

The appearance of the DH 110 (which became the Sea Vixen) and the signing of the development contract which resulted in the appearance of the N 113 (which eventually became the Scimitar) showed that those in Admiralty's Directorate of Naval Air Warfare (DNAW) at this time realised that the Wyvern was a very poor contender for its supposed role as a 'Torpedo/ Fighter' aircraft, and likely to be equally useless as its predecessor, the Firebrand. But when the Wyvern was finally scrapped in 1958, no one could say it had not given of its best in its strike role at Suez; albeit in good weather, in daylight and in conditions of complete air superiority.

Back at Manby in May 1953, Pilot's Notes for aircraft usually started off with a pilot's check list of about 100 items. These were divided into headings of about twenty basic items, each of which had to be checked before and after take-off and before and after landing. For example:

Checks before take-off:

Trimming tabs;	Elevator neutral without flap, (½ div. nose-up with flap); rudder neutral; aileron neutral.
Throttle;	Flight Idle Gate, friction adjusted.
Fuel;	Main tanks, check contents, fuel pressure normal, engine torque warning test.
Flaps;	30 degrees – max lift.
Airbrakes;	In.
Wings;	Spread and locked, warning light out.
Hood;	Locked closed.
Harness;	Tight and locked.
Tailwheel;	Locked central.
Compass;	Check gyro setting.
Altimeter;	Check mb's setting.
Oxygen;	Supply and pressure.
Windscreen;	De-icing pump.
Hydraulics;	Check handpump, dial readings.
Drop tanks;	Jettison lever locked.
Flying controls;	Full and free movement.
Ejector seat;	Pin removed.
Pitot heater;	On.
Cockpit;	Heater and pressurisation on.
. . . and so on.	

The 4,100 hp axial-flow Python in the Wyvern S4 – as it was now called – was started by compressed air. Sixteen eight-foot-long compressed-air bottles were loaded on a trolley, a tractor was then engaged to tow it to the aircraft and a twenty-foot hose from four of these bottles was connected to the aircraft's starter turbine. With two men each holding the four chocks in place, with the pilot having selected 'brakes on' and given the 'thumbs up', the ground crew opened the four valves to a deafening sound of rushing air. The eight-bladed propeller gradually speeded up until the main turbine was doing about 3500 rpm, at which stage the pilot opened the high-pressure fuel cock and the main jets ignited – with a long flame appearing from the jet pipe and a noise like a dozen elephants trumpeting denoting success.

If a full-power engine run was required with the Wyvern, the aircraft had to be tied down to ring bolts in a concrete blast pen, otherwise the ground crew holding the chocks in place could become airborne and tend to disappear over the far hedge. This sort of thing actually happened on board *Albion* when Wyverns of 813 Squadron were returning to Portsmouth from Malta – mentioned in detail later.

Climbing up the 14 feet into the Wyvern's roomy cockpit was an awe-inspiring business. However, the cockpit was well laid out and the view in every direction was good. With the double-thickness 'teardrop' hood closed, external noise was minimal and the start up and taxy out easy and comfortable.

I found that take-off was smooth and all three flying controls responded well with small movements and light stick forces. The aircraft flew off the ground at about 120 knots and once the flaps and wheels were up it accelerated quickly to 200 knots, its best climbing speed. Ten thousand feet was reached in 2½ minutes at the light load at which I was flying. I throttled back to carry out some stalls, flaps up, flaps at 'max lift' for take-off, flaps fully down, power on, power at 'flight-idle', wheels up and wheels down. Then, at 15,000 feet I did a few steep turns at full throttle until stalling incidence was reached – managing to pull a steady 4G without having to reduce height or speed below about 180 knots throughout. This minimum turning circle would have been nearly twice the radius of a Seafire 47 or Sea Fury, and the Wyvern would have presented both of them and many other fighters with a sitting target.

The Wyvern was a classic example of how it is impossible to 'get something for nothing' in a 'multi-role' aircraft. It could lift only 30 per cent more bombs than a Fury and go only 50 miles further towards its target with them. Yet, unlike the Sea Fury it could not take on the mantle of a fighter once it had dropped its load, for its power/weight ratio was half, and its wing-loading double that of a Sea Fury in a similar condition.

Its 'ceiling' at a weight of 24,000 lb was 25,000 feet and the extra drag of a steep turn – an essential manoeuvre to try and avoid enemy fighters in a dogfight – would immediately slow it down to the stall, requiring a large loss in height to retain flying speed. However, sea-level fuel consumption trials at Manby showed that the Python prop-jet combination was economical in miles-per-gallon at low altitudes compared with a pure jet of the same weight, so that the Wyvern's radius of action over the sea under the enemy's radar – about 400 miles – would be more acceptable.

In fact the Wyvern's sea-level approach pattern completely baffled the Navy's radar defence arrangements in the absence of AEW Skyraider support for, when we flew it in 813 Squadron in the Mediterranean the following year, we always managed to get into rocket-firing range of HM ships before a single gun had been turned in our direction. Even if they had seen us coming, their larger AA guns could only be traversed at the speed of a Swordfish and would have been ineffective in any case.

The fact that the earth's curvature screened our approach from their radar beyond a distance of about 20 miles did not appear to worry the average Navy gunnery officer at that time, although this had become fully apparent to all German FW 190 fighters/bombers the first time they were used as such at the landings at Salerno in the war. We had not forgotten it either, for we always used the low level approach. We had also combined this sea-level attack method with the author's near-invention of modern-day 'lobbing', (first taught by 738 Squadron four years later and called the 'LABS' attack system). This method allowed the weapon to be fired out-of-range of lethal close-range gunnery weapons and allowed an easier withdrawal. Twenty years later it was adopted as the only practical method of air-delivery of the A-bomb from a low-level approach.

The Wyvern's approach and landing was as easy as the take-off. It had a good forward view, with the nose acting as a perfect incidence indicator needing only an occasional glance at the airspeed indicator to check the airspeed on the deck approach. With a long tailwheel strut and a long-stroke 'trailing link' undercarriage shock absorber system, the Wyvern sat down and stayed down on the deck in all touchdowns not above a vertical velocity of 14 ft/sec. Above this the undercarriage would fail, the metal prop would strike the deck and slivers of steel would fly everywhere. Following the death of one of the flight deck party during deck trials, an Admiralty Fleet Order was issued forbidding anyone to be near the Wyvern during decklandings. This included the usual crowd of aviators watching from 'Goofers Gallery' on the Island – 300 feet away!

The relative touchdown speed of about 80 knots was nearly twice as fast as that of the Seafire, so that controllability and fast reactions from the pilot to advice from Nick Goodhart's 'magical mirror' were essential. But speed control was easy to maintain throughout the entire approach with very small throttle movements, the contra-prop, powerful rudder and lockable tailwheel ensuring straight landings and take-offs, even when taking off from airfields in strong cross winds.

On trying out the various effects of using the airbrakes in dives and on the landing approach it was found at Manby that there was still too much vibration when they were used with the flaps and undercarriage down, and there was such a huge reduction in lift and increase in drag in this condition that nearly full power was required to maintain height.

When checking the Wyvern's maximum indicated airspeed, I found that at all the weights that I flew it, it only managed about 300 knots at maximum power at sea level when carrying wing stores, not the 345 knots at sea level stated by the makers. This was a bit too slow to loop and roll off the top after lobbing a bomb or rocket – the normal method adopted in the LABS (Low Altitude Bombing System), so the Wyvern had to break away by steep turning.

Even at 300 knots indicated airspeed the Wyvern's high wingloading (its 70 lb/sq/ft being double that of the Seafire 47) limited its turning ability to a huge radius at no more than four sustainable G, making it an easy target for computed, light AA fire should it ever get near enough to a Russian ship to release its weapon; neither would it stand much chance in a dogfight against any fighter, piston or jet.

About twenty hours flying was needed to gain enough experience of the Wyvern to write Pilot's Notes. Having only simple navigation devices and needing no observer to accompany the pilot to operate the ever-more complicated electronics about to be fitted to the Scimitar and Sea Vixen, the Wyvern was extraordinarily easy to write about. The usual flights were made to check miles/gallon, lateral control with bomb hang-ups, night landings and control in the dive up to about 560 knots indicated and up to 0.76 Mach at which speed the prop tips were supersonic and people in the Lincolnshire pubs wanted to know what all the noise was about!

At about this time we heard of the true cause of Lt/Cdr Dave Hanson's death in a Wyvern crash. The canopy had come off in a high-speed dive test and it had hit the tailplane. This knocked off the rudder and half the fin and put the aircraft into a violent yaw, causing the contra-props to enmesh and the engine to be torn from the structure. Hanson pulled the ejector seat but as the control column had jammed against his right leg, he suffered pain on the descent, probably leading to unconsciousness. Then, because there was no automatic seat release and auto-deployment of the pilot's parachute, he crashed to earth still in his seat a few seconds later and was killed.

On 20 May 1953 – the usual meeting we had with RDT3, Ministry of Supply at St Giles Court in London finalised the Wyvern's Notes and the S4 was granted an initial one-year's CA release for Navy use from land bases and 813 Squadron was formed with Lt/Cdr C.E. Price (8 ETPS) in command at Ford in Sussex. A second Squadron – 827 – formed at Ford a year later under Dicky Richardson, with two more – 830 amd 831 – a year after that. These two were in time to take part in the Suez operation aboard *Eagle*. The last Wyvern went to the breaker's yard in April 1958. It was the last flight made by 813 Squadron – then under the command of Lt/Cdr R. Abraham – which has not reformed since.

The next Naval aircraft requiring a Pilot's Notes re-write at Manby was the Attacker FBMk 2. The 'Fighter/Bomber version was the latest Mark of Attacker about to be adopted by 800 and 803 Squadrons reforming at Ford to go aboard *Eagle* in June 1953.

The first large order for 80 Attackers had been given by the Admiralty in early 1951. No. 806 Squadron was the first to embark aboard *Eagle* with the fighter version where it showed itself to be a good formation-flying and demonstration aircraft but a disappointing fighter plane. The remainder of the eighty Attackers ordered were converted to the fighter/bomber role and remained in service until October 1954.

Jeffrey Quill had taken the first prototype Attacker into the air from Boscombe Down on 27 July 1946. Mike Lithgow flew the second prototype from Chilbolton a year later and Les Colquhoun had continued with development testing until it came out of first line service in June 1954. It was Les Colquhoun who was awarded the George Medal for landing the prototype 'navalised' Attacker after one of its wings had folded in the air, jamming the ailerons.

As the Attacker – like the Sea Hawk – had the 5,000 lb static thrust Rolls-Royce Nene 3 engine and as the fighter version of the Attacker weighed only twice this engine thrust, I was expecting it to climb at twice the rate and at twice the speed of a Seafire. This turned out to be too optimistic a guess, even for the first 15,000 feet, and above this height the thrust progressively fell off until at about 30,000 feet it was barely sufficient to keep the airspeed high enough for the steep turns essential for fighter combat. Although faster than the Sea Vampire and a little faster than the Meteor IV and with a better rate of roll than both with its power-boosted ailerons, the Attacker was not sufficiently far ahead in performance as a fighter by 1952 and it was soon relegated to the fighter/bomber role.

The FB version which arrived at Manby was therefore equipped with bomb racks, a 250-gallon belly tank and rocket launchers. All that was necessary was to find out its fuel consumption, check on its 'Machery' handling and do some landings with bomb and rocket 'hang-ups' and add this information to the current Pilot's Notes for the fighter version.

In a dogfight with a Sabre IV one day, it was noticeable that the Attacker's controls seemed to be far too heavy for a fighter – after the delights of a Seafire – and above about 15,000 feet, it seemed to lack sufficient lift from its 'laminar-flow' ex-Spiteful wing to out-turn this much faster American fighter – which, having shot the author down, dived away easily, leaving him to struggle to retain enough elevator control to pull out in time before hitting the ground at a Mach number no higher than about 0.78M. It was probably due to the Attacker's habit of 'tucking its nose down' and not responding to elevator above Mach 0.82 that led to the death of 'Spike' King-Joyce – and later of Lt.Cdr Malcom Orr-Ewing – characteristics which added to its unsuitability as an interceptor fighter. Neither was it as easy to deckland as the nose-wheeled Sea Vampire. It certainly needed the assistance of the newly invented gyro-stabilised mirror landing sight installed in *Eagle* to allow it to operate from a carrier without too many accidents.

From about March 1953 onwards, the Attacker was withdrawn from front-line service in 800, 803 and 890 Squadrons and was replaced with the Hawker Sea Hawk F Mk1, beginning with 806 Squadron. Most of the remaining Attackers were given to 736 jet training Squadron at Lossiemouth or allotted to two of our excellent RNVR Squadrons – 1831 and 1832. Unfortunately, three years later on 10 March 1957 and in spite of their magnificent help in the

Korean war, all RNVR Squadrons were abolished by the 'Sandys Axe' and their remaining Attackers and other aircraft were transferred to Fleet Requirement Units to provide targets for gunners until their end in 1958.

The next Pilot's Notes task was the Sea Venom, a type already in service with the RAF as a night-fighter. The Navy could see no embarked operational future for the very few Sea Hornet NF 21s still in service afloat in *Eagle* with 809 Squadron and with enemy night attacks becoming a future possibility a replacement night fighter was urgently required.

Night air warfare and the ability to navigate and intercept enemy aircraft at night and in all weathers was becoming a much easier proposition than in the days of 'Cat's-eyes Cunningham' in Mosquitos. Air-to-air interception radar – AI – was replacing human eyesight for the last few miles of the night chase and new navigation aids – including radio altimeters, air-ground radar and navigator/fixers, were making all-weather flying much safer. A start was being made in the practice of 'Carrier Controlled Approach and Landing' (CCA) in – almost – fog conditions and at night. Weapon aiming was becoming even easier by computer-sights and, by making use of another invention of the author's, the 'head-up display' (HUD) system, whereby the pilot could read his attack and navigation instruments while looking straight ahead through the windscreen, the workload on a single-seater fighter pilot – without assistance from his observer – was becoming more reasonable.

The pilots' and observers' cockpit environment was also much safer. Well-warmed and fully pressurised and de-iced cockpits were now the norm and air-operated anti-G suits were becoming a normal part of a fighter pilot's flying gear. By the year 1960 Martin-Bakers would have made 'single-action' ejection at zero altitude/zero flying speed possible. (Zero altitude ejection trials on a runway take-off were first live-tested from a Meteor on 3 September 1955.) With a single pull of the ejector seat firing mechanism, many of the high-performance military aircraft coming on the market by 1960 would automatically jettison their hoods, (or the seat would break through the hood without injury to the pilot), the control column would 'break' clear of the pilot's knees, auto-seat-separation would take place immediately after getting clear of the aircraft, the pilot would have an auto-supply of oxygen during the descent, he would then have auto-inflation of his dinghy after a sea-landing and the automatic switching-on of a radio rescue beacon to tell the air/sea rescue helicopter – by this time hopefully alerted – where he was. Thanks largely to the School (now the 'Institute') of Aviation Medicine at Farnborough, and by such people as J.S.P. 'Doc' Rawlins, RN and, of course, Herbert Ellis and many other thoughtful agencies engaged in preventive medicine, flying dangers which had so rapidly increased with the appearance of the jet engine and had accounted for the deaths of 57 ETPS test pilots by the end of 1954, began to decrease.

On 4 January 1954 the author collected the seventh production Sea Venom Mark 20 (WM507) from Hurn. It had now been renamed the FAW Mark 20, the initials standing for 'Fighter, All Weather', having been fitted with rocket and bomb racks in addition to its four 20 mm cannon and Gyro gunsight, for a second and third role – that of daylight fighter/bomber operations! The RAF had ordered about a hundred night-fighter versions which they called their NF Mk2. These had been delivered a few months ahead of our version which was due to arrive for 890 Squadron's use at Yeovilton by May 1954.

The RAF must have been encouraged to order the Venom in 1949 by witnessing John Derry's memorable aerobatic display of the first prototype only three days after its very first flight – perhaps one of the few occasions when the designers had not said those fatal words: 'Ah me. It's back to the drawing board.' (It was so sad that three years later in what was to be a similar type of demonstration of a de Havilland fighter at the 1952 SBAC display. John Derry's DH 110 – the prototype for the Sea Vixen and the Venom's replacement – disintegrated over the crowd, killing John Derry, Tony Richards his observer and 29 spectators.)

The Sea Venom had been delivered to Boscombe for deck trials in April 1951. The first four prototype Sea Venom NF Mk20s had then appeared in public for the first time at the Queen's Royal Naval Review Flypast at Lee-on-Solent on 13 June 1953, led by Commander 'Dicky' Law, the CO of 'C' Squadron at Boscombe.

For a single-seat fighter pilot, the twin, side-by-side seating arrangements in the Sea Venom FAW 20 which we now had at Boscombe Down (as Handling Squadron had moved there on 1 April) took a great deal of getting used to for daylight fighter operation. The pilot now had to depend on his observer to look out to his right, but as the latter would be spending much of his time looking at his AI 10 radar screen and at his maps and charts, the job of flying this aircraft as a daytime interceptor/fighter was going to be difficult.

The Ghost engine in the Sea Venom had to propel 1½ tons more aircraft through the air than the equally-powered Attacker, but as it had about 40 square feet more wing area and a thinner wing, its top speed and climb performance at high altitude were equally as good as the Attacker and it could out-turn it as well in the day-fighter mode. Its climb to 40,000 feet took four minutes less than the Attacker if a slow climb-airspeed technique was used. Speeding up to a useful interception speed at 40,000 feet took another five minutes at full power. Its 'critical' Mach number was much higher – about 0.81 Mach (0.82 with geared-tab aileron controls) – before aileron flutter called a halt to anything faster. All-round view had, in any case been much improved by the fitting of a clearview canopy, directional control had been improved by additional fin and rudder areas and the frequent incidence of aileron flutter was finally cured in the later Marks of Sea Venom by the introduction of power-operated ailerons.

When carrying out ADDLS (dummy decklandings at an airfield) the Sea Venom's undercarriage shock absorbers worked exceptionally well, with half the bounce of a Gannet after a heavy landing. However, the offset pilot's position needed getting used to when lining up for the catapult and, with a maximum decklanding weight into *Ark Royal*'s arrester gear equivalent to only 150 gallons of fuel remaining, she would always have to operate within 60 miles of a friendly airfield in case hook trouble or a crash-on-deck required a diversion ashore.

The deck trials in 1952 with the FAW Mk 20 had failed to show up an unsuspected weakness in the deck hook, stressed as it now was to enter the wires at speeds up to 95 knots instead of the usual 65 knots of a Sea Fury. Several serious accidents – including a fatal accident to Frank Cawood – made some strengthening essential. These improvements were added to the later batch of Mark 21s, of which 160 were built. Later versions still were fitted with M-B ejector seats and Maxaret brakes. The Mark 21s in 892 and 893 Squadrons in *Eagle* and 809 Squadron in *Albion*, took part in the Suez and Yemeni operations as day-fighters – and later as rocketeers – with only a single accident and no casualties. Forty Mark 53s were bought for use by the Australian Navy – mostly in 808 Squadron – and these were also fitted with a clearview sliding hood.

In January 1959, 893 Squadron with Mk 22s under Eric Manuel, was equipped with the new Firestreak missile. The Sea Vixen FAW 1 became available by September 1960 and most of the remaining Sea Venoms were then transferred to training duties or for carrying out 'Electronic Counter Measure' (ECM) trials.

Fourteen hours of flying the Sea Venom 20 were largely uneventful – apart from two minor occurrences. One was on 19 January when doing 'Machery'. The starboard aileron nearly disintegrated due to flutter at about Mach 0.83 in a 40-degree dive at about 20,000 feet. The wingtip tanks were springing up and down through a foot or more and the ailerons were crashing up and down in a blur of grey rivets with the stick not knowing which way to go in the cockpit. On landing, the ailerons were changed for new ones, complete with spring tabs and, on flying it again – this time to only 0.82M – things functioned perfectly.

The other incident was when the wingfold warning light suddenly glowed red – signalling that the main wingfold bolts were unlocked. As this had just occurred during a Sea Hawk take-off, the thought that the same thing could happen in a Sea Venom when airborne was a bit frightening. CP/O Tunks could find nothing wrong with the wing bolts on landing – after a gentle return to the airfield – but it was taken back to Hurn for new ones to be fitted, just in case.

Leading half-a-dozen Sea Venoms in a 60-plane Naval 'Balbo' over the Solent on the occasion – on 14 May 1954 – of the Queen's homecoming from a visit abroad – with the remainder of the formation mostly consisting of remains of the 700 Fireflies and the 500 Sea Furies built over the last 5 years – we Sea Venoms arrived back at Boscombe in near darkness, taking about four circuits to slow down to landing speed. This 'slow-down' procedure took us over the Officers' Mess and most of Amesbury a couple of times. Needless to say we got into trouble with the Commandant for shooting up the Mess in this way but we were sure that had Prince Philip known of the Commandant's disapproval, justified though it was, he would have stuck up for us. Having raced against him often at Cowes in Flying Fifteens and had a beer at the Island Sailing Club afterwards, our Naval Prince would have thought nothing of it and 'par for the course.'

At about this time we five pilots at Handling Squadron visited RAF Kemble to fly a Sabre F-86K. In competition with the MiG-15 over Korea, the Sabre F-86 A and E had become the best fighter of its age. Equipped with airbrakes, powered controls, all-flying tailplanes and fully pressurised cockpits, 6 × 0.5-inch guns, able to carry 2 × 1000 lb bombs, it had a radius of action of about 200 miles, half of which could be flown at speeds of 650 mph. It had almost as good a top speed and turning performance as the Hunter F Mk 4 fitted with the Avon 100 of about 6000 lb thrust – but as its power/weight ratio was 10 per cent less than that of the Hunter and about 20 per cent less than that of the MiG, its rate of climb suffered at high altitudes. However, because its designers had used all the aerodynamic knowledge to be gained from their study of the German Me 262 jet after the war, the Sabre's transonic performance was superior to either aircraft, requiring only a very shallow dive from 25,000 feet to pick up a speed of Mach 1.2 and only loosing 5,000 feet in the process.

The Sea Hawk was the last aircraft besides the Gannet needing a full re-write of the Notes. Fitted with the Nene 101 with about 5000 lb of thrust, the first prototype (VP101) set a good example on 30 July 1949 when 'Wimpy' Wade, Hawker's CTP, and Neville Duke flew it round a closed circuit at a record top speed of 536 mph. An order was placed on 22 November 1949 for 150 Mark 1s. By February 1950 it had completed decklanding and RATOG trials in *Illustrious* with a lengthened hook and underwing drop tanks. Our pilots had a very high opinion of the Sea Hawk as a carrier-borne fighter. It was reliable and remarkably easy to maintain aboard ship. Pilots who flew it found it a joyful release and probably gave birth to the saying used on emergence from the carrier's briefing room: 'Kick the tyres, light the fires – and the last one off's a sissy'

The Hawker 1052 – a swept-back version of the Sea Hawk – was also flying at this time and many in the FAA thought that it should have been chosen instead to give the Navy a supersonic capability. The Mark 1 Sea Hawk first entered service with the famous 'Ace of Diamonds' 806 Squadron where the first eight aircraft, led by Pat Chilton, took part in the 150-strong FAA Coronation Review Flypast on 15 June 1953.

The Mark 3 Fighter/Bomber version of the Sea Hawk came to Manby in January 1954. It was due to enter service in July in five squadrons – 806, 800, 801, 811, 897 amd 898 Squadrons. The only incident worthy of note was when the author flew WF241 which had just been fitted with Maxaret brakes. The runway surface at Ford where the trials were carried out was 20 per cent puddles and, on touchdown, the wheels tobogganed, failed to speed up to work the 'flywheel' system (whereby brake pressure can only be applied to the wheels if there is no difference between the flywheel and the landing wheels' rotation speeds), and so failed to prevent brake application from jamming the wheels, solid. Skidding along for a few hundred yards without any of the wheels turning – apart from the nosewheel – it would have overshot had not the brakes been released for a few seconds in a dry patch of the runway.

Probably the greatest enemy of good wheel-braking in aircraft is excessive heat. This causes distortion and the formation of carbon on the brake discs which acts as a good lubricant, causing the well known lorry-driver-rolling-on-hills' nightmare of 'brake fade'. The heat energy evolved from a Sea Hawk pulling up on brakes alone would lift a 4½ ton elephant up to a height of 600 feet.

As any racing car driver knows, tyre friction – or lack of it – limits the retarding or acceleration forces which he can apply when stopping, starting or cornering. The force required to push an object along a road or an ice skater along the ice at a constant speed depends on the force of friction (and, of course, air resistance proportional to V-squared) resisting motion. The maximum amount of force transmitted through an aircraft's tyres to slow down an aircraft by wheelbrake brake application when it is on its landing run on the runway depends entirely on the limiting force of friction between the tyres' surface and the runway. The greater the force (usually gravity) holding the object in contact with the runway and the better the 'grip' of the rubber tyres on the runway surface, the greater will be this force of friction and the less will be the distance required for stopping provided the brakes apply a constant force no larger than this retarding force and do not 'lock' the wheels – which would seriously reduce their effectiveness.

Thus an aircraft requiring to use its wheelbrakes to stop its motion after landing must expect the brakes, the tyres and runway surface to satisfy several conditions if stopping distance is to be minimal. The simple relationship between the braking force 'F' (or 'limiting force of friction') available on each wheel is governed by the simple formula:

F = u multiplied by 'N', where
u = the 'coefficient of friction' and
N= the 'normal reaction' or the 'pressing down' vertical force of the tyre on the runway.

'u' can never be more than unity – unless 'stickyness' or 'ratchet action' or a surface cutting action is employed as in ice skates, between the two surfaces. However 'u' can approach unity in situations where a dry rubber tyre is in steady contact with a firm, hard, tarmac runway or road surface. That is to say, the two tyres of a Sea Hawk can have their rotation braked to a maximum retardation force of their combined vertical weight on the runway. The maximum deceleration from wheelbrakes alone (or acceleration from a four-wheeled-drive car) can therefore never be more than 1 G unless other forces are employed to increase 'N' without increasing the 'mass' of the object, car or aircraft to be stopped, accelerated or cornered.

Likewise, a racing car cannot be stopped quicker or cornered with a greater deceleration than 1 G unless the tyre's downforce on the road is artificially increased by the use of 'wings' giving negative lift or an extra downforce – 'N' – on the car without adding significantly to its 'mass' or inertia. Even then, 1 G deceleration can only be exceeded slightly if braking forces on each wheel are adjusted to conform with the actual 'N' force at the mini-second they are applied. This is, of course, the aim of the 'Maxaret' system.

In the case of a typical Formula One car, the downforce on the back wheels can be increased by half-a-ton when it is travelling over 80 mph airspeed. Thus considerable extra retardation forces can be applied when braking and, more important perhaps, the car can be cornered at much greater speeds without the back skidding, due to the extra 'N' force fore-and-aft holding it down on the road. Racing drivers often report high sideways 'G' forces in turns. Average side-force maxima are obviously governed by the above formula, so that figures of 5 G sideforces often quoted can only be caused by 'jerks' and not by a steady side force. Likewise, it is possible to apply more than one G deceleration to an aircraft if aero-negative lift is applied by means of reverse or upward thrust from jet power or airbrakes.

Tobogganing and skiing values of u are probably about 0.01 or less, depending on the finish applied to the ski runners and the snow conditions. As u – the surface friction coefficient – does not increase much with speed in straight downhill sledging or skiing – or when lugeing or tobogganing – maximum speeds attained depend entirely on runner finish and areas and, at airspeeds above about forty mph, on air drag. Thus the heavier skier, the heavier the toboggan and the smaller their frontal areas to the airflow, the faster they will travel downhill. Thus the 'tuck' position is vital, just as is the streamlining of the toboggan itself plus its occupants.

In the case of the Sea Hawk skid, not only was u a fraction of what it should have been due to both tyres aquaplaning due, in turn, to incorrect tyre-tread patterns failing to expel the water, but aero lift might have *reduced* 'N' due to the lift from the nose-up attitude of the Sea Hawk when all wheels were on the runway. The situation might be similar in effect to a lorry attempting to apply its brakes with normal ferocity when on a steep incline. For instance, if the lorry is on a 25 per cent incline, its 'N' factor will be reduced by about the same amount although its 'F' factor remains the same. It will therefore have about a 25 per cent increased tendency to skid.

Initial aerodynamic dissipation of touchdown energy is obviously much better in propeller-driven aircraft as they had immense prop drag particularly in the tail-down attitude and can usually use the V-squared law for the first third of the landing run to dissipate three-quarters of the energy without touching the brakes at all.

In the case of the Sea Hawk, it had very little inbuilt aero-drag and early wheelbrake application was essential. Brake cooling was just adequate to prevent overheating if the windspeed was above about 15 knots. But if the windspeed was near zero, the extra 15 knots doubled the heat produced and at the very least, caused immense brake and tyre wear. Reverse jet thrust is now used for the first half of landing runs by commercial jets in addition to extension of large airbrakes. Wheelbrakes are seldom used until the runway speed is reduced to an airspeed lower than 50 knots, below which aerodynamic retardation forces become less effective.

Further complications – such as aquaplaning, ice on the runway and having the wrong tyre tread for wet runways not fitted with emergency arrester gear, as the Sea Hawk had at that time – made the risk of overshoots inevitable. In the case of the RAF's Lightning, the tyres had to be so thin to fit into the wing when retracted that the rubber area touching the runway was only about 60 square inches, needing a tyre pressure pumped up to 200 lb/sq/inch to support the weight. Incidentally, this sort of tyre pressure 'dented' the runway surfaces in many places throughout the world and an extra layer had to be applied. Very long runways were becoming essential to allow jet fighters to stop and this greatly added to the expense of operating them from airfields.

The Sea Hawk's high-subsonic behaviour was much more predictable than the Attacker's. Its power-operated ailerons and elevator plus a later version of the excellent Martin-Baker ejector seat probably made all the difference to pilot confidence when flying in this region. However, in spite of having vortex generators fitted at one-third chord along a portion of its mainplane top surface to reduce the thickness of the boundary layer, and an uprated Nene 103 giving 5300 lb static thrust, the highest Mach number to which the Mark 3 could be safely flown was 0.79M and some of us regretted that the Navy had not chosen the P 1052 sweptback version of the Sea Hawk. The sweepback had reduced Hi Mach drag sufficiently to allow the same engine power to give it maximum speed of 0.89M and made it superior in all-round performance to its USN counterpart – the FJ-2, a navalised version of the F-86E Sabre used by the USAF over Korea.

However, in a short dogfight with a Sabre, it was found that above 30,000 feet the Sea Hawk could climb faster than the Sabre and could keep going faster at low and medium altitudes when compressibility drag was not the main factor in speed limitation. It could also out-turn it at any altitude in a conventional dogfight setting where each aircraft tries to get on the tail of the other.

Towards the end of the Sea Hawk's 20 years of RN service – 450 having been produced – a 'long-range' bomber version was tried out with the idea of using it, when at full load, from the latest high-powered steam catapults. However, because its runway take-off performance was disappointing and the automatic fuel transfer system from its four underwing tanks was unreliable, the idea was dropped.

There was only one design characteristic which made the Sea Hawk dangerous if the pilot failed to watch his instruments closely. With its engine having been placed at about the CG position, the Sea Hawk's internal fuel supply had to be accurately weight-positioned at either side of the CG. This led to balancing problems during flight. Lt Derek Taylor crashed into the sea off Spurn Head in 1954 and in order to find out the cause, the wrecked aircraft was raised by two Navy minesweepers and inspected by the Accidents Investigation Unit. It was found – as suspected – that the automatic fuel transfer system from the aft tank had not worked properly leaving all of its 170 gallons still in the aft tank. This made the aircraft uncontrollably tail-heavy and unstable and cause it to crash. Regrettably, the pilot had not used his manual override balancing switches in the cockpit, possibly because the fuel-balance warning system was not working. It is possible that he was unable to bale out because of the very high 'G' loadings in the ensuing spinning dive.

The remaining Mark 1s were operated by 1832 RNVR Squadron and Cdr (A) G. McRutherford was the first RNVR pilot to deckland a jet – which he did during a training session in *Bulwark* just before she took part in the Suez operation.

The Sea Hawk's part in the Suez operation – with 5 Squadrons embarked in *Albion*, *Bulwark* and *Eagle* in the 'ground attack' role – proved its effectiveness. It may well have been the most popular of all British-designed fighter aircraft to have seen service in the Navy up to that time, not only for its reliable structure and ease of maintenance and safe handling in the air but its cockpit safety features, its good decklanding qualities, its wide undercarriage, its effective airbrakes, its easy stalling characteristics, its good allround view from the cockpit and the well-balanced feel and effectiveness of its power-operated controls. A typical Sydney Camm winner if ever there was one.

The author collected the eighth production Gannet AS Mk 1 from White Waltham on 27 March 1954 and produced the 'Provisional Pilot's Notes' for it in time for the first delivery of this excellent aircraft to 703X Flight at RNAS Ford for 'intensive flying' trials. The CO of this Squadron at this time was Lt/Cdr Frank Cowtan who had been on the same – Number 20 – entry Course at St Vincent in November 1940 with the author and had afterwards flown Swordfish A/S aircraft on Atlantic convoy protection in *Biter*, *Avenger* and *Argus* during the war and later, in 1942 he was in 836 Squadron on anti-E boat patrols from RAF Thorney Island. Following trouble with engine compressor stalling in the Double-Mamba prop-jet combination in the Gannet Mk 1, similar in its cause to the control problems in the Wyvern prop-jet combination, the author flew WN336 to Fairey's factory at White Waltham for them to cure it. This took about three weeks of flying there and delayed the decktrials to be carried out by 703X Squadron in *Albion* until August 1954.

A third mid-fuselage seat had been inserted behind the observer's seat by this time and a two-seater pilot trainer had been authorised, for ex-Firefly pilots now taking over the Gannet were not all used to jet-powered contra-prop twins, particularly where it was possible to fly on either engine, wind-mill-start the second engine on the ground or in the air or make single-engined decklandings at night quite safely and as a matter of course.

The first two operational squadrons to fly the Gannet AS Mk 1 – replacing Mark 6 Fireflies and Avenger AS Mk 4s in January 1955 – were 824 and 826 Squadrons based at Eglinton in Northern Ireland. Gannet AS Mk 4s were eventually replaced by the Westland Whirlwind HAS Mk 7.

Fairey's now received an order for 45 Airborne Early Warning Gannet aircraft to take over in 1960 from similarly equipped (with AN/APS 20 F radar) Skyraider AEW 1 aircraft, the Skyraiders having operated afloat in 849 Squadron in this vital job for the past six years.

The protype AEW Gannet made its first flight on 20 August 1958. The Double Mamba Mk8 of 3875 ehp was fitted with an airstarter – much more popular than the cartridge starter version – and the pilot's cockpit had been redesigned with side-by-side seats for the observers. A feature of this design was the centralised warning system, the 'percentage' power indicators instead of rpm gauges plus full engine and airframe de-icing.

AEW Gannets were in constant demand until the rundown of the carrier force started in 1970 with the final 849 Squadron flight of Gannet AEWs disbanded in December 1978 and the remains of their AN/APS radar given to the RAF for installation in twelve Shackleton MR Mk2 aircraft.

Writing the Pilot's Notes for the Gannet was a very straightforward process and only took about 15 hours flying. Most of the work concerned single-engined overshoots, fuel consumption trials, take-offs with full load with simulated engine failures – to establish the minimum safe climb-away speed – stalls on one engine and dummy decklandings on one engine.

On 31 October the author received a signal detailing him to take over 813 Wyvern squadron from Lt/Cdr Pridham Price (8 ETPS) in Malta.

CHAPTER 10

813 SQUADRON IN *ALBION* and *EAGLE*

A few days before I was due to take over 813 from 'Pridham' Price, I found that a Wyvern – the first to be fitted with a Coffman cartridge starter instead of using compressed air – was at Lee-on-Solent and wanting someone to fly it out to Malta. I climbed in the night before I was due to leave to give it a practice start to see if everything was OK. The WRN mechanic had just inserted two immense cartridges into something the size of an Austin Seven engine just behind the main air intake so I was expecting something exciting to happen especially as it was a few days before November the 5th.

When I pressed the starter, there was an immense hissing sound and the props started to turn. Just as I opened the high-pressure fuel cock to light up, there was a colossal bang and a sound like someone having thrown some milk churns into a harvester. I closed everything I could think of in the cockpit and the props came to a grinding halt. The WRN rushed up with a fire extinguisher and discharged it down the air intake and all was quiet once more apart from the usual hissing sounds like when a snake is cornered and the crackling sound of cooling metal.

Apparently, unburnt cordite gas from the starter cartridges had been drawn into the main combustion chambers where it exploded, blowing the back spinner into the front spinner turning in the opposite direction, and sucking the bits down the air intake, where it wrecked the compressor turbine. It was disappointing for the WRN Mechanic who had now seen her good work come to naught, with streaks of molten aluminum scarring the fuselage where it had blown out of the jet pipes. A much modified cartridge starter was refitted in June next year and it worked perfectly.

I arrived in Malta a week late by Dakota in the evening, joining a party of five of the twelve Squadron pilots at Jimmy Dowdall's restaurant at Birzebbuga on the shores of Marsaxlokk Bay, home of six Sunderlands and a large fishing community. 'Turn-over' from Pridham took the morning of the following day and after meeting the Captain of Hal Far Naval Air Station – Gratton-Cooper – we joined up with the Senior Pilot and our 'Carrier-borne Army Liaison Officer' (C-Balls for short) – Captain Colin Wallis-King, RA – and went on a risky ride in his jeep to visit Colin's Army Club where we played croquet until bar-opening time. Finally, some of us ended up at midnight at a flat in Valletta hired by the Armstrong-Whitworth engine representative attached to the Squadron, where we stayed the night.

Things were very relaxed in 813 Squadron, partly because we liked it that way and partly because 813 Squadron's nine Wyverns had been put ashore from *Albion* as 'unsafe to operate from a catapult' and our C-Balls had not yet fixed us up with any army 'battles' to join in on on the African mainland.

Pridham told me the history so far. *Albion* had been fitted with a 5½-degree 'interim' angled deck and had left the Tyne for Spithead to commence trials five months previously. After the completion of 'wire pulling' and finding that her BH 5 catapults did all their makers said they would, trials were also carried out on her newly fitted decklanding mirror using a Sea Hawk. Lt/Cdr W.I. Campbell had brought his 12 Sea Hawk F 3s of 898 Squadron on board and Lt/Cdr W. 'Doc' Ellis, AFC, RN– a genuine flying doctor from the School of Aviation Medicine – landed on with his 'own' Sea Hawk F1 fitted with an 'audio' airspeed indicator, the first of its kind. (This device issued a steady medium-pitched note for 'speed OK', the note altering in the pilot's earphones, high or low, loud or soft, intermittent or steady, to warn the pilot of the rate and amount by which his airspeed on the landing approach was deviating from the correct speed).

After this, 'Jock' Elliot had made a sonic boom or two before doing half-a-dozen 'touch-and-goes' in one of the prototype DH 110s from Boscombe and then Pridham had arrived with his Wyverns and 813 did DLPs (decklanding practice) for the next three or four days. Then, *en route* to Malta Lt Bruce MacFarlane, a New Zealander, had been catapulted off *Albion* in a Wyvern S4 and he had a 'flame-out' when going off the port catapult. The Wyvern had crashed into the sea almost under the ship's bows and the ship ran over him. His account read:

> Catapulting is always a startling experience and I usually find myself off the bows before I collect my wits enough to be aware of anything and take control of the aircraft. In this case my first realisation was a loss of power; I tried to open the throttle, but this was of course already locked in the open position.
>
> The next instant I hit the sea at about 70 knots, wheels down, of course, and flaps in the take-off position. I knew that the Wyvern had very poor ditching characteristics and I had in fact witnessed a fatal ditching about 18 months ago when the Wyvern had entered the sea and disappeared immediately without any hesitation at all before sinking.
>
> This memory flashed through my mind just before hitting the sea and I felt that I had no chance of escape. The impact with the sea stunned me to some extent.
>
> When I had collected my wits again I was underwater and it was getting darker. My nervous system seemed to have disconnected my body from my brain – except for my left hand. The yellow 'Emergency Canopy Jettison' knob filled my whole vision. I was grateful for its colour and position. I hit it with my left hand and the canopy became unlocked and green water poured in all around its edges. I did not notice the canopy actually go and it may have been more or less in position when I ejected. I pulled the ejector seat 'blind' handle with my left hand only immediately after hitting the hood jettison lever.
>
> Tears on my flying overall and on my Mae West could have been caused by the ejection up through the canopy. I was wearing a crash helmet (bone dome) and

the actual jettison seemed identical to the practice we had on the test rig. I then pulled the firing handle once more to fire the seat. I blacked out immediately and the next awareness was of being out of the aircraft. Ejection did not bring me out on the surface – from a position when I fired the seat perhaps 20 feet under and with the cockpit at about 30 degrees nose down.

I learnt later that the ship had cut the rear fuselage in two – the tail and a collapsed fuselage tank had been seen to pass down the ship's starboard side. I assume I was out before the ship hit the aircraft. I was not aware of any collision with the ship. As soon as I collected my wits again after ejection I became aware of being tumbled over violently in light green sea and becoming entangled in the seat and its yellow drogue chute. I had choked in quite a lot of water by this time and the prospect of drowning was no longer unpleasant – just like drinking fresh water.

Eventually the tumbling ceased and I thought I was going to live, and then, with the most bitter disappointment, I began to be dragged slowly down, deeper and deeper. I must have reached an advanced stage of drowning as I was dreamy, relaxed, comfortable but in a sad state, slowly 'floating' deeper. I had given up the struggle.

Suddenly all the tangle freed itself, a spark of life reached my brain – but the dinghy halyard (fastening the dinghy to the Mae West) was still pulling me down. I followed my hand down and pulled the release and after two attempts it came adrift and I began rising. For the first time I had a desperate need for air; I tried to swim upwards. I suddenly remembered my Mae West and I pulled the toggle to inflate it. I popped up like a cork, into the sunshine. I surfaced astern and to port, about 200 yards from the ship. The helicopter with the strop lowered was already there waiting for me.

My overall conviction from this was that but for the ejector seat I would never have got out of the aircraft as the water pressure would have held the canopy on and I could not have lifted it. My experience on the 'practice' ejector seat rig was much appreciated. Crash helmet and inner helmet not only protected my face and head but my ears as well.

By some miracle, Bruce MacFarlane had nothing but a broken collarbone and minor cuts and bruises. (The author is grateful to him for allowing the printing of his report in this book).

Following a fatal accident off the catapult seven years later in a Buccaneer on catapult trials in 'C' Squadron where the pilot and observer could not get out, three years research on underwater ejection systems eventually produced a safe answer and it became a practical possibility.

The cause of MacFarlane's engine failure had been a total fuel stoppage in the main supply pipeline leading forward from the tanks to the burners. This horizontal supply pipe was about six feet long, but because fuel was being *sucked* along it to the burners by a pump in the front, instead of being pushed along by a pump in the back, a vacuum was caused in the pipe whenever the horizontal forward 'G' of about three and a half times gravity was applied to the aircraft as it was accelerated off the catapult, cutting off the fuel supply completely for about two seconds, sufficient time for the engine not to relight when G conditions returned to normal. An identical failure had also occurred in the Double-Mamba-engined Gannet. The fault was corrected in this case by inserting a small 'recuperator' tank of fuel in the circuit, *forward* of the burners, which was sufficient to keep the flame alight for the two seconds acceleration off the catapult.

After MacFarlane's accident, the squadron had been sent ashore to await modifications. Pridham had only lost one other Wyvern so far and that had been the tragic loss of Lt P.R. Banner when he crashed into the sea after having taken off from Hal Far. The reason for this was not certain, but it may have been engine stoppage due to propeller bearing failure again.

After we had said goodbye to Pridham who was appointed to ETPS as a tutor, flying continued from Hal Far, Bizerta or Idris with the squadron taking part in army and fleet exercises. On one of these we took all 11 serviceable Wyverns into the air and made a pretence rocket attack on the cruiser *Jamaica* who had requested C-in-C Med for a bit of gunnery practice. As we had found out that she would be about 50 miles north of Cape Bon – some very high ground on the North-African coast which would mask her radar – and, lacking any 849 Squadron AEW support to give her warning of a low-level approach, we made a combined 'attack' on her from this direction. Not a gun moved, for her defence system was not even at Action Stations. She never saw us coming. Feeling very pleased with ourselves we made some practice strafing attacks on Filfa range with our four 20mm cannon on the way back and then got into the Squadron's three-tonner and went to Jimmy Dowdall's pub at Kalafrana for a beer.

After Christmas – which I do not remember a thing about – Colin Wallis-King and I flew to Idris to fix up an army exercise with the 14/20 Hussars who were camped in the desert near Tripoli. Driving there in the Hussar's jeep which came to meet us, we mounted the escarpment south of Tripoli and, after about twenty miles of nothing but sand I spied an army private sitting on a chair miles from anywhere and having a haircut – so we knew we were getting warm. He lowered the *Daily Mirror* he was reading and directed us to the officer's mess tent about half a mile away. We arrived just in time for lunch at a laid table with a snow-white cloth. After a gin-and-tonic we sat down at table and were served with a magnificent roast lamb main course and red wine by deferential stewards in white coats and gloves.

Having fixed up a date when we would be available for an 'attack' on the Hussars' formation in the coming 'battle', Colin and I were driven back to our Meteor and we returned to Halfar.

When the day came for us to strike the Hussars' enemy – the Lancers – Colin, pointing to a position on the desert map fifty miles from nowhere near the confluence of two 'wadis' – said:

> If I know Charles. . . (this was not the real name of the Colonel-in-Command of the 17/21st Lancers who was our 'enemy' for this exercise). . . he'll be here and if

we get there at lunchtime, his Lancer chaps'll be consuming the unexpired portion of the day's ration, with their transport round them and their eyes up their a... ...s.

So, with much merriment we climbed the 14 feet into our cockpits, took off and set course in radio silence for Colin's suggested map-reference position 290 miles distant. Needless to say, we found Charles and his chaps exactly where Colin had said, 'strafed' them with our cameras – to prove to them later that we had actually been there – and returned to Hal Far having been airborne for only two hours and fifteen minutes.

We had 93 men in the squadron, 10 Chief Petty Officers, 15 Petty Officers and two Engineer officers assisted by two senior Westlands' representatives.

Towards the end of February 1955 our C-in-C wanted 813 Squadron to take part in Operation SEA LANCE – flying our Wyverns from Bizerta airfield. We were going to be part of Black Force – the baddies – and we were attacking Malta supposedly defended by Red Force – the goodies. I went to see my Commanding Officer for this exercise to find out how our 12 Wyverns based at Bizerta could help him capture Malta from Red Force. He was a 'Submariner' so he was open to any ridiculous suggestions as long as they had a chance of catching Red Force with their pants down, preferably by an underwater weapon of some sort.

I suggested that our Wyverns should drop 'practice mines' at the entrance to Grand Harbour between St Elmo Point and Fort Ricasoli. Any 'invasion' force would have to pass through this gap to enter harbour and our magnetic mines would wreak theoretical havoc upon them, winning us the battle with no casualties on our side at all! If done at night, it would be free of any interruption by the RAF's Meteors at Luqa who were 'Red Force's' fighter defence. We would light up our target by firing parachute flares from a low-level LABS attack, approaching from seaward.

Night-flying was not a popular sport at Hal Far in 813 as our night vision was usually ruined by contractor's lorry headlights engaged in runway lengthening, and Hal Far's runway lighting was still at wartime standards and still using paraffin flares in places. However, we were able to fly to Bizerta during the first week in March together with half our men and do our night flying practice from there.

On the night of our attack we had just loaded up at Bizerta with our flares and four dummy mines when a French Air Force officer ran out from the flying control building and handed me a message in a cleft stick. This cancelled our mine dropping 'due to risk of practice mine marker-floats damaging *Britannia*, the Royal Yacht'.

Apparently she would be entering Grand Harbour in a ceremonial fashion rather than a warlike one before our mines could be removed, and, particularly as she was brand new and much in the news, there was a risk that the phosphorous mine-marker flares, which would automatically be released as a ship passed over them, might ruin her topside paintwork. We had to be content with dawn shoot-ups of Floriana using nothing but noise.

On 22 March *Albion* put to sea *en route* back to Portsmouth via Gibraltar. After saying goodbye to Hal Far and to their Commander 'Air' – Percy Heath, who had flown Swordfish in the old *Eagle* in 824 Squadron in the war and who had been very helpful and patient with us Wyverns during our stay there – we landed aboard *Albion* without incident.

Because of the unreliability of our air-starter supply we had devised a similar scheme to that of the Gannet by using prop slipstream from two Wyverns to start a third. Two Wyverns were therefore securely tied down with their tails converging at an angle of about 30 degrees. The Wyvern to be 'windmilled' was then positioned about 25 yards behind them. The front two were started and run at full power such that their resultant slipstreams hit each other and, in doing so, gained height as well as speed sufficient to cover the entire 18-foot diameter of a Wyvern's prop and to rotate it fast enough for the pilot to open his high-pressure fuel supply and press the relight button. When we used it, it saved having to leave anyone behind when his cartridge starter system failed.

Our 'land-on' went well. This was good work by the squadron because we had had no mirror sight at Hal Far to practice with and *Albion*'s single mirror on her port side was in line with the setting sun at the time of our land-on and invisible for most of the time. Furthermore, the batsman, still in charge in case the mirror misbehaved, fired so many 'round again' red Very lights at every-one that he ran out of supplies and we had to wait until someone produced some more from the ship's ammunition locker.

Eventually, we asked the ship to alter course so that we could see the rather dim horizontal datum lights. This made the angled deck even more out of wind so that our approach had to be from starboard of the centreline. This hid us from the nervous view of Commander Air. As no one had yet been allowed to watch Wyverns landing-on because of the propeller splinter hazard, it was some time before we had any useful criticism of our landings, for even the batsman was seen to be crouching down behind the armour plate with just two wild eyes visible over the top and a Very pistol sticking out sideways.

Several of us did 'bolters' – a word derived from the game of skittles and a descriptive name for 'missing all the wires and going round again for another try'. Bolters were quite safe, of course, as there was no barrier now that we had an angled deck. We took our own decision whether we would bolt or not. We ignored frantic signals from the batsman because his signals were too late for the engine to pick up in time before running out of flight deck. In fact bolters were encouraged, for coming in too fast and too high was infinitely safer than coming in too slow and too low and risking a collision with the round-down.

When twin mirrors were eventually installed on both sides of the deck, the pilot could obtain clear and continuous information on his height/angle-of-approach and centre-line accuracy by a steady gaze at the mirror/projector sight. Nothing could be gained by suddenly transferring his gaze to a batsman or other objects at different distances and directions, because a pilot's eyes took time to re-focus and the brain took time to digest and act upon new information. This second's delay was sufficient to throw the pilot off course, causing him to make unsafe corrections at the last moment.

Albion's patient and thoughtful skipper – Captain 'Bill' W.A.F. Hawkins, DSO, DSC & Bar – came down to see us in the wardroom afterwards to tell us the ship's programme. 'Umtum-Tiddly's* engineers were aboard in strength and with the help of our own highly skilled and hardworking riggers and fitters, they would be modifying our fuel systems to allow catapulting. He then told us that 813 would re-embark in *Eagle* with 827 Squadron on arrival at Ford when *Albion* took us all back to Portsmouth at the end of March 1955 and we should probably not be required to fly on the way home except for 'beating-up' North Front at Gibraltar together with 898's Sea Hawks as we passed by.

When taking off for this 'attack', the Wyverns put their foot in it. It had been a sporting move on the part of the Captain to have allowed us free take-offs – as we still could not use the catapult – so we had been ranged well aft on the flightdeck to allow a 600-foot take-off run. Down went the green flag and Charles Bush's Wyvern ahead of me, the first to take off, blew his two chock-men over the round-down with his slipstream. I can vouch for the fact that there were two for I counted them as they passed under my starboard wing, moving at about 45 knots, two or three feet up.

The S-51 'chopper' immediately hovered over their two splashes and was able to deposit them both on the flight deck a few minutes later. They had then made a beeline for 'Fly One' up in the bow where they carried out their duties for the remainder of the trip.

This was a lucky outcome for a possible tragedy, for the two men only just missed my Wyvern's propellers as they swept past. The incident reminded all of us of the dangers of passing anywhere near a Wyvern's 250 mph slipstream when it was delivering its full 4,000 horsepower. (The V-squared 'lift' from this slipstream on the crouching human body is about 500 lb, or a 'push-force' of about 150 lb on every square foot of his body exposed to it. If there were about three square feet of body in its way, the Wyvern's prop slipstream would impart an acceleration four times that of gravity on the human body, equal to the G from the ship's catapult on an aircraft)!

The ship took five days to reach the Nab Tower off Portsmouth where she flew us off to Ford. The flight to Ford airfield took about ten minutes, five of these being spent in a brief 'goodbye' to the ship – i.e., trying to blow Bill Hawkins' hat off.

On landing from *Albion* at Ford we heard that our sister Squadron – 827 – had already flown aboard *Eagle* a day or two previously for some decklanding practice. But she had had to return to Portsmouth with one of 827's Wyvern engines sticking out of her funnel. This delayed the ship's work-up pro-

---

* Navalese for Armstrong-Siddeley

gramme and S/Lt Jarret – the lucky Wyvern pilot who survived with little harm – and the remainder of 827, went back at Ford for more practice.

It took a fortnight to repair the funnel after which it was 813's turn to embark with our nine aircraft and 90 men. This allowed us first pick of the accommodation. The two 'new boys' in the squadron did a few decklandings, but Lt (E) 'Joe' Norman was not considered to have passed the test by Barry Nation (Cdr Air) or by our Skipper (Captain E.D. Lewin, CB, DSO, DSC & Bar). Pleading with the Captain to allow us to give Joe another chance was useless. The Wyvern was not so dangerous to deckland now that we had the angled deck and Joe would soon have gained confidence with a bit more practice. However, such was the general fear of the Wyvern – with its past disastrous history and the image of the dartlike Wyvern in *Eagle*'s funnel passing again before our Captain's eyes – that he decide against being allowed another try.

Both Wyvern squadrons behaved very well in this magnificently built and happy ship and in the next few months we completed about 1,000 decklandings without a single crash. One in ten of all these landings was preceded by one or more bolters, but no one minded in the least; in fact with the deck sometimes pitching through 24 feet at the round-down (equivalent to a 3½ degree bow-down pitch) it was much safer to do a bolter than risk a heavy arrival and risk more propeller shrapnel.

Nevertheless, two tragedies were caused in this way. In the second one, a flight deck Petty Officer was looking up at the pilot of a Wyvern he was directing and signalling it to park behind a Gannet. He forgot the Gannet's steel hook sticking out from behind its rudder by a couple of feet and the Wyvern's propellers smashed into it. Minute steel splinters flew off the propellers killing him instantly.

The decklanding and catapult intervals compared well, weight for weight, with the Sea Hawks on board and the Wyvern stood up well to rough weather on deck, for seven of them formed a permanent deck park. However, the ten-ton Wyvern could easily tow the ship's small tractors about if *Eagle* was rolling and we often had to drag many of our men away from servicing them to ask them to help push.

On our arrival at Malta the ship was visited by the press, the army and other dignitaries. Our decklanding performance had given the Captain much more confidence and he had allowed a few selected 'goofers' onto the *Eagle*'s 'island' as long as they stayed forward of the funnel. The 'air show' included Sea Hawks in tight formation, rocket attacks on a splash target towed astern, decklanding twelve Wyverns in five minutes. But the best entertainment might have been our Wyverns doing a cartridge start. In fact it should not have been allowed. Enough smoke and flame was evolved from a dozen of these ten-ton monsters starting up, to give away the position of the fleet. In the ensuing holocaust on the flight deck, dim figures could be discerned, coughing horribly in the cordite-laden air as they staggered and strained every muscle to try to position these huge aircraft to safe positions. As the smoke cleared, grim faces were revealed and startled eyes. Hoarse shouts rose above a crescendo of noise as the green flag went down. The cynical eye of the Flight Deck Officer giving the 'full throttle' signal to the Wyvern leader on the catapult. The surprised look of achievement on the face of his number two as he felt his aircraft wheels come up against the loading chocks of the other catapult – tailwheel dead-centre.

Then there was the land-on in an hour's time. Wyverns were meat and drink to the hardened goofer. Heads would poke out of every hole along the island and eyes would range behind the armoured glass on the bridge. A line of brave goofers would appear from behind the funnel, ready to retreat if things looked nasty. The wires would reset, the mirror angle altered to four degrees descent path. There would be a plume of white smoke from the rear of the funnel and a plume of black smoke from the forward part and no one on the bridge could find which engine-room was to blame. The ship's doctor is on the bridge, the stretcher party 'closes up.' Commander (E) John Rae explains the cause of the funnel smoke to the Captain so that he can tell the Admiral if he complains. Speed is increased to 30 knots and the whole ship vibrates under our feet.

The first Wyvern approach is a wave-off. This is usual stuff and is done more for effect than safety. The next one is perfect and the hook catches number two wire. Those in Flyco pass a dry tongue over a stiff upper lip and take another nervous drag – the Captain having given permission to smoke during this time.

Perhaps the only person who is not too worried at this time is the Wyvern pilot. With a steady 100–102 knots on the clock, the Wyvern's irresistible, steamroller-like approach is as steady as a rock. The only deck accidents we had were caused by tailwheels being knocked off due to a construction weakness. On one occasion the tailwheel strut caught a wire and the twenty-ton retardation force pulled the entire tail askew. However, the spare tail had been made so accurately at Westlands that the replacement, out of packing cases, fitted perfectly in the existing holes within a hundredth of an inch.

As our aircraft got older and with so much low flying over the sandy deserts of North Africa, we found that their roughened surface at the wings' leading edges caused stalling speeds to rise (as fast bowlers have found out when wanting to impart more swing to a cricket ball), with tail buffeting starting some ten knots earlier as the stall was approached. They were accordingly smoothed up by Westlands and coated with a special 'rubber' finish on the first two inches of wing upper surface which cured the problem entirely and also discouraged ice formation.

Our two squadron Air Engineer Officers (ours in 813 were Lt (E) David Rose and Lt (L) C.D. Hodgkinson) were wizards at improvisation and had the essential sense of humour and patience to keep our difficult aircraft flying. That using part of the ship's company – our squadrons' ratings in 827 and 813 – worked in conditions worse than a car factory for long hours and their minute attention to detail deserved our thanks a hundred times a day.

Exercises continued in the Mediterranean during June, July and August 1955. During the hot weather we wore the latest 'ventilated suit' at skin level in an effort to keep cool in the Wyvern's un-airconditioned cockpit. The suit was a mass of terylene fabric and plastic piping, designed to allow air under pressure from a small compressor to blow cooling air over the parts of the body that other air couldn't reach. Although we were grateful to the doctors who had thought of this idea, the suit itself was made of semi-impervious material so that it allowed body moisture to build up under it until it ran into our boots, so we tended to wear Gieves' absorbent cotton vests instead.

During our stay in Malta and while we were aboard, we were visited by designers and other scientists from the firms who had manufactured the Gannets, Sea Hawks and Wyverns we were flying. The experience was invaluable for them to see how the Navy operated their products and for them to have some warning of future design problems. One of the chief scientists was Mr N.E. Rowe or 'Nero' for short, the Technical Director at Blackburns. He was most intrigued to know what we thought of the Wyvern, because his firm's Project Design team was busy designing what they hoped would become the Wyvern replacement in three years time. 'Nero' had told me in a whisper that his firm had obtained preliminary information in December 1953 of a new strike aircraft – destined to become the NA 39 Buccaneer concept the Navy might want to replace the Wyvern. I remember telling him that what was wanted above all was a *single-purpose* design, not an 'all-singing, all-dancing' model which was designed to do everything and would end up doing very little – like the Wyvern and Firebrand. What the Navy needed was a genuine, low-level, long-range aircraft, subsonic – but capable of going supersonic in a shallow dive if need be –which could get *under* the defences and deliver its weapons from a safe distance, be they rockets or bombs. The idea of dropping torpedoes – which I had already been ordered to practise but as yet had had no time – should be forgotten completely. Getting anywhere near as close as 2,000 yards to a Sverdlov cruiser – with or without MiG defence – and having to slow down to 200 knots to drop it, was similar in its madness to sending Swordfish to do the same thing against the *Scharnhorst* and *Gneisenau* up the English Channel on 12 February 1942 in daylight when the brave Esmonde and his 825 Squadron met their death. The air-dropped conventional torpedo just wasn't on. It was extraordinary that anyone at the Admiralty still thought that it was.

In June I was told to attend a Naval Air Staff meeting at C-in-C's office, Malta. Captain Smeeton – about to take command of *Albion* – was also there plus officers from the Admiralty. The subject was *Strike aircraft for the Royal Navy*. When I was asked to comment – not daring to say anything unless I was asked – I repeated what I had said to 'Nero'. Perhaps several of those at this important meeting may have had the same opinions as myself as it was three weeks after this meeting – on 30 July 1955 – that Blackburns received their first contract for the NA 39. Exactly a year after that, a top-level meeting was held with the Defence Minister – Mr Duncan Sandys in the Chair and with DDNAW, Captain Gibson and the First Sea Lord, Lord Mountbatten present. This meeting is described later.

Having said goodbye to the aircraft manufacturers, the ship sailed from Grand Harbour on what is best described as a 'Discovery' cruise round the Mediterranean, calling in at Naples, Taormina, Catania and finally Messina – where our Wyverns posed for F 24 photographs over Mount Etna.

While operating with the American 6th Fleet we had 183's first airborne incident. This was when S/Lt Steers ejected from his Wyvern over Capodichino while photographing Latina on 12 August. The remains of his aircraft were dug up and its engine taken to Farnborough. On dissecting the engine, they found that its 'verge ring' had 'picked up' on the main rotor of the compressor and the whole thing had broken up. This occurred when Steers was flying at about 15,000 feet in hazy cloud formations and, so he said, was presaged by engine stalling and vibration. The ejector seat plus all its gear (including auto-hood ejection, leg restraint tightening, harness tightening, auto-oxygen supply, seat separation, the new 'bone dome' helmet etc.) had all worked perfectly. This success replenished our confidence.

But it set us all thinking too. Several of us in 813 had experienced the same sort of vibration when we had been flying in formation through very thin stratus cloud at about 12,000 feet over Idris one day. This happened to be at air temperatures of about zero degrees C, too. Steer's engine break-up – and our 'vibrations' over Idris – could have been caused by ice formation in the reverse-flow part of the air intakes with bits of ice breaking off and disrupting the airflow in the combustion chambers causing mini-explosions there and breaking up the turbine. This was no more than conjecture, of course, as all signs of the ice had disappeared by the time we had landed and there could be no proof of our theory. (Similar engine breakup has since occurred in a number of civilian jet aircraft flying in similar weather.)

Towards the end of August the ship started to make her way back to UK via Naples. Naples and Vesuvius were great attractions. The yacht harbour and Yacht Club welcomed our ship's sailing boats and *Iff* (my Flying Fifteen which the Captain had given me permission to bring aboard at Malta) for which they lent us free mooring space just for the asking. It was heaven sailing round to the famous Grotto and taking off for a 20-mile sail to Capri, sleeping the night aboard *Iff* in the warm, moonlit harbour. On the next 'day off' I and Charles Bush sailed her to Ischia, about twenty miles northwest of Naples. Having insufficient wind to get back in time for supper, we thumbed a lift from a passing motor-boat – which happened to be one of *Eagle*'s returning by the same route – and she towed us behind her at 15 knots and it was more exciting than landing a Wyvern.

Life in the Navy can have its ups and downs, but our time in *Eagle* must have been the happiest peacetime job of all. We arrived at Harwich on 12 September and did a 'strike' on the ship herself after 'minelaying' the harbour entrance. During this two-hour trip several of us had our 'reverse torque' warning lights show while flying at ice-formation height at about 15,000 feet. This 'compressor-stalling' behaviour reinforced our suspicion that it was the ice in the air intakes which caused explosions of steam in the combustion chambers which blew the flame out.

Three days later and with the ship by now off the north coast of Scotland and going north-west to Norway, we had another Wyvern incident. In this case Lt Charles Bush pulled the blind of his Martin-Baker automatic seat at 700 feet above the sea (he had just taken a wave-off from his decklanding approach) and his parachute had opened with about 200 feet to spare. His immersion-suit boots had come off with the ejection 'G' as he had forgotten to put his feet on the seat bars before pulling the blind.

When he answered the question on his accident report form, 'Did you notice any peculiar sensation?' he said, 'As usual,' for it was not his first use of the M-B seat, having had to leave a Sea Venom a year earlier. The cause of the second Wyvern bale-out was assumed to have been the failure of one of the aileron operating arms. Two others were found to have cracks in them and were hurriedly replaced. Following a further incident 10 days later when Morris Hedges made an emergency landing ashore due to engine trouble, our Captain began to lose confidence and called Dicky and I to his sea cabin. He proposed cancelling all Wyvern aviation until the reason for the failures had been discovered.

After a long discussion – at which we pointed out that Morris Hedges' trouble had probably not been icing but oil cooler 'coring' (where the centre of the oil cooler freezes up solid, thus causing the engine to overheat) and not quite so serious – Dicky and I told the Captain that everyone was keen to continue as morale was still very high in the two squadrons. So the Captain agreed to continue.

Our trip round the North Sea included visits to Orlandet, Bergen and Oslo. From 22 September to 11 October we took part in a NATO exercise called SEA ENTERPRISE together with *Centaur*, *Albion* and *Bulwark* – all with angled decks by now. Wyverns, with navigation assistance from AEW Skyraiders, carried out strikes on Orlandet and Vaernes – places well known to Skua pilots in the war. Our Sea Hawk Squadron – 898 – landed ashore at Gardermoen airfield where they said that the Norwegian 'enemy' were very friendly and after partaking of much wassail, they spoke better English than we did.

We had a few Russian 'spy ships' hovering around and the ship's 'Intelligence Officer' told us that he had overheard their radio conversation telling their 'agents' in Tromso or somewhere that they had bugged all our signals and were 'swanking' that they knew more about our movements than we did ourselves. Our Force Commander encouraged the use of flag semaphore signalling between ships in close company after that, as the Russians could not understand this Nelsonian method of communication.

In the air we found we could out-manoeuvre the heavily-loaded Norwegian Airforce Thunderjets (controlled by their own AEW) but only if they approached from a dive too fast to turn with us.

At this time we were using the new TACAN navigation aid centre at Lossiemouth which was now classed as an 'All-Weather' station.

We could probably have been sent twice the distance to our targets – i.e., 300 miles there and 300 miles back – and still have had no difficulty in managing the daylight navigation for ourselves. But none of our strikes would have reached their targets unless our Sea Hawks had already established 'air superiority' over the target areas before our arrival and during our retreat for the Wyvern was easy meat for the Norwegian fighters. Neither would our pilot navigation alone be sufficiently accurate, especially when flying at night or in poor visibility at low altitudes. Small errors in heading when flying a jet at 450 knots had a greater affect on navigation accuracy than when flying at a Seafire's 240 knots. A timing error of one minute's flying in a Firefly cruising at 180 knots would mean a distance error of only three miles. At 40,000 feet with a ground speed of 450 knots the same error in time in a jet would result in a navigation error of nearly eight miles. Errors due to wind would have less effect on jets due to their higher speed, but this could be offset when flying at high altitudes where wind velocities were often 50–60 knots and, in jet-streams, wind speeds could be up to 120 knots or more. (Another reason why we could never understand faith in high-level bombing accuracy). It was obvious that a strike aircraft of the 50s would have to take an observer along as well as the pilot – if only for him to work all the new electronic gear making its appearance in the back seat.

At this time we Wyverns were trying out our new form of attack on shipping called 'lobbing'. It involved releasing the bombs or rockets while in the early stages of a loop. Because the bombs or rockets could then be released at three times the usual range from the targets, the attacking aircraft could be on its way home within seconds. Provided that aiming accuracy could somehow be preserved, this 'lobbing' method might catch on. It might even be possible to fire torpedoes in this way, provided they could be slowed down with small parachutes before they entered the water or they could sprout small wings with an in-built autopilot to guide them, for the lobbing would need to be done at the aircraft's maximum speed.

Bomb-lobbing had special problems in the Wyvern, for the aircraft was not fast enough to clear the target area in a loop after doing so. Rocket lobbing was feasible however, as the increased firing range allowed a steep turn away from the target which would probably keep it out of lethal – i.e., close – 20–30mm AA gunfire range.

The most important factors affecting whether you hit a stationary target or not when lobbing were likely to be aircraft's speed, altitude, range and angle of elevation at the moment of firing the rockets – and, of course the target's speed and direction as well.

Speed was always 300 knots for the Wyvern – its only speed, flat out at sea level, come what may.

Altitude was also easy to fix accurately – sea level. No mistakes possible so far.

Range was fixed by using the Mark 13 radar ranging device already fitted to the Wyvern for firing torpedoes at ships. This was now altered by Lt

Hodgkinson, our electrical officer, to give the warning to fire at 4000 yards range instead of the 2000 yards – which was the range for dropping torpedoes.

Angle-of-elevation was the tricky one; but by connecting the aircraft's artificial horizon to the firing circuit, 'Hodge' made it fire the rockets at a predetermined, nose-up angle of 20 degrees to the horizon. Knowing the rocket's average speed to the target, this was the angle that was needed for it to hit the target at a 4000 yard firing range.

Our results were staggering – nearly as good – on a splash target towed astern of *Eagle* at 20 knots – as those fired conventionally from a 30-degree dive at a quarter of the range. Additional accuracy was obtained when firing at moving targets or in windy weather by using the gyro gunsight with its precision input reduced to allow the correct deflection at 4,000 yards range instead of the normal rocketry deflection allowance setting of about 1,000 yards.

Fired in this manner at about 2 miles from the target and miles outside accurate 20–30mm AA range, we could look forward to a reasonable survival rate from the guns of a Sverdlov and a better survival rate than in any Swordfish. Knowing that some very large, long-range rockets were being tested at this time, we expected that, provided the Wyvern could depend on 'air superiority' fighter protection from our Sea Hawks, the Wyvern might be useful in a future war. We carried out several 'attacks' on splash targets towed astern of *Eagle* and it did not take a genius to see that this 'lobbing' idea would immediately catch on.

The Captain forwarded my ideas to the Admiralty – dated 23 January 1956 – through the C-in-C's Office, HMS *Tyne*, at Gibraltar, with a recommendation for an award to myself and Lt Hodgkinson from the 'Herbert Lott Naval Trust Fund.' The C-in-C at Gibraltar forwarded our Captain's letter with mine to the Admiralty on 23 January. In his letter he said:

> This invention is an excellent example of the type of co-operation to be encouraged, an Executive officer's proposed new tactics and a technical officer's effort to give him the means. It is considered that Service trials must be carried out to prove the value of this form of attack before any award can be made, but it is already apparent that low cloud and/or bad weather could force the Wyvern to use this form of attack, even though only superficial damage to the enemy could be expected. An award is strongly recommended.

Back came the reply, dated 12 April 1956 (and I still have the copy):

> By Command to Their Lordships – the proposed technique has been considered but in view of the time-scale of Wyvern aircraft the project will not be proceeded with. The officers are to be congratulated . . . etc etc.

This was an 'all-weather' attack method. The lack of interest shown by the Admiralty was probably because they had wrongly assumed that this attack method was only intended for use in bad weather!

This LABS attack method may have been unpopular with the Navy's gunners because it might have cast official doubts on the effectiveness of their new 'Sea Slug' missile as a means of surface/air protection from missile-firing aircraft. (Please see Appendix 1, Air Defence: Naval gunnery or fighters?)

Identical LABS (Low Altitude Bombing System) lobbing techniques in Scimitars, using weapons such as 'Bullpup' and 'Sidewinder' were eventually adopted by pilots seven years later in the Buccaneer (as instructed by 764 Squadron at Lossiemouth two years earlier) and twenty years after that the Sea Harrier used the technique in the Falklands.

By the middle fifties, it became apparent to some scientists that the day of the big gun and high-altitude bomber were over and that below-radar approaches to the target by aircraft or missiles would be the safest and by far the most accurate air-delivery method in a defended area for all types of weapon in the near future. The French were already designing their 'zero-height' 500 mph, 50-mile range self-guiding 'Exocet' and by this time the Navy were considering whether to replace the air torpedo with the 'Bullpup', rocket-propelled, low-level guided missile. This was a slight improvement as it had a five-mile range but had to be guided by the pilot who fired it.

Air-delivery methods for the A-bomb – which had yet to have a 'stand-off' capability – might be in the form of a near-supersonic loop with the bomb being released as the aircraft was approaching the vertical; the idea being that the aircraft would then roll off the top of the loop and dive down for cover, in the direction of home. Such an aircraft would need to have a very high power/weight ratio to allow it to retain near-supersonic speed throughout the delivery manoeuvre so that it could remain ahead of the nuclear blast wave and keep outside excessive radiation levels after the bomb exploded.

In 1962, strike aircraft of that era, including the Buccaneer, were painted white to reflect this radiation as much as possible. When we first saw this whiteness and realised its purpose, not one of us had yet thought of the hazards of getting caught up in the explosion ourselves or how we could keep out of the way of the huge blast wave and its radiation.

Rocket lobbing was not our 'swansong' in *Eagle* for just before flying ashore to disband, our squadrons carried out a 'Shop Window' display for the benefit of the press, manufacturers and others who came aboard to watch. About 200 sorties later – which included the dropping of live 500/lb bombs and rockets – we assembled in the Wardroom for a party and entertained our guests by playing the game of 'High-cock-a-lorum.' There can be no accurate description of this delightful schoolboy game except to say that its basic aim is to collapse the opponent's team by jumping on them.

Someone then decided that the Wardroom officers should try to show their gratitude to the Wardroom stewards for their fine service by doing the clearing away and washing up. *Eagle*'s washing-up machine was 'Admiralty Pattern' and built like a battleship. It had a moving belt on which the plates were set. The plates, knives, forks, cups, glasses, napkins, cigar ends and ashtrays disappeared through two rubber 'doors' – and that was the last we saw of them. After five minutes, as nothing had come out the other end, we summoned John Rae, the Chief Engineer for his opinion. He lifted an inspection window and we saw nothing but a grey sludge, with the occasional bent spoon swimming past the window. John said that we should have been warned that it did not like certain sizes of plates and had therefore rebelled.

Baron, the famous photographer, came on board with about five beautiful cameras and took pictures of life aboard *Eagle* – including pictures of us playing games in the Wardroom after dinner. Intrigued, and expecting to get our faces in *Tatler* next month, we asked him how many he intended to publish. His answer was 'Perhaps one or two'.

On 19 November 1955 the Squadron was disbanded and we all went on leave. However, this was not until after 813 Squadron had given a 'lecture' to an assembled multitude in the station cinema at Lee-on-Solvent. All the usual staff officers were there – about a hundred of them. The Gannets and the Sea Hawks gave their expositions first. We then came on stage and, to show just how brave we had to be to fly a Wyvern against the Russian navy, we had made up a playlet, the scene being:

A typical squadron briefing aboard *Eagle* before a dawn strike in the North Atlantic against four Sverdlov cruisers believed to be advancing towards us in a following gale but with nine Wyverns of 813 Squadron armed with conventional torpedoes ready to stop them.

Our pilots were sitting in a row on the stage in their Mae Wests. Each was suitably pale and subdued, eyes set and thinking of England.

As if this tragic setting was not enough to get the audience's sympathy, I was also shaking with genuine fright myself for I had to read my briefing on the stage a few feet from a line of Admirals in the front row, dreading that our playlet might incur their displeasure. The audience thought that my fright was good acting so we were on to a winner from the start. Further pathos was when I briefed the squadron on the air/sea rescue arrangements we could expect if the Russians shot us down. At the mention that the sea temperature was nearly zero and we had no helicopters, a pilot pulled his Mae West inflation knob as a reflex action, disappearing behind it as it inflated. He then pretended to be sick in a bucket. When 'Seaweed', the Met Officer, came on stage to give us the weather – his isobars of course being in the shape of a naked lady – he 'accidentally' got his foot jammed in the sick-bucket. He crashed round the stage and eventually asked Commander (Air) – complete with huge brass hat and who had come round the door to wish us God's Speed – to help him pull it off. This started a mini game of 'high-cock a lorum' on the stage between 'A' and 'B' Flights who naturally tried to help as well. Then, when 'Action Stations' sounded on a distant Tannoy, everyone ran off stage and the curtain came down.

When we took our leave from our Captain – who had done us all proud – we went ashore to Ford where our aircraft were soon being repainted with 830 and 831 Squadrons' markings and were taken over by their new COs, Viv Howard and Stan Farquhar. They re-embarked for a second cruise and 830 Squadron was later involved in operation MUSKETEER at Suez.

CHAPTER 11

INTERLUDE ASHORE

To resume the narrative: the Army had taken the first initiative amongst the three Services to give their officers a year's break from Regimental duty to study Army management at a Staff College at a midpoint in their careers. Officers recommended for the Course were usually those chosen for promotion to the rank of Major and beyond. The course instructors, or Directing Staff (DS), were more concerned with instructing us on how to organise a battlefield rather than advising us on weapons and how to use them. They taught us how to write good English free from journalese, how to plan a battle and when to give clear, reasonable orders leading to an equally clear military objective within sight. Weapon performance was demonstrated on Salisbury Plain but was not often mentioned in the excellent lectures at the College. Neither were the DS (Directing Staff) much concerned with 'combined battles' involving the other two Services at this time, and the use of Fleet Air Arm aircraft or ships' bombardment was hardly mentioned.

When we joined on 4 February 1956 the author was one of three Navy and two RAF officers, all of us feeling our way amongst the traditional setting of the College at Camberley and its 'overflow' at Minley Manor. The head Tutor for the Minley Manor class was the well-known Colonel Richard Clutterbuck DSO, MC, of the Royal Engineers, one of the few who was interested in scientific and technical matters as well as organisational problems in soldiery.

When we were given typical military problems to solve – such as how to make a heavily-defended river-crossing in daylight – the airmen amongst us always managed to include massive air support of course.

'Splosh' Jones, (General Sir Charles Jones, GCB, of the Royal Engineers) was the Commandant of the College at that time. He accompanied us on one of our expeditions to Normandie – on what was known as the 'bottlefield tour.' Our Tutor at that time was Lt/Col 'Bobby' Steele, DSO MC who, on occasion, lent his yacht to several of us and which, on this occasion we took to Ouistreham for him on the start of one of our European tours.

Towards the end of September we became more and more aware of trouble brewing in the Suez Canal. It appeared that Colonel Nasser, who had taken over as dictator in place of King Farouk, had nationalised the Suez Canal.

Unknown to us at the time, London and Paris were in collusion with Israel. All three countries knew that Nasser would refuse to obey their ultimatum and clear out of the Canal Zone and that Egypt would continue to fight the Israelis. We and the French could then butt in, ostensibly to divide them but actually to seize back the Suez Canal without offending America, and so ensure future free passage for our third of the world's shipping which wanted to use it.

Accordingly, on 31 October, British and French planes attacked Egyptian bases. Five days later – during which time the media deplored such action – airborne and seaborne forces landed round Port Said.

In spite of the somewhat gentle approach of our forces plus our careful choice of targets and weapons to try to avoid hitting civilians, the invasion aroused much criticism especially in America where there was an election in progress, making it difficult for either President-to-be to be seen supporting Eden's action.

Accordingly, under this pressure, France and Britain halted their action on 7 November and a United Nations peace-keeping force was sent to the canal to take over.

Although 10 per cent of our budget was spent on defence at this time and the army still had about 350,000 men, it was clear from what we had learned at Staff College that the army was not trained or equipped for 'police actions' outside Europe or Northern Ireland and, lacking indigenous air support, was unable to act quickly enough to forestall public opinion in UK from bringing such action to a halt before the military aim could be properly achieved. Given a quick enough response to Nasser's action, British public opinion would have supported Eden, American support would have been forthcoming and collusion with Israel would not have been necessary.

As for the air battle itself, it was evident that although the Egyptians had been well armed by the Russians they had not yet developed the needed infrastructure of radar direction, warning systems, aircraft and armament maintenance and other operational techniques essential when actual fighting was necessary.

The first strike of forty Sea Hawk 6s and Sea Venoms from *Eagle* and *Albion* took off before dawn on 1 November. They strafed airfields along the canal, each pilot doing about four sorties each on that day. RAF Hunters and Venoms from Cyprus supplied 'top cover' with Wyverns attacking two coastal airfields. All dispersed aircraft targets at these airfields had been destroyed by the evening of 1 November and there was no need for further action by Canberras or Valiants. In the words of Lord Hailsham, then First Lord of the Admiralty:

> The aircraft were largely Naval aircraft, the land forces were largely Marines and of course, the carriage was largely by sea.

He could, however have criticised Naval 4.7in. gunnery accuracy which missed its proper targets by a mile or more on at least one occasion.

Six Sea Hawk squadrons, five Sea Venom squadrons and a single Wyvern Squadron took part. The standard procedure for fighter/ground-attack sorties was to take off in twelves every hour or so, climb to 20,000 feet, let down 'on track' and attack the targets with cannon, rockets or bombs and retire at zero feet to the coast. Then a climb to 5,000 feet to receive homing signals from the ship and a land-on via the AEW 'picket'. Naval aircraft claimed 102 aircraft destroyed on the ground in 1,300 sorties on the first five days of operations, the ceasefire coming at midnight on 6 November. The two magnificent Princess flying boats laid up on the slipway at Calshot were not ready in time to take part and sadly, these lovely craft were finally broken up a year later.

The end of the course in the College came all too soon and after a stirring speech from General Montgomery we trooped off back to our homes and awaited the next buff envelope. The author's was to appoint him Naval Tutor to relieve Pridham Price on Number 16 Course at ETPS.

Needless to say, the lunchtime conversation in the ETPS Mess was just the same – aeroplanes, fast cars and other exciting pastimes. There were 28 student pilots on Number 16 Course. Group Captain R.E. 'Paddy' Burns CBE, DFC was our Commandant. He was in place of the outgoing 'Sammy' Wroath – who had been the 'founder' of ETPS in 1943 and had been its Commandant for the past three years as well. Other tutors were Squadron Leaders Pete Baker and 'Bill' Morrison of 7 and 12 Courses respectively. Besides four Canadians, three Americans and two Indians, there were Dutch, Australian and French students. There were also two US Navy students and five Royal Navy, one of which – Lt Ted Anson and one of the author's 'pupils' – later made Admiral. (Vice-Admiral Sir Edward Anson, KCB.)

At this time, ETPS lectures included the latest progress information on weapon and aircraft development. On 15 March 1956, Peter Twiss – Fairey's Chief Test Pilot – had just flown their Fairey Delta FD-2 at 1,000 mph. We learnt, with trepidation, that the 'V' Force would soon have to contend with surface-to-air weapons with a 60-mile range up to heights of 60,000 feet with a 100 per cent hit capability. (Gary Powers was shot down at 60,000 feet by a similar weapon on 1 May 1960). However, the Americans were developing Polaris fired from submerged submarines to take the place of the V-Force and 'stand-off' and guided nuclear bombs were no longer on the development list after December 1962. However, we heard that a Captain Philip Saumarez had joined Hawker Siddeley Dynamics to advise on their development of the Sea Slug and Sea Dart seaborne guided weapons which, as the first generation of seaborne guided missiles, the Navy expected would take the place of fighter aircraft in the defence of our fleet in accordance with the then Minister of Defence's opinion – that manned aircraft would phase out and be replaced by guided weapons!

Fifteen Course's 'end-of-course' party had assembled a glittering throng. The students had made the ladies powder-room particularly attractive, for there was a beautiful Greek statue standing there, his nakedness suitably covered by a hinged fig leaf. When the fig leaf was lifted, a microswitch operated and a tape played various comments from a loudspeaker placed in the ceiling, saying such things as: 'I say, do you mind' or alternatively: "Ere, 'av yer doone?' This was relayed to the bar so we could all take part and see who emerged from the doorway afterwards.

The twelve different types of aircraft for use by ETPS had not altered much since 1948 apart from the addition of a Seamew, a Canberra T4, and S51 and an S55 helicopter.

Although the Seamew's fore-and-aft control was heavy handed and it had a somewhat ineffective elevator at the stall, it had a marvellous view for the pilot and observer, a steady decklanding approach and a well-absorbed touch-down. Unfortunately, by the time 'Brookie' and 'Wally' Runciman (who sadly crashed in the Seamew and was killed) had taken it to 'C' Squadron for trials in 1954, the Navy had already decided to use helicopters for anti-submarine search duties and as India – the only other potential customer – followed suit, Shorts were told to stop production after number 6 and the idea was scrapped.

We also had an opportunity to fly the Gloster Javelin 1. From four trips it was not possible to give a proper opinion on its effectiveness as an 'all-weather', night/day fighter/ground attack aircraft in competition with the Navy's Sea Vixen, but compared with the Scimitar, it lacked its easy handling and its climb performance. It was slow to take off and accelerate, it was lazier in roll and, except for elevator forces which were light but unresponsive at slow speeds, its controls were far heavier. Its rate of climb was about 20 per cent less than that of a Scimitar and its turning circle at 40,000 feet consisted of a series of near pitchups and skidding recoveries. I felt even sorrier that Pete Lawrence had been killed in one for it seemed he had lost his life for nothing.

A further note about the Canberra T4 is perhaps worthwhile. Designed mainly by Teddy Petter, it was the RAF's first jet bomber and was probably intended as a replacement for the Mosquito/Welkyn when it entered RAF service in 1951. Designed mainly for high altitudes like the V-bombers, it had been given a thin wing of large area. (The designers had learnt their lesson with the Welkyn which had been given a 'thick' wing for high lift in the 'thin' air at high altitude with the designers not realising that this would lower its critical Mach number to a speed lower than its best climb speed!).

The Canberra therefore had a small turning circle and reasonably good aileron response for its large wing span at 40,000 feet at which height it was capable of 550 kts TAS (true air speed) at maximum cruise power from its two Avon 101, 6500 lb thrust engines. It had a better power/weight ratio than a Meteor IV and it could out-turn it above 25,000 feet when lightly loaded. However, perhaps because we had grown used to sitting in a fighter cockpit with a good all-round view, we found that sitting side-by-side in the huge Canberra T4 cockpit was like sitting in a large, deep, bath with a glass dome over the top and where the all-round view was dangerously restricted.

It is doubtful whether English Electric had given as much thought to the problem of baling out of the Canberra T4 as the American firm of Martins had for their B 57 version which we flew later from Edwards Air Force Base in California and which had a hinged hood. Entry for the British version was from below in the T4 so that the fighter pilots amongst us felt claustrophobic, particularly when it became insufferably hot in the summer sun. Later versions of the Canberra allowed easier hood jettison, entry from above and a 'stickbreaker' which prevented serious injury if the pilot ejected.

The Canberra's Avons inexplicably delivered their three tons of thrust well out on each wing, so that when practicing engine failures on take-off, it was essential to have achieved a 'safety speed' of at least 135 knots before 'cutting' one engine, otherwise rudder power was insufficient to keep straight. If the power failure was real and occurred before a take-off speed of more than 135 knots had been attained before one engine failed, and if no 'zero-altitude' ejector seats were fitted for the crew, a landing straight ahead would be essential. (Fl/Lt L.A. Coe of the preceding 14 Course had been killed in 1956 when attempting a late practice overshoot when the 'dead' engine failed to pick up in time.)

Having used the Canberra in torpedo-dropping trials from Yeovilton in 1957, the Navy bought a few more modified Canberra B Mk 2s in 1961 to act as pilotless 'drone' targets for the Navy's new ship-to-air missile – the Sea Slug. These beautiful aircraft were taken off and landed without anyone aboard them, from Hal Far in Malta. They were remotely controlled by a pilot from 728B Squadron sitting in air traffic control. The reason for using such expensive 'drone' targets was for it to photograph the Navy's new 'Sea Slug' missile as it went past the target, with the timing of each exposure marked in milliseconds so that 'Sea Slug' could be assessed for its accuracy later on. Other target practice was also carried out against V-1 rocket-propelled targets simulating enemy missile attacks.

Whereas the Canberras were landed back at Hal Far by remote control, the V-1s were ordered to stop their rocket motors and stream a parachute. They then dropped obediently into the Mediterranean and were sometimes picked up by crane from a Navy tug and used again.

Ending up as a target for HMS *Girdle Ness*'s Sea Slugs was a most undignified use for the Canberra aircraft and it must have been a disappointment to 'Teddy' Petter, its designer. However it seemed to us that it would have been easy meat for an active 'homing' missile or even a fighter such as the Hunter, Swift or Sabre with front guns, if flown within air defence radar cover just as all the V-bombers were. By 1954, it seemed to us that anything flying above 100 feet over the earth's surface was living on borrowed time. The Canberra Mark T22 air-to-air target-towing version continued to operate in this role from Yeovilton until 1992.

Back at ETPS, we tutors had to show students how to test aircraft behaviour after simulated engine failure. Instruction in aircraft such as the Vickers Varsity was a stressful occupation. Losing half its power with its 'critical' engine failed, it had all the handling difficulties of a Manchester wartime bomber.

Needless to say, most fighter pilots preferred single engines – such as the Hunter T-7s – at ETPS. The Hawker Hunter could cut circles round the Canberra and because of its reliable stalling and spinning behaviour, the T-7 2-seater version was used to instruct us Tutors in the art of *inverted* spinning in a swept-wing aircraft – the first of any in the world at that time. Inverted spinning is not just entering a spin while upside down, but involves reverse wing-loading, pulling the stick *back* to recover and a very uncomfortable ride.

Coming back to Farnborough in a Lincoln one day, we smelt petrol in the cockpit. On looking out we could see fuel splashes on the starboard inner engine nacelle and we immediately feathered it. Making an emergency landing and slowly coming to a halt to avoid setting fire to the fuel leak from sparks under the wheels, we stopped the remaining three engines opposite flying control and waited for the fire engine. The fire engine was beaten for speed by several car owners on the course armed with gerry cans – which they proceeded to fill from the jet of green 100-octane pouring from the engine nacelle over the starboard undercarriage. I managed to get hold of some of this and I tried it out on my own car – another 20 hp Rolls-Royce which I had bought for £625 from a shop on the Basingstoke bypass. Although I had fully advanced the ignition timing, the 100 Octane fuel burnt the exhaust valves badly and cost me £70 to have them reground.

We had several gliding sessions at Lasham and, in complete contrast, we also had several hours in the driving seat of an S 51 'chopper'.

Westlands had been the first to build helicopters of United States' designs in this country, their first 'copy' being of S 51 Dragonfly which had first flown in the States in January 1947. Number 705 Naval Air Squadron had then taken their first delivery of the British version on 13 January 1950. The Dragonfly was fitted with an Alvis Leonides engine of about 500 hp and it was used in Korea as 'Plane Guard' rescue instead of Sea Otters from 1951 onwards until 1967.

Flying helicopters was not popular with most fixed-wing pilots and some of us thought that had God intended it He would have made birds with revolving wings. In particular, apart from the dangers of trusting yourself to a flimsy collection of aerofoils held spread only by centrifugal force and lashing around overhead, there was (a), the need to ensure their rotation speed to within very narrow limits to prevent either their collapse or the stalling of the rear-going blades by insufficient revs or (b), the need to fly within the aircraft's true airspeed limits of below 200 knots set by the dangers of stalling the rear-going blades or exceeding the speed of sound by the forward-going blades or (c), the lack of 'wing' area and the growing risk with increase in altitude that the forward-going blades would become supersonic, all of which limited altitude to about 15,000 feet and (d), their feeling of uncertainty – especially if a forced landing should become necessary due to engine failure – if an 'auto-rotative' landing had to be attempted. All this required additional skills of a high order, the airborne cost of training for which could only be justified if the 'chopper' could be made to do things which no fixed-wing aircraft could do.

The 'chopper' is a marvellous example of the workings of the 'V-squared' law as understood in 1934 by Cierva's *auto-gyro*. Here, the blades were windmilled by the forward motion of the plane imparted by a conventional propeller. Because their average speed through the air was about 300 mph, Cierva discovered that he only needed about 10 square feet of aerofoil-sectioned planking whirling overhead to provide the same lift that could be expected from about 100 square feet of fixed wing in a conventional aircraft. Then, he invented the true helicopter by dispensing with the propeller and connecting the engine direct to the rotor. The windmilling action to keep the auto-gyro blades revolving, achieved by tilting the rotor disc upwards at its leading edge, was no longer required.

Lift could now be provided from a standing start and vertical landings could be guaranteed. Lift/power settings were controlled by a 'collective' lever in the cockpit – up for increased lift and vice versa, with the handle providing a twist-grip for throttle opening/closing, as necessary to maintain adequate rotor speed. Bank, pitch-up and pitch-down movement were controlled by a 'cyclic' alteration of blade angle of attack by means of a convention pilot's stick control.

The torque reaction of the engine driving the helicopter blades – say – clockwise, is counteracted by the anticlockwise sidethrust of a small propeller on the tail of the helicopter. This was geared to the main shaft, with its pitch – and thus sidethrust – controlled by the pilot's feet on the rudder bar. In case of engine failure, auto-rotation was kept up by energy obtained from height loss, where the upflow of air through the blades 'windmilled' the blades to a high enough speed to ensure that their centrifugal force kept them fully extended.

If engine failure occurs, the helicopter pilot had immediately to 'unload' the rotor to an 'auto-gyro' condition so that its rotation speed is maintained. By purposely losing height to maintain safe rotor revs in this way, the pilot can 'glide' the helicopter with zero engine power while he picks a suitable forced-landing area. If sufficient height is still available he can build up rotor speed to maximum revs and use rotor inertia to supply upthrust at the last moment before touchdown. He does this by pulling up on the 'collective' lever before hitting the ground. If he judges it correctly, he can guarantee a gentle touchdown.

Top speed of a helicopter is governed by the forward-moving blades remaining subsonic and the aft-moving blade retaining enough airspeed to prevent it stalling. Thus, in a 40-foot diameter, four-bladed rotor, the top speed of the rotor would be limited to between 180 and 250 rpm if the limits were to be safely preserved. Height limits are about 15,000 feet – mainly because of relative air density reductions reducing lift and Mach effects limiting the forward speed of the rotor tips.

Helicopters, although immensely useful on the battlefields and oceans of the world – not only for search, rescue and transport but for accurate weapon delivery in all weathers, night and day – cannot, however, be safely operated unless air supremacy prevails in an airspace controlled by friendly fighters and with friendly surface/air defences in positions known to the airmen beforehand.

Nowadays, civil duties such as air/sea rescue, traffic control, ambulances, criminal search, firefighting – and so on – would alone seem to justify single or twin helicopter common use, particularly as cheaper training methods are available by using simulators instead of real live aircraft. The use of the heavy, twin-engined 'choppers' by the army as an extension of the tank (itself an extension of the horse as a highspeed weapon carrier on the battlefields) was perhaps as inevitable as its use by the Navy, in the anti-submarine search-and-attack role to replace the A/S Gannet.

The magnificent Sea King HAS 2 with its two 1,660 hp Rolls-Royce Gnome h.1400 jet engines has a hover ceiling of about 5,000 feet and a top speed of about 130 knots at sea level and a range of about 800 miles. Attack helicopters are now equipped with 'fire-and-forget' heat-seeking weapons, night visibility devices and an instant response capability at speeds nearly double that of an express train. If shielded from enemy fighters from above and close-range fire from below, it would seem to provide a marvellous substitute for the armoured car and tank transporter. Larger versions make use of contra-rotation with twin rotors to cancel the need for tail rotors and so give them the lifting power to act as heavy transport to the battlefield. The attack 'chopper' is also an essential weapon for the Hussars and Lancers as well as for the Royal Armoured Corps itself, and it may well be worth the additional flying hazards which all chopper aircrew bravely encounter while flying them.

During the 'fifties' the Farnborough Air Show displayed a helicopter which was powered with ramjets at its rotors tips. It would doubtless have scooped the market if only the jets could have been made less deafening to those on the ground.

The close connection between aviation and sailing became apparent once more at this time at ETPS. Sqn Ldrs Tony Svensson and Lionel Taylor – two students on the course – joined with Major Peter Knott – from Staff College days – and the author on many sailing visits to France and the West Country in two of the Navy's 'strength-through-joy' ex-German yachts: the 50 Square Meter *Seehexe* and the 100 Square Meter *Merlin*.

Up to the year 1955 the Royal Navy had been slow to adopt the teaching of 'the science of sail', preferring to use their ship-borne whalers, gigs and cutters in intership competitions rather than taking part in Yacht Clubs' regattas. However, the Duke of Edinburgh had set a Naval example by making use of his own Dragon and Flying Fifteen at Cowes Regattas for the past two years. Naval sailing skills were of a very low standard at that time but Admiral Sir Manley Power – C-in-C Portsmouth – was keen to set a good example to his troops.

The day had dawned at Cowes in a flat calm and Admiral Power had signalled to one of the 70-foot Motor Torpedo Boats to give him a tow to the starting line. Keen to carry out his Admiral's wishes, the MTB skipper started up his twin Merlins, cast off and took the Admiral's yacht in tow. However, the towline had been passed round the yacht's mizzen mast and this came down with a crash enveloping the Admiral at the wheel.

Nothing daunted, Admiral Power's head came out from under the sail and he was heard to say in good Nelsonian style: 'Very well then, we'll go as a sloop'. So he did – and won, too, for the loss of his mizzen mast reduced his handicap.

Dartmouth College had then taken on several fast yachts for its own instructional and regatta use and by 1956, yachtsmen on the lawn of the Royal Yacht Squadron at Cowes were no longer muttering: 'The three things I never allow aboard my yacht are: a cow, a naval officer and an umbrella.' The Royal Naval Sailing Association was now becoming highly respected.

Tony Svensson was later appointed as test pilot to a Royal Australian Air Force Squadron in Australia. When writing the Pilot's Notes for the French supersonic Mirage 1110 at Avalon near Melbourne he was flying it at about 35,000 feet when, having initiated some manoeuvres at Mach 1.5, the aircraft got out of control. He finally ejected, severely injuring himself in the process owing to the huge aerodynamic forces hitting him when struggling to leave the aircraft when it was still in a supersonic, spinning dive. (See Appendix 4 for his own story.)

In December 1957, at the end of Number 16 Course at ETPS, we tutors were taken across the Atlantic in the new Constellation to Edwards Air Force Base where we were the guests of their Test Pilot's School and Test Establishment. (The USN had a separate test establishment of its own three times the size of Boscombe Down at Patuxent River in Connecticut.) Here we were treated to ten days of delight by our USAF hosts. We flew the F-86E, the T-28 and USAF's version of the Canberra – the B-57.

The Americans were well ahead of us in supersonics with their F-100 Super Sabre. Their 'run-o'-the-mill' Sabre F-86E which we flew, was experimentally fitted with 'reheat' (another word for an 'after-burner') which added about 40 per cent more power for short periods for take-off and acceleration. This also allowed it to go supersonic in the climb, a feat only possible at that time in Britain in the English Electric Lightning interceptor fighter being developed for the RAF. We felt very safe flying the Sabre transonically as it had fully powered controls with an 'all-moving' – or 'slab' – tailplane – an absolute 'must' in transonic flight. At this time in Britain the latest Mark of Sea Hawk had already been fitted with an experimental 'slab' tailplane and the new DH 110 – to be called the Sea Vixen – would also have this essential improvement for transonic/supersonic longitudinal control.

Very high altitudes and Mach numbers of 0.95 had been achieved in the three British types of V-bombers at this time and the Vulcan had been flown supersonic. However, partly because the crew did not all have ejector seats, the V-bombers would cause the death of 71 crew in 16 crashes during the next ten years.

The United States' Martin Aircraft Company's version of the Canberra – the B-57 – had a simple cockpit layout and the pilot and navigator could enter through a hinged canopy. It had an experimental emergency hydraulic pump system which was driven by a small windmilling propeller which automatically 'popped out' into the airstream if the main hydraulics failed. The B-57 seemed to be underpowered compared with the Canberra T-4 and, probably because of its awkwardly high stick and rudder forces when flying on one engine and its 'rudder tramping' at Mach numbers above 0.79, the USAF made little use of it by day or night. Nevertheless it appeared in the Vietnam campaign alongside the Australians in their Australian-built Canberras possibly because of its excellent aerodynamic features compared with anything they had to offer themselves at that time.

The Americans were, as usual, kind and generous to us six tutors during our visit. We had talks given by Captain O.C. Kincheloe Jr, DSO, SS, DFC, AM, USAF, who had been a student on No 13 Course at ETPS. He was currently testing the Lockheed F-104 Starfighter (also eventually built by Mitsubishi, Fiat and Messerschmitt). This was a knife-edge 'thin wing', unswept fighter having about the same wing area as the tailplane of a Gannet. It was probably the first aircraft built to have BLC air blown over its wing flaps to allow it to land at a sensibly low speed. Kincheloe said that without both BLC and 'fly-by-wire' auto-safety inserts into the flying control system to prevent 'pitch-up' in steep turns, it would not be safe to fly. It was sold widely in Europe because of its good supersonic and low-level performance but it occasionally still suffered from 'roll-inertia coupling' and 'pitch-up' in steep turns. (Kincheloe was tragically killed by the F-104 a year later after we had returned to UK as its ejector seat had not allowed him to get clear at 600 knots indicated airspeed.)

Edwards' and NASA's boffins were designing a new Mach 3, 60,000 feet high-altitude fighter where the whole cockpit – complete with aircrew – was ejected if the aircraft got into difficulties. Separation occurred when the 'capsule' had been slowed sufficiently by a small stabilising parachute of its own and at a lower altitude.

We also saw the huge 220-ton B-52 bomber, designed to deliver the 'stand-off' H-bomb direct to Russia and return. We wondered how long it would survive with fighters about. We also wondered why it was needed at all when the A-bomb could now be delivered from low level, using the 'LABS' lobbing techniques with the new 'Head-up' displays to ensure safe low flying with clear target indications to the pilot. There were also rumours that the Americans were building a nuclear-powered submarine that could deliver the A-bomb from under the water from anywhere in the world. This would surely put the high-level A-bomber out of business entirely.

The choice of Edwards as a Test Establishment was a good one, for pilots in difficulties could use an 'airfield' the size of Hampshire for their emergencies – a level piece of hard desert sand stretching as far as the eye could see in every direction and with an emergency runway laid down for a distance of four miles in two directions.

The test pilot's own families at Edwards lent us their spare cars and we drove north-east up the endless desert highway to Las Vegas. Although the 4-litre engines of these spare cars only managed about 15 miles to the gallon, as it only cost 19 cents a gallon in Los Angeles garages, travel up to Las Vegas cost very little. We spent our money – 15 dollars a day 'American allowance' – on the pool tables, roulette wheels and fruit machine at the 'Golden Nugget' saloon, using real silver dollars.

We also went to see a show at Caesar's Palace Hotel where 'Custer's Last Stand' was the title of one of the sketches. Suffice it to say that the scene opened with Custer in bed with his bedsheet in the form of a tent.

When we were leaving our hotel and paying the bill, I asked whether I could take an ash tray with the hotel's name – 'The New Frontier' – upon it as a souvenir. The man behind the counter replied: 'Son, you take anything that ain't nailed down.'

On return to UK the author discovered that he had been promoted to Commander and because there was no flying job available at ETPS in this rank, he had been appointed in charge of Naval Air Equipment and Photography at the Admiralty. The job involved the modernisation and improvement of aerial 'stereo' photography and interpretation methods in the Navy. Moral was high for, among the letters of congratulation on surmounting this promotion obstacle with only two years as Lt/Cdr, I received one from Charles Evans and Dick Janvrin.

A Scimitar (XD227) was fixed up with three of the latest type of reconnaissance F-95 cameras and the author got permission from his desk at Rex House in Regent Street in London to fly it at Boscombe Down using 'C' Squadron facilities. The Scimitar F Mark 1 was originally intended to be used as an interceptor/fighter, but its role had been changed by 1957 after it had completed its proving trials and it became a low-level strike aircraft capable of dropping an A-bomb using the Low Altitude Bombing System (LABS) or 'lobbing' procedure.

Photographic Reconnaissance was now becoming more specialised and its use more urgent, particularly in 'Limited War' conditions such as at Suez where careful target identification was essential before an attack was authorised for fear of accidentally hitting civilian targets and causing a public outcry. The F-95 cameras in the test Scimitar also had 'image movement compensation' (IMC) and an f2 lens with a very wide angle and a maximum shutter speed of 1/2000th/sec. What this really meant was that the pilot could fly his Scimitar past his target within a hundred feet at ground level at 600 knots in almost any light conditions and the F-95 would take automatic pictures at 1/5th/sec intervals in perfect focus and without a suspicion of blurring due to camera movement. The results could then be used to give stereo 'vision' to the photographic interpreters. The IMC device was a simple system which automatically wound the film across the frame within the camera at the same speed as the image swept past the lens and at the same instant that the shutter opened. The F-95 cameras were also fitted with 'auto-iris' controls. This device measured the object's light value and set the iris automatically without action from the pilot.

Photographic enhancement also depended on the finest possible grain size for the film in use to improve the stereo interpretation on much magnified black-and-white prints. To reduce time delay, a TV device was tried out whereby the F-95 negatives alone were used straight from the developing fluid to produce a positive image on a large screen in the aircrew briefing room aboard the carrier.

'Humph' who had been our ETPS Chief Ground Instructor in 1947 on number 6 Course was now in charge of Boscombe's Phot. Section. He stood alongside the main runway with his 'target' boards as the author flew past at ever increasing speeds up to 0.9 Mach with the 'oblique' F-95s switched on. On the last two 'passes', the aircraft's drag could be felt to change momentarily with changes in air temperature as it came up against a 'wall' of compressibility under a thick fog of condensation.

These camera trials lasted, off-and-on, from February to July 1958 after which the author only had to be another year sitting at a desk in Rex House before receiving another buff envelope telling him to relieve Pridham Price (yet again), as CO of 'C' Squadron – probably the top job in Naval test flying.

CHAPTER 12

BOSCOMBE DOWN AGAIN

Having spent the last year sitting on a chair at Rex House, I needed a few hours general flying on arrival at 'C' Squadron to catch up with the latest standards and to qualify for a 'Green Ticket' – without which a pilot was not allowed to fly in instrument flying conditions. Sq/Ldr Tony Svensson, a great chum to find at Boscombe but soon to go to Australia on another test job to help the RAAF fly their Mirages, 'passed me out' in a Meteor T7.

'Cliff' Evans (ETPS 16 Course) and 'C' Squadron Senior Pilot, then showed me the taps in Buccaneer XK523 – one of the first six development versions of the Mark 1 produced – and, with Lt Jimmy McPhee as Observer in the back seat I did a few circuits and bumps. It was evening before it was ready for flight so the last few landings were made in near darkness using Boscombe Down's 'HILO' mirror sight on runway 24. It took another 10 hours of flying before I, or anyone, could have done sufficient exploration to know much about the 'Narner' (so-called because the Buccaneer's original design number contained a few Bs, Ns and As) but its salient features were obvious from the first flight. It 'answered the helm' smoothly, particularly when low flying in turbulence, and it had exceptionally small trim changes when altering flaps and undercarriage positions or airspeeds, good control 'harmonisation' and a natural feeling of stability at all speeds including supersonic dives. These excellent handling characteristics had been evolved from the results of some marvellous test flying – led by Lt/Cdr D.J. 'Block' Whitehead (13 ETPS) since he had made the first flight as Blackburn's Test Pilot on 30 April 1958 with his Observer Bernard Watson, from Holme-on-Spalding Moor airfield. Blackburn's design office had been led by Barry Laight since the Naval Staff Requirement – NA 39 – for a low-level, long-range, nuclear-strike aircraft, had been issued by the Admiralty in September 1953. The NA 39 requirement had initially been outlined in all its brilliance by Captain 'Ben' Bolt and his Deputy, Commander F.M.A. Torrence-Spence, (OC Flying, 6 ETPS).

In addition to many design changes since 1953 under the general technical direction of Blackburn's N.E. 'Nero' Rowe, the firm's test pilots – under their Flight Test Manager Joe Stamper – had made some great improvements to the NA 39's handling in the air. Tailplane, aileron and rudder gearing alterations had been made to cater for the huge changes in air loads over its speed range, the required stick-force changes all achieved in flight by the input of a 'Q'-feel' (indicated airspeed/stickforce) monitoring device, and the insertion of a 'viscous damper', designed to prevent over-control by the pilot between both extremes of the speed range. The only easy criticism of it was that, compared with, say, the Scimitar, Sea Vixen or even the Canberra, the 'Narner' was underpowered.

Next day I said goodbye to Pridham once again. He was going to America for his next appointment – his full title becoming: 'Naval Air Representative, British Joint Services' Mission in Washington.'

There were five Test Pilots in 'C' Squadron plus myself at this time. They included Maurice Hedges who had done ETPS since our time in 813, Cliff Evans, John Cross, Bill Newton, Peter Barber; with Trevor Spafford, Nick Bennet and Alan Deacon and Brian Davies joining them later. There were also four Observers and Lieutenant Ben Rice as Staff Officer. The four Observers were Jimmy McPhee, Ed Beadsmoor, Tony Walsh and Di Jones.

On the maintenance side we had Lt/Cdr (E) Peter Rippon and Lt (L) Dennis Slater in charge of the 85 skilled Naval Ratings which the Navy allowed us (the RAF employed civilians) and we also had the advice of aircraft manufacturers' engineers where prototypes were involved. Senior Naval administration dealing with service conditions, etc., came under the nearest RN Captain – at Yeovilton. Otherwise we were locally subject to RAF discipline at Boscombe Down, enjoying living conditions in their comfortable accommodation. The RAF were responsible for flying safety and for administering the various handling, performance, radio and armament test programmes demanded by the Ministry of Supply under the command of the Superintendent of Flying – Group Captain Ian MacDougall. The Ministry of Supply (now the Ministry of Defence, Procurement Executive) actually owned the Establishment here and at RAE Bedford and Farnborough, and had its headquarters at St Giles' Court in central London.

We had our own 'Naval' hangar and office block next door to 'A' Squadron. The RAF were busy in 'A' Squadron with the Lightning fighter and next door to them was 'B' Squadron which tested the V-bombers and military transport aircraft including the Blackburn Beverley.

Looking out of my office window past our ancient Vauxhall 14 Saloon – 'C' Squadron's chauffeur-driven car with its RN numberplate – I could see a line of three Buccaneers – XK429, 523 and 527 – a Scimitar F Mk 1 XD227, a Sea Vixen FAW Mk 1 XJ564 and our Meteor 7 used for long-distance Squadron transport. Sea Vixen XJ516 and Scimitar XD212 were in the hangar having flight-refuelling systems installed.

Mr Dennis Higton came to see me. He was 'C' Squadron's own scientist/engineer/aerodynamicist, with his office in Boscombe's Technical Office. He had joined the 'C' Squadron team in 1955 at the request of Cdr 'Stan' Orr, the CO of 'C' Squadron at that time. He was a well-trusted friend as well as a superb scientist/engineer, who used his vital knowledge to help secure our recommended action from his firms' designers, from the Navy or from the Ministry of Supply. He joined in all our 'jollys' (social gatherings ashore) including sailing. As a marvellous communicator with us aviators, he rose to the very top of his profession within the Ministry (Director-General Military Aircraft Projects and Superintendent of Performance Division) before retiring to the countryside in Wiltshire where, as if to prove his versatility, he is now taking a Fine Arts degree!

Boscombe's full title at that time was the 'Aircraft and Armament Experimental Establishment' – abbreviated to A&AEE. Dennis told us that the first of these 'E's' now stood for 'Evaluation' – for the tasks which Boscombe was now required to do were concerned more with collecting data from flying trial results (and, through consultation, making a judgement and reaching a conclusion on an aircraft's serviceability and safety in its intended role) rather than pure experimentation flying which was RAE Farnborough's job.

Dennis and I were soon called to Brough (Blackburn's factory airfield in Yorkshire) to discuss arrangements for two of our Buccaneers to fly out to *Ark Royal* off Malta to continue with the deck trials which had been interrupted ten months previously because of refuelling troubles in the ship.

These deck trials were to begin in a fortnight's time on 2 November 1960, their aim being to highlight any handling faults in the aircraft and check on engineering and safety when catapulting and decklanding.

This might be a convenient moment to go back in Buccaneer history a little to see what progress had been made since the signing of a small design contract in 1956 following N.E. Rowe's visit to us in *Eagle* in July of that year when its future role was finalised.

The 'go-ahead' for building the first 20 Buccaneers had been made a bit later in 1956. This was at the classic meeting at the Admiralty between Duncan Sandys, the Minister of Defence, Captain Donald Gibson (DNAW) and Lord Louis Mountbatten, the First Sea Lord, at which Mr Sandys gave the 'go-ahead' for building the first 20 Buccaneers.

Captain Gibson has given the author permission to reprint the following 'conversation' from his book *Haul Taut and Delay* (Spellmount Ltd).

> The Minister of Defence, having arrived at the meeting, sat down and asked:
> 'You have the Sea Vixen – how far will it go?'
> The question was so naive that Captain Gibson was at first taken aback but he gave an answer. He says that he did not bore the meeting with details about its role, weight of weapons, fuel, etc.
> Once again the Secretary of State asked;
> 'How far will the NA 39 go?
> Once again Lord Louis asked Gibson to answer. The Minister of Defence then said something like: 'Gentlemen, you have your aeroplane.'

The first four prototype Buccaneers were to be delivered by April 1958. XK486 arrived by this date, and the remaining 19 were delivered during the next 16 months.

Blackburns and 'C' Squadron had made good progress with flight tests. Brief initial handling tests had been completed and by January 1959 it was time for the first decklanding – or 'carrier suitability' – trials to begin. However, the first date set for these was cancelled due to an unexplained fatal accident which occurred a few days beforehand. Until the cause was known, the Navy refused to proceed further at that time.

The Navy's nervousness could be explained by a number of factors, one of these was its fear that any further unexplained fatal accidents would frighten off other potential buyers of the Buccaneer – notably the RAF who were more interested in the 'Multi-role' combat aircraft project (MRCA) and/or the TSR2 than anything the Navy could provide. Another reason for the Navy's nervousness about adverse publicity for the Buccaneer was their memory of the RAF's cancellation of any possible interest in the Sea Vixen after John Derry's tragic accident at the SBAC show. (This was when the DH 110 proto-type disintegrated over the SBAC crowd, killing him and his observer Tony Richard and 29 spectators, probably due to a structural failure in the port wing.)

It might be worth having a look at the proposed role of the Buccaneer. The Buccaneer concept was the result of clear thinking on the part of those who were appointed to the Directorate of Naval Air Warfare at this time. They did not pretend that the Buccaneer could ever be a 'multi-role' aircraft like the Wyvern or the MRCA, but a straightforward, single-purpose, 0.85 Mach cruising, 500 mile radius, low level strike aircraft capable of deck operation and loaded with tons of weapons plus overload fuel in the bomb bay and under the wings; a huge weapon load which could include two self-propelled 'atomic torpedoes' capable of sinking a Sverdlov Russian cruiser.

The NA 39 Operational Requirement was not only the best Naval Air Strike project the Naval Air Staff had ever thought up, but the Buccaneer Mark 1 and 2 were probably the best-ever response to a Naval OR by any member of the British aircraft industry during the preceding twenty years. In their OR, the Navy had specified a need for easy transonic handling plus low gust response at high speeds at low altitudes. The 'Narner' also had to be capable of flying very slowly for deck-landing and catapult purposes – incompatible require-ments indeed. The first would need sweepback and a thin wing of very small area and the second would need a 'high-lift' wing of large area to lift 15 tons of aircraft onto the flight deck at airspeeds of no more than 110 knots.

Its designers had to convince the protagonists of Vertical Lift (VTOL) that their VTOL schemes would not be needed and that the NA39 – as the Buccaneer project was called – could operate quite comfortably from a flight deck fitted with powerful catapults and also from an airfield ashore if required, using RATOG.

No one knew at this time in 1959 whether the 'Narner' would come near to satisfying the RAF requirement for a bomber. We now know that the RAF were looking for an aircraft capable of delivering a four-ton weapon-load a distance of 850 miles and for it to return safely, by day or night, fair weather or foul, and that it would be able to do the last few hundred miles to the target at zero altitude at speeds up to 600 knots. This was, in fact, what the more pow-erful Mark 2 Buccaneer achieved by August 1965 when loaded to 62,000 lb – its maximum take-off weight – and catapulted off the US Navy's aircraft carrier *Lexington* with Dennis Higton in charge of the results and Geoff Higgs (13 ETPS) in the cockpit. The trial also included single-engined aborted deck-landings and carriage of the new wingtanks.

The development programme for the Mark 1 involving a new 'light-weight' engine and an airframe incorporating the new 'boundary layer control' system, had been shared between nine of the pre-production batch instead of the usual two or three, with each airframe having specific performance test jobs to do – engines, deck trials, armaments, electrics, aerodynamics, radar, flying controls and general handling.

The first series of test flights dating from 30 April 1958, took place two and a half years after the initial 'go-ahead' from the Admiralty. Derek Whitehead made the first Buccaneer flight on 30 April 1958 in XK486 (later assisted by 'Sailor' Parker – Blackburn's second test pilot) and these had shown up exceptionally few handling faults in airfield operation and none which would, so far, require more than routine modification.

Blackburn's design team had introduced two innovations to reduce high-speed drag and increase low-speed lift. The first was called 'area rule', whereby the fuselage contours were 'indented' where the wings joined in order to preserve a smooth change in velocity of the airflow at that point. This also prevented large trim changes occurring and delayed 'compressibility drag' until 0.9 Mach was reached – allowing a max-cruise speed 80 knots above that of the V-bombers.

The second innovation was called Boundary Layer Control (BLC). It had the effect of lowering the stalling speed of the aircraft by 15 knots in the landing and take-off configuration which its high wingloading made essential if it was ever to be safe to operate from a carrier.

As mentioned above, the first deck trials in XK523 and XK489 – the first 'navalised' prototypes with arrester hooks, folding wings and improved airbrakes – had been cancelled because of an unexplained fatal crash a few days before they were due to begin, in October 1959. A brief mention of the causes of this crash might help to emphasise the sort of problems which arise on the first flight of a prototype and prompt the saying: 'Ah me. Back to the drawing board.'

The Americans at NASA had helped Blackburns with the BLC and 'area-rule' innovations. Accordingly they had sent over their Bill Alford from America to fly the Buccaneer and check its performance for themselves. Both the American and his English observer – John Joyce – were killed when flying XK490 over the New Forest on 12 October 1959, a few days after this aircraft had returned from the Paris air exhibition and a few days before it was due to begin the first deck trials.

The wreckage was immediately recovered from the 12-foot-deep hole it had made in the New Forest and it was taken to Farnborough. Here the Accident Investigation Unit, assisted by Blackburns and the information from the flight recorders in the Buccaneer at the time of the crash, attempted to discover the cause. They came to the initial conclusion that it was pilot error – the usual assumption when scientists are baffled. They considered that the American pilot had 'exceeded his briefing by carrying out single-engined flying at slow speeds'.

Single-engined flying at slow speeds was not thought to present any problem in the Buccaneer as it had its engine thrust almost on its centreline. Moreover, testing single-engine handling and performance of a twin was the usual routine test expected of a skilled test pilot – even on his first flight. So that, unless there was a known fault in the system which would have prohibited the pilot shutting off power on one or the other of the two engines (which would have been 'entered' as a fault in the aircraft's Form 700 and signed as having been read by every pilot before take-off can be made) the American pilot may not have been to blame.

As mentioned above, the Buccaneer's slow-flying behaviour had, so far, turned out well, mainly due to the manufacturer's use of BLC. This was high pressure air blown from spanwise slits over the top surfaces of the wings and flaps and ailerons when the latter were lowered into the 'maximum lift' positions for landings and take-offs. In the case of the Buccaneer, BLC was also used under the *lower* surface of the tailplane to improve its negative lift in the landing and take-off configurations.

The main action of the BLC air was to 'speed up' the normal airflow over the top surfaces of the mainplanes, keeping it in close contact with the wing for much longer and so adding to its lift and reducing the stall tendency at high angles of attack and, in effect, 'making the wing believe it was going much faster than it really was.'

The reduction in stalling speed of 15 knots brought about by NASA's invention – BLC – made it possible for its small wing area of 508 sq/ft to support its decklanding weight of 15 tons at speeds as low as 110 knots instead of about 125 knots which it would otherwise have been. An approach indicated airspeed of 125 knots would have given a hook entry speed of about 100 knots, about double the hook entry speed of most other contemporary aircraft in naval service at that time and the wire would probably have parted. BLC also made it possible for the underpowered British steam catapults then installed in *Victorious*, *Hermes*, and *Ark Royal* to have some chance of accelerating the Buccaneer's twenty-ton weight to a safe airspeed at the end of a catapult run, even in light winds and in tropical temperatures.

BLC takes its air supply from the main engine compressors. It is piped at high pressure through to each wing, over the wing-fold junction and into the slits via two valves operated automatically when flaps are selected by the pilot. Engine rpm must be kept high when it is in use to ensure equal, high pressures on both wings' slits. To ensure high engine rpm on the approach, the makers had installed very large airbrakes which are fully extended for all approaches and landings.

BLC pressures achieved were registered on two instruments in the pilot's cockpit. BLC and flaps were, of course, used for take-offs as well, and 'lift' was further increased by 'dropping' the ailerons.

The accident investigation team at RAE Farnborough discovered that Bill Alford had lost control of XK490 in very odd circumstances. It seems that when he had closed the throttle on one engine, the other's higher pressure BLC air supply had blown back through a faulty non-return valve straight into the idle engine's compressor, putting its flame out entirely, making it impossible to relight and failing to give BLC at the correct pressure to the other wing. The wing without BLC immediately lost its extra lift, and if Alford had been flying at or near the normal landing approach speed with BLC 'on', this wing would have stalled completely when it lost its BLC and the aircraft would have inverted and spun. The flight recorder showed that such a stall had indeed occurred at about 10,000 feet – too low for a spin recovery and probably too near the ground for successful ejection from an inverted position.

A year later, the firm announced that they had discovered a fault in the BLC air-supply system of the Buccaneer which – through failure of a non-return valve to function – could shut off BLC air from one wing without giving the usual warning to the pilot. A 'centralised' emergency warning system was then made part of an improved cockpit layout and the BLC system was modified to prevent a recurrence of Alford's mishap. We in 'C' Squadron were of the opinion that the firm may have originally omitted a non-return valve in the system altogether.

The second attempt to start deck trials in January 1960 was only partially successful. Pridham had managed to get two Buccaneers aboard *Victorious*, but flying time was again cut short, not only because of poor winter weather but because the 'Narners' were continually running short of fuel. The fuel supply fault was not in the aircraft but in the refuelling method used, resulting in the pilot taking off with some of his aircraft's ten fuel tanks half-empty and then having to demand a 'panic' landing before fuel ran out. With no flight-refuelling system yet in operation in the Buccaneer, and with the ship out of wind at the time, or, if into wind about to run into shallow water in Lyme Bay, such demands were unpopular aboard *Victorious*.

However, in spite of this, 'C' Squadron made 31 landings and enough faults were discovered in the hook design, the rebound ratio in the undercarriage, the tailskid damper and the 'auto-stability' gearings, to have made the trials worthwhile for the designers. (*Victorious* later began a long refit and did not appear much again until 1965.)

Ten months later, as if to emphasise the risky nature of the aircraft business, just as we were about to embark on the second deck trial scheduled at our meeting at Brough – this time in the Mediterranean autumn weather aboard *Ark Royal* – we heard through the 'grape vine' that there had been yet another serious accident and Blackburns' test pilot – 'Sailor' Parker – and his Observer had had to (successfully) eject. He had, apparently, got into a 'roll-inertia coupling' situation (although neither he nor any of us knew the nature of this phenomenon until the latter part of 1961) while he was carrying out some autopilot tests in cloud in XK486, the first prototype. Loss of control was stated to have been caused by 'blind-flying' instrument failure and, as this was not a design fault, our deck trials were allowed to go ahead on time.

As *roll-inertia coupling* was the cause of Parker and his observer finally losing their lives two years later in a Buccaneer and the cause of many other accidents since then to military aircraft worldwide – a short explanation of this phenomenon is included as follows:

The 'official' definition of roll/inertia coupling is that it is: 'a function of the inclination of the axis of the aircraft to the line of flight and of the rate of roll'. That is to say, if an aircraft is rolled while it is nose-up or nose-down to its line of flight, the nose-upness or nose-downness will rapidly increase uncontrollably if the pilot rolls the aircraft rapidly.

Perhaps the best way of trying to describe this is to suggest a way of constructing a simple 'model'. This could be done by nailing one stick to another at roughly their mid points, taking the longer by its two ends between the thumb and fingers of the left and right hands and twisting it rapidly round its axis, watching what happens to the other stick. If the nail is sufficiently loose in its hole in the shorter of the two sticks and it is free to rotate, it will do so, flying out at right-angles to the longer stick. By imagining that the longer stick represents the flight direction and the shorter stick represents the nose-to-tail direction of an aircraft's fuselage, we can see how, if the shorter stick is slightly out of line with the longer stick when it is first revolved, it will immediately fly out at right-angles to the longer stick.

Likewise, an aircraft which is rolled rapidly, unless its flight direction is exactly in line with its fuselage 'nose-to-tail' direction all the time it is being rolled, the nose will fly further out of line, requiring instant application of – usually – nose-down elevator to stop it. The more rapidly it is revolved by aileron, the more it will fly out of line, until the whole aircraft will pitch up violently, perhaps overstressing itself in the process and breaking up in the air.

A typical situation leading to a roll-coupling disaster is when G is being pulled at the moment that a pilot makes a rolling pull-out after a dive-bombing or strafing manoeuvre. The aircraft's 'angle-of-attack' – and thus its nose-up angle – will be all the greater. Such conditions also apply when rolling off the top of a loop, where the airspeed is low, the angle of attack is high and the roll rate is high – even if it is only for 180 degrees.

A Buccaneer pilot was court martialled in 1963 for disobeying the aerobatic rules for the Buccaneer. The Pilot's Notes stated clearly that rolls must be limited to 180 degrees only. The pilot was practising for an 'air day' and thought he would get round the rules by doing a 360 roll with a 'hesitation' in between. In fact, what he did made 'roll coupling' more likely, not less, as he rolled from the inverted, level, flight condition (i.e. with a negative incidence of about 5 degrees and with the nose higher than normal above the flight line) through 360 degrees to the inverted flight condition again, 'hesitating' – to beat the rules – in between. The Buccaneer's inverted wing-loading increased due to the roll inertia as he rolled upright again. Negative G then increased to the point where the aircraft entered an inverted stall condition, one wing 'dropping' at the moment the pilot re-applied full aileron after his 'hesitation' such that it entered a spin. Both crew managed to eject through the hood and this saved their lives.

The author was ordered to be the court marital president as he had written that part of Pilot's Notes himself and might have known the reason why! Next day was spent writing up the evidence with the aid of a WRN stenographer. We did this in an office at 'C' Squadron, the remainder of the Squadron being on leave. The air-conditioning was not working in the sound-sealed office and we each smoked our way through about four packets of duty free Galloise Bleue which the squadron had just brought back by yacht from Cherbourg. This cured me of smoking cigarettes for life and it can be recommended as a good method.

The court martial results did not appear in print in time to save the life of poor 'Sailor' Parker and his observer in Buccaneer XN952. He and his observer – G. Copeman – died when doing no more than Sailor's usual roll off the top of a loop over his home airfield at Holme-on-Spalding Moor, about a week later.

This accident led to modifications to the Buccaneer's aileron gearing and pilot's aileron 'authority' and we did about a dozen separate flights at Boscombe to help Mr Roy Boot – now Assistant Chief Designer at Brough – to find out what these limits should be.

So, ten months after Pridham's first deck-trial, 'Cliff' Evans and I with our two Observers – Lts Coleman and Walsh – climbed into XK527 and XK489 respectively and set out from Boscombe for Hal Far in Malta for the second try.

About halfway there, at about 35,000 feet, warm and comfortable in the Buccaneer's quiet cockpit at about 0.82 Mach, I heard Cliff say he would have to return to Boscombe as he had a fuel transfer problem. I told our friendly Canberra – who had been told by Group Captain Ian MacDougall, our Superintendent of Flying at Boscombe, to act as consort – that we would race him back to Boscombe, hoping there was still time for us to make a second attempt that day after lunch. The Narner easily outstripped the Canberra and we were having our lunch at Boscombe by the time he got back.

As Cliff's problem could not be put right immediately, I and Coleman went on alone again that day, landed at the French Air Force base at Orange and spent the evening round the bar in the mess trying to talk French. The Buccaneer created much interest and we had a warm send-off after lunch next day, arriving over the Maltese cliffs to land at Hal Far at about tea time, with the Captain – Alfie Sutton – a wartime Observer of 815 Swordfish Squadron which led the raid on Taranto on 11 November 1940 and then with us in *Implacable* in the Pacific as Commander (Ops) in 1944/5 – there on the tarmac ready to greet us, complete with journalists and a photographer from the *Times of Malta*.

Next morning the paper was full of headlines such as:

Pirate in Malta. The Buccaneer, still under security wraps, landed at Hal Far. This chubby, twin-jet giant, with rotating bomb-bay capable of swallowing nuclear missiles, is powered by a brace of de Havilland Gyron Junior turbo-jets . . .

etc., in the usual dreadful journalese. It went on:

> It appears that the Buccaneer has escaped being festooned like a Christmas tree in and out of season with varied excrescences. True, it sports a dielectric radar nose, but this can be bent out of line like a boxer's pug to lie fore and aft along the port fuselage when the Buccaneer goes down the lift. The split-type rear fuselage airbrakes are normally opened on deck to reduce overall length to 62 feet four inches . . .

Finally, we read:

> When the commander and his observer managed to extricate themselves from the stratospheric-looking cockpit via a long ladder, they were greeted by Captain A.W. Sutton, DSC & Bar, CO of HMS *Falcon* and Commander S. Laurie, the RNAS' Commander (AIR). Weights and performance figures for the Buccaneer are still secret.

Cliff arrived next day in XK489 with Tony Walsh and after a few practices 'MADDLS' (Mirror Assisted Dummy Deck Landings) on the following two days, we joined *Ark Royal* somewhere off the south coast of Sicily, landing on at about 1000 hours. Our maintenance crew with Peter Rippon (Air Engineer Officer) and Dennis Slater (Electricals) with Jimmy Cross and 'Ozzie' Brown (Senior Pilot), having travelled down from Boscombe by Valletta to Hal Far, had preceded us in helicopters and it was good to meet on *Ark Royal*'s flight deck. Summoned to the bridge, I met *Ark*'s skipper – Captain Hill-Norton, a non-aviator. He was annoyed because we were a few minutes late for land-on and this had disrupted the ship's programme. He said:

'Crosley, your b. . . Buccaneers gave me the f. . .g sickups.'

He continued to complain to me each day:

'Why the two Narners on the flight deck were not "covered with screw-drivers" '. I read later of the cause of his annoyance – as follows

> Those of the ship's company who had been licking their lips in anticipation of a 'self maintenance period' in Toulon had their hopes dashed by delays in the trials of the Buccaneer. Eventually the Buccaneers embarked with their host of retainers and completed, somewhat spasmodically, a series of launches and recoveries on board whilst the ship's own squadrons enjoyed once more the delights of Hal Far.

Knowing by now that the 'Narner' was underpowered, we had considerable misgivings when we taxied up to the catapult on board *Ark* at this time. True, the hydraulic deck rollers shoved us into the catapult grooves and the deck crew could hook on the 200-ton wire strop and attach the 'holdback' gear as if they knew what they were doing. But when, after having the nose raised twenty feet off the deck as the strop tightened, we cautiously opened up to full power and re-checked BLC pressures, trim positions, temperatures, flaps, undercarriage locks, hood and seat jettison levers and counted our beads, we could not help having our misgivings as we gave 'thumbs-up' signal while waiting a long half-second for the stab-in-the-back of the 3½ G acceleration to see if we made it without hitting the sea ahead.

During the acceleration lasting about a second or so, I kept my right hand behind the stick – which tended to sway back with the 'G' – and my left hand behind the throttles. I watched the 'strip' airspeed indicator. It was hovering around the 115-knot mark as the strop fell off into the sea. The airspeed barely altered at all for the first 10 seconds or so – so different from the Seafire or the Sea Fury which would have gained 50 knots by that time. The Narner's acceleration was abysmal. We could expect it to be slower still when we came to do 'minimum launch speed' trials on the next deck clearance tests. This was because drag increases the slower you are travelling below an aircraft's 'speed for minimum power' (VIMP). This, for the Narner, was about 130 knots at the take-off weight and configuration that we were using. VIMP was the American's minimum launch speed for all their aircraft at that time, and showed by how much our catapult powers had fallen behind the Americans' in spite of ourselves having invented the steam catapult.

However, there was no problem whatever in decklanding the Narner and the only improvement we suggested was to reduce its aileron droop angle to prevent adverse yaw effects when using large amounts of aileron necessary in rough weather on the approach. But when watching Ozzie and Cliff do a few take-offs, it was frightening to see their aircraft sink off the end of the catapult each time. Besides its obvious lack of power from the two Gyron Juniors, the Narner seemed to need a greater lift coefficient than it had available with take-off flap only, and we eventually lowered the flaps fully for take-offs, which not only reduced the 'sink' problem but did so – thanks to BLC – without increasing drag significantly.

We managed to complete 36 decklandings in a week: but on five occasions, either or both aircraft had to land back at Hal Far for repairs or replacements to faults in their hook attachments, tailskids or engines. The final blow came when Ozzie and Cliff each had an engine fail for identical reasons at the same time and had to make single-engined landings at Hal Far. Apparently, one of their two Gyron Junior engines had each suddenly lost all power and had failed to answer to the throttle, the rpm winding back to idling revs.

After a brief talk with John Edwards, DH's Chief Engineer, and bearing in mind that if these engines had both failed in the same aircraft, Ozzie or CLiff would have had to swim for it, we flew back to UK, leaving our two Narners at Hal Far to be repaired by some of our engineers in their own time and the *Ark* free to take her holiday.

At the usual post-deck-trial conference, the engine-failure problem was the main subject of conversation. DH's Gyron Juniors gave about two horse-power for every pound of engine weight. One of DH's methods of extra weight saving had been its adoption of a new kind of fuel system employing 'half-ball valves, rubber rings and microscopic orifices' as one engineer rudely put it, instead of Rolls-Royce's usual fuel system designs involving much heavier construction materials. DH's system worked well in the laboratory but Pete Rippon and ourselves had no faith in its working on a flight deck with salt water everywhere and in a gale of wind. The two engine failures on our last deck trial had been caused by microscopic pieces of dirt in the fuel having lifted a half-ball valve off its seating by a thousandth of an inch or so. This had been sufficient to render the pilot's throttle movements ineffective and had 'stagnated' their engines at idling rpm.

Returning to 'C' Squadron after this conference, the Narner's clearance trials were continued – bomb doors, 'wet contacts' in-flight refuelling, 'buffet boundaries', Hi-Mach flying, carriage of 'Blue Parrot' guided weapons, rates of roll, aileron 'gear-changing', 'roll-with-G' to check 'roll-inertia coupling' limitations in XK527, incidence checks at low airspeeds and high indicated airspeed (HIAS) and handling up to 650 knots.

The next aircraft to arrive at 'C' Squadron was the Mark 2 version of the Sea Vixen. Although it weighed about 15 tons, it was basically a fighter and as such, it had to pass a spinning test before being allowed into squadron service and we were not looking forward to having to do it.

Here is a brief word on the progress of the Sea Vixen so far in the Navy. The Sea Vixen (DH 110) had had a slow start – particularly following the RAF's refusal to adopt it in 1953 – but once the Admiralty had been given the politicians' 'go ahead,' the first 'hooked' version had been taken aboard *Albion* for initial deck trials in September 1954. Stan Orr, CO of 'C' Squadron, had then done the deck trials in April 1956 in XF828, the third DH 110 to be built. With a maximum decklanding weight of 27,500 lb – 10,000 lb lighter than that of the Narner – and having the benefit of large Fowler flaps and nearly twice the engine power, the DH 110 had no problems on the flight deck.

Thirty-six arrested landings were done and 15 catapult launches, the remainder being free take-offs. Pilots found that the DH 110 was a simple and pleasant aircraft to deckland and with certain minor modifications to the control systems would be even better by the time it entered squadron service.

Minor improvements were made. One was to install nosewheel steering; a second was to modify the 'Maxaret' brakes to prevent the anti-skid device from acting on a single wheel (and so swinging the aircraft off the runway) and a third was to install an automatic trim-change 'corrector' to operate if the pilot selected the 'barn-door-sized' airbrakes at high speeds when wanting to slow down to shoot at a slower enemy aircraft. (This had become a requirement from our Korean MiG 15 experience where large airbrakes were seen to have been needed by a MiG's pilot to give him a chance of quickly slowing down to the speed of a Sea Fury he was attacking to allow him to take a shot at it. The MiG pilot was unable to do so and, as recounted in an earlier chapter, got shot down himself).

De Havilland's test pilots, John Cunningham and John Derry, had had much experience with transonic flight tests in the DH 108. They knew that immense elevator power was necessary to retain sufficiently positive fore-and-aft control when aiming weapons in the transonic region of flight. The power-operated controls, which had to work very large ailerons and a fully-moving tailplane with its trailing-edge flap in all flight conditions in the Sea Vixen, were given variable 'Q' feel such that the pilot could not apply excessive amounts and risk breaking the aircraft when travelling at high indicated airspeeds. Neither would he have to put up with excessive stick forces if, transonically or at very low speeds, he needed to use very large control movements to keep accurate control. ·

The result was that the Sea Vixen could be flown from subsonic to supersonic flight with complete confidence, the powerful controls able to cope safely with the usual 'wingdrop' at 0.84 M or thereabouts. Controllability was so good when subsonic that differential aileron power alone was sufficient to control the aircraft when flying on autopilot.

Design requirements in AP 970 – the standard aircraft 'bible' – state that all Service *fighter* aircraft should be capable of recovering from a two-turn spin. Model spinning tests in the Farnborough wind tunnel allowed an assessment to be made of the chances of recovery from a new project, so that test pilots who had to do it for the first time were not put at too much risk.

Prototypes to be spin-tested have to have special instrumentation fitted. 'Hussenot' recorders take a permanent record of stick forces, rates of roll, yaw, pitch, tailplane, rudder and aileron displacement. All these measurements are transmitted to a radio-telemetry hut on the ground and recorded so that discussions can take place after the flight. Height-sensing devices are fitted in the cockpit to tell the pilot when to start recovery and a tail parachute is fitted for use as a last resort. About twenty spins are usually needed to establish behaviour and to allow the test pilot to recommend reliable recovery procedures.

Starting at about 40,000 feet – for aircraft like the Scimitar, Hunter or Sea Vixen – the aircraft is trimmed for straight flight at about 180 knots IAS. Power is then reduced to 'flight idling' and airspeed reduced to 'pitch-up'. The speed at which this took place varied with weight and sometimes did not occur at all. Speed could sometimes be reduced some 25 knots below the pitch-up speed in the Hunter before the stall occurred. At the stall, the right wing dropped sharply and the aircraft pitched nose-down, rolling in the direction of the dropped wing. Recovery from the stall was immediate on allowing the stick to return to the central position. Height lost in the stall was about 7,000 feet. Wing rocking at the stall made lateral control difficult and if more than about 3 degrees of aileron was being carried at the point of stall, the aircraft rolled sharply against the aileron. A full 360-degree roll occurred at one time when I happened to have 5 degrees of aileron on at the stall.

Bill Bedford's trials in the Scimitar had already shown that the most reliable spin recovery technique in this fighter was to apply full opposite rudder and *free the control column* to its pre-spin position. When I tried my first spin in the Scimitar I reduced speed to 110 knots and applied full rudder and pulled the stick hard back. The first half turn of the spin which then occurred took about half a second, with the nose dropping into a steep dive. The rotation rate decreased in the second half turn and the aircraft raised its nose to near horizontal flight again with rotation ceasing. On taking recovery action – opposite rudder and a stick released to central – the nose pitched into a dive once more but rotation stopped. Speed was allowed to build up in the dive to 200 knots before any attempt was made to pull out of the dive.

A two-turn spin was then tried and this was more exciting as it carried on spinning for two turns after recovery action was taken, losing 4,000 feet more height in the process. It showed how easy it would be for pilot's to leave baling out too late in such circumstances and why the cockpit height warning – giving a flashing-light minimum safe recovery height of 20,000 feet – was fitted in test aircraft. Height lost in a two-turn spin in the Scimitar was about 15,000 feet.

'Spinning in' from a steep turn was a common occurrence in modern jet aircraft so that it was necessary for us to warn pilots of 'G'-stall dangers in all aircraft. Speed was reduced to about 200 knots in a 40-degree banked turn at 40,000 feet with power at 85 per cent. The pitchup in the Scimitar occurred at about 160 knots. Speed was further reduced by heaving back on the stick until, at about 130 knots and with full back elevator, the aircraft 'flicked' upside down and did two turns of a spin before recovery was possible, requiring 12,000 feet to do so.

The next test required us to try 'normal' recovery action to the Scimitar. (Normal spin recovery is by applying full opposite rudder and easing the stick forward until rotation – hopefully – ceases.) We found that if the stick was moved forward of central in the Scimitar, there was a 50/50 chance of it entering an inverted spin. Thus, by applying *normal* recovery techniques to the Scimitar the pilot could end up with a disaster.

More than adequate stall warning was given by the Scimitar and provided that the pilot relaxed sufficiently to make sure of the direction of rotation and that he did not apply stick forward of central when recovering, no harm would come to him.

Inverted spinning – that is to say where the spin is due to *negative* G wing loading – is not permitted. Recovery – by applying full back stick and opposite rudder – was not usually effective. However, it was important that test pilots could recognise an inverted spin when they saw it, because many of us tended to confuse an upside-down normal spin with a true inverted spin.

A pilot would always know if he had spun inverted for he would be 'hanging on his straps' with negative G throughout and he would have to apply 'stick back' to recover, not stick forward. We were taken up in a dual Hunter by Hawker's Chief test Pilot – Bill Bedford. He was kind enough to show us how to enter one and recover from it. The Hunter was a superb demonstration aircraft for this and was the only fighter aircraft cleared for the purpose.

We start the *inverted spin* in the Hunter by inverting the aircraft at a speed just above normal stall speed and easing the stick forward. When flying level and totally upside down, apply a little rudder in the required spin direction and then encourage it to start autorotation by applying a little down aileron to the 'inside' wing, to encourage that wing to stall if it had not already done so. Autorotation then starts. Autorotation occurs in a spin because the 'inside' wing remains more stalled than the faster-travelling outside wing. It is the inside wing's greater drag that keeps the rotation going and it is because it develops much less lift than the outside wing, the aircraft remains in a fully 'yawed' condition towards the inside wing and so 'autorotates', until the pilot takes recovery action to (a) stop the yaw and (b) to unstall both wings.

Attempts to recover from a spin depend considerably on rudder/fin effectiveness. The usual cause of an aircraft failing to recover after the correct action has been taken is usually that the fin/rudder assembly is fully stalled or, particularly in the case of the elevator, is in a turbulent part of the airflow behind the wings/fuselage and is only partially effective when the pilot pushes the stick forward to unstall the wings. Another cause of recovery failure is that the inside – or slower-moving wing – is discouraged from unstalling itself because the pilot has inadvertantly retained some positive aileron on that side. The increased aileron drag in the stalled state will ensure that rotation towards it will continue regardless of the power of the fin/rudder combination fighting against it.

The *inverted* spin recovery, therefore, requires the pilot to 'unload the wings' by *pulling the stick back* – the reverse of normal. Recovery may also necd much more room so that minimum height for a recovery in the Hunter was set at about 20,000 feet.

The sequence of events for inverted spin recovery for the Hunter is first, by centralising all controls, then applying back stick and opposite rudder and then centralising the moment autorotation stops – otherwise the aircraft will start a spin in the other direction. The main difficulty is being able to recognise the direction of the spin. A quick look at the 'turn and bank' indicator will tell the pilot, i.e., the 'turn' needle points to the spin direction at all times and in all cases.

The Mark 2 Sea Vixen – XJ474 – which was waiting for us at 'C' Squadron to do spinning trials on our return from the Narner deck trials in *Ark*, was a re-built Mark 1. The Mark 2 version had extra fuel tanks of 100 gallons added to the forward tail booms, forming large ridge-like structures over the wings' top surfaces. Although the firm had not thought it necessary to conduct new spinning trials, Boscombe's 'Tech. Office' wanted to find out what changes, if any, had been made to the spin recovery by the addition of the pinion tanks on XJ474. Wind tunnel tests had shown that the Mark 2 had normal spinning characteristics and recovery so that unless the pilot did something wrong, there should be no trouble.

'Hussenot' recorders were fitted to take a permanent record of indicated air-speeds, heights, G, stick forces, rates of roll, yaw, pitch, tailplane, rudder and aileron movements. Most of the above measurements were transmitted automatically to the ground telemetry hut on the airfield so that if the pilot got into difficulties, a permanent record of the reasons would be available. Height warning signals were given and a tail parachute was carried. Observers were not required to descend into their 'sightless' seats for this venture. it would have been too cruel to have asked them.

I did a total of ten spins in two trips lasting an hour each. In order to get on friendly terms it was necessary to do a few stalls, power off, from about 40,000 feet, the last two using full back elevator. At the stall, the left wing dropped sharply and the aircraft pitched nose-down, rolling as it did so to the inverted position. (I was not carrying an observer, so I did not have to worry how he was feeling.) Recovery from the stall was immediate on releasing the stick. Height lost was about 10,000 feet, most of it in the dive recovery. Spinning to the left was started by applying full rudder towards the direction that I chose to spin. The spinning characteristics were almost identical to those of the Scimitar, starting by swooping out of the fully inverted position, hesitating for what seemed like two or three seconds in a near horizontal flight attitude before starting a proper, conventional spin earthwards. Centralising the stick carefully, and watching the desyn instruments to make sure I had done so, I applied full opposite rudder and, when nothing happened for another two turns, I pushed the stick forward. The spin stopped, and I breathed again. For one dreadful moment – the aircraft having done two full turns before showing any signs of recovery – I thought I might have done something wrong.

I climbed up and did three more in both directions, using exactly the same technique and not risking any aileron movement until I had seen the traces at the telemetry hut. These showed that the Vixen needed stick-forward to recover. If any of us had done that in the Scimitar it would probably have entered an inverted spin immediately. Bill Bedford's trials in the Scimitar had shown that the most reliable spin recovery technique in this fighter was to apply full opposite rudder and free the control column to its pre-spin position.

The second flight included the use of out-spin and in-spin aileron applied while in the spin. This had some exciting effects. A few degrees of out-spin aileron entirely prevented any sign of recovery after four turns. In-spin aileron slowed the rate of spin but did not effect recovery. But when applying full in-turn aileron at speeds near the G stall, the results were frightening. The aircraft entered a G-stalled high-speed spin with about 2 G applied and the spin became ominously flat. Carefully centralising the controls I applied full opposite rudder with fully-forward stick. Nothing, seemingly, happened for two turns until, when applying in-spin aileron slightly the spin slowed down and finally stopped – after losing 20,000 feet of altitude. That was quite enough and I came home to write my report. In it I suggested that the irregularity and hesitating, random nature of some of the spins could be accounted for by engine gyroscopic forces.

The Sea Vixen had originally been designed for all-weather fighter duties like the Javelin. So, following tests carried out by Ian Normand (15 ETPS) on

Ark Royal in 1956 it was fitted with an 'auto-throttle' engine control system on the port motor which automatically retained speed control on decklanding and airfield approaches, so that the pilot could concentrate more on his instrument-flying approach path. The Sea Vixen was only 60 per cent of the weight of a Narner and with 75 per cent more thrust to urge it along it could, with its large wing area, easily out-turn and out-climb any opposition except the RAF's new interceptor, the Lightning and, perhaps, the Navy's Scimitar. It had been designed to fire four of the two types of heat-seeking air-to-air missiles – the Firestreak and Red Top – and it was armed with 4 × 20 mm cannon and could also carry conventional rockets and bombs for a distance to the target of 500 miles and back. The only disadvantage was the seating arrangement for the observer who was unable to see ahead and had to sit to the right of the pilot with his head on a level with the pilot's lap, staring at a mass of instruments and a large radar screen.

At this juncture, Maurice Hedges and Cliff Evans left the squadron to take up squadron posts. Lt/Cdr Nick Bennet and Lts Bill Newton and Pete Barber joined us from ETPS No. 18 Course. 'Ozzie' Brown became Senior Pilot in place of Cliff Evans.

During June 1961 we did a considerable amount of flying to check single-engined behaviour, re-lights, low level/high speed flying, and 'dummy' flight refuelling with the new probe installed in Buccaneer XJ524 for the first time. We were all pleasantly surprised how unaffected by 'air bumps' the Narner was – compared with the Sea Vixen and Scimitar – when low-flying at very high speeds. When doing 'stick-force-per-G tests, we wore the latest anti-G suit. This replaced the Franks suit used in Seafires during our bombardment spotting duties over Normandie. The Franks suit required two gallons of water to be emptied into a waterproof garment laced round the lower limbs. On application of G, the water equalised the pressure on both sides of the skin and thus effectively prevented excess blood from flowing in to the lower limbs and starving the brain and retina. Our latest suit used air instead of water to supply the pressure – the more G the more air pressure. Besides the normal straps connecting the aircrew to their dinghy/parachute and ejector seat, there were now five more connections. The connection to the air supply for the G suit was the fifth pipe. A sixth pipe assembly secured the aircrew's oxygen supply (normal supply and emergency) to their oxygen masks. Radio connectors and leg restrainers were the seventh and eighth connections. Four of them were combined into a single plug-in fitting.

At about this time Pete Rippon and I were flown out by BOAC to an airfield on the Island of Bahrein to discover whether it would be suitable for a Buccaneer to do a tropical trial there in a month's time. We travelled first class in the forward seats of a beautiful Comet, with free drinks and every attention from two air hostesses. When the Comet went unserviceable at Beirut on the way, we spent two nights in a luxury hotel by the beach. Bahrein had some very cheap shopping but no facilities for a Buccaneer so we returned to Boscombe. One of the reasons why Bahrein was unsuitable was because the

Buccaneer's 450 lb/sq/in tyre pressure would have cracked the perimeter track's concrete – like the Lightning's.

Blackburns were already two months late in getting their C of A handling release for the Narner from Boscombe Down and the deck clearance seemed to be even further off. Much time was spent on checking their idea for a retractable flight-refuelling probe which resemble an Indian snake-charmer trick as it unravelled itself from its stowage along the starboard nose fairing. It was nearly impossible to get its probe into the drogue, for whenever the drogue came near the probe, the drogue sheered off due to its proximity to the nose 'bow wave' and sometimes disappeared round the other side and threatened to enter an air intake. Several of those in the new Intensive Flying Development Unit (700 Squadron – Z Flight) at Lossiemouth who had by now received their first Narners and, like us, were using the new 140-gallon 'Buddy' refuelling pod carried under a Sea Vixen's wing, had also failed to get it in. Blackburns quickly replaced it with a sensible non-retractable device which extended forward of the bow wave and gave the pilot no trouble.

Then came the third Narner deck trial. This time we knew that we should be asked to determine the 'minimum safe launch speed at ever increasing weights. The 'end speed' achieved by a catapult working at its maximum steam pressure depended upon the weight that it was being asked to accelerate and the distance through which it shoved the weight forward along the track. The 80-ton pull of the strop connected to the steam-driven piston of Ark's catapult was hardly helped at all by the mere eight-ton total thrust of the Buccaneer's two Gyron Juniors during the second or so it travelled along the catapult track. Neither would RATOG have made much difference. For an aircraft of the weight of a Buccaneer – about the same as a B-17 – each foot of catapult would only add about half a knot to its speed. Its rate of acceleration under engines alone would only have been about 2 knots over the whole distance and of no significance. A 'free' take-off of a Seafire over the same distance would have gained a speed of about 50 knots. In other words, the jet-engined Buccaneer's acceleration was only a fraction of that of a comparably power/weighted prop-driven aircraft.

By adding ship's speed to wind speed, and knowing the weight of the Buccaneer to be catapulted, the boffins and Deck Officer would be able to work out exactly what 'indicated airspeed' (IAS) the pilot should have 'on the clock' by the end of its run. By adjusting the Buccaneer's weight or ship's speed after each test to give an ever decreasing IAS at which the pilot still had good control of the aircraft, a complete list of figures could be produced covering all wind speeds, ship's speeds, aircraft weights, temperatures and weather states, day or night, so that 'minimum end-speed' graphs could be prepared for each type of aircraft borne in the carrier.

The Americans had avoided most of this palaver by designing their steam catapults with sufficient energy to guarantee safe catapult launches for all their types of aircraft at their maximum weights and at speeds fifteen knots higher than their minimum tested speeds – thus leaving an adequate safety margin. The Americans' *minimum* 'end-speed' figure was, however, an absolute emergency figure.

Starting with the *Forrestal* and *Kittyhawk* in 1960, by 1962 they had their C-13 catapults using steam at 800 lb/sq/inch to our 375lb/sq/inch and with lengths up to 253 feet compared with our maximum of 151 feet in *Hermes* and *Ark Royal* and 200 feet in the refitted *Eagle*. At the time we, who had invented the steam catapult, were struggling to get a lightly loaded Buccaneer airborne in 15 knots of natural wind plus a thirty-knot speed provided by the carrier at full throttle, the Americans were able to shoot off such aircraft as the A4D Skyhawk, F4H Phantom, A3J Vigilante, W2F Hawkeye (AEW) and the F84-2NE Crusader, in harbour and with no natural wind with enough fuel on board to make the nearest US Navy airfield ashore.

The reason why Britain had fallen so far behind was the unwillingness on the part of Director-General Ships (DGS) at the Admiralty to find £8 million pounds to lengthen two out of our three Fleet Carriers' catapults by 36 feet and bring them up to standard of *Eagle* – until 1969, when he agreed to modify *Ark Royal*'s. DGS was only able to provide a six-degree angled deck instead of a 10-degree angle, thus limiting parking/catapulting space forward and slowing down aircraft take-off intervals.

Back at 'C' Squadron in August 1961, after checking out the two test Buccaneers intended for *Hermes*' deck trials, we flew 529 and 530 aboard her and started our 'minimum launch speeds'. I and Ozzie Brown – with Lt Jones and Mr Mather as brave Observers – completed 20 landings and 'squirts' each on the first two days. The third day dawned with only five knots of natural wind. This limited our catapult weight to 34,000 lb, 10,000 lb lighter than the Buccaneer's full design weight. Having done the usual landings and 'squirts' without incident at 34,000 lb take-off weight – it was Ozzie's turn.

I watched from the bridge and saw his aircraft rear up, drop its port wing slightly in a stall and hit the water within 10 seconds of its take-off. It had only its airbrakes showing as it passed down the port side, about 100 yards distant.

It stayed like this for about a minute as if its nose had stuck into the sea bed, and then slowly dipped forward and disappeared below the surface as the easterly tide took it. We were shattered. Was it the tailskid collapsing that started a nose-up pitch which Ozzie could not stop? According to the instrument recording Ozzie had applied full available nose-down elevator one-eighth of a second after leaving the catapult. Was the end-speed dangerously low? (We all knew on board *Hermes* that the acceleration of the Narner off the end of the catapult had been as low as half a knot/sec on some of the occasions that it had been measured.) Was BLC failure the cause? Was it because the tail-down launch posture adopted by the Navy was too nose-up for airflow to fully establish itself? Finally, was it because the wire strop attached from the shuttle to the aircraft aligned *below* the aircraft's CG, so tending to rotate the aircraft nose-up/tail-downwards and collapsing the tail skid at the last moment?

All further flying was cancelled and XK530 was left onboard, no one daring to authorise any further catapult take-offs until the causes of Ozzie's and his Observer's (Mr Terry Dunn's) deaths were known.

Having visited poor Ozzie's widow in Wales and attending Ozzie's funeral I went to the official enquiry at Portland. It was concluded that Ozzie had pulled back on the stick, promoting a pitch-up and stall. The reason why he could not correct the pitch-up was through lack of available nose-down elevator power to correct the pitch-up.

At a preliminary meeting on board I said I thought that the three-degree pitch-up had occurred on the catapult due to the tail skid having collapsed. It was the exciting cause of the pitch-up which was not Ozzie-induced as I had seen no up-elevator movement during the launch. The inertia from this three-degrees-per-second pitch-up could not possibly have been stopped by Ozzie shoving the stick fully forward – as he did – as the elevator nose-down authority available to him was almost nil. It would have had no effect.

In fact, because of the built-in hydraulic restrictions in the elevator's movement range, Ozzie's maximum nose-down elevator angle was only +2 degrees, insufficient to make much difference at that speed. Peter Rippon also pointed out that the use of the wrong grease in the wing-fold bolts had caused misalignment in the port, rear wing-fold bolt, possibly leading to partial loss of BLC on that side. This could have explained why the port wing stalled first after the pitch-up. Pete also said that he had authorised the aircraft to fly with auto-hood-jettison not operative, otherwise it was fully serviceable.

When the wreckage had been raised from 50 feet of water and inspected on the quay at Portland (and before it went to Farnborough for a closer inspection) it was found that Ozzie had jettisoned the hood underwater. He was found out of his cockpit but with his foot firmly jammed by the Observer's ejector seat after it had fired accidentally.

The observer had also been trying to get out of his cockpit at the same time, but, at the time his seat fired, the aircraft had already turned over onto its back, thus driving him downwards and injuring both of them.

I and Dennis then met the firm's designers who had just completed their inspection of the wreckage and the salvaged flight recorder at Farnborough. It showed that because of corroded BLC switches and wing-fold damage, BLC pressure on the port side might have been lower than that on the starboard and, because of the corrosion, the cockpit instruments may not have shown this to the pilot. This may have tended to lower the port wing and encourage the pilot to apply correcting aileron. This may, in turn, have increased the stalling tendency of the port wing at a difficult time. The tail skid was still in one piece but it may have collapsed. Several witnesses had said that, because of steam escaping from the shuttle during the launch, all they could see were the usual sparks as it trailed on the deck and could not see whether it had collapsed or not. I pointed out that I thought that because the aircraft's CG was higher with the bomb bay empty, the 80-ton drag on the accelerator strop – of which my schoolboy physics told me a fifth would have been vectored vertically downwards – would have applied an additional ten-ton load to the tailskid. If it had then collapsed, this would have increased the Buccaneer's tail-down incidence by three degrees, making an angle-of-attack of nearly 20 degrees. If the collapse rate had been for a second's duration as the aircraft sped down the catapult, the nose-up rotation rate imparted by the collapse would have been three degrees/sec and probably beyond pilot's correction by elevator, even if this was applied 1/8th of a second after launch.

Although Ozzie's last launch was not at 'minimum end-speed', the extra nose-up pitch probably caused by the tail-skid failure, caused the aircraft to have far too large a nose-up angle to have allowed a proper establishment of airflow over the wing as speed increased in the one and a half seconds on the catapult run, particularly in the turbulent airflow forward of the ship. A Comet had just crashed because the pilot had 'rotated' too soon on take-off and we were always being told by our instructors never to 'wrench it off' in the three-point attitude. The tail-down launch configuration was asking for trouble if such large incidences and such slow end-speeds were to be used. The prospect of being discharged into the blackness of a night at only 50 feet off the sea and with marginal acceleration and even less elevator control filled us all with horror. There was no doubt that unless someone had a bright idea, the 'Narner' would not be allowed into Naval carrier-borne service and the production order of the Mark 2 with more powerful engines had yet to be signed.

As if to reinforce our opinion, we next heard that the Ministry of Supply Project Officer had declared that the Admiralty would not accept the Narner into service with such obvious handling difficulties when catapulted at minimum launch speeds. However, having talked amongst ourselves at 'C' Squadron we managed to convince the doubters that a 'hands-off' take-off technique seemed to have worked well on the single occasion I had tried it, and if the aircraft was given more nose down stick authority than the seven degrees it had been given by Blackburns so far and if we could use full landing flap to increase lift at the present tail-down incidence, the aircraft would fly itself off the catapult much better than the pilot could for the first five seconds of flight.

We all knew that the Buccaneer 1 was underpowered and that this had made it difficult to handle after launch. Even if our scheme worked, it was becoming obvious that the Buccaneer would need more power if it was to operate off the catapult in hot weather or when heavily loaded in flat calm wind conditions.

After this tragedy, Dennis asked the firm to ensure that the tailplane control in our Mark 1s was given much more nose-down authority (clearly lacking in Ozzie's case) and that full flap should be allowed to be used off the catapult. He also ensured that Blackburns mass-balanced the entire tailplane control circuit so that it would not shift during five G horizontal forces being applied during catapult launches, whether the pilot's hand was on the stick or not. 'C' Squadron would try the new 'hands off' launch technique at the next deck trials if the Ministry would give us the chance and agree to keep the Buccaneer in production. We required that the 'hands off' tailplane trim position should be set at minus seven degrees at normal take-off C of G loadings and marks should be painted on the tail fin to tell the ground crew and catapult officer that the pilot had trimmed it to this figure before he was allowed off the deck.

Top level meetings with the Ministry always had a mixture of people sitting round the table, half financial management and half technical. I sat alongside Dennis at these meetings and he would press the *facts* button when he intended to answer the scientists and he would press the *emotion* button when I was required to speak to non-scientists. Between us, we stuck up for the Narner quite well for we were determined to see it succeed.

Ministry permission was accordingly given to proceed with the deck trials as soon as a carrier could be found. So that, nine months after Ozzie's accident, Brian Davies (19 ETPS) and I, plus our two brave Observers – Jimmy McPhee and Lt Di Jones – took off in XK530 and XK536 to do some 'hands off' trials using the catapult ashore at RAE Bedford before landing aboard the *Ark* once more for the fourth deck trial starting on 16 May 1962.

We found from the readings of a G-meter in the cockpit that the catapult at Bedford was applying up to six G for very short periods in a series of jerks on the take-off run, its average being only five G. The jerky behaviour actually broke the G-meter fitting in the cockpit and it nearly hit Brian Davies in the face.

The peaks and troughs in the acceleration pattern and its consent lack of smoothness would seem to be the reason why the catapults in our carriers were only allowed to use low steam pressures compared with the Americans, for fear of overstressing the aircraft. 'Wet' liners and rotary valves partly cured this jerkiness in future years, but those in charge of ship engineering in DGS were not able to achieve American pressures. These rose to double the 400 lb/sq/inch pressure available in our carriers in future years.

To show that all of us had confidence in the 'hands off' scheme, Dennis bravely sat in the back of XK530 with me and did the first one. Having climbed down the ladder afterwards without assistance it seemed that he was well satisfied, as we all were. Blackburns had done an excellent job on mass-balancing their tailplane circuit and had given the pilot nine degrees of nose-down authority instead of the usual seven.

'C' Squadron would try the new 'hands off' launch technique at the next deck trials. We set the 'hands off' tailplane trim position at minus five degrees at normal take-off centre-of-gravity loadings and marks were painted on the tail as we had requested.

On 16 May 1962, nine months after Ozzie's accident, we repaired on board *Hermes* once more with two white-painted Buccaneers and carried out about 40 landings and 'squirts' without the smallest incident. It only remained now, to check this out at full weights and at minimum launch speeds and the Narner S Mk 1 could be saved.

Since March 1961, 700 'Z' Squadron had been formed at Lossiemouth for crew training with early production Narners with 'Spiv' Leahy in command. This became 809 Squadron in January 1963 embarking in *Victorious* for deck-landing practice in July 1963 following clearance by the Ministry of Supply having been granted after 'C' Squadron's successful deck trials in February of that year.

Meanwhile, 801 Squadron had formed under Ted Anson in July 1962 (about six months before 700 'Z' became 809 Squadron) so becoming the first operational – as opposed to training – Squadron in the Fleet Air Arm. Following the successful – and final – deck trials of the S Mk 1 'C' Squadron at Boscombe Down in February 1963, 801 Squadron increased to ten Buccaneer S Mk 1s before departing in *Victorious* to the Far East. Permission was also given to Blackburns in February 1963 for them to build 40 Mk 1 Buccaneers for delivery between April 1963 and February 1964.

The final deck trials of the S Mk 1 had taken place in *Ark Royal* on 5–15 February 1963. Jimmy McPhee and 'Ed' Beadsmore were our two observers this time and Nick Bennet and Brian Davies the other two pilots. We had received a signal at Boscombe Down the night before to be on board at 1000 hrs on the 5 February, complete with aircraft and ratings plus Dennis Higton and the firm's reps.

We discovered that a foot of snow had fallen on Boscombe's runway during the night. A strip 300 yards long and about the width of a cricket pitch was therefore cleared of snow to prevent the nosewheel from splashing snow down the two air intakes. Jimmy told me afterwards he was holding his breath in the back of XK536 as he could hear the snow smacking against the fuselage as we disappeared in a white cloud up the two-mile runway. But the nose-wheel lifted clear of the snow after a couple of hundred yards and we landed at Culdrose 25 minutes later. Who should walk up in the sunshine but Captain Jooef Bartosik – late of HMS *Loch Scavaig*. He had been appointed Captain of Culdrose a year previously.

Jimmy McPhee takes up the narrative at this point:

> On arrival at Culdrose a look of near petrified fear came over you when it dawned on you that the Captain was a rather enthusiastic Polish gentleman with whom you had had some unfortunate anchor-dropping experiences in the past. You decided that the best form of defence was attack, so this non-aviating Captain was invited to take a flight in my observer's seat. I was detailed to brief him. You said: 'Be careful. Jimmy, watch out for the gas-chamber smile!'

Jimmy continued:

> I met the greatcoated figure on the hardstanding the following morning. He seemed to me to have the bonhomie of an OGPU general and the 'cockpit brief-ing' had all the conviviality. My greatest mistake was to offer him a sick bag – just in case.
>
> The circuit cleared, you took off and disappeared seawards below the horizon of the Cornish hills only to return at floor level and great speed. A couple of 'upward charlies', a roll off the top and an inverted run followed. Thence out of sight again for five minutes as, we presumed, you were giving him a close-up of the seals basking on the beach.

During this five minutes we had flown to the Isle of Scilly and back in a mock A-bomb lobbing sequence. Josef's voice remained icy calm as he remarked on the wingtip trails and the cloud of vapour at about 0.85 Mach as I applied about six G on the pull-up from zero feet over the sea and he even continued normal conversation as we did the roll off the top at about 12,000 feet a few seconds later. (Of course, this was not as sensational as the performance of an F-104 pilot a few years previously at Edwards Air Force Base when we had watched him as he pulled up at zero feet in a true vertical climb and at last disappeared from our vision still vertical, at about 50,000 feet – saying afterwards that he had at last run out of 'puff' at about 100,000 feet altitude and had had to relight! But it wasn't bad for the Narner to get to 12,000 feet, was it?) The Narner was so beautifully smooth to fly at Mach 0.8 low down that it was obviously a great pleasure for him as well myself.

Jimmy continues:

> After the landing I watched you taxy back with trepidation in my heart as your manoeuvres would have made all but the most hardened of observers queasy to say the least.
>
> I climbed up to the cockpit to unstrap him and to consider how best I could clean up the mess. He greeted me with a rare smile: 'McPhee' he said, 'until today I have not lived'. There cannot have been a more sudden conversion from salthorse to airman since the days of Saul of Tarsus.

This very popular skipper even came out to say goodbye to us as we set off for the *Ark* the next morning.

Captain D. Gibson, DSC had now taken over from Hill-Norton in *Ark Royal* and we received a warm welcome from all on the bridge on 5 February 1963.

Three of us completed 85 landings and catapult launches in *Ark Royal* without the smallest hiccup. While we were on board her, she gave up a small portion of her deck on 8 February 1963 for initial 'compatibility' trials of the Hawker P1127 in XP831. We watched this V/STOL fighter-to-be settle comfortably onto the aft lift for its first-ever decklanding, scarcely crushing a pork pie with its wheels as it touched down. It came down vertically for the last 15 feet with such little disturbance that the hundred or so goofers were disappointed, having expected flames, explosions, noise and confusion and with the *Ark*'s paintwork on fire.

I met a fully relaxed Bill Bedford – Hawker's Chief Test Pilot – on the flight deck, and I took him up to the Captain – who said that he hadn't got any money to buy one just yet but it obviously had a great future as an Admiral's Barge. (Bill Bedford returned to a new *Ark Royal* 25 years later to the day and hour, this time flying in the back of a two-seat T4N Harrier piloted by Lt Alistair MacLaren of 899 Naval Air Squadron from RNAS Yeovilton. On landing, Bill was greeted by the Captain – Mike Harris – and commemorative plaques were exchanged.)

Little did any of us know in 1963 that the P 1127 – the initial outcome of four years testing by Tom Brooke-Smith and others on the 'flying bedstead' concept mentioned below – would eventually produce the magnificent Harrier FRS 1 in time for 27 of them in 820, 800, 801 and 819 Royal Naval Air Squadrons – and No. 1 Royal Air Force Squadron – to defend our Argentinian offensive against the 200-strong Argentine Air Force.

But returning to February 1963 aboard *Ark Royal* once more, the Navy still had doubts about the possible usefulness of V/STOL and the P 1127 at the time of Bill Bedford's arrival. The Admiralty also feared that it might make the large carrier less necessary, forgetting of course, that the Navy would in any case still need large carriers to operate effective AEW aircraft.

The Americans also had tried out various schemes for V/STOL during 1950–1955. They produced their Ryan XC-142, powered by four prop-jets driving 15-foot diameter propellers fixed to a wing which turned through 90 degrees. Then there was the Convair XFY-1. This was powered by a large Allison turbo-prop and was an example of the 'tail-sitter' type of VL aircraft, using variable pitch, large diameter contraprops to supply the vertical lift instead of helicopter rotors. Its take-off was normal, but for landing the pilot had to pull the nose up to a vertical position over the runway and make a verti-cal, tail-first landing on four wheels sticking out of his wingtips and fins. Although this might have been feasible for a prone-pilot sitting position, it seemed to us to be asking too much from a normal aviator unless he had eyes in the back of his head. It seemed about as sensible as Farnborough's 'rubber deck' idea with the Vampire.

At this time – 1952–4, and the time of the first 'H'-bomb – Britain had been trying out a testing 'vehicle' for what eventually became the P 1127 concept. This was a framework supporting a pilot, a few fuel tanks and two Nene engines built by Shorts and Rolls-Royce and bravely 'flown' by Tom Brooke-Smith. It was soon known as the 'Flying Bedstead'. Its two Rolls-Royce Nene jets had their exhausts ducted through 90 degrees to discharge downwards, their gyroscopic forces cancelling each other by placing them facing opposite ways in the fuselage. Control movements in yaw, pitch and roll were effected by compressed air from the Nenes being squirted through a number of nozzles to act as ailerons, rudders and elevators as the pilot demanded through his control column and throttle levers. The Bedstead showed that provided a single engine could be found of sufficient power to lift, vertically, a useful load of about 20,000 lb, a fighter might be developed with V/STOL (vertical and short take-off and landing) capability which would be of great use to the army as it could then operate in the frontline of battle without the need for air-fields.

The Navy were not keen on this idea in the early 'fifties' as the government had made it clear that if the RAF adopted this idea for their fighter replace-ment for the Lightning, the Navy would also be required to use a V/STOL fighter-type to replace the Sea Vixen. With the increased power now available from catapults, jet afterburners and BLC, plus the likelihood of variable sweep wings of increased area to give slower decklanding speeds in the future and with drooped leading edges to the mainplanes with jet deflection and BLC added, it was considered that the navies of the world could easily do without V/STOL. All they would need for the jet age would be more powerful catapults to get them airborne and, by 1960, this is exactly what the Royal Navy had been planning to have, with a new series of 40,000-ton carriers, starting with CVA01.

With politics involved as well as these new technical factors, the progress of V/STOL was slow. Before making irrevocable decisions on a replacement for the Scimitar and Sea Vixen fighters, the Royal Navy wanted to learn of progress made in carrier-borne fighters in the United States Navy. We would also be required to fly the USN's new AEW aircraft, the twin-engined Grumman Hawkeye W2F. In the next chapter, I will try to describe what I, Nick Bennet and Dennis Higton did on our visit to Patuxent River, where we had been sent by the Admiralty to find out what the USN might be prepared to offer and how they expected to be able to cope in the ten years which lay ahead – without V/STOL.

Following the fifth decktrials from 5–15 February 1963, the Mark 1 entered service with a clearance to operate from a carrier up to a weight at take-off of 44,000 lb. Besides the forty Mark 1s which were then ordered, further permission was given for construction of the more powerful Spey-engined S Mark 2, the first of 86 deliveries to begin in June 1964.

The Spey 101s in the Mark 2s delivered 11,000 lb of thrust each (9,100 lb with BLC). This compared with 7,000 lb from a Gyron Junior and was achieved by Rolls-Royce with only a ton's increase in weight per engine. The first two prototypes had become available to the firm's test pilots earlier than the main order for the Mark 2, because two Mark 1s – XK526 and XK527, last flown by 'C' Squadron in July 1961 had been re-engined in May 1962.

Although our catapult performances were never up to American standards – who could catapult all their different types of aircraft off in zero wind in harbour with a considerable fuel load – it was at least encouraging to know that, given a catapult of the expected performance of *Eagle* after her refit, we should be able to operate the Mark 2 Buccaneer at a take-off weight of 50,000 lb from *Victorious*, *Ark Royal* and *Eagle* at sea, anywhere in the world in a few years time. Although this was still 10,000 lb below the full capability of the Mark 2 demonstrated aboard the USN's *Enterprise*, if the RN had been given permission to build the new carrier – CVA01 – in 1966, this combination would have given the RN a worldwide nuclear and conventional strike capability comparable with the USN.

The 'hands off' system had been in service use for all deck take-offs from our carriers until the Buccaneer had gone out of Naval service in 1978. It is used by USN carrier pilots, with inputs from 'fly-by-wire', to this day. There were only two catapult accidents reported – in June 1966. This was when a Mark 2 pitched up off the catapult and crashed in a similar manner to Ozzie – but with both crew ejecting this time, being equipped with a 'zero-zero' M-B seat. Lt Dave Eagles from 'C' Squadron went out to the ship to put matters right but did the same himself!

The probable cause of both accidents was because, with wing tanks fitted, the Narners were being launched in an out-of-trim nose-up condition, the change of trim probably being due to a change of airflow characteristics over the mainplane caused by the airflow around the tanks. The wing tanks had been tested for the first time off the USN's *Lexington*'s powerful catapults a year previously, but no out-of-trim changes had been reported at that time. The new wing tanks were faired into the wings' leading edges in such a way that they had probably altered the airflow to cause a nose-up trim change equivalent to about minus two degrees of elevator – thus causing the pitchups.

On 15 February 1968 I received a £150 cheque from the Herbert Lott Naval Trust Fund for the 'hands off' invention which '. . . secured a safe catapult clearance to a useful operational standard for the Buccaneer.'

Thirty two years after the first Buccaneer Squadron was formed, six hundred of those who had flown or operated the Buccaneer in the Royal Navy and Royal Air Force gathered at Lossiemouth in Scotland as guests of 208 Squadron to this marvellous aircraft. A brief history – an Eulogy – was given at the end of this service by Group Captain T. Eeles, BA, RAF, Commanding Officer of RAF Station, Linton-on-Ouse. With his permission, this is reproduced as follows:

It is always a sad occasion when one says goodbye to an old friend for the last time, and indeed this weekend will have seen the odd tear in many a hardened aviator's eye, especially after watching the flying on Saturday afternoon. The regret we must all feel at having to say farewell to that outstanding aircraft, the Buccaneer, must also be tinged with many memories, hopefully most of them happy ones.

The Buccaneer has always generated the fiercest of loyalties and inspired the utmost devotion and enthusiasm amongst the air and ground crews of the Royal Navy, Royal Air Force and South African Air Force, who were privileged to fly and work on such a splendid aircraft. A demonstration of that loyalty has been the exceptional number of people who have come here this weekend to say their last farewells. There has always been something special about the Buccaneer, from the day it was first revealed to the public at Bedford in April 1958 in the form of the prototype NA 39, right through to its final day's service in 208 Sqn here at Lossiemouth. Even the name was perfect, but it was well known that the principal reason for there being two seats in the Buccaneer was that only 50 per cent of the aircrew who flew it could spell it properly.

The Buccaneer was arguably the finest naval aircraft ever flown by the Fleet Air Arm. It was operated from the carriers *Victorious*, *Eagle*, *Hermes*, and *Ark Royal*, and was flown by the Royal Navy in many areas of the world where we don't go nowadays. Sadly, the 1960s turned out to be an era of withdrawal from overseas, and by 1971 there was only one fixed wing carrier left. In 1978, conventional fixed wing carrier flying ceased in the Royal Navy when 809

Squadron disembarked for the last time and HMS *Ark Royal* sailed to the breaker's yard and out of history.

Another aspect of the Buccaneer story that we should remember was the sale of the Mark 50 version to the South African Air Force. In 1963 the Republic of South Africa ordered 16 aircraft, which were basically similar to the Mk 2. Initial training was carried out here at Lossie and 24 Squadron first formed in November 1965. Twenty-four Sqn flew their 16 Buccaneers for over 25 years, the aircraft retiring in late 1990 – and that was a tremendous achievement which reflects much credit on the South African Air Force and the Buccaneer.

Since 1969 the Royal Air Force has also had a long and happy association with the Buccaneer. Although the Royal Air Force was initially reluctant to take on its first-ever ex-naval aircraft, Royal Air Force aircrew who flew the Buccaneer rapidly became just as enthusiastic as their dark blue colleagues about the robust qualities of their jet propelled near-sonic bulldozers. The Squadrons, based at Honington and Laarbruch, soon established a formidable reputation for employing aggressive and highly effective operational tactics and were the envy of many less capable outfits.

However, in the 1980s, following the discovery of serious fatigue damage and two fatal accidents, the fleet size was reduced and the Germany-based squadrons were disbanded. The force returned to its spiritual home at Lossiemouth where it has remained ever since. Notwithstanding its relatively small size, the Buccaneer force's contribution to the Royal Air Force operations over the last 25 years has been considerable. The introduction of the Royal Air Force's only tactical air-to-surface missiles, Martel and Sea Eagle, the first participation in Flag exercises in the USA, the pioneering of the delivery techniques for Laser Guided Bombs and of course, the enormous contribution to victory in the Air War in the Gulf, are some typical examples.

But now we have come to the end of the Buccaneering years. The Buccaneer was a formidable aircraft which still has an unsurpassed performance at low level; it has remained a most potent aircraft right to the end of its Service career. To misquote slightly: 'in it we slipped the surly bonds of earth, and danced the skies on laughter-silver'd wings. Sunward we climbed – but not very far – and chased the shouting wind along, down in the noise-filled valleys'.

The Buccaneer's unique shape is unlikely to be seen in the air for much longer; most will die at the hands of the scrapman's torch. Luckily several examples will remain preserved for posterity in various aviation collections, including the Royal Air Force and Fleet Air Arm Museums. It is, of course, the last combat aircraft to have been designed and produced solely in this country. Inevitably, as with any high performance combat aircraft, especially when flown to the limits, there have been accidents and losses, and we should remember at this time all those aircrew, British, American and South African, who gave their lives in the service of their country whilst flying the Buccaneer in the Fleet Air Arm, the Royal Air Force, the South African Air Force and as Service and civilian flight test aircrew.

And so it is time for us to say farewell. The Buccaneer has served us magnificently, and we have enjoyed superb flying and comradeship on our various Buccaneer squadrons, having made friendships and taking with us memories that will hopefully last for many years.

To conclude, I can do no better than to finish by saying: well done, thou good and faithful servant.

CHAPTER 13

PATUXENT RIVER, USA

Patuxent River was the United States Navy's equivalent of 'C' Squadron at Boscombe Down. The USN airfield covers an area many times that of Boscombe Down and had about 100 USN aircraft under test at that time, of fifteen different types.

The visit lasted 10 days during which six of the latest prototypes of aircraft were flown, water ski-ing and golf attempted and the 4th of July celebrated. The weekends were spent 'resting-up' as the guests of the Naval Staff and Pridham in Washington. By the end of the trip we three – Dennis Higton, Nick Bennett and myself – were in good training but feeling a trifle sleepy, 'dutch-rolling' our way back to England in a Boeing 707. Dennis did not improve our jet lag by celebrating his birthday twice, once at US midnight and again at UK midnight – with 'fillers-up' in between.

The flying hours available on the series of test aircraft which we flew were insufficient to get more than a cursory glance at the performance of each, but valuable impressions were gained, particularly in the high supersonic, sub-sonic cruise, low level and landing regions.

Once settled into our luxurious quarters at the airfield in Maryland north of Chesapeak Bay, it was decided with our kind American Navy hosts to eschew all thoughts of aviation until the 4th of July celebrations were over. During the inevitable lull on the morning of the 5th, opportunity was taken to look through the lengthy Pilot's Notes. Verbal briefing consisted of innumerable cups of tea, anecdotes of past mishaps to other aircraft and discussions of last night's party, interspersed with a rundown on systems and emergency pro-cedures dwelling only on the most important features.

Next was a visit to the aircraft. On climbing into the cockpits of the Phantom, Crusader and the Vigilante, it quickly became apparent that so much test instrumentation had displaced the standard instruments that Pilot's Notes bore no resemblance whatever to the cockpit layouts of the aircraft we were to fly; so that it was necessary, and remarkably easy, to forget all about it and start again. Working round from left to right it took about half and hour.

The briefing, although light-hearted was nevertheless adequate – or so it turned out. Such irrelevances as, 'In case of twin flame-out, reduce speed to Mach 1.1 or to 515 knots IAS, whichever is lower . . .' were nice to know but not essential in our case as a chase plane was always provided and the chase pilot could better be relied upon to thumb over the pages of his copy of Pilot's Notes under these exceptional circumstances. However, there was always a dreadful feeling in the back of the mind that we had missed out something important.

On at least one occasion I had hoped that some shattering unserviceability would develop, thus dispensing with the need to fly at all that day. But the time inevitably drew nigh when it was necessary to open the throttles and blast off down the runway. After all, we had come a long way and it would hardly be good manners to chicken out at so late a stage.

Before 'getting airborne' in this brief narrative, it might be worthwhile to say a few words about USN safety equipment compared with ours at that time. Their flying harness was integral with the parachute and it was part of their flying overall – which they gave us to keep. Their negative-G restraint was better than ours but their upper harness was less rigid and allowed a great deal of side sway in bumpy air. To add to this, their oxygen supply plumbing was unwieldy as it had the oxygen 'economiser' attached to the face mask. We needed chameleon-type eyes to look round the cockpit as it was usual to snag the facemask if the complete face was moved. There seemed to be no means of knowing that our oxygen supply had failed apart from a complete inability to breathe. The whole thing was as difficult to adjust as a lady's hat.

British Martin-Baker seats were used in the F8U-2N Crusader and the F4H Phantom. These seats were the only ones there at that time which had zero-height ejection through the hood. The A3J Vigilante seat had been made by the aircraft manufacturers and it made use of hydraulically operated leg and arm-restraint bars but had no face blind.

The first aircraft I flew was the McDonnell Douglas F-4H Phantom II. This was the main purpose of the visit so that I could report on it to the Admiralty who were, at that time, intent on buying it to replace the Sea Vixen and Scimitar to operate off CVA01.

The F-4 has to this date served in 12 countries and, up to the time of the appearance of the F-18 series is considered to have been the world's most successful post-war fighter design ever built. The last one came off the production line in 1981, 28 years after the McDonnell Company first tendered for this USN requirement – for a supersonic, carrier-based fighter; at first unsuccessfully, as Chance-Vought got the initial contract to build the F-8U-3 Crusader. The Phantom first flew on 26 May 1958 in the hands of McDonnell's Chief Test Pilot – R.C. Little. It was designed to carry four Sparrow missiles radar-guided from the back seat and the F-4B version quickly proved its combat superiority over the MiG 17s and 19s in Vietnam. By the time I first flew it on 5 July 1962, it had done 1,606 mph on a straight course, 1,390 mph on a closed circuit and, as early as 6 December 1959 it had zoomed to an altitude of 98,558 feet in the hands of Cdr Lawrence E. Flint, USN.

The version which we flew at Patuxent River was the F-4H, carrying front guns as well as missiles, leading-edge slats and Boundary Layer Control (BLC) lift augmentation. These latter two devices gave increased manoeuvrability in dogfights and slower decklandings and catapult end-speed requirements. Better speed control on the approach was achieved by fitting larger airbrakes and, with air-search radar in the front and with the observer's cockpit raised so that he could see over the pilot as he controlled a mass of electronics, the F-4H was capable of all-weather and day/night operation from a carrier, its steam catapult able to discharge it with a total weapon load equal to its empty weight. Its maximum permissible take-off weight was 62,000 lb, the weight of eight Seafires and the weight eventually achieved by the Buccaneer Mk 2 when using the US Navy's more powerful catapults.

Power was supplied by two General Electric J-79s with afterburners each giving 18,000 lb of thrust at sea level, more than equal to the aircraft's maximum permissible decklanding weight of 34,000 lb so that the pilot could go round again in a loop if he felt like it!

As in the North American A3J Vigilante, the dicky seat of the F-4H we flew at Patuxent was crammed full of black boxes and this meant I was on my own. However, I and Nick were always watched by a pilot in a chase plane. Thus it befell that a puff of white smoke was seen as I started off down the runway. This was thought to be a burst tyre but it was the effects of the after-burner exhausts on the runway marking. Airborne inspection of the tyres by the chase pilot revealed no fault, but as a seamanlike precaution it was deemed advisable to make a landing into the arrester wires which happened to be in use on the dummy deck and steam catapult area of this huge airfield. The deckland-ing circuit 'drill' at Patuxent for the F-4 required an entry to the traffic pattern at 300 knots, a 60-degree banked left turn downwind with speed brakes out, undercarriage down at 200 knots, flaps down at 180 knots, with speed reduced to 145 knots (the deck approach speed for the F-4) on 'finals at 1 mile-to-go at 250 feet altitude. The fact that this was no sweat was not only due to the mag-nificent cockpit refrigeration system but to the extreme 'grooviness' of the F-4H in the decklanding configuration. (Pilots told us that the F-4 was not as 'groovy' on catapult launches due to the ease with which it could be over-rotated. However, this did not worry pilots too much during daylight because there was always sufficient engine thrust available to accelerate the aircraft out of trouble before it hit the sea – unlike the Buccaneer. A USN test pilot even demonstrated this to us at the time of our visit by doing a loop and a roll off the top immediately after his catapult launch on the airfield.)

There was the added advantage of a 'head-up' airspeed indicator in the F-4 with a large angle-of-attack meter alongside. The advantage of having an angle-of-attack meter was that it registered exactly how near the aircraft was to the stall regardless of its weight, height, barometric pressure or any other variable and regardless of the G that was being applied at the time. 'G' stalls and 'spinning-in' on the approach to land in the Phantom and other US naval aircraft were unheard of as a result and an identical instrument was later fitted to most other naval aircraft including the Buccaneer.

The F-4H version of the Phantom that we flew was classed as an 'attack interceptor fighter'. Auto throttles, 'approach-power compensators', weapon avoidance radar and enemy search radar were not fitted on the aircraft we flew. Both it and the Vigilante – each costing five times as much as a

Buccaneer and twenty-five times the cost of a Seafire 47 but only half the cost of the RAF's new TSR-2 – had twice the rate of climb and level speed of the Buccaneer and both were far superior in every respect to our Sea Vixen and Scimitar. The F-4H and the A3J made use of 12 per cent of their twin NJ79-4 engines' thrust to supply BLC air when taking off or landing. (The Buccaneer used 18 per cent.) Owing to the mechanical reliability of the American's BLC system, no cockpit instrumentation was necessary and failures were unheard of. The Americans were very pleased with their emergency hydraulic/electrics system in their aircraft. Instead of individual emergency switches, dials and levers in the cockpit, the pilot had nothing to do if the undercarriage, fuel jettison, radio, cockpit lighting, brakes or flaps systems suddenly failed to work. All he had to do was wait for the wind-driven turbine to automatically 'pop-out' from the wing root leading edge to recover full hydraulic and electric power immediately.

My second F-4H trip was more useful than the first as some supersonic handling was possible. It was extraordinary to see an *indicated* airspeed reading of 600 knots at about 40,000 feet and the *true* airspeed indicator pointer still moving rapidly clockwise past the 1,300 knots mark on its dial. It was difficult to tell whether the aircraft was supersonic or not by the handling alone and there was so much power to spare that it was necessary to make a conscious effort to avoid going supersonic on the climb.

After about five minutes at 40,000 feet in after-burner the aircraft was allowed to slow down. This took a further 60 miles or so down Chesapeak Bay and allowed a few steep turns at speeds above Mach 1. Buffet warning of the G-stall was more than adequate and 'rudder shakers' provided additional warning if I attempted to turn too steeply. It was obvious that the designers of the F-4H and the A3J Vigilante were more interested in providing the pilot with supersonic manoeuvrability than subsonic, for the former was nearly as good as the latter, although, of course, turning circles were immense compared with piston-engined fighters owing to the much higher wing loadings – 90 and 72 lb/sq/ft respectively compared with, say, the Sea Vixen FAW-2 of 52 lb/sq/ft or the Hunter's 41 lb/sq/ft.

The F-4H has a 3–4 per cent thickness/chord ratio (the Buccaneer had 7 per cent, the Seafire about 8–12 per cent and the Hurricane about 15 per cent) and unless the F-4H's wing is travelling very fast indeed it produces very little lift. Thus, when manoeuvering, it is normal to increase the effective thickness of the wing by lowering leading-edge droop. The F-4H and A3J versions at Patuxent, plus the Crusader, all had this so that the pilot could gain another 25 per cent lift per square foot of wing area as a result and so able to out-turn many other fighters, which had nominally greater wing area, in a dog fight.

It was also interesting to see a sophisticated arrangement of hydraulically operated and computer-controlled ramps and restrictors in the engine air intakes – something not attempted in the Buccaneer which made do with variable-pitch guide vanes to assist engine air intake efficiency at Hi-Mach.

Lateral control of all three types of aircraft at high speed was by the use of lift spoilers (first tried out in the Attacker in Britain in 1951, but for different reasons). The Crusader-2N and the F-4H Phantom also made use of aileron droop like the Narner when landing or catapulting. In this way, adverse yaw effects were eliminated but I found that the aircraft could emulate a falling leaf if alternate and coarse use were made of lateral control on the approach. So much for the Phantom. With a dry weight of about half a ton less than the Buccaneer and a total static thrust in after-burner of about 14 tons – which was 2 tons more than its usual landing weight – there were no handling problems off the end of the catapult. This marvellous performance was demonstrated to us by a USN pilot at Pax river doing a loop and a roll off the top straight after a catapult launch on the airfield, with his undercarriage and flaps still down.

In spite of the F-4H's single-purpose design as a day/night all-weather interceptor carrier-borne fighter, it could carry a far greater military load twice the distance and at much greater speed than any British naval aircraft flying at that time. This was not only because of its much greater power and size but because it could easily be assisted into the air at these huge weights by the USN's use of immensely powerful versions of the steam catapult from their large carriers. The strategic advantage of being able to overload interceptor fighters for the strike role in this way – and, on dropping their load on the enemy becoming interceptor fighters once more – was not lost on the USN; their F-14 Tomcat series and their F/A 18s being the latest example of the worldwide versatility which this powerful combination has given them and eliminating the need for land bases overseas.

The A3J Vigilante (number 146697 – the sixth development aircraft singled out in the test programme for 'carrier suitability' trials) was the next aircraft which I was permitted to fly once at Patuxent. It carried nearly twice the fuel load of the F-4H but I flew it with a mere 2,000 gallons on board and at a take-off weight of 45,000 lb – about 5 tons below its normal offensive load weight but still slightly heavier than a fully-loaded B-17 Flying Fortress of World War Two.

The A3J had the same engines as the F-4H but as its basic weight was about two tons more, its low level performance was not so startling. However its high altitude climb and turning performance was better, perhaps because it had 770 square feet of wing area compared with the F-4H's 550.

Its main interest to the test pilot was its unique system of 'fly-by-wire' pitch augmentation. Its designer – Frank G. Compton – who had started work on the Vigilante in 1953 and had also been responsible for the P-51 Mustang, the B-25 Mitchell and the F-86 Sabrejet – was America's first designer to incorporate 'computer controls' in aircraft. These were far less sophisticated than present 'fly-by-wire' systems in civil airliners and they were far less intrusive, too, for they could be safely disconnected at any time that the pilot wanted, by his pressing a red button on the control column. Reliability of today's systems is assured by having up to four systems in series, so that if one goes wrong, the next one automatically takes over. However, this reduces the chance of a quick disconnection if the pilot wants to override a manoeuvre which he has not programmed correctly and which has led to several accidents so far.

Needless to say, the 'fly-by-wire' system is here to stay and with such safety assurance, a designer can nowadays design a basically unstable aircraft – if this saves money and improves performance – which is still safe to fly as the pilot no longer has to rely on inbuilt stability or conventional skills to avoid stalling, roll coupling effects, landing errors and so on.

The Vigilante's all-moving fin and tailplane were, of course, power-actuated and they moved through 8 degrees and 30 degrees respectively. Ailerons are very little used at high Mach compared with lift spoilers; so these 'spoiler-deflectors' were placed midspan and at three-quarter chord. Their use instead of ailerons allowed perfect banked turns – avoiding the usual need to use rudder to counter the adverse yaw effects of ailerons. The spoilers worked as airbrakes when flaps were not in use. Lateral trim was altered by 'twisting' the tailplane.

The A3J I flew (production number 146697) was crammed with electronics and other gadgets so that its 70-foot long fuselage had a high moment of inertia in the pitching plane. The pilot and observer sat at the extreme forward end of this structure, some 40 feet forward of the CG and entirely unbuttressed by the usual jet engine intakes and free to react to every sideload that came along in turbulent air. The engines were about 40 feet behind the pilot and I could not see or hear them at all from the cockpit. As the pilot sat about 10 feet ahead of the nosewheel and 35 feet ahead of the mainwheels, his height judgement when landing was difficult for a beginner. My seat was about 60 feet above the level of the runway just before touchdown.

The A3J's role had been fixed in 1956 as an important means of delivering the USA's strategic nuclear deterrent. The USAF disagreed and built the B-36 and other long-range bombers to compete with the USN. Their disagreement stemmed from the post-WW 2 US defence policy which prevented the storage or handling of nuclear weapons on foreign soil (except Britain). This created the dilemma at that time – and before Polaris submarines came on the scene ten years later – of having targets not physically accessible to USAF planes. These targets thus became the responsibility of the USN's carrier-borne planes – giving birth to the Vigilante. (It also allowed the Royal Navy to claim that the Buccaneer Mark 2 was the only British V-bomber with world-wide cover.)

The A3J had therefore been designed with a 'toss-bomb' capability, releasing its A-bomb while in a loop when pointing vertically skywards from a position exactly over the target and from an internal bomb bay situated between its two jet exhausts. The bomb was entirely enclosed within the fuselage structure and was loaded through a hole in its tail. The bomb was pushed up the fuselage on rails to the forward end of the 'tube' and the remainder of the space was then taken up with jettisonable fuel tanks and the necessary compressed air devices to expel the bomb and the tanks rearwards, when required.

The Vigilante had been designed with this special feature to allow it to escape more easily from the lethal A-bomb blast which, with the advent of the H-bomb, spread farther and wider than the one used over Hiroshima and Nagasaki. When the bomb was expelled, the bomb would then continue upwards for a few thousand feet before turning 180 degrees earthwards. The A3J would then have time to complete its loop towards the ground and escape at zero feet the way it had come. Speed in afterburner would never be less than 0.9 Mach and it would thus remain well clear of A-bomb blast and radiation during its escape manoeuvre.

Not so the V-bombers or the American's B-36s etc. These, it seemed to us, would have no chance of escape unless they dropped their A-bombs from a height well above that at Hiroshima on parachutes or they had fitted the bombs with delayed-action fuses. Whatever their escape and bombing plan, the heavy V-bombers were certainly much more vulnerable than a Buccaneer or an A3J. Unless the V-bomber could approach unseen by enemy radar and the A-bomb had a very long-range and sophisticated 'stand-off' capability when released from zero altitude a hundred or so miles from its target, we considered the heavy V-bomber to be a dead duck. (The last active Victor ended its days at RAF Shawbury on 30 November 1993.)

Toss-bombing accuracy from the A3J was expected to be assured by using its rearward ejecting system operated by a command from various air data systems. Navigational accuracy would be assured by using 'cross-coast' fixers, inertial navigation systems and head-up displayed terrain clearance aids. The all-weather decklanding aids already installed in the four, 60,000-ton Forrestal Class carriers in use in the USN included a blind approach system with six-mile acquisition range. An autopilot control system could be engaged to fly the aircraft down the glide path and, if need be, to within a few seconds flying time of the deck itself.

However, the Vigilante was not, after all, to become a potential A-bomber, its intended strategic duty being take over almost entirely by the Polaris submarines. Its bomb-loading capacity and release arrangements were found to be unreliable and its fatigue life, for aircrew and airframe alike, ruled it out for low flying missions in air turbulence. This serious disability also applied to some other long-fuselaged aircraft having the pilot/observer at the front end. I found that when seated at the end of this 70-foot 'pole' in the A3J, the slightest air bump caused the whole cockpit to shake viciously. Flying in conditions that the Buccaneer could hardly feel, I found that that Vigilante's cockpit was shaking sideways and up and down three inches. My eyeballs – which were obviously not mass-balanced – nearly left their sockets when trying to read any of the instruments.

The designers of the Vigilante had placed the pilot's cockpit at the front of its 70-foot fuselage to allow him to see the entire horizon and also to have a good view downwards and forwards on his level approaches to the target area. They seem to have forgotten that low-level aviation at speeds of 600 knots would have to take place through exceedingly rough air on most occasions and that these turbulent air patterns could cause side gusts as well as vertical gusts. Vertical strengthening and rigidity was usually built in by habit to allow the airframe to withstand 'G'. The human frame can also take vertical 'G' loadings without excessive disorientation. However, side gusts had not been allowed for in the structure of the airframe or the human body. Low flying on a hot day over the desert at 600 knots, sideloads of several tons were hitting the nose on alternate sides at a frequency of half a second or so. This felt like sledgehammer blows in the Vigilante, more so than in, for instance, the Buccaneer, because the Vigilante's fuselage was slabsided rather than curved and a shape totally unsuited to absorb or deflect the crushing blow of the airflow past it whenever this was even slightly from one side or the other.

I would have had to suggest that the RAF test pilots and navigators from Boscombe Down 'A' Squadron should come and fly the A3J, for they would obviously have the same problem with their TSR2 which was scheduled to appear for the first flight at Boscombe a few weeks later, for – but for its cancellation– the TSR2 aircrew would also have been sitting in the front of a similar long and even more slab-sided and 'un-buttressed' fuselage than the A3J's.

It seemed that aircraft designers, although aware of *vertical* stresses caused by sharp-edged air bumps, had not been told at this time by their test pilots that bumps also came sideways in equal proportions. In fact, before about 1962, no other aircraft designers had placed the pilot as far forward in an 'empty' fuselage as in the TSR2 and A3J, so that test pilot experience of the huge side-forces caused by air obeying the V-squared law had, up to that time, been insignificant. It only takes a brief moment to work out what these sideloads could be; e.g., assuming 30 square feet of fuselage at even a small incidence to the airflow at 600 knots, one could guess that the total 'lift' or sidethrust on that part of the fuselage nose might be as much as 10 tons for a split second or two. It must have come as no surprise to the designers of the A3J that its fatigue life was insufficient when perhaps thousands of such stress reversals might be suffered on every flight at low level. Even the Buccaneer 2 had some fatigue failures and required minor redesign action following its visit to Patuxent for low level trials in the early sixties.

Steep, subsonic turns were not easy in the Vigilante because of its huge, undamped pitch inertia and because its tailplane was so near its CG that it needed large tailplane angles to secure the necessary leverage. The 'fly-by-wire' computer inserted into the Vigilante's longitudinal control circuit – the first of its kind in the world – was intended to ensure maximum response to pilots' inputs consistent with safety in any flight conditions. In other words, the pilot could be as ham-handed as he liked but he would not be able to over-stress the aircraft or get into a roll-coupling situation at any time. Thus, at transonic speeds when control effectiveness was at its minimum and when large control movements were required to produce an adequate effect, the computer automatically increased the stick/tailplane gearing so that an inch stick movement at Mach 0.95 would produce the same result as an inch stick movement would at, say 0.7 Mach.

Perhaps the most important benefit obtained from the Vigilante's fly-by-wire system was that it prevented any possibility of the pilot applying excessive rates of roll when the aircraft was flying at high angles-of-attack when doing a rolling pullout. But, like all computers, it lacked personality and would sometimes insert a 'slow-down' just when it was least needed. But it was less intrusive than the present-day fly-by-wire systems in airliners, because the A3J pilot could safely disengage the Vigilante system at any time by pressing a red button on his control column. Thus, when subsonic turns degenerated into a series of mini-pitchups with the computer trying its hardest to iron out the pilot's hamfistedness but never entirely catching up, it could be safely disengaged. Nowadays the fly-by-wire intrusiveness on some airliners seems to be getting out of hand. Pilots are losing control. When something goes wrong on the flight deck of a 1995 jet airliner, the Captain no longer asks: 'What shall we do now' from his engineer. He is more likely to ask: 'What's the b. . . . computer making the aeroplane do now and how can I stop it?'

Automation can fail unpredictably and can sometimes help to create errors much worse than those it is designed to prevent. It encourages pilots to look at screens in the cockpit at times when they would normally be looking outside. The computer has no ingenuity to compare with a human's when faced with uncertainty and perhaps it should be designed for safe disengagement by the pilot at any time that he thinks fit – just as we could in the Vigilante whenever the 'fly-by-wire' system was becoming intrusive, unhelpful and dangerous.

Although the Vigilante would give the pilot and his radar intercept officer sitting behind him a prohibitively rough ride low down or in clear-air turbulence high up, it was as smooth as silk at all speeds from subsonic to Mach 2.2 in good air conditions. It would accelerate to about 1.65 Mach within 5 minutes in level flight at heights of about 45,000 feet when after-burner was selected. (Its record 'zoom' height was 90,000 feet.) It was therefore retained for use for about seven years as a high-altitude reconnaissance and ECM aircraft. It was not used in the low level role so that V-bomber capability was ruled out. It seemed to prove the point (although variable sweep may now have eased the problem a little) that it is very difficult to design a supersonic high/low aircraft which performs well in both environments.

In spite of its size (its designed maximum take-off weight being 80,000 lb) the Vigilante was a pleasure to fly on the approach and provided the sun was not shining on the dust and flies which accumulated on its windscreen, with its good view over the nose and good engine response and in spite of the pilot height over the landing gear, it was possible for even a beginner like me to make a near-perfect touchdown, exactly where intended. The brakes were excellent – showing no signs of fade or overheating – the cockpit air-conditioning was marvellous, but I found that the vision ahead was sometimes very poor because of the almost total opacity of its radiation-shielded, angled-back windscreen when the sun was shining obliquely at it. View to the rear was almost non-existent. Presumably the observer had rear-vision radar at his service in order to warn the pilot if there was anyone behind.

I heard that the Vigilante had cleared its prototype deck trials aboard USS *Saratoga* in July 1960. The first operational Squadron went aboard her in August 1963, a few weeks after we returned to Britain. One hundred and fifty-six were produced and the last one went out of operational service in 1968, although many were still flying from shore stations until 1978.

The next aircraft I was allowed to fly was the Chance-Vought F-8U-2N Mark 2 Crusader, just about to go into service in the USN. It was classed as a 'hot ship' in 1957 but was fast becoming a back number with aircraft like the Phantom F-4H about and by 1962 had lost the competition for an attack fighter role. However, its main attribute was its low cost and its small size and its adequate 1.2 Mach cruising performance at 50,000 feet. It could carry 6 × 500 lb bombs, 8000 lb of internal fuel in eight tanks plus 600 rounds of 20mm ammunition at it AUW of 32,000 lb. The Mark II, together with its attack and search/warning radar, probably had a superior interceptor/fighter performance than English Electric's Lightning in Britain. It was, moreover, so simple to fly and maintain that it was known at Pax River as the 'last of the fun airplanes'. Its designers had reduced its high-speed drag, made it easier to rotate after a catapult launch and improved over-the-nose visibility when landing by building the F-8 with a variable, two-position incidence wing. We had to pull a large lever on the right of the cockpit when selecting flaps and undercarriage for a landing. This 'wound down' the fuselage out of sight of the pilot and it had the disadvantage of removing any aircraft attitude information from his gaze – which took much getting used to.

However, it was otherwise a pleasure to fly – although, once again its subsonic turning performance was poor even when leading-edge droop was selected. With 8,000 lb of internal fuel for its single engine it had an impressive range and a four-hour endurance on Combat Air Patrol, complete with guided weapons. It looked after itself well in the Vietnam war, most of its losses occurring through fuel shortages when it was used in the low-level attack role.

We were a few weeks too early arriving at Pax River to fly Chance-Vought's latest creation – the A-7 Corsair II. This was a single-place fighter/attack aircraft – the idea that may have given birth to the Wyvern ten years previously. There was never any thought of making this a supersonic aircraft as in the A3J's concept. The USN had learnt its lesson – that supersonic attack aircraft not only cost three times the price of a Corsair II, but, when manoeuvering – ostensibly to avoid enemy missiles at low altitudes – they consumed four times the fuel and took four times the air space to turn through 180 degrees at that speed. If, then, they slowed to subsonic speeds, their wing area was insufficient to allow steep turns, so that the same lack of low-level manoeuvrability applied. In fact, the USN were spelling out to us just why the TSR-2 would be a failure and why the Buccaneer – although subsonic in the cruising mode – would be a success. Not having flown the Vigilante themselves, the RAF were still telling the RN that if they were made to accept the Buccaneer instead of their TSR-2, they would insist that it be made supersonic, so ensuring that it would probably suffer from the same faults as their TSR-2 was found to have had.

Performance figures for the USN's Corsair II were very impressive and compared well with the Buccaneer. Designed for close interdiction and close air support for troops, Chance-Vought were given the contract in February 1964. It had a shorter, fatter fuselage than the Crusader and its wing was fixed but otherwise it looked the same. It weighed 16,000 lb empty, could carry 15,000 lb of external ordnance under its wings and belly and had a take-off-the-catapult-in-zero-wind weight of 38,000 lb – about 6,000 lb lighter than a Buccaneer Mark 1. It had a ferry range of 3,500 miles without refuelling and a 1,000 mile combat radius of action from its target when operating from a carrier. By 1965 the Pratt & Whitney TF30 turbofan had been replaced with the British-designed Allison (Spey) TF41 of 14,500 lb thrust – with no after-burner. It did 600 knots 'clean' at zero feet (560 knots carrying weapons). It did exactly double everything that the Wyvern did – except crash – and cost about half as much. It seemed to us at that time that the USN – at three times the size of our own RAF –were leading the world.

The fourth aircraft flown was the A4D Skyhawk – a later version of which was used by the Argentinians in the Falklands war. The initial requirement in 1952 had asked for a carrier-based 'attack bomber' capable of speeds of about 0.8 Mach and able to carry up to 10,000 lb offensive load and the total weight not to exceed 30,000 lb – about two-thirds the weight of a Buccaneer Mark 1.

It was so simple to fly that I was convinced I had forgotten something. There was no aircraft storage battery, everything therefore burst into life only after the engine had been started by its plug-in starter. It was a strike aircraft and of course without reheat, lacked the electric performance of a fighter. In spite of its small size and weight, it had a three-hour endurance on a high-level sortie making its radius of action a full five hundred miles carrying a 5,000 lb weapon load with two 20mm cannon as well.

Its British-designed engine was uprated to 8,500 lb of thrust by 1972, and this was just sufficient to give it supersonic level-flight performance. It was basically a weight-lifter, having a 5 per cent t/c delta wing, a fuselage dry weight of 12,000 lb and, by 1975 it had the ability to carry 9,000 lb of fuel plus weapons which could include a 300-gallon overload fuel tank. With flight refuelling it could deliver two 2,500 lb guided weapons a distance to the target of five hundred miles with the last hundred miles being at zero feet.

The version we flew at Patuxent with the J 52 engine was barely transonic in a shallow dive and, compared with the F-4H, it gave me a feeling of complete nakedness when flying it in clear air above ground level. It also lacked the auto-navigational and enemy missile auto-protection devices that such a 'naked' aircraft would need and seemed to present a very easy target if flown within fighter range above ground level by day or night. About 2,700 were built by the mid 70s, its final AUW having nearly doubled to a maximum – using the powerful steam catapults by then available – of 27,000 lb.

The last aircraft we flew at Patuxent was the W2F Grumman Hawkeye. The

Grumman Company never seemed to have made a bad aircraft and this was no exception. Its entire purpose was to take a powerful long-range radar aerial into the air complete with a fighter-direction crew of four people to process and transmit its information. One of its two Allison turbo-prop engines could keep it airborne for about ten hours, if necessary at any height up to 20,000 feet. It was, of course, fully air-conditioned in a shirt-sleeve environment, where three fighter directors in the rear fuselage worked at three large 'television' screens on which was the processed information received from the 60-foot diameter aerial revolving above them. They could carry out twenty interceptions at the same time and maintain the plots of up to 70 different 'echoes' on their screens. This was about equal to the capability of a complete crew in the *Ark Royal* at that time working their 984-type radar.

The Hawkeye AEW set-up was the most impressive thing I have ever seen from close range. On the trip we were on, the crew were constructing an interception exercise using USN fighter taking off from a carrier 150 miles east of Long Island and using as their 'targets' the crowd of civil aircraft taking off from Idlewild. Although the radar showed interceptions taking place, the fighters' targets were actually 'displaced' by fifty miles or so for the purpose of the exercise, so that the fighters kept entirely out of their targets' way. We were flying on one engine at the time and had enough fuel to stay airborne for six more hours if necessary at this height. The Hawkeye seemed to be just what we wanted in the Royal Navy aboard our new carrier – the CVA01 – to replace the Gannet AEW whenever that became necessary. Present-day versions can transmit the relevant radar 'picture' direct to the head-up displays in the fighter/attack F/A 18s they are controlling up to 200 miles away over the battlefield. Target marking (by Buccaneers during the Iraq war) completed the picture for the F/A 18's pilot to fire his guided weapons accurately once he had got safely to the target area.

On our return to Boscombe Down, we were told some tragic news. Five days before we got back to UK, Willy Newton, who was in charge of flying while we were away in the States, had crashed in a Buccaneer. He had taken up the 'armament' test aircraft on bomb-carriage trials, using the wing stations. One of the tests was to see if the aircraft could be safely decklanded with a 1,000 lb bomb 'hung-up' on one wing – the alternative being a 'fast' landing ashore or a bale-out. In order to save time and bombs, he had taken off with the asymmetric load already in place. The aircraft dropped its 'heavy' wing sharply on rotation on take-off and its remains had ended up in the flying position on IFDF's hangar roof, with Willy having suffered an eye injury and his Observer – Di Jones – having sadly been killed.

On 23 May 1963, the same day that the Spey-engined Buccaneer Mark 2 first flew from Holme, I flew a replacement 'armament' test Buccaneer XK923 having a single 1,000-pounder on the starboard wing. I experienced the start of Willy's difficulties only when flying near the stall in the take-off configuration, BLC on. In this condition, the aileron angle to hold up the 'heavy' wing seemed excessive and large amounts of rudder were required to prevent yaw towards the heavy wing and to maintain lateral control. It seemed that Willy may have got into trouble by using take-off flap only and then rotating before reaching full flying speed i.e., before the airflow had fully established itself over the wings. It is also possible he may have had a crosswind from port to add to his difficulties. Raising the nose on take-off might also have caused gyroscopic-induced yaw and roll effects in the same way that gyro effects caused the same thing to occur during the 'Flying Bedstead' V/STOL prototype trials. (Gyro effects may also have led to similar unpredictable behaviour in rolling-pullouts and might further have complicated some of the 'roll-inertia coupling' misbehaviour.) Bob Helliwell then joined the Squadron to replace the tragic loss of Di Jones. He and my replacement – Geoff Higgs – completed the clearance of the electronic package for the Mark 1 and 2 Buccaneer during the next two years.

At about this time a Wing Commander Ken Wallis arrived from Norfolk with his single-seat autogyro which he had designed and built. This consisted of a bath-tub-sized open cockpit with a 'pusher' propeller behind; a small high-wing suspended overhead, a rudder and a tricycle undercarriage – all held together by suitably stressed struts and wires. The two-bladed autogyro speeded up quickly on the short take-off run and it seemed to us to be both pretty and safe as it banked steeply so near the ground that the rotor seemed to be mowing the grass and with Ken Wallis obviously enjoying himself. We heard later that a spare one of these little machines was used in a James Bond film and, thirty years later, they are still flying!

There was very little work to do at 'C' Squadron after we returned from the USA in December 1962. Apart from the arrival of an AEW Gannet, a photographic Sea Vixen and some very interesting Bullpup firing trials, I only flew ten hours per month for the last six months I spent at Boscombe. Lieutenant Allan Deacon who had joined us from 20 ETPS in 1962, Pete Barber who joined us with Nick Bennett and John Spafford from 18 ETPS and Brian Davies from 19 ETPS all did excellent work for 'C' Squadron. All continued with test flying afterwards, mostly as civilians within the aircraft industry after the demise of the Fleet Air Arm in the early seventies. Allan Deacon became CTP at Shorts in the 1970s until his tragic death at the age of 58 in a Tucano when its tail came off during aerobatics over the Irish Sea.

In my report of our visit to Patuxent I had – after long deliberation and talks with Nick Bennett – decided to include mention of the main reason why the USN had no use for the Vigilante in the 'high/low low/high' A-bomb delivery role. This was mainly because of the bumpy ride it gave to the aircrew and electronics when flown at low altitude. The vicious sidewise buffet cause by rough air was much accentuated in the Vigilante because the aircrews' cockpits were at the front end of a long, slabsided fuselage, unsupported by the usual air intakes or wingroot junctions and free to oscillate from side to side through three or four inches, causing the pilot's and observers' to lose control of their eyeballs! The Vigilante's layout was so similar to that of the TSR-2 that I said in my report that TSR-2 pilots should go to Pax River to fly the

Vigilante before they took the TSR-2 into the air so they could see what they might be letting themselves in for. The cockpit vibration had probably ruined the chances for the Vigilante to be used in the now mandatory low-level role and it might also be a problem with the TSR-2, the purpose of which was to carry out an identical job to that for which the Vigilante was produced for the USN.

Needless to say, I should not have done this for the RAF could well do without such criticism, especially from a Naval test pilot and by someone who had not flown the TSR-2 and was never likely to. No mention was ever made of my report on this 'gust response' problem affecting the TSR-2 so that its mention may have been struck out on its way to the Ministry. It may not have been a significant problem with the TSR-2 anyway. It did not, however, make us any more popular at Boscombe at the time.

The TSR-2 first flew from Boscombe on 30 September 1964. 'Roly' Beaumont and Don Bowen, the Navigator, reported 'shaft resonance'. Their second trip was on 31 December 1964 and they reported 'severe airframe vibration causing the human eyeball to topple'. The third trip was made at reduced power early in the new year and on the 14th the TSR-2 flew supersonic. The 20th flight had been completed by 12 March. Mr Callaghan cancelled the project in his Budget speech on 6 April 1965.

I had heard in January 1963 that I would be relieving Pridham in Washington. It was not to be, however as once again my domestic circumstances would not allow it. I could therefore hardly complain when they sent me back to a job at the Admiralty – Director-General Aircraft – 'Bases' Section. My three years and three months at Boscombe Down had come to an end, the last two weeks being made particularly enjoyable by 'C' Squadron hosting a return visit from USN Patuxent River test pilots.

CHAPTER 14

THE FATAL DECISION

This book has been centred on my experiences as a test pilot. Chapter 13 would have been a fitting conclusion, ending as it does on a high note. But a closing chapter several octaves lower has been penned by the hand of fate, in the form of a file on the carrier building programme, which was passed to me when I was serving on my second Admiralty tour just before retiring. The contents of this file seemed to write *Finis* not only to this book, but also to the efforts of generations of Naval aviators whose inventiveness had given us the angled deck, the mirror landing system and the steam catapult, which together are capable of providing deck operation of top of the range fighters at weights giving them a true multi-role capability. This file had already gone to the Chief of the Defence Staff and, although I had no idea why it was sent to me at that time, it was of interest then and perhaps it is still of historical interest now.

In it there was a paper headed: *'The Future of the Carrier Force'*, signed by the Defence Minister of that time. The paper stated that the RAF had already 'lost' their TSR-2 (first publicly announced on 6 April 1965 but secretly decided in January of that year) and it was now up to the Navy to show some equal savings on the defence budget which was limited that year to £2,000M. It then went on to say:

> Although the cost of the carrier plan which includes the building of CVA0-1 could be reduced by building only one new carrier, the effectiveness of such a force with only three carriers [*Hermes, Ark Royal* and CVA0-1] would be disproportionately less from about 1970 onwards and would cease to be viable by 1980.

The Navy had apparently argued that if only one new carrier were built, its carrier fleet could then have been less cost-effective than building three new ones. In effect this was tantamount to their saying that if they could not have three new carriers they did not want any. They had failed to perceive the advantages of accepting a single new carrier as a possible 'foot-in-the-door' allowance of further carriers if a future politician relented. Furthermore, they had failed to realise that by scuppering their chances of having a carrier fleet in the years after 1973–5, they would be entirely dependent upon the RAF Coastal Command or the Americans to provide essential AEW aircraft throughout the world to take the place of the AEW Gannet. Then a few years later, having been granted permission to build three 'through-deck cruisers', they failed to insist that these were built of sufficient size to allow the fitting of essential deck-arrest and catapult systems to allow the operation of fixed-wing AEW aircraft of the size of the Gannet or the Hawkeye so that the few Sea Harriers that they could accommodate would be able to operate with full effect in modern air warfare conditions.

Under the heading : 'Operational Implications', the paper continued:

The Effect on our Strategic Options after the Carriers Phase-out in 1975

Because carriers are our most powerful naval units, a decision to phase them out might well be interpreted by our potential enemies and trouble-makers as a sign of our economic and political weakness and of our probable intention of dis-engaging east of Suez. This could hearten and stimulate such countries as Egypt, Iraq, Indonesia and Afro/Asian supporters to make increasing demands on us.

We must recognise that when carriers phase out we will have lost an element of our forces which is particularly suitable for fulfilling tasks which cannot be predicted, particularly in the maritime area of the Indian Ocean – e.g., the East African and Rhodesian crises.

Then, in spite of having been told by the Admiralty that if the Navy had to equip the fleet with Surface-to-Air (SAM) missiles and the RAF had to increase the size of Coastal Command's AEW and Anti-submarine aircraft (by adapting the beautiful Nimrod) to try to compensate for the Navy's loss, the total cost would be far greater than the three new carriers they were asking for; the Defence Minister went on to say, in conclusion:

I believe that it is impossible to reconcile the maintenance of the full range of our present military capabilites on a worldwide deployment through the 1970s, with a reduction of the defence budget to £2,000M.

I recognise that we have a valuable asset in our existing carrier force, and I should be reluctant to abandon carriers any sooner than we have to. There are in any case especial risks in attempting to do without carriers for the next ten years or so.

However, I believe that in the longer term it should be possible for us to reduce our commitments (surely a contradiction in honest terms*) in such a way as to minimise our dependence upon sea-borne air power; and so to make heavy capital expenditure on the Fleet Air Arm – and on CVA0-1 in particular – unnec-essary at the present stage.

I propose therefore to cancel CVA0-1 and to reduce expenditure on the Fleet Air Arm to what is necessary, in effect, to work out the lives of our existing carri-ers.

An essential part of my plan would be:

The Government should work towards a reduction in commitments in the mid 70s, bearing in mind the military restrictions which would follow from the loss of the carriers.

We should face up to the probable need for substantial inducements to Fleet Air Arm aircrew in order to ensure, so far as possible, that the carriers do not fade out prematurely.

*Authors comment

> That expenditure on additional RAF aircraft and on additional ships and weapons for the Navy – also allowed for in OPD(65) – should be accepted.

The very senior members in the Admiralty had obviously failed to make a strong case for the new carrier(s) because they may have imagined that the Fleet could protect itself from the air with their new surface-to-air missiles and forgetting, of course, that without indigenous AEW, even their Sea Dart missiles would be useless against low-flying enemy aircraft outside a range of twenty miles – the maximum 'seeing' distance of their masthead radars – and would give them only two minutes warning of an approaching enemy 'Exocet' missile fired from 60 miles away. They also failed to make the obvious point that carriers of the size of CVA0-1 having catapults of the necessary power would be essential for an effective AEW, such as the Hawkeye, to operate at all.

The Army's statement in 1965 that it would be unable in future to mount an operation against opposition out of range of an RAF base without the support of at least two CVA0-1s and the Navy's reply that it would need at least four carriers to guarantee such support at short notice, prompted the following Ministerial reply:

> This, therefore, is the type of operation that will no longer be undertaken! The gaps in our defence will be filled by the F-111 and other RAF aircraft.

In May 1967 – a year later, Captain F. Torrens-Spence – now retired – wrote:

> The RAF, having consistently refused to have anything to do with the Buccaneer, now had no comparable weapon. Had they adopted it, it would have become even cheaper and might well have been exported in quantity.
>
> Instead, £200 million has been wasted on an aircraft intended to go one better all round – the defunct TSR-2. It is now proposed to spend a further £280 million over 10 years on 50 F-111s in aid of the American aircraft industry.
>
> To pay for all this the Government has decided not to replace the Navy's aircraft carriers, thus depriving Britain's shipyards of much needed work and reducing the Navy to future impotence. How crazy can you get?

This book has included word-for-word descriptions of how, and in what circumstances four important decisions were taken concerning air matters in the Royal Navy in the past 50 years. Those who took the final decisions on fighter supply in 1941; design of carrier aircraft in 1943; the 'go-ahead' for Buccaneer production in 1956 and the cancellation of the Royal Navy's carriers in 1966 had no personal knowledge whatever of the performance capabilities of present or future aircraft or how they would operate from carriers worldwide in the years to come.

Now, fifty years later, the technical know-how of those in charge of the Royal Navy on new methods of operating aircraft from carriers and their likely cost-effectiveness in their defence of the fleet and the army ashore in its Mobile Strike Force (MSF) role, is reduced to the same level as that which applied at the start of WW2 i.e., some twenty-two years after Lt Dunning had done the first-ever decklanding aboard ship and which first sparked off the Admiralty's air-thought process.

At the time of writing there are some hopeful signs of a resurgence in science/engineering education in Britain. Britain's aerospace industry still has a very important stake in worldwide air technology and still leads in some of its departments. But the decision to invest and exploit science research to match other countries in this field still largely depends on the whims and expediencies of arts-educated politicians rather than on those who have any scientific or practical knowledge of the future usefulness of the discoveries that science has made. Neither do most leaders in politics and industry yet seem to possess sufficient powers of engineering leadership to effect the introduction of the many British new inventions into service. An improvement in the use of new Information Technology is, however, likely, for the Royal Navy recently engaged a senior management within the Ministry of Defence whose job it will be to arrange for much wider use to be made of this Information Technology, to spread new ideas amongst the rank and file, to improve their fighting efficiency and perhaps allow easier and more accurate dissemination of Naval news through the media to the taxpayer.

At the time that the politicians took the fatal decision in 1956 to cancel the carriers, the senior members of the Royal Navy, lacking superior technical knowledge of the air matters on which they had to make their case in competition with the RAF, also seemed to have taken little notice of the supreme cost-effectiveness of carrier-borne ground-attack planes exemplified by the United States Navy.

Looking back at this period and bearing in mind that effective fighter-direction of any fighter aircraft, VTOL or not, would have to be supplied from an aircraft of the size and capability of the Hawkeye W2F which we flew at Pax River in 1963, and that this indigenous, 'look-down' radar director could only operate from an aircraft carrier of the size of the proposed CVA0-1, it seems a pity that those in Fleet Air Arm who had had a 'lifetime's' experience in the AEW Skyraider and Gannet from 1951 onwards, were unable to bring this point to the notice of the Admiralty ten years later to give force to the Admiralty's argument against the Defence Minister's intention to cancel the building of CVA0-1. Their insistence on the need for AEW direction and control from large aircraft such as Hawkeye – or even the much smaller Gannet – could have produced an infallible argument for the Navy to continue with the large carrier, not only because such an aircraft would require a catapult and conventional flightdeck arrangement, but because any landbased substitute for the Hawkeye or Gannet would be unable to guarantee the use of a friendly adjacent airfield at short notice from which to operate, because of the fear that the owners of these neighbouring airfields might find themselves involved in a war not of their choosing.

Without a carrier of the size of CVA0-1, no effective AEW could be supplied, either by V/STOL aircraft or by helicopter. The latter would need to be operated in conditions of complete air supremacy and freedom from all sorts of groundfire if they were to avoid having huge casualties in a real shooting war, and they would not have the endurance, range, speed, electronic or crew capacity or ceiling capable of 'seeing' for more than a 100 miles from their targets, when a distance of 400 miles is required in most warlike circumstances. Neither would their maximum operating height allow them to fly clear of icing conditions at all times, a factor which cancels their all-weather reliability.

It is a hard world and perhaps the Royal Navy had no one but itself to blame for the loss of its large carriers and for making such a poor case for their retention, the inevitable consequence clearly displayed by Galtieri's action a few years later.

The Falklands War would not have happened if we had had a fully effective Mobile Strike Force available. Victory was only achieved because *Hermes* was still accidentally available and her Harriers, with those from *Invincible* were immediately armed with an effective airweapons system donated by America. In a series of engagements from April to June 1982, 22 Sea Harriers operating in the air defence role from *Invincible* and *Hermes* were set against a total of about 140 A4D Skyhawks, Mirage 'Daggers' and a few Exocet-carrying Etendards. Possessing unique manoeuvrability in the chase, due to its directive jets, the Harrier had outstanding success. In 2,376 sorties flown by 800, 801, 809 and 899 Naval Air squadrons – of which 280 were flown at night – lasting on average 1hr 10 mins each, the FRS 1 Harrier pilots shot down 20 Argentinian aircraft in air-to-air combat and claimed four others as 'probables'. Six Sea Harriers were lost with four pilots, but only two of these were shot down by enemy action. (Two ditched, two collided in fog and two were destroyed by enemy ground fire.) Naval Sea King Mk 4s flew 12,021 hours, Wessex Mk 3s flew 5,090 hours and Lynx Mk 2s and Wasp Mk 1s flew 3,042 and 994 hours respectively in a total of 10,381 sorties. Losses in helicopters totalled fourteen. Five were destroyed by accidents or groundfire and one was hit by an albatross flying into its rotor. Nine were lost when *Coventry*, *Atlantic Conveyor*, *Glamorgan* and *Ardent* were bombed or struck by Exocets from enemy aircraft.

By 1992 the more capable and agile Sea Harrier FRS 2 had begun to replace the FRS 1, with the older airframes withdrawn for easy conversion. The FRS 2 is now equipped with a look-down shoot-down Blue Vixen radar and by 1995, the FA2 version has advanced medium range air-to-air missiles (AMRAAM), and Sea Eagle. The Sea Eagle is an air-to-surface sea-skimming missile intended in carrier operations for long-range use against shipping targets. The air-to-air weapon and radar improvements allow the Harrier to fire at longer ranges than before so that its lack of speed in pursuit of the enemy is not a great disadvantage. Provided it can be controlled and directed by our own, or American, Naval fixed-wing AEW aircraft, the Sea Harrier or its replacement will be able to use its complete inventory of hitting power for fighter defence, medium-range shipping strikes, air-to-ground attacks and for recce duties. It also has the unique ability to operate off short runways if operating from land. Its maximum, short-range offensive load is likely to be 9,000 lb – the weight of a nuclear bomb.

Many of the 'changes' now proceeding within the Fleet Air Arm are exceedingly complicated and are bound to lead to future changes in training procedures and airframe/engine modification patterns and standards. For instance, the pilot's cockpit of the FA2 bears no relation to convention. The HOTAS ('Hands-on-throttle-and-stick') control by the Harrier FRS-2 pilot requires no less than nine separate buttons on the stick and a further seven on his throttle control. Cockpit instrumentation consists of multi-purpose radar displays, missile control panels, engine display panels, head-down and head-up displays for navigation and weapon-firing purposes plus a tactical information system which gives secure voice and data links in the aircraft plus a radar warning capability.

With the FA2 in operation the results in the future should be even better than those achieved off the Falklands provided that AEW Direction is available from fixed-wing aircraft and, bearing in mind the ever-present need for the Services to retain public support and minimise casualties (and in spite of the Royal Navy's traditionally abysmal handling of press relations which usually make a naval victory look like a defeat) the Fleet Air Arm should have the chance of proving its worth to the taxpayer (as it has done off Bosnia) and deserving of replacement carriers capable of operating at least 50 fighter/attack aircraft supported by their own fixed-wing AEW.

The main advantage of a carrier-borne airpower is its ability to cover most of the earth's surface without having to ask permission from adjoining countries in a war situation, whether or not they can use their largest airfields. These airfields would doubtless need to offer a very long, all-weather day/night runways and a complete technical back-up brought out from Britain by sea transport defended and paid for by the Royal Navy. For instance, the United States Navy's fighters and fighter/ground/attack aircraft, directed by their own AEW aircraft flying in safety up to 200 miles from the battlefront on a 24-hour basis, were able to wreck Iraq's air opposition and pick off military targets one by one with incredible accuracy, thus clearing the political way for Saudi Arabia to allow US and British aircraft – including the Buccaneers of the RAF – to operate from her sufficiently nearby airfields to assist in and complete the process without delay. Within this combined air attack sweeping all before it and with a clear military objective in sight, the 220,000-strong ground forces were able to land in safety and proceed to their targets, bringing the main war to an end in a fortnight with insignificant casualties both to ourselves and to the civilian population.

The second major advantage that carriers have over airfield operation is through their use of the catapult. The immense power of steam catapults can launch a fighter with a weapon load and a fuel load of which any landbased strike aircraft would be proud. The F-18 of the USN is a true 'multi-role' aircraft because it is a carrier aircraft and based on a fighter's required performance and not based on a strike aircraft's. Once it has dropped its load it becomes a true, interceptor fighter, the task for which it was designed in the first place. It is able to take off in its overloaded state only through the power given to it by the ship's catapult plus the 30-knot windspeed over the deck which can always be guaranteed in large carriers. Runway take-offs by the same heavily-loaded fighter/strike aircraft would probably not be possible on runways less than three miles long, and if there were no natural wind, the necessary unstick speed might be so high as to lead to tyre failure due to over-rapid rotation – to say the least! Steam catapult power gives aircraft such as the F-18 a true, dual-purpose role without limiting its performance in either mode. If this could be made available to the Royal Navy, it would pay for itself within a few years by allowing a halving of the expenditure on the Eurofighter and would probably reduce the need for a replacement for the Tornado.

The Establishment still seems to be unaware that a powerful force of carriers can compromise the most important single military asset that a country can possess, whether for the unprovocative protection it can give to food supplies to the population in a civil war situation, the powers that it has as a Mobile Strike Force to impose a ceasefire between two or three warring factions, or for its instant help to any friendly power threatened by aggression anywhere in the world without having to rely on adjacent friendly airfields and having to delay action by the huge transport requirements needed for their setting up and maintenance. The carrier force can accomplish all this and can use its aircraft for any necessary assistance to the army once it has established air-superiority – as in Iraq – and without the need for inaccurate shore bombardment with its inevitable risk to civilians.

By 1979, when there were no fixed-wing aircraft remaining in the Navy, the First Sea Lord at that time was still saying that we had a 'balanced fleet', capable of protecting itself anywhere in the world from air attack with its new surface-to-air missiles. Not even the Argentine Air Force believed that! The only reason why the Argentinians were overcome was because the 1960's decision to phase out the carriers had, through persistent lobbying by a few serving and retired Naval Aviators, been modified to the extent of allowing the Navy a few fixed-wing V/STOL Harrier fighters – using Air/Air missiles hurriedly supplied in the emergency by the Americans – to operate from a resurrected *Hermes* and the 'through-deck cruiser' *Invincible*.

Official Naval comment on the Sea Harrier's task in the Falklands battle was given by Sir Henry Leach, First Sea Lord. He said: 'Without the Sea Harrier, there could have been no task force'. After the Falklands war, *Invincible* was promoted to a 'carrier' instead of a 'through-deck cruiser' and she was withdrawn from sale. Searchwater radar was fitted to Sea Kings, but it needs several of these vulnerable aircraft to do the work of a single Hawkeye. The Royal Navy is still missing its safe, long-range eyes and cannot be deployed safely in any military situation short of having air supremacy, courtesy of the United States Navy.

It is generally recognised now that the mobility and flexibility of naval seaborne air power in the form of the USN was well demonstrated and was the deciding facet in the political and military success of the Iraq operation. Additional close air support for the army came later from Saudi Arabia airfields friendly to the Allies once they could see how the battle was progressing. Once the army had been put ashore safely and in the excellent flying conditions for low-level interdiction which is a feature of this part of the world, the result was a foregone conclusion.

The United States Navy then demonstrated its air power 50 miles off Yugoslavia where it could provide the necessary protection of the United Nations aid convoys without, this time, becoming involved in the civil war itself. However, all air-only operations, in addition to requiring a unified military command in charge having clear military objectives, also need AEW direction, reasonable weather and a terrain clear of a large civilian population so that they can use their 'all-weather' weapon systems against proper military targets with the exact accuracy achieved by laser marking. Although the Royal Navy carriers were able to lend a hand on the 'cab rank' air patrol over Bosnia, they may have lacked the sophisticated weapon systems of the United States Navy aircraft to enable them to make an accurate attack in all weathers, and this reduced their effectiveness in this civil war environment. Such action requires an aircraft of the size and performance of a F-18 together with Hawkeye or AWAC control and direction.

In any military situation the final solution can usually only be made by troops-on-the-ground. But before they can be landed, they must have complete air protection. The vital need for this essential air domination can best be provided in a Mobile Strike Force situation by carrier-based aircraft. This requirement for air domination before a landing can be made or a land battle can begin proves, if anything does, that naval air power is not just another weapon system or another 'layer' of fleet defence but a vital pre-requisite for any Mobile Strike Force operation. The flexibility of movement and nearness to the land battle which carriers allow makes their possession vital to a country's military effectiveness.

Perhaps it would be appropriate here to place on record some of the arguments for an improved Carrier Force made recently by retired members of the Fleet Air Arm and which have also been addressed to those in Government.

1. Introduction. Over the past forty years or so, misinformation has deluded many people, including politicians and senior naval officers, into believing that a medium sized Strike Aircraft Carrier (CVA) of about 45,000 tons would cost more than the nation could afford. The absence of a CVA has led to a major imbalance on our defence posture with far too much money being expended on an immobile organisation of shore-based aircraft and infrastructure which has seldom been used. In the same period, the Royal Navy has been stretched to the limit, dealing with several shooting wars and many crises in distant parts of the world, having to make the best use of inadequate equipment and recently, with inadequate manpower.

2. *Commitments.* Britain has military commitments to the United Nations, NATO and the Commonwealth. In order to meet these, a Mobile Strike Force with world-wide capability is essential. The Royal Navy has been able to supply a balanced MSF for every conflict until the Gulf War. Without a carrier force of its own, Britain had to deploy the RAF with other Allied Air Forces making use of other country's airfields. Such a deployment turned out to be expensive, dangerous, unreliable and politically sensitive. The RN had to arrange for the safe lift of 80 per cent of all the necessary supplies besides assisting in its defence. Because such trouble spots around the world are much more approachable from the sea than from the land, it is likely that this support would have been more cost-effective and flexible if the Combat Air Squadrons had been seaborne in aircraft carriers.

3. *Present-day Carriers in the Royal Navy.* The present plan is to retain two out of the three Invincible Class carriers as fully operational. These 20,000-ton ships were designed to operate in the Atlantic with a maximum of 22 aircraft compromising Sea Harrier fighters and Sea King helicopters, the latter for use in the anti-submarine, rescue, troop/stores and AEW roles. In effect, we have not possessed an adequate MSF since our strike carriers were scrapped in 1960/70.

4. *Future Carrier proposals.* Studies have been underway for some time in the Admiralty to produce a suitable replacement for carriers of the Invincible class. They would probably be equipped with an improved Harrier type if this was available and would be of the order of 30,000 tons. They would not have the essential catapults and arrester gear to allow operation of an effective fighter/attack aircraft of the F-18 type neither would they be capable of operating an effective AEW aircraft having the performance of a Hawkeye. A CVA of about 45,000 tons is preferred, as ships of this size could be used effectively in the strike role. Their catapults would allow the operation of 50 aircraft in the strike role and their structure would be of sufficient strength to withstand a hit from an enemy Exocet without being put out of action.

5. *Future naval aircraft proposals.* Although the Sea Harrier is a superb aircraft, it lacks the range and weapon systems to allow it to be effective in the strike role. The lack of range is mostly due to a lack of catapults in our present-day carriers. The 45,000 ton carrier would allow the fitting of powerful catapults to allow strike aircraft to take off with their necessary heavy fuel load. Although the American Marines still use a version of the Sea Harrier, they are against continuing with a ASTOVL replacement as its

assisted take-off and vertical landing when used from carriers severely limits its range, endurance and weapon-carrying ability. If the American Marines do not order the ASTOVL, this will probably scupper the Royal Navy's present plans for an Invincible replacement programme. It would also increase the cost of production for a similar British-built replacement for the Sea Harrier. The only other alternative to opting for the F-18 might be the French Navy's Rafale fighter which is expected to be in service from French carriers by the year 2000.

6 *The cost of carriers.* A 'private' study of the cost of a 45,000-ton carrier with 50 F-18 or similar fighter/attack aircraft with a radius of action of at least 600 miles plus a weaponload of 4,000 pounds plus AEW and ECM aircraft of the performance of a Hawkeye, has been made by Captain George Baldwin. The figure agreed amongst the shipbuilders for a single carrier of 45,000 tons is 'of the order of' a billion pounds. Considering the immense political and operational power of such a vessel, this cannot be considered expensive, particularly when compared with the following:

Nuclear submarine	£900 M
30 Euro-fighters	990 M
2 destroyers	900 M
300 Challenger Tanks	900 M
1 penny/litre on petrol/diesel tax during building	900 M

7. *The cost of aircraft.* The all-through cost of building a modern aircraft is very high in terms of both money and manpower and such a project undertaken in countries apart from the USA requires a consortium before it can be afforded. The cost of the McDonnell-Douglas F-18 – already in service in several other countries besides the USA – is much less than the cost to the Ministry of Defence of the Eurofighter which is standing at £33M each at 1995 prices compared with the cost of an improved version of the F-18 which will be no more than £26.5M each.

8. *Conclusion.* Should the principle of the MSF be approved and adopted as a Naval requirement and meet with government approval, it is logical that the orders for the Eurofighter amounting to 300 aircraft could be reduced to about 150 and the money saved to support an F-18 plan. The cost of three CVAs – which should be built with all haste to eliminate the long lead-time involved with current proposals and save costs – would be no more than the cost of a nuclear submarine each or one penny on the tax of a litre of motor fuel each during the time of their building.

If there are still some Royal Navy officers willing to look upwards and not only along the barrel of a gun as they did in the days of Jutland, then there should be some hope for this fine Service in the future. Perhaps those in command of our defence will then be able to follow the example of the President of the United States. Before the start of each day, he requires to be told the position and status of all United States Navy's carriers – such is the importance of this information for the preservation of world peace to the leader of the most powerful nation in the world at this time, half of whose naval officers have 'wings'.

Appendix 1

Air Defence; Naval Gunnery or Fighters?

Only three weeks after the Battle of Jutland – a battle almost lost because of lack of knowledge of the enemy's whereabouts – Admiral Sir John Jellicoe wrote:

> The first requirement is for the Fleet to be provided with sufficient carriers and efficient seaplanes for scouting and spotting, manned by trained personnel.

He did not realise that the enemy would doubtless do likewise and we should therefore need fighters as well – not only to intercept and destroy the enemy's 'scouting and spotting' aircraft but to defend our own reconnaissance aircraft as well. However the Royal Navy seemed to have had complete faith in its own 'intense AA fire' if the enemy ventured within shooting range of our fleet and only very few fighters were added to the Royal Navy's air defences. These had the sole job of taking care of those enemy 'shadowers' who were sensible enough to carry out their reconnaissance out of gunfire range.

As time went on and with RAF advice, it became clear that, in addition to their reconnaissance role, naval aircraft would also be required to make day and night attacks on the enemy fleet with bombs and torpedoes. However, escort fighter protection was not provided as it was thought that they would be able to look after themselves by their own defensive armament in the same way that our own fleet thought it could protect itself with its own gunnery. This led to the Royal Navy ordering the Blackburn Roc and Skua and the Fairey Fulmar. The Skua and Roc aircraft were very effective dive-bombers but only if there were no enemy fighters about. Likewise the Fulmar could not defend itself against the Me 109 and it, too, suffered unsustainable losses early on in the war.

The average Royal Navy fighter pilot – of which there might have been a total of twenty at the start of the war in 1939 – could not understand how anyone could imagine how a bomber, such as the Skua or Fulmar, could be expected to become an interceptor fighter once it had dropped its load on the enemy and was turning for home. It was about as sensible as expecting a heavy lorry to turn itself into a racing car after unloading.

The initial alternative to the 'multi-role' Skua or Fulmar aircraft was to supply enough single-purpose, interceptor fighters to go with them as close escort. Even this had its drawbacks, for the interceptor fighters were largely ineffective without radar direction – that we so miraculously had in the Battle of Britain – and if used as escort fighters they were equally ineffective. Both the Germans and ourselves quickly found out that in order to remain in contact with the bombers *en route* to the target, the fighters had to slow down to the bombers' speed and come down to their altitude, so sacrificing their speed and height superiority when enemy fighters came in to attack the bomber formation. The Germans, in the Battle of Britain in particular, complained of being clobbered easily from above – even by the slower Hurricanes and with their own Me 109 escort nowhere to be seen. Likewise, when the CO of 249 RAF Squadron was told in 1941 that he would have to accompany 6 Blenheims on a bombing raid in December 1940 as *close escort* with two other fighter squadrons – at 7,000 feet – he said:

> We all wanted offensive action, but this was ridiculous. We had the Spits above us, yet we Hurricanes, slow and low as we were, had to fend off Me 109s coming from above and with twice our speed, and we were caught entirely with our pants down every time, all our attention having been taken in keeping formation with the Blenheims – which shouldn't have been there anyway. We were entirely useless and we lost four of our boys on that trip alone.

The Americans tried it, too, in their Flying Fortresses. We, in the RN, tried it over Norway and Japan – close-escorting the slow, heavily-loaded Avengers in our Seafires. Although close escort fighters were popular with the 'bombers' – for they could look out of their cockpits and see us – the difficulties of doing so have to be experienced to be believed. As most of the Naval planners on the admirals' staffs afloat had not flown fighters, the difficulties of close escort were never properly appreciated by those in command.

During such operations – over Norway or over Japan – our eyes were constantly diverted from spotting the enemy fighters by avoiding clouds, collisions or other confusions. Our planes were slowed to the bombers' 160 knot speed of advance making it impossible for us to accelerate in time for us to catch the attackers when they came upon us, as they always did, unexpectedly. If we maintained a sensibly high speed, we then had to weave all over the place and so consumed more fuel. Bad weather, or if the strike leader flew through cloud, made close escort impossible.

No one would ask a swallow to formate with a vulture, but that is what we were being asked to do. All we could give the bombers – for most of the time – was 'area support'. Without our ground radar telling us where we were, where the enemy was or even where our strike party was, even supplying an effective area support was difficult. In these circumstances our best solution was to arrive in the target area at exactly the same time as the strike aircraft and provide 'top cover' or 'area support' during their bombing runs, proceeding home independently.

Perhaps those who issued Staff requirements for multi-purpose aircraft had a point or two in their favour, but their constant error – as with the Wyvern in particular – was to concentrate on a basic strike capability rather than on a basic fighter capability when they issued their specifications to the designers, for they failed to realise that until fighter *supremacy* is obtained, tactical use of purely strike aircraft at any stage of a war cannot be economical. Even then, if fighter air *supremacy* is established – as it was over most of Japan during the final onslaught – fighters themselves can carry out most ground attack and interdiction duties as effectively and probably more efficiently than any 'multi-role' strike aircraft provided they can get airborne by powerful catapults with a suitable warload and sufficient fuel.

The United States Navy completely avoided the 'multi-role' error during the 1940s by building very large numbers of powerful fighters – the Corsairs and Hellcats. Then, having won air superiority over their own fleet they set about winning it over the Japanese fleet as well and only bringing in their specialist strike aircraft on the few occasions that this had been done – with superb results and the winning of the Pacific war from Pearl Harbor onwards.

The USN then transferred many of their fighters to the ground attack role, loading them with bombs and rockets and assisting the ground battle in all its stages. If attacked by the few remaining enemy fighters, they could then get rid of their bombs and rockets and could become interceptor fighters within seconds and carry out their primary role almost without interruption.

A Corsair fighter was test-loaded to 22,000 lb – i.e., 6,000 lb of bombs plus additional fuel – and flown from a catapult. This fighter thus proved its ability to carry nearly the same offensive load as a Wellington bomber for about the same radius of action and, once having dropped this load on its target with equal accuracy, it could revert to its original designed purpose again – an interceptor fighter!

Several of these fighters could be fitted into the same hangar space as a single bomber. Even if powerful catapults were not available, their large numbers made up for their lighter loads, they spent less time in the air, their sortie rate was nearly double that of the 'bombers' and their loss rate was minimal.

It is therefore only possible to sympathise with those who support the 'multi-role' aircraft concept if the multi-role specification starts life as a single-purpose, interceptor fighter!

Fifty years later, the RAF have the Tornado – a brilliant strike concept if only for its variable sweepback which allowed it to cope with both high and low supersonic flight problems and so make full use of the latest weapon delivery methods assisted by a highly skilled observer/navigator using information sent down from AEW aircraft direct. (The fighter version of the Tornado was, predictably, a relative failure and the RAF has had to proceed with the 'Eurofighter' accordingly – a 'single-purpose' interceptor.)

The United States Navy, cashing in on its powerful catapults to launch its heavily-loaded F/A 14 and 18 single-seat fighters and by using its own AEW command and control aircraft overhead as target indicators (where the relevant information is transmitted direct to the attack aircraft's own head-up display) is able to retain air mastery over any battlefield in the world today. In fact, if trouble occurs anywhere, the first thing that the United States President now asks is: 'Where are the carriers?'

The Royal Navy, before it lost its carriers, had the Buccaneer as its single-purpose strike aircraft and a sufficient proportion of single-purpose day/night fighters to protect a given airspace with indigenous AEW Gannets so that it could operate within it – albeit only at low level – without United States Navy support. The American Navy is now the only air force in the world that has a world-wide capability with a powerful and well-balanced, single-purpose fleet of strike and fighter aircraft available. It seems to have continued where it left off in the Pacific, its aim being first to achieve air superiority – as in Iraq – and only after this has been done, to allow the army to move towards their objectives. Only then would it be possible for the army/marines to summon their own specialist United States Air Force strike aircraft and helicopters to assist in the interdiction and destruction role, borrowing adjacent and now friendly airfields, for this purpose. Meanwhile, the entire tactical battle would be controlled from the skies, by the use of Airborne Command and Control and AEW aircraft, operating up to 200 miles from the battlefield itself.

As for the Royal Navy's present air-defence posture, its present 95 per cent reliance upon the missile coupled with its almost total lack of effective AEW, places its air defence posture entirely off balance and dependent upon the Americans.

AA defence, whether in 1942 or in the Falklands, whether by gun or missile and whether visual or radar directed, is no more than an additional layer of defence for the fleet, a morale booster for the ships' companies and a grand sight for media photographers. It is not and can never be a defence system by itself.

INACCURACY OF LONG-RANGE NAVAL GUNNERY

There are many naval officers about to-day who still believe in the effectiveness and accuracy long attributed to long-range Naval Gunnery. Yet anyone who has studied physics up to GCSE standard can see why this cannot possibly be so. Long-range naval gunnery accuracy – and therefore its military cost-effectiveness – is a complete myth and a waste of money.

The simple truth is, that in ranges over a time-of-flight of more than about 20 seconds, the shell begins to tumble and only luck allows it to hit the ground point first or pierce its armoured target or keep to a calculated flight path.

When the shell begins its flight from the barrel it is spinning like a huge gyro at about 3000 rpm. It will therefore continue to point in its barrel's direction for the remainder of its time in the air unless, of course, it is affected by an outside 'tilt' force. This outside tilt force is supplied by the airflow almost from the moment it leaves the barrel. This aerodynamic force is in the form of a nose-up tilt derived from the aerodynamic lift acting on the nose of the shell which, due to gravity, steadily increases its angle of incidence to the airflow.

The necessary incidence angle to secure this lift is caused by the gradual change between the shell's direction through the air and the angle at which its 'fuselage' is forced – by gyro stabilisation to point. Gravity naturally acts on the shell the moment it leaves the barrel – giving it a downward acceleration of 32 ft/sec/sec. By the time it has travelled for about 10 seconds – say, halfway to its target – it will have fallen vertically through a considerable distance, and unless the gun barrel had been raised to a fairly high angle before the shell was fired, the shell will obviously hit the ground well before getting anywhere near its target. Thus the gunner has to raise the gun barrel to an angle he has calculated will ensure that, at about halfway to the target, the shell will be at its highest point – say 3000 feet in our case.

The shell will then still be pointing upwards but beginning to drop earthwards, following the path of a huge, but unsymmetrical parabola. Provided that its flight path and 'pointing direction' remain at a sensible aerodynamic lift value, say between about five and 20 degrees, the airflow over the nose of the shell continues to exert a very considerable lift centred well forward of its CG and which therefore attempts to tilt the nose of the shell upwards.

However, this 'tilt' force will not succeed in tilting the shell *upwards* at all but – as any gyro behaves when 'tilted' – it will immediately cause the shell's nose to 'precess' to the left or right – depending on the direction of the shell's rotation.

This 'precession' movement is exactly the same as when we try to tilt a child's spinning-top/gyro by pushing its 'north pole' sideways. The top refuses to go in the direction we push it and, if it moves at all, it will move *at right-angles* to the direction we wish it to go. It will then begin an increasing rotary movement.

Our shell behaves in a similar fashion to a tumbling gyro top. Like the top, it will begin to tumble, rotating round its CG until all predictable movement 'capsizes' and it becomes completely unstable. It will then be travelling sideways or end-over-end in a haphazard manner through the air and no scientist or gunnery expert could possibly guess where it may land or in what direction it might be pointing when it does so.

Luck alone will then secure a 'point-first' entry to its armour-plated target and no one, not even the cleverest computer, knowing upper-air wind speeds and directions, cordite and air temperatures, speed and direction of the target, rolling effects of the gunnery platform, or even the engine-driver's name, could possibly depend upon any accuracy. It will be sheer luck if it gets within a mile of its target – as we saw for ourselves over Normandy in 1944 – and, it may have perhaps a five per cent chance of hitting the ground – let alone its target – point first. It seems extraordinary that those who complained about the failure of our shells to pierce the German ships' deck armour at Jutland – even if they managed to hit them – could not have known the reason why. A cursory study of elementary schoolboy physics could have told them the answer.

Having been on the receiving end – airborne at 3,000 feet or above – of complete broadsides from *Warspite, Ramillies, Nelson, Rodney* etc., at ranges of 20,000 yards, when only one shell in every sixteen exploded and when the remainder, spread over several different corn fields, only managed to raise a small puff of dust as they landed up to two miles from their target, we can have no faith whatever in long-range gunnery as a means of making war compared with the use of dive bombing or missile-firing aircraft. In fact, medium or long-range shore bombardment before a beach landing should be forbidden, as it will surely kill civilian targets and cannot be relied on to do vital military damage to the enemy forces particularly if they are expecting it and hide on the reverse slopes of adjacent hills.

We tend to believe what we are told by our experts in the Navy so that it was not until I actually used a gun myself aboard *Loch Scavaig* that I began to think that the reason that I was given by the experts for the D-Day inaccuracies could have been wrong. The reason that I was given for the poor shooting was that the battleships' guns had worn their rifling smooth! This, if it was true might even have improved matters and have increased *Nelson* and *Rodney*'s accuracy to that of the round shot of Nelson's day!

It is interesting to note that, in to-day's long-range army gunnery, smooth-bore guns appear to be in use in some American tanks, their shells probably fitted with 'spring-out' tail fins. These shells would then behave as they should – and as the media still imagine all shells behave – by landing point first like a pub dart, having travelled through the air continuously pointing in the exact line of flight all the way to the target. Perhaps the 'pop-out' tailfin idea may catch on and we might see an improvement in long range naval and long-range army gunnery in the next fifty years. Our gunnery experts may at last have to admit they spoofed us all for the past 80 years.

APPENDIX 3

HIGH-ALTITUDE BOMBING ACCURACY

High-level bombing during the war was notoriously inaccurate. In the fifties the Royal Air Force had the V-bombers. But they had soon realised that for them to reach most Russian targets with the A-bomb in the jet age (Polaris submarine delivery was still a few years off) they would have to go most of the way at high altitude. They needed all the range they could get. Right up to 1958, V-bomber aircrew knew that they would not be able to carry enough fuel to get back. In fact one officer was advised by his CO: 'Carry on flying east and come down by parachute somewhere deep in the country and snuggle up to a Mongolian women for the rest of the war.'

Looking across Boscombe Down airfield from 'C' Squadron we could see the V-bombers dispersal, ready at ten minutes notice to take-off to drop the A-bomb on Russia if the need ever arose. What bravery, we thought – for this was well before the day of the 'stand-off' bomb. Thank goodness it wasn't us who had to do it. However, a year later we were carrying out the deck trials of the new Buccaneer which had been painted a reflective white colour – to reflect A-bomb radiation! So we would be required to deliver it as well.

Careful thought on this point produced an even more fatalistic answer. The V-bombers could at least hope to keep clear of the explosion – if the MiGs had not shot them all down by then – by maintaining their release height of 50,000 feet. If they went in low, they might avoid the MiGs but they would all then die in the ensuing holocaust. What they needed was a means of delivery from zero feet and enough speed to get away ahead of the blast. This needed a high-speed, low-altitude aircraft able to apply after-burner power sufficient to pull up vertically into a loop from ground level at near sonic speed, release its bomb just before reaching the vertical, carry on with a roll-off-the-top and hare back home in a dive, the way he had come, keeping ahead of the bomb blast and outside lethal radiation intensities.

We then wondered how the Royal Air Force intended to use its V-bombers for high-altitude non-nuclear bombing with ordinary, free-fall bombs. It was obvious that their Javelin would not have the range or the load-carrying ability to out-distance the Fleet Air Arm's Buccaneer at high or low levels, for a 'Narner' had just flown across the Atlantic non-stop. They would have to use their V-bombers.

High-altitude bombing was notoriously inaccurate – almost as inaccurate as long-range naval gunnery. The reasons for this high-level bombing inaccuracy are many. First, the bomb leaves the aircraft horizontally. The bomber does not know its position in space with a greater accuracy than about 100 feet sideways, 200 feet fore-and-aft and, perhaps as much as 100 feet vertically. This is because an error of half a degree in its compass direction, an error of two mph in its speed input to its computer, an error in the meteorological office's wind speed and direction at the time of release, an error of two degrees out-of-horizontal in the bomber's flight path – plus a quarter-second delay in the bomb release switch gear plus the bombs unpredictable behaviour as it enters the slipstream from the bomb bay itself – all these variables could add up to a miss of quarter of a mile by the time it reaches the earth 30 seconds later. Proof of this miss distance was available from the photographs of the results of the V-bomber raids on the Falklands, 20 years later and from the equally poor results from the Valiants at Suez.

When comparing the high-level bomber's accuracy with a 16-inch shell fired from a naval gun – at anchor – at a target 15–20 miles away, at least the gun knew where it was when it was fired, so that source of error would not apply.

There is little doubt that had the invention of lobbing been taken up in the early fifties and then further improved by use of the head-up display (HUD), using 'stand-off', self-propelled heat-seeking guided bombs and missiles, air torpedoes and an automatic aiming and firing system incorporated into the 'LABS' system (taught by 738 Squadron later by 1962/3), it would have drawn further attention to the dangers and inaccuracies of high-altitude bombing. The Fleet Air Arm's Buccaneer – the first of its type – would have swept the board, for with flight refuelling it could deliver an A-bomb – or its weight in ordinary bombs – over a distance of 3,000 miles on a one-way journey and would not have to fly above enemy radar height. It would also be able to keep clear of the bomb's blast and radiation at the time of delivery. The Buccaneer's conventional bombing – dive-bombing or lobbing – would also have been more accurate from low level than anything that a high-level bomber could do.

SQUADRON LEADER TONY SVENSSON EJECTS FROM A MIRAGE AT 750 KNOTS INDICATED AIRSPEED

After ETPS in 1958 I spent two years at 'A' Squadron Boscombe Down and gained invaluable experience on the Lightning flight trials. I then had the good luck to be posted to Australia with my family, to help the RAAF with the flight trials of a Marcel Dassault Mirage 111-0 (prefix A3-1) supersonic fighter recently imported from France and which the Australians themselves intended to build for their Air Force in their government factory at Fisherman's Bend near Melbourne in the years to come.

The Mirage 111 had first flown in France in November 1956 and had completed its flight trials there in the next two years. Further trials were now required in Australia which centred round engine handling problems associated with the Australian tropical conditions where temperatures decreased much more rapidly with increase in height than in Europe.

Most jet engines at that time had their fixed air intakes designed to give minimum drag and maximum intake of air at high speeds and at high Mach. However, when flying at high angles of attack the engines' intake guide vanes tended to stall (not being of variable pitch) causing turbulent flow into the compressors which immediately caused 'engine surge.' This manifested itself by producing bangs from the engine, a drop in RPM and a rise in jetpipe temperatures. It was then necessary to close the throttle, dive to increase airspeed and decrease wing angle-of-attack, and hope that the RPM would build up once more.

It was during one of the engine handling trials on 7 December 1964 that I flew into big trouble.

Three flights were planned for this day. The first two were timed supersonic accelerations at 50,000 feet up to Mach 1.8. On the third flight I got airborne and climbed to 47,000 feet above Avalon for the first of three 'surge' runs at 250 knots. Descending to 36,000 feet for the third run and reducing speed once more to 250 knots I applied 'surge' conditions by a hard pull on the stick – and suddenly, things were not the same as usual. Instead of the usual pre-stall judder – after which by relaxing back pressure on the stick the aircraft would normally resume normal flight – this time, there was only a very brief judder and the aircraft flipped over to port in a steep nose-down attitude, yawing to port. In accordance with the French Pilots' Notes – translated into English – I centralised the controls – and waited for the promised recovery. The 'pause' period of the recovery action i.e., centralising the controls, *must* have had time to work, I thought.

But time seemed to have stopped. The rotation hadn't. I applied full 'in-spin' aileron but the spinning continued with increasing ferocity. I was becoming disorientated and I had the impression I was sitting at the centre of a rapidly rotating kaleidoscope. Recalling a comment in the French report of the Mirage spinning trials which said: 'Do not despair,' I maintained in-spin aileron as they suggested. My sight was blurring. I tried to concentrate my focus on the altimeter – 9,000 feet already – and it was most definitely time to despair.

I reached for the ejector-seat face screen handle and pulled hard. The indicated air-speed – which I did not know at the time – was registered on the flight recorder as 750 knots indicated airspeed. This was 150 knots faster than the maximum permitted ejection speed allowed for the seat and the slipstream force acting on it and myself as I left the aircraft was 1,640 pounds per square foot.

The hood had shattered immediately it had come free and from this time I can remember nothing more – for the next nine days. In fact, unconsciousness seemed to have been the best state to have been in.

The seat design had incorporated leg-restraint straps but no arm restraints. The leg restraint system consisted of two reinforced nylon cords, each connected to the cockpit floor by a shear pin designed to pull away on ejection at a load sufficient to hold the legs against the forward edge of the seat. The other end of this cord was passed through snubbing units fixed to the seat, crossed over, passed through steel rings attached to the pilot's legs by a strong garter and fastened to the harness release box. The cord was automatically tightened as the ejection took place and only released when the seat occupant had separated from his seat and before his parachute was automatically streamed. In my case, these cords had not been crossed over as tests in the Mirage in Australia had already found that at certain positions they could snag the control column. This was a bad decision – as I found to my cost. As the seat had moved up the guide channels the leg restraint cords had not pulled my legs together and as the blast hit them, it forced them apart causing pelvic and groin injuries. The seat immediately buckled downwards, my flying-boot toes hit the wind-shield, both arms flailed behind me – breaking my left collarbone and the right upper arm – and inner and outer flying helmets, gloves and watch were torn off.

When the seat drogue had fired at an estimated speed of 500 knots, the deceleration of the seat plus occupant had been about 20 G. This shredded the drogue and removed my right flying boot. After three seconds of this, the automatic barostat mechanism sensed this excessive G and locked the seat separation sequences until the G had reduced to 4 G – equivalent to the retardation force at 300 knots. Five-and-a-half seconds had elapsed since ejection before the main parachute was streamed after the seat had dropped away. Unfortunately, my right leg was still attached to the seat as one of the leg restraint cords had jammed the release mechanism on that side.

The opening shock when my parachute opened was about 20 G at 300 knots. The seat's inertia at this speed would have jerked my right leg with a force of 1½ tons before it broke the leg restraint garter – breaking my right leg at the same time.

After the seat and I were finally separated and the parachute deployed, I continued downwards at the usual rate of about 24 ft/sec. Being unconscious, I had not lowered the seat pack on its line so that my parachute was not stabilised and quickly developed a large oscillation. I hit the ground 3½ minutes after ejection on a downward swing and fractured my left femur.

The Mirage had taken four seconds to cover the same distance as myself and had buried itself in a crater 25 feet deep and 45 feet wide, 600 yards from where I landed. From the records of Martin-Baker, this had been the highest speed at which recovery of an aircrew had ever been made.

As I had landed two miles from the airfield the RAAF ambulance soon arrived and I was transported to number 6 RAAF Hospital in Laverton, one hundred yards from our married quarters and my wife Pam. She had been hanging out the washing at the time of the crash. She had heard the explosion from 20 miles away and knew it was the Mirage. Having reassured her beforehand that I would not hesitate to eject if things went wrong, she was not particularly surprised when my Commanding Officer arrived at our house and told her that I had ejected but had suffered only a broken arm. I expect he was trying to break the news gently.

Recovery took two and a half years. I was in intensive care for 10 days, eight of which I was in a coma. Holes were drilled above each temple to relieve brain pressure and Pam had to wear winter clothing to keep warm – as I was being 'stored' at low temperatures – while she tried to talk to me to trigger a response while I lay unconscious.

After passing through an hallucinatory stage of nearly a month, many operations were carried out including leg pinning. The day then came when I was presented with my first wheel chair. It had been modified by the Squadron and looked suspiciously like an ejector seat. They asked me to carry out a test evaluation, particularly of their pilot's relief tube (PRT) mechanism. (This was similar in design to those used in bomber cockpits in the war. All too often the aerodynamic effects had blown or sucked – according to the airspeed at the time of use – and this had often had unfortunate effects on the user's equipment or on the hygienic state of the cockpit at the time.)

I complained in my report on the PRT that its tube was too short and could result in personal injury if used in emergency from a seating position. The Squadron Flight Sergeant who had designed and built the mechanism said·

> We apologise for the inconvenience but we could not obtain your vital measurements in that area at the time so we assumed that yours would be the same size as the average Australian pilot.

After much work in the station gymnasium I was found fit enough to be flown back to UK in May 1965, being given a full medical examination *en route* at the RAF hospital at Changi, Singapore and kindly accompanied there by Flight Lieutenant Peggy Mallon, one of Laverton's hospital sisters. Pam, and my seven-year-old son Mark, had travelled home a few weeks beforehand in luxury in SS *Canberra*.

In September my medical category was re-assessed A4, G5 and Z5 – virtually good for nothing anywhere and, even more depressing, both legs had to be re-broken and re-set. I could then walk on crutches – an improvement.

I then had the luck to meet an old friend – Wing Commander Peter Bardon – who I had met at Boscombe and who was now Chief Instructor at ETPS. He got me a posting back to ETPS as a 'supernumery' tutor.

On 27 April 1967 I was re-awarded a full flying category and flew solo again. It was wonderful being back in the hot seat at last – a Martin-Baker one, of course.

APPENDIX 5

ROLL-INERTIA COUPLING

Perhaps the best way of trying to describe this is to suggest a way of trying it out ourselves. This could be done by nailing one stick to another at roughly their mid points, taking the longer by its two ends between the thumb and fingers of the left and right hands and twisting it rapidly round its axis, watching what happens to the other stick. If the nail is sufficiently loose in its hole in the shorter of the two sticks and free to rotate, the shorter stick will do so, flying out at right-angles to the longer stick. By imagining that the longer stick represents the flight direction and the shorter stick represents the nose-to-tail direction of an aircraft, we can see how, if the shorter stick is slightly out of line with the longer stick when it is first revolved, it will pitch up, or pitch down even more.

Likewise, an aircraft which is rolled rapidly, unless its flight direction is exactly in line with its fuselage 'nose-to-tail' direction all the time it is being rolled, the nose will fly further out of line, requiring instant application of elevator to stop it. The more rapidly it is revolved by aileron, the more it will fly out of line, until the whole aircraft will pitch up violently, perhaps overstressing itself in the process and breaking up in the air.

If G is being pulled at the moment that the pilot makes a rolling pull-out, the 'angle-of-attack' – and thus the nose-up angle – will be all the greater. Such conditions always apply when rolling off the top of a loop, where the airspeed is low, the angle of attack is high and the roll rate is high – even if it is only for 180 degrees.

LIST OF COMMANDING OFFICERS, 'C' SQUADRON, BOSCOMBE DOWN

Captain E.M.A. Torrens-Spence, DSO, DSC, AFC*	1944–45
Commander D.R. Robertson, AFC.	1945–46
Rear-Admiral J.A. Ievers, CB, OBE.	1946–48
Commander L.G. Kiggell, DSC.	1948–50
Commander G.R. Callingham.	1950–52
Captain D.B. Law, CBE, DSC.	1952–54
Commander S.G. Orr, DSC, AFC.	1954–56
Captain P.C.S. Chilton, AFC.	1956–58
Captain C.E. Price, AFC.	1958–60
Commander R.M. Crosley, DSC*	1960–63
Commander G.R. Higgs, AFC.	1963–66
Commander N.T. Bennett, AFC.	1966–68
Commander F. Hefford, DSC, AFC.	1968–71

Programme for the disbanding of 'C' Squadron 7 May 1971

2030	Mourners to muster.
	Dress: Sackcloth and ashes or black tie.
2100	Requiem and Beating of Retreat by the band of HM Royal Marines, Flag Officer Naval Air Command.
	Funeral Director: Bandmaster D.A. Drake, LRAM, RM.
2130	Musical laments and dispensing hemlock in the main anteroom. Special dirges in the discotheque.
2200–2300	Wake in the dining room.
0200	Last rites will be served in the dining hall.
0300	Hearses.

Postscript

In 1993, an Operational Evaluation Unit was formed at Boscombe Down to develop procedures for the Sea Harrier FRS1's new weapon system. (Blue Vixen radar/AMRAAM will provide simultaneous engagement of four targets beyond visual range and the ability to 'look down, shoot down' at targets flying low over rough sea).

HEAD-UP DISPLAY PATENT

PATENT SPECIFICATION
Inventor: ROBERT MICHAEL CROSLEY.

662,987

Date of filing Complete Specification: May 12, 1950.
Application Date: May 13, 1949. No. 12809/49.
Complete Specification Published: Dec. 12, 1951.

Index at acceptance:– **Classes 4**, K; **and 106(iv)**, IIa.

COMPLETE SPECIFICATION

Improvements in Aeroplanes

We SHORT BROTHERS and HARLAND LIMITED, a British Company, of Seaplane Works, Queen's Island, Belfast, Northern Ireland, do hereby declare the invention, for which we pray that a patent may
5 be granted to us, and the method by which it is to be performed, to be particularly described in and by the following statement:—

This invention has for its object to provide in an aeroplane new or improved means whereby it
10 becomes possible to avoid the disadvantage that the pilot in landing the aeroplane upon the deck of an aircraft carrier, or in other analogous circumstances, must avert his eyes from the batsman on the deck of the carrier to consult a stall warning or
15 airspeed indicator or other instrument in the cockpit to enable him correctly to adjust his flying speed for a safe landing. The necessity for such provision is the more apparent when it is remembered that in certain existing aircraft the airspeed indicator dial
20 is located not more than two feet from the pilot's eye and is set at right angles to the forward line of vision, as the result of which arrangement the pilot is compelled during the landing approach, when it is desirable that his eyes should remain focussed on
25 the batsman situated up to 300 yards distant, to move his eyes as nearly instantaneously as possible through an angle of 90°, re-focus them on the airspeed indicator dial two feet away and note the reading of a vibrating pointer on what may be an
30 unsuitably calibrated dial. Even though the better

placing of the instrument would represent a slight improvement, it will be appreciated that the necessity of the alteration of the focal distance of the pilot's vision is responsible for the greater loss of time and is therefore the more likely to give rise to accident due to a misjudgment of one or more of the conditions which must be observed simultaneously to avoid a premature stall or over-shooting of the deck.

The present invention proposes to achieve the object referred to by providing in the aeroplane cockpit means for projecting an image of the airspeed indicator dial and pointer, or of the stall-warning indicator, upon the inner surface of the windscreen at such a position that the pilot may read the instrument without averting his eyes from the batsman, such image being brought to an infinite focus to avoid the necessity for alteration of the focal distance of his vision.

An embodiment of the invention is illustrated by way of example in the accompanying drawing, which is a diagrammatic representation of the interior of an aeroplane cockpit in which a light beam, is projected from a source A through the translucent dial B of an airspeed indicating instrument, or of a stall-warning indicator, and a collimating lens system C so that an image of the dial B and the pointer D associated therewith is reflected upon the inner surface of the windscreen E to the pilot's eye F. As will be seen from the drawing, the image of the dial and pointer appears in alignment with the line of the pilot's sight, indicated at FG, and he is accordingly enabled to note the reading of the pointer on the dial without averting his eyes from 65 the batsman.

What we claim is:–

1. In an aeroplane cockpit, means for projecting an image of the dial of an instrument, such as the air-speed indicator or the stall-warning indicator, 70 upon the inner surface of the windscreen in a position such that said image will be visible to the pilot looking through the windscreen.

2. In an aeroplane cockpit, the combination with an air-speed indicator or a stall-warning indicator, of a translucent dial for said instrument, a light 75 source located behind such dial, and an optical system adapted to project an image of the illuminated dial upon the inner face of the windscreen at a point appropriate for the purpose stated.

3. The combination claimed in claim 1, includ- 80 ing in the optical system means for bringing the image to an infinite focus.

Dated this 12th day of May, 1950.
BREWER & SON,
Chartered Patent Agents,
5/9, Quality Court, Chancery Lane,
London, W.C.2

PROVISIONAL SPECIFICATION

Improvements in Aeroplanes

We SHORT BROTHERS and HARLAND LIMITED, a British Company, of Seaplane Works, Queen's Island, Belfast, Northern Ireland, do hereby declare the nature of this invention to be as follows:–

This invention has for its object to provide in an aeroplane new or improved means whereby it becomes possible to avoid the disadvantage that the pilot in landing the aeroplane upon the deck of an aircraft carrier, or in other analogous circumstances, must avert his eyes from the batsman on the deck of the carrier to consult a stall warning or airspeed indicator or other instrument in the cockpit to enable him correctly to adjust his flying speed for a safe landing. The necessity for such provision is the more apparent when it is remembered that in certain existing aircraft the airspeed indicator dial is located not more than two feet from the pilot's eye and is set at right angles to the forward line of vision, as the result of which arrangement the pilot is compelled during the landing approach, when it is desirable that his eyes should remain focussed on the batsman situated up to 300 yards distant, to move his eyes as nearly instantaneously as possible through an angle of 90°, re-focus them on the air-speed indicator two feet away and note the reading of a vibrating pointer on what may be an unsuitably calibrated dial. Even though the better placing of the instrument would represent a slight improvement, it will be appreciated that the necessity for the alteration of the focal distance of the pilot's vision is responsible for the greater loss of time and is therefore the more likely to give rise to accident due to a mis-judgment of one or more of the conditions which must be observed simultane- 35 ously to avoid a premature stall or over-shooting of the deck.

The present invention proposes to achieve the object referred to by providing in the aeroplane cockpit means for projecting an image of the air-speed indicator dial and pointer, or of the stall- 40 warning indicator, upon the windscreen at such a position that the pilot may read the instrument without averting his eyes from the batsman, such image being brought to an infinite focus to avoid the necessity for alteration of the focal distance of 45 his vision.

According to one embodiment of the invention, the airspeed indicator, or stall-warning indicator, may have associated therewith an optical projector arranged to project a light beam through a suitable 50 graticulated translucent dial and a lens system, whereby an image of the dial and pointer is reflected by the inner surface of the windscreen to the pilot's eye.

Dated this 13th day of May, 1949.
BREWER & SON
Chartered Patent Agents,
5/9, Quality Court, Chancery Lane,
London, W.C.2.

Leamington Spa: Printed for His Majesty's Stationery Office, by the Courier Press.–1951. Published at The Patent Office, 25, Southampton Buildings, London, W.C.2, from which copies, price 2s. per copy; by post 2s. 1d. may be obtained.

662,987 COMPLETE SPECIFICATION I SHEET

This Drawing is a reproduction of the Original on a reduced scale

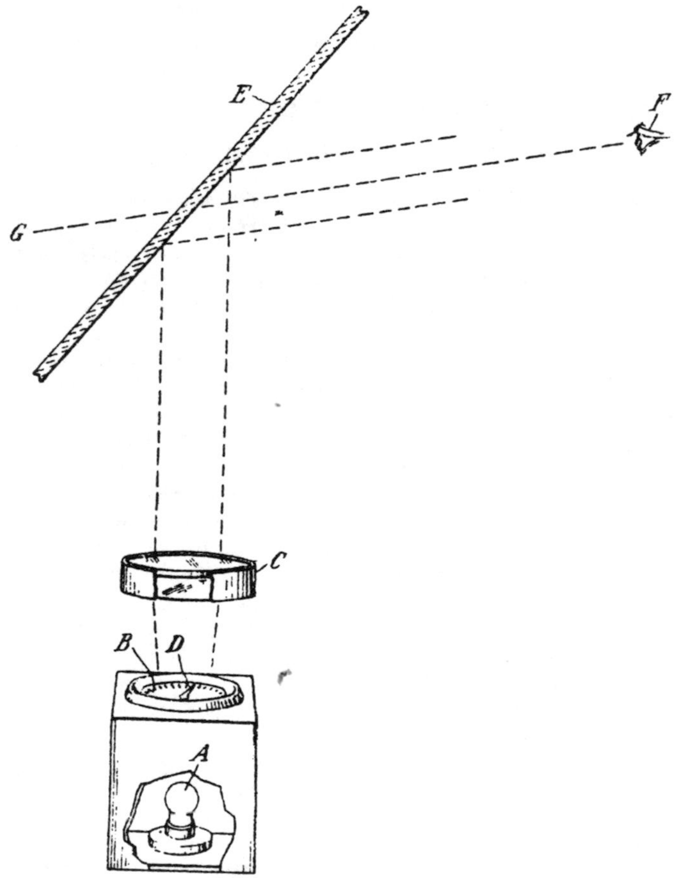

1020-M.M.P. LTD-1951

C SQUADRON BOSCOMBE DOWN AIRCRAFT 1941–1971

Fixed Wing Aircraft

Martlet	Bermuda	Wyvern S-4
Chesapeake	Beaufighter	Attacker F-1
Swordfish	Tarpon	Sea Vampire F 20
Havoc	Seamew	Sea Meteor T7 and TT 20
Fulmar 1–2	Hellcat	Hawker N7
Hampden	Mitchell	Sea Hawk FGA-6
Boston	Firebrand 1–4	Seagull
Oxford	Helldiver	Blackburn YA5
Botha	Wildcat 4	Sea Prince
Wellington	Corsair 1	Fairey GR 17
Beaufort	Seafire 1b–FR47	Swift
Hudson	Spitfire 1	Griffon
Mosquito	Tigercat	Athena
Buffalo	Harvard	Gannet AS 4 and AEW 3
Barracuda 1	Sea Fury FB II	Balliol
Sea Otter	Meteor TT 20	Sea Venom FAW 22
Avenger TR1-AS4	Barracuda 5	Midge
Henley	Vampire	Acquilon
Albacore	Firebrand	Sea Mew SB-6
Kingfisher	Martin-Baker	DH110
Whitley		N113
Baltimore	Seafang 32	Sea Mosquito TR 33
		Scimitar FG1
Walrus	Rapide	Sea Vixen FAW 1 and FAW 2
Ventura		
		Sea Hornet NF 21 and F 20
		Sea Devon C 20
Intruder	Firefly F1–AS6	Sea Fang 32
		Sea Heron C 2
Taylorcraft	Spearfish	NA 39
B-25	Tiger Moth	Hunter T8 and GA 11
Albemarle	Magister	Buccaneer 1 and 2
Vengeance	Sturgeon TT-2	Phantom F4
		Harrier FRS-1

Some Naval Helicopters, from 1951

Hoverfly 1 & 2.
Dragonfly S-51 (First ASR January 1951).
Whirlwind S-55 – HAR 21s (Malaya – 848 Sqn 1953).
Whirlwind HAS Mk 22 – Dunking Sonar – (1953).
Wessex Mk1–Mk3.
Wessex HU Mk 5 (Cdo).
Wasp Mk 1.
Sea King HAS Mk1–2.
Sea King HU Mk 4 (Cdo).
Westland Gazelle (Training).
Westland Lynx Attack/AS.

INDEX